What does the Lord require of you
But to do justice,
To love kindness,
And to walk humbly with your God?

Micah 6:8
Revised Standard Version

LOVE KINDNESS!

The Social Teaching of the Canadian Catholic Bishops

(1958-1989)
A Second Collection

Edited by E.F. Sheridan, S.J.
The Jesuit Centre for Social Faith and Justice (Toronto)

Editions Paulines
and
The Jesuit Centre for Social Faith and Justice

Phototypesetting: *Éditions Paulines*

Cover: *Jean-Pierre Normand*

ISBN 2-89039-469-7

Legal deposit — 2nd quarter 1991
Bibliothèque nationale du Québec
National Library of Canada

© 1991 **Éditions Paulines**
  250, boul. Saint-François Nord
  Sherbrooke, QC, J1E 2B9

  Jesuit Centre for Social Faith and Justice
  947 Queen Street East
  Toronto, ON, M4M 1J9

CONTENTS

THE DOCUMENTS

8 *Contents*

Section III   **LITURGY — WORSHIP**

Section IV   JUSTICE — WAR — PEACE

**Section VI   AT THE WORLD SYNODS OF BISHOPS
SYNOD OF 1971   PRIESTHOOD — JUSTICE**

SYNOD OF 1974 — EVANGELIZATION

ACKNOWLEDGEMENTS

I am very grateful to the Executive Committee of the Canadian Conference of Catholic Bishops for their cordial permission to begin this compilation and for a subsidy towards its completion. I am grateful too, to the then President of the Conference, Archbishop James M. Hayes, for the right to use all the documents here published.

I must acknowledge as well many courtesies and services of the Conference staff, of its General Secretary, Father Wm. F. Ryan S.J., of Miss Patricia McKale, Documentation Secretary, and of many others, to whom I had to appeal for information or help — never in vain.

Of my colleagues of the Jesuit Centre for Social Faith and Justice, the Director — until very recent date — Father Michael Czerny, S.J. was most encouraging at times when my own energies or enthusiasm tended to flag. He will be sorely missed but we are proud that he has accepted an appointment to the Central American University (UCA) of San Salvador, to reinforce the department of philosophy so tragically decimated in late 1989.

All the Centre's staff were unfailingly helpful, especially Eve Leyerle, office manager and mainstay, for advice as to the potentialities and peculiarities of computers. Norine Pigeau and Sandra Kowalchuk were also ever generous and patient.

I should make special mention of Ann Goodwill, my free-lancing secretary, for generous assistance and valuable literary and editorial judgment.

This sort of book, while serving useful purposes, is not likely to prove a best seller, though it involves many hours of rummaging around and running down vaguely cited authorities. It would have been impossible without generous subsidies from the Ontario State Council of the Knights of Columbus, through the good offices of Mr. R.J. Cadeau, State Deputy; from the F.K. Morrow Foundation of

Toronto; the Canadian Province of the Society of Jesus, through the Provincial Superior, Father Wm. M. Addley, S.J.; from the Loyola Jesuits' University Fund (Montreal), and the Jesuit communities of St. John's, Newfoundland and of St. Paul's College, Winnipeg.

I thank all the above and many others not mentioned by name. Without them the book would simply not be. They surely share largely in any good it may serve.

Edward F. Sheridan, S.J.

INTRODUCTION

I — SOCIAL TEACHING — SOCIAL JUSTICE — SOCIAL LOVE

1 — Social Teaching and Social Justice

In a first English collection of statements, briefs, letters etc. of the Canadian Conference of Catholic Bishops (*Do Justice! The Social Teaching of the Canadian Bishops*)[1]. I limited the selection largely to a somewhat restricted sense of social teaching which had become common. In this sense it is the Church's ethical teaching on the so called "social question", the complex of problems addressed by Pope Leo XIII in his encyclical letter *On the Condition of the Worker* (1891), and by successive Popes to the present day. The latter expanded their purview beyond the situation of European industrial workers, to comprehend agricultural and all other workers in the so called free world. This is the sense of *social teaching* in the U.S. Bishops' comprehensive Pastoral Message, *Economic Justice for All: Catholic Social Teaching and the U.S. Economy*[2] of 1986.

I have been asked why *Do Justice!* has no document on abortion, for example, a basic violation of justice, yet one protected by law and favoured by the social institutions of many countries. The reason is that abortion did not fall within the "social teaching of the church", as this had been more commonly understood by Catholic moralists and writers in the sense above.

If one understands *social justice* as it is widely and — I think — best understood by ethicians, as the virtue which disposes and prompts a person, individual or corporate, to reverence and promote those social institutions and patterns of conduct necessary or very conducive to the common good (whether enshrined in law or only in common usage), then social justice imposes a very wide area of obligation. Humans are social beings, called to live in society and to find their full human development in social interaction. Benefitting from life in society and good laws and customs highly favourable to such development, every citizen is morally obliged to observe such laws and respect such customs, to promote their introduction and observance.

Social justice is thus the virtue of the common good, of the good citizen as citizen (individual or corporate), disposing and prompting to serve the common good, as a demand of justice, *owed* in view of the benefits derived from membership in a well-ordered society. As looking to the common good, perhaps a great good of a large number, the obligations (preceptive or prohibitive) of social justice are binding in conscience and can be seriously so.

Love of God and of neighbour is the first and greatest commandment (Dt. 6:5; Lev. 19:18; Mk 12:30f) and absolutely basic to Christian ethics. In a very beautiful and cogent way, the Second Vatican Council, in *The Pastoral Constitution on the Church in the Modern World*, argues from the data of revelation, from the natural law and the essentially social nature of human kind (nn. 24-25) to the obligation of promoting the common good.[3]

Reflecting revelation and the increasingly prevailing secular humanistic ethic of the western world, the Constitution stressed the dignity of the human person, obliging us to reverence the same in absolutely everyone.[4] The Council concluded that much more is required than an *individualistic* ethic. Having castigated those who make light of social laws and directives, the payment of just taxes and fulfillment of other social obligations, the Council sanctioned such obligations in a sweeping and serious way:

> Let everyone consider it a sacred duty to count social obligations among his or her chief moral duties today and to observe them as such... This challenge cannot be met unless individuals and their associations cultivate moral and social virtues, and promote them in society. Thus with the necessary help of divine grace, there will arise a generation of new men and women, artisans of a new humanity.[5]

This is the call of the Council, integral to the mission of the Church and of every Christian.

2 — The Gospel of Justice and Love

My primary purpose in editing *Do Justice!* was to make accessible to any interested the considerable volume of social teaching of the Bishops' Conference as contained in their very varied statements since the early 40's to 1986. I thought it useful to include as Introduction a brief indication of the sources of the Bishops' teaching, a few of their fundamental principles and some notes on the structures of the Conference.

My present purpose is nearly identical, taking social teaching in a somewhat wider sense. These statements, briefs, etc. are often unreported in the secular press, seldom completely in the religious, not widely distributed and appear in very disparate formats. They are difficult to locate a few years after publication. I add some reflections towards understanding their teaching and on the possibilities and conditions of its effective proclamation, as well as practical acceptance by the Roman Catholic constituency and perhaps others.

The social teaching of the church from the late 19th century through Pius XI, Pius XII and John XXIII had stressed the fact that the socio-economic orders of many countries, as well as structures of international trade, were characterized by a radical social and distributive injustice. The Second Vatican Council was but echoing the conclusions of earlier Pontiffs when it proclaimed:

> While an enormous mass of people still lack the absolute necessities of life, some, even in less advanced countrties, live sumptuously... While the few enjoy every freedom of choice, the many are deprived of almost all possibility of acting on their own initiative and responsibility, and often subsist in living and working conditions unworthy of human beings. [6]

This is an iniquitous perversion of the finality of a socio-economic order and of its productive capacity, whose fundamental purpose must not be mere growth,

> ... not profit or domination, ... but the service of persons and indeed of the whole person, in terms of their material needs and the demands of their intellectual, moral, spiritual and religious life. And when we say persons, we mean every person whatsoever and every human group, of whatever race or part of the world. [7]

Obviously, in an ethic inspired by the Gospels and Christian theology, the obligations of charity, of compassionate love of neighbour (and in what a wide sense!) could never be neglected, but it is true that in the papal encyclicals and documents, as well as in the social teaching of theologians, the insistence was on the obligations of *justice*, on the rectification of a social order which was *unjust*, which did not recognize what was *owed* to individuals and groups by reason of their essential dignity as human beings. Perhaps it was a sound pastoral strategy, concerned that those delinquent in the inauguration of social structures and institutions demanded by social justice — by the common good — be not permitted to leave necessary public welfare services to private charity, perpetuating unjust social structures and the *status quo*.

It was inevitable that under the influence of the magnificent theological anthropology and sociology of the Pastoral Constitution, *The Church in the Modern World*[8] and perhaps due to a revival of biblical studies, subsequent social teaching would begin to associate social justice and charity, while maintaining the distinction between the two. In scholastic teaching, the moral virtues, justice, fortitude etc., are in the service of charity, for its preservation and perfection — "but the greatest of these is love". (1 Cor. 15:13)

As far as I know, it was Paul VI who coined or at least preached the ideal of a "civilization of love"[9]. John Paul II was to return to that phrase later (cf. below), but even in his first encyclical, *The Redeemer of Mankind* (1979), he indicated the necessary association of justice and love. Speaking of the contrasts of our consumer civilization, capable of producing a surplus of necessities for entire societies and the whole human family, while other peoples hunger, millions dying annually of starvation and malnutrition he wrote:

> This is a drama that can leave no one indifferent. The person seeking maximum profit and the person paying the price in damage and injury, are both man, always man... The remedy requires daring, creative resolves in keeping with authentic human dignity, but the task is not an impossible one. The principle of solidarity in a wide sense must inspire the effective search for appropriate institutions and mechanisms.[10]

This solidarity which is so stressed in John Paul's letter *On Human Work*[11] (1981) is much more than a close knit and disciplined political activism. It seems clearly to be an expression of the *social love or social mercy,* developed in his letter *Rich in Mercy* (1980) of the previous year:

> The experience of our times demonstrates that justice alone is not enough, that it can lead to the negation and destruction of itself, if that deeper power which is love is not allowed to shape human life in its various dimensions. This does not detract from the value of justice nor minimise the significance of the order based on it. It only indicates the need to draw from the powers of the spirit conditioning the order of justice, powers still more profound. [12]

The whole of the final section (VII) of this letter (*Rich in Mercy*) is a beautiful and powerful development of the relation of social justice, mercy and love. True mercy is the most profound source of justice. Accepting that, as Paul VI had frequently indicated, the "civilization of love" must be the goal of all efforts in the cultural and social fields, as in the economic and political. He insisted that the goal cannot be reached if we stop short at the criterion of justice. "In every sphere of interpersonal relationships justice must, so to speak, be 'corrected' to a considerable extent by love." The Second Vatican Council speaks repeatedly of the need *to make the world more human,* the mission of the church in the modern world. Society, however, can become more human only if there is introduced into interpersonal *and social relationships,* "not merely justice, but also that merciful love which constitutes the messianic message of the Gospel." [13]

The Fifth Section of John Paul II's letter on *The Social Concern of the Church* (1987) is a *Theological Reading of Modern Problems.* He finds a *positive and moral value* in the growing awareness of the interdependence of individuals and of nations — a reduction of the obstacle to conversion of hearts of stone to hearts of flesh. (Cf. Ez 11:19)

> When interdependence becomes recognized in this way, the correlative response as a moral and social attitude, as a "virtue", is *solidarity,* … not a vague compassion or shallow distress at the misfortunes of so many… but a *firm and persevering determination* to commit oneself to the *common good,* the good of all and of each individual, because we are *all* really responsible *for all.* [14]

This is a perfect realization of St. Thomas' definition of love (charity in the Christian sense, biblical *agape*), "to will the good of another", (*amare: velle alicui bonum*) found throughout the *Summa Theologica.* [15]

3 — Option for the Poor: Social Love at Work

Gregory Baum has written eloquently and wisely in the CBC Massey Lectures, [16] sketching the recognition of world wide interdependence in his own Roman Catholic confession, but paralleled in all the mainline and some other Christian churches. The Second Vatican Council was the event in which the Catholic church discovered its co-responsibility for society and social structures, its mission of service to the world, a service not only religious, but as wide as the category of truly human goods. [17]

In the Medellin (Colombia) Conference (1968) gathering all the Latin American Bishops, this insight and new consciousness of the Council, led to a re-reading of the "signs of the times", a perception, scrutiny and critique of national social situations from the perspective of the vast majority of the citizens, poor and oppressed by a very small minority of the wealthy and their relatively few agents and supporters of a tiny middle class. The bishops recognized their obligation to support the poor and oppressed in their struggle for freedom and justice, to make an effective "preferential option for the poor", if not in so many words. That formula would become explicit in the Third Conference of Latin American Bishops (Puebla, Mexico, 1979), at which the newly elected John Paul II would be present.

The Canadian Roman Catholic Church was particularly open to these currents, since there had been a national program of pastoral action and help in Latin America by the Canadian church since 1960. Since then hundreds of Canadian bishops, priests, religious and laity had visited many countries, often engaging in pastoral and social work for varying periods. [18]

Baum rightly recognizes Medellin as a second phase or moment in the development of liberation theology, of solidarity with the poor, which was greatly accelerated and widely diffused by the stance adopted in the Second General Synod (1971), representing the Bishops of the whole church. It proclaimed:

> *Action* on behalf of justice and participation in the transformation of the world fully appear to us as a constitutive dimension of the preaching of the Gospel, or, — in other words — of the church's mission for the redemption of the human race and its liberation from every oppressive situation.

And again:

> For unless the Christian message of love and justice shows its effectiveness through *action* in the cause of justice in the world, it will only with difficulty gain credibility with the men and women of our times. [19]

Baum distinguishes two senses of option for the poor: [20]

— first, *adoption* of the optic of the poor, *their* perspective as they observe *their* socio-economic situations of poverty and powerlessness in societies which could provide them a standard of living in accord with social justice and human dignity;

— "a second, an activist dimension", which calls for effective collaboration in their struggle to rise from such servitude.

There is no doubt that the option of the Latin American Bishops, at Medellin and again at Puebla, as also in the quotations from the Synod on Justice immediately above, included the second sense. This was and has continued to be the understanding of the Canadian bishops in many statements and pastoral messages.

So too Paul VI understood it in his great Apostolic Exhortation, *Evangelization in the Modern World* (1975). That letter begins with a biblical-theological account of the *liberating* mission of Jesus Christ, liberation from everything which oppresses people — not only spiritually, but politically, socially, economically — as part of the Good News, of evangelization. He recalled with sympathy how many of the bishops of the Third World, in the Synod on Evangelization (1975) described the struggle of their people to rise above famine, chronic disease, illiteracy, poverty, injustices in international relations, especially commercial. He continued:

> The Church has the duty to proclaim the liberation of millions... many of them her own children — the duty of assisting at... this liberation, of giving witness ot it, of ensuring that it is complete. This is not foreign to evangelization. [21]

This clearly requires much more than a rhetoric of liberation and implies active promotion of a more just social order.

It is hardly surprising that, as Baum remarks, "the preferential option for the poor is often opposed in the Church and in society". [22] There is reserve in the *Instruction on Certain Aspects of "Liberation Theology"* (1984) of the Congregation for the Doctrine of the Faith, approved by John Paul II; an impression not altogether dispelled by its later Instruction, *Christian Freedom and Liberation*

(1986), similarly approved, which avoids "option for the poor" and prefers to speak of "God's special love of the poor" (n. 22) and "the Church's love of preference for the poor" (n. 68)[23]

It would be long to trace the change in John Paul's appreciation of liberation theology and of the "preferential option", but it can be noted that in a series of addresses in 1984-85, he was evidently chagrined that he was thought to have been opposed to it. To a group of cardinals in Rome, Dec. 21, 1984, he protested:

> I do make this option. I identify myself with it. I feel it could not be otherwise, since it is the eternal message of the Gospel. That is the option Christ made, the option made by the apostles, the option of the Church throughout its two thousand years of history.[24]

It seems that Pope John Paul II became ever more strongly and personally committed to the cause of the poor and oppressed in visits to the urban slums, the landless farmers and the oppressed workers, in his journeys to Mexico (1979), Brazil (1980), Haiti (1983), Ecuador and Peru (1985) and Colombia (1986). Love of preference for the poor (n. 68), special option for the poor (*ibid.*) are prominent in the description of *The Liberating Mission of the Church*, the title of the Fourth Chapter of the *Instruction on Christian Freedom and Liberation*.[25] It seems irrefutable that this option and liberation theology, as understood in the developing tradition of the Church by their best proponents — including very many episcopal conferences — have achieved orthodoxy in the Church.

Baum calls the preferential option "the startling message from the Latin American Church... a profound challenge to the church in the developed world."[26] That would mean we of the First World have been, are being, evangelized by the churches of the Third World. The Canadian bishops were remarkably prompt in their reply to the challenge. "Preferential option for the poor" first came to explicit formulation in the Puebla meeting of the bishops of Latin America in 1979. By 1982, it had become a basic principle of the most important and influential statements the Bishops have produced[27] and is operative implicitly in two other documents, *Defending Workers' Rights* (1985) and *Supporting Labour Unions* (1986).[28]

But the principles of *The Constitution on the Church in the Modern World*, of the responsibility of the church and of each Christian effectively to reverence and promote the common good, with particular regard for the poor, had inspired the social teaching of the Canadian bishops from the close of the Council in 1965. [29]

4 — A Changing Emphasis ?

This energetic response to the call of the Council and to later church teaching has been thought by some to be waning. Causes advanced are: a prevailing neo-liberalism in economics and political science, with decline of the ideal of the welfare state; the gradual thinning of the ranks of bishops who had lived the experience of the Council; the alleged nomination of more "conservative" clerics to the episcopacy in many parts of the world and the reserve of John Paul with regard to liberation theology, to clerics in politics or in radical social advocacy, the area of action of the laity, etc.

However, in his apostolic visits to very many Third World countries the Pope has not hesitated to state boldly the evident need for fundamental economic reform — sometimes very specific — and for social and political change. Visiting Canada he quoted verbatim, a number of the principles of the Canadian Conference in the strongest language of their social teaching. [30]

In the last decade the Bishops' Conference has been preoccupied with other business, four World Synods, the arms race, peace and war (especially in the early '80's), abortion legislation, refugee policies and rights and the Papal visit.

If there has been any slackening on the part of the Conference of Canadian Bishops in the proclamation of the gospel of compassion and solidarity, I don't think it can be attributed to a declining faith in the teaching of their predecessors. All the mainline churches in Canada and the U.S.A. have experienced difficulty in gaining *effective* popular acceptance of this social teaching. [31] I think that difficulty and inertia were only to be expected.

It is precisely in the area of religious beliefs and practice that people are most reluctant to change. What has been held as satisfactory faith and practice over a period of years, will not be lightly changed. In most parishes the affluent or comfortable members of the congregation — management personnel, professionals, entrepreneurs of varying grades — will often be the most influential. They will have little spontaneous sympathy for the idea that the social order needs fundamental change, much less with any active promotion of the same by the church. Some twenty-four years have elapsed since the Council and the majority of clergy in charge, have been educated and probably served some years before the Council was concluded. With all good will, conversion of heart and mind, and *much more* of pastoral style and *praxis*, would not come easily. Perhaps it is necessary to look, not so much at the proclamation of this social teaching — forceful and persevering on the part of the Conference — as at its strategic promotion, for an explanation of its slow appropriation.

5 — Education for Social Love and Justice

The late George Cardinal Flahiff, CSB, then Archbishop of Winnipeg and delegate to the World Synod (1971) on *Justice in the World*, read the assembly an important lesson in formation for social justice.[32] It was very influential in the Synod and for its final Statement, which in turn has been one of the key post-Conciliar documents on social justice and evangelization.[33]

The cardinal, a scholarly and pastoral educator on many levels, said:

> When we ask ourselves, sometimes with no little anxiety, why the social teachings of the Church have had so little impact, I believe we may have to admit that we have too often believed that an academic knowledge... was most important, if not sufficient. Our basic principle must be: *only knowledge gained through participation* is valid in this area of justice; true knowledge can be gained *only through concern and solidarity*... We have too frequently separated evangelization from social action and reserved social involvement to elites and eventually the clergy. Unless we are in solidarity with the people who are poor, marginal or isolated we cannot even speak effectively about their problems.[34]

There was much more in the way of quotable quotes. On the specific role of the Church in justice:

— Christianity liberates from sin, not only personal but also and chiefly from social sin, a situation wherein individual sin becomes easy and acceptable;

— Christianity believes in man, knowing him a sinner, but expecting the gift of salvation, and a coming. We are not mere critics; we are fashioners of hope.

— Christianity cannot be content with minimum proposals, defending minimal rights, since it sees human rights as dynamic, evolving, and demands the maximum development for all.[35]

He went on:

Hence it follows that the lines of action should be these:

a) to encourage at all costs, the *practice* of justice, knowledge by participation... effective instruction begins not in school, from theory, but from life, involvement and solidarity.

b) to promote social animation, and thus conscientization. Only by experiencing and grappling with injustice locally, will people come to an effective understanding of injustice among the poor.

c) to encourage the responsibility of all, — not paternalism only on the part of pastors and elites.[36]

This is very insightful and a valid analysis of the necessary conditions and qualities of effective education for social change. It is borne out by the Canadian experience, for example, of the Extension Department of St. Francis Xavier University, Antigonish, N.S., in consumer, producer and marketing cooperatives. Other examples could be cited. On a massive scale it has been the experience of the Latin American church. I should say churches, for the same is true of non-Catholic confessions, under the leadership of the World Council of Churches.

In Latin America there has been the stimulus of a certain desperate need for radical social change, of the self-interest of millions to whom the inequity of their national socio-economic orders was agonizingly evident. The small ministerial or apostolic teams of lay persons which sprang up everywhere to substitute for a diminishing clergy, were often catechised by priests and sisters or brothers, local or missionaries from abroad, who knew the social situation, had themselves studied the social teaching of the Second Vatican Council and could not fail to draw conclusions. Elements of liberation theology were already circulating, even before the Council (1962-65); the latter gave it legitimacy and impetus, burgeoning in Medellin (1968). The revival of the study and preaching of scripture in our Church, the discovery of Yahweh as a God who frees and saves his people, who hates injustice and oppression, provided these lay preachers with themes which could not help but suggest action for social transformation.[37] It was inevitable that ideologues would use this development in theology for their own purposes, but no theologians of stature have been seduced into revolution or the idea that the Reign of God can be ushered in by social activism.

What is the practical possibility (and what the conditions?) of the church — ecumenically, for all Christian churches — making an effective contribution to the establishment of a more just and compassionate socio-economic-political order in Canada? In some sense the question, for the Christian of faith, hope and charity, does not call in question whether the church or the individual Christian should engage in the endeavour. The answer has been given for Canadian Catholics by the clear call of Vatican II, notably in *The Church in the Modern World* (1965) and in the persevering teaching of the church, universal and national, ever since. The task may be, *is*, daunting, but "Woe to me if I do not preach the Gospel!". (1 Cor 9:16) And both Paul VI and John Paul II have repeatedly urged that serving the Gospel of justice *is* integral to evangelization.[38]

As sequel to the Synod on Evangelization (1974), Paul VI chose *Catechesis* for the theme of the Synod of 1977. His death occurred after its conclusion but before he could complete the Apostolic Exhortation he contemplated on the subject. That was issued by John Paul II, making use of Paul's notes. The title is *Catechesis in our Time* (1979).[39]

> Catechesis is education in the faith of children, young people and adults... with a view to initiating them into the fullness of Christian life. It is a moment, — a very remarkable one — in the whole process of evangelization. (n. 8)

Central to the work of catechesis, "its principal form", is that of adults whose faith must be continually enlightened and renewed, "so that it might pervade the temporal realities in their charge. It would be quite useless if it stopped short just at the threshold of maturity". (n. 43)

Turning to consider the locale of catechesis, — parish, family, school, organizations (lay associations, movements, groups), he remarks that catechesis can be given anywhere, but that in the Synod, many bishops felt that the parish should continue to be "the prime mover and pre-eminent place for education in the faith". John Paul agreed, in spite of difficulties which would require new structures. Large parishes or groups of smaller parishes have the serious duty to provide such catechetical leadership, personnel and equipment for catechesis in all its aspects. (67) Clearly this will lay a heavy material burden on the parish, not to mention demands on a clergy, ageing and reduced in numbers.

I would recall here the conviction of Cardinal Flahiff, shared by the Synod of 1971, that such education to be effective must be education in action, by experience, in solidarity with the poor or marginalized, those seeking justice in situations of injustice. There is no lack of such in Canada but, fortunately, no lack of groups in active solidarity with them.

During his visit to Canada in 1984, the Holy Father gave an important instruction very pertinent to our subject, little remarked by the press as less newsworthy than those at Flatrock, Midland or Fort Simpson. It was a homily at Front Mountain Road, Moncton, N.B. [40] He spoke of Christian communities, parishes, and the need to deepen the faith of members through the continuing formation of adults; about efforts in sharing, justice and charity, which one could call — he said — "social love".

He insisted that a well-understood faith involved all the commitments of active charity, enumerating them at length, a litany of the obligations of social justice and solidarity:

— respect for persons, their freedom and dignity;

— respect for human rights — to life from the moment of conception, to development, to freedom of conscience;

— concern for the less favoured, women, labourers, unemployed, immigrants;

— social measures for greater justice and equality for all, regardless of influence or privilege;

— concern for simplicity of life, sharing, rejection of consumerism and of the urge to accumulate;

— greater openness to the needs of poor countries, lands of hunger, malnutrition, without minimum health care (n. 8).

All this activity of solidarity you will accomplish individually, or by your Christian associations and by taking part in the initiatives of... civil society. With the Christian motivation which sees in the other a brother or sister in God, a member of Christ, you will be the leaven raising society to a level of greater justice, concerned solidarity and social love (n. 8).

All sorts of action groups are necessary for such varied activity, the better to manifest the vitality of the church and to further widespread participation. And here

... the parish plays a unique role. For all groups, its vocation "is (quoting from *Catechesis in our Time*[41], n. 67) to be a fraternal and welcoming family home, where those who have been baptised and confirmed become aware of forming the people of God... From that home they are sent out day by day to their apostolic mission in all centres of activity of the life of the world." Let us not forget the fullness to which God calls us (n. 9).

Such a parish, a centre of adult evangelization, of formation to a vital spirituality, able to sustain active apostolates, and of education for justice to which the needs of church and world call the laity,[42] is something of the sort of parish which began to appear throughout Latin America, during and after Vatican II and the Medellin Conference.

Very influential in this evolution were the lay assistants, men and women, recruited to supply for the dearth of ordained ministers in the conduct of Sunday liturgies of Communion and the Word, for catechesis and a variety of religious ministries. These soon constituted basic church communities (BCCs) stable groupings of families, with such leadership as could be recruited locally in villages or workers' districts, or as could be sent periodically by a parish, or a diocesan centre. The majority of the hierarchy have favoured their development and they have increased rapidly in numbers and influence. This is especially true in Brazil where they have had the greatest success, being systematically promoted by the hierarchy as a principal pastoral strategy, now numbering more than eighty thousand groups with total membership of between 1.5 and 3 million.[43]

It would probably be naive to think that this development would have taken place without the strong motivation of self-interest on the part of millions, desperately poor, dispossessed and powerless. Of course political parties and ideologists have seized every opportunity to fish in troubled waters but neither national churches nor dioceses have been seduced into support of violent revolution.

The question of interest, however, is this. In a prosperous, consumer society like our own, in which the proportion of poor (below the poverty line) to non-poor is approximately 15% to 85%, by Stats Canada's reckoning — just about the reverse of the ratio in the more prosperous countries of Latin America — what is the possibility of

transforming any sizeable proportion of Canadian parishes in the model proposed by John Paul at Moncton? It is precisely this sort of conversion and renewal of which the churches of our North American First World stand in need, faced by triumphant consumerism and secularism. They go together!
Reflecting on the feasibility of a vigorous and widespread BCC movement in Canada, sociologist W.B. Hewitt judges

> that until the Canadian Catholic hierarchy moves... to an understanding of BCC activism which stresses the necessity of active elite intervention, no base community phenomenon of significant proportions will develop in Canada... Only a well organized, actively promoted programme... supported by the entire institutional structure, will result in a thriving BCC movement. The Canadian Church has long planted the seeds for the birth of this movement through its post-Vatican II involvement with the cause of social justice.[44]

The promotion of justice from 1965 to 1985 can yet bear fruit.

Futurology is hazardous but of this we may be certain. Such an ecclesial development will not be achieved if the effort be not made. I would venture to say that it will not be achieved without parish renewal, involving much more lay leadership and participation of the kind John Paul II preached at Moncton. In the Synod of 1985, marking the twenty fifth anniversary of the conclusion of Vatican II, Bishop Bernard Hubert, President of the CCCB, speaking on *The Practice of Justice in the World*, remarked on

> ... the challenge we are meeting and are trying to meet more successfully: how to assure better participation on the part of our Catholic communities and specialists in evolving, preparing and finally welcoming these statements (on social justice)... how to help our people go beyond a purely individual ethic and defend the moral dimensions of all human activity, economic, political, religious, scientific, cultural or military.[45]

Challenge indeed! — to the acceptance and appropriation of the whole *Constitution on the Church in the Modern World*.

6 — At Stake in this Challenge

At Moncton John Paul remarked that our religion is undergoing a *profound transformation, a test*. Urbanization and a socio-economic crisis are affecting local communities, religious and secular, involving "a spiritual crisis, a crisis of values".

You can look to the future with serenity, if you stand firm in faith in the Risen Christ, if you allow his Spirit to form in you the response to the new challenge, if you show solidarity with one another, if you accept being a leaven in the Church and in society... And your Christian communities will immediately take up the challenge if they are able to form and deepen the faith of their members... a faith that is a personal attachment to the living God and takes account of the whole creed. [46]

There followed that description of *action* inspired by social justice and social love cited above. Clearly in his mind such solidarity is the fruit of formation in action and for action. "Neither circumcision nor uncircumcision is of any avail, but faith working through love" (Gal. 5:6), including social love. No Christian liberation theologian believes that any human endeavour can usher in the Reign of Christ. As John Paul said at Moncton: "We toil with courage and strong love to construct a new world, more open to God and more of a human family, one that offers some sketch of *the world to come*." n.9. [47]

The highest ecclesial authorities in our church have affirmed that appropriation of the teaching and spirit of the Second Vatican Council is the path the church *must* follow for its renewal. It is fruitless to debate which of its decrees is the most important. A good case could be made that the decree which aimed at the most sweeping effect was undoubtedly the *Constitution on the Church in the World*, which greatly influenced so many other decrees (e.g., on *Communication, Ecumenism, Religious Life, Laity, Religious Freedom*) and their implementation in the life of the church. It presented a new vision of the church and, I think, more than any other, sent the bishops back to their pastoral charge galvanized to new action and fresh hope.

The Synod of 1971 (*Justice in the World*) in its deliberations and statement strongly affirmed the whole ethos and teaching of the Constitution. The Synod on *Evangelization* (1974) and Paul VI's *Apostolic Exhortation* on its theme (nn. 25-39) accepted that ecclesial orientation in its essential work of proclaiming the Good News. (Cf. above *Preferential Option etc.*, I, 3.)

Announcing the Synod of 1985, Pope John Paul II said:

The Second Vatican Council remains the fundamental event in the life of the contemporary church, fundamental for deepening the wealth entrusted to her by Jesus Christ... We must ceaselessly refresh ourselves at this font... The aim of this Synod... is above all
— to revive in some way the extraordinary atmosphere of ecclesial communion which characterized that assembly;
— to exchange and deepen experiences and information concerning application of the Council;
— to favour deepening and constant application of Vatican II to the Church's life in the light of new needs. [48]

The Synod's *Message to the People of God* [49] is a fervent expression of gratitude for the grace of the Council and an aspiration to deeper insight into its teaching, "to respond to the world's new challenges and those which Christ ever addresses to the world." The list of challenges was almost exclusively in the area of the teaching of the *Pastoral Constitution on the Church.* It concluded:
We are made to love God... for God himself. For humankind there is a path — and we already see signs of it — which leads to a civilization of sharing, solidarity and love; to the only civilization worthy of men and women. We propose to work with you towards this civilization of love, God's design for humanity as it awaits the coming of the Lord.

The Final Report of the Synod (II,D,1) [50] affirmed the great importance and timeliness of the *Pastoral Constitution on the Church.* It confirmed the preferential option for the poor — "not to be understood as exclusive" — and proclaimed the Church's obligation prophetically to denounce every form of poverty and oppression, "everywhere defend and promote the fundamental and inalienable rights of the person, especially in defense of human life from its very beginning" (*ibid.* n. 6).

I think that the most vital and apostolic elements in the church of the western world, the *forces vives,* are those who have regarded *The Church in the Modern World* as the statement of its vocation for our times and have tried to appropriate it, live it, implement it, as well as God's people — still a sinful people — can. If this lamp, lit in the church, should fail to light our way, then the darkness will be dark indeed.

The *Canadian Catholic Organization for Development and Peace* has recorded more than twenty years "to promoting active solidarity between Canadians and the peoples of the Third World". Its record is one of which the CCCB as its founding body, the organizing members, nationally and locally, in nearly all dioceses and many parishes, and the overseas volunteers may be justly proud.[51] In 1987 there were more than 230 local CCODP groups of active support.

The limitation of its work lies in the fact that it looks essentially to the Third World and there are relatively few Canadians who have the freedom for any lengthy active experience of solidarity with the poor and disfavoured abroad. In its parameters, its educational effort has been impressive, but for most it necessarily lacks much of that element of personal involvement with the victims of injustice or misfortune which Cardinal Flahiff and the Synod on Justice judged necessary for effective education to solidarity and compassion.

Is there not need for a similar effort and national organization in dioceses and parishes, not in competition with CCODP, but in emulation, having as its aim education *and local practice* of such love and service? How else might a parish become a community, a communion, the sort of parish John Paul II sketched at Moncton? much more than a place of love and worship of God, of sacramental nourishment — precious and essential as these are — but a centre of love of God in God's daughters and sons, the image *par excellence* and the glory of God?

One thinks of the needs of single parents, a situation desperately aggravated by housing shortages and the frequent dearth of child care assistance, of poor seniors without the support of families, of lonely chronic or temporary invalids, of refugees with children, jobless in a new and strange country, of food banks and soup kitchens, hostels for abused mothers and children, so many other needs which social workers could identify. There are more public justice and solidarity issues, housing, taxation, public health and environmental concerns, labour conflicts, minimum wage laws, welfare and unemployment benefits, workmen's compensation — the list could continue — on which parishes and dioceses could educate for social justice.

Many of these should be services of public welfare, but it is only in the *experiential* knowledge of the deficiencies and gaps in welfare programs that people are educated and stimulated to remedial action for improved social structures. There are always the cases that slip through the safety nets, however well designed, but which must be cared for by the Christian community, confessional or ecumenical, if it is to merit that name. Otherwise it is a community which

worships communually and loves God in some sort, but hardly *effectively* as a community of concern for God's daughters and sons.
Though they have not used the papal terms "social love", "civilization of love", the Canadian bishops have been exhorting to this concern for others, for the common good, ever since the close of Vatican II. This has been a call to love, social love — a rose by any other name! The reality has come to more overt and explicit expression in the presentations of our and many other bishops at the most recent Synods (1985 and 1987), that the Church — for most, the parish — must become and be seen to become, a *communion*, a religious-spiritual community, of effective and affective support, solidarity if we cannot quite digest the traditional words love and charity. [52] This call is the faithful echo of the voice of the Church in its most authentic and authoritative teaching, conciliar, papal, synodal.

It is not easy to discern widespread signs of such a renewal of the only church communities which most Catholics know, their parishes, nor any frequent evolution pointing in new and hopeful directions. In a secularized culture, fascinated by applied science and technology and dedicated to acquisition and consumption, Christian communities of fervent faith, hope and active love will be very counter-cultural indeed, quite out of step with the times, struggling against a current in spate.

Perhaps the church, as the sacrament of Christ in the world *must* be counter-cultural, at least in our western world, distinguished by its nature from the *sæculum*, the world in a Pauline or Johannine sense, not triumphant but quite humble; a small light but very bright by contrast.

Bishop John Sherlock (London, Ont.) said at the Synod of 1987 (*Vocation and Mission of the Laity*):

> Many voices in this synod have been urging lay Catholics to embrace their call to live fully in the world... as a mission of transformation, a mission which passes by way of the cross... Transforming the human world is a work of suffering, sometimes of helplessness, like that of Jesus crucified. It will identify those who dare to try it with His self-giving. The least we can do is to offer those brothers and sisters our own lives as pastors. [53]

II — A CONSISTENT ETHIC OF LIFE

The decision of the Supreme Court of Canada, January 28, 1988, striking down the existing abortion legislation exacerbated the existing situation of passionate division on this issue in our country. At the time of writing, December, 1989, it seems predictable that no new legislation will win peaceful acceptance backed by a solid consensus.

Though hard evidence is lacking, I think a majority of voters would be dissatisfied — from vaguely to very strongly — with a simple Pro-Choice legislation, leaving the decision to the expectant mother and her qualified medical advisor, subject to certain public health regulations, e.g. performance of the abortion in an acceptable hospital or clinic, by a qualified physician or surgeon, not after so many weeks of gestation certified thus and so, etc.

On Sept. 23, 1989, the leaders of several mainline churches signalled to the Prime Minister that they *"unequivocally* oppose a gestational approach".[54] It is uncertain what percentage of the *members* of those churches would be equally opposed. Nor is there clarity what percentage of the electorate would be happy with restrictive legislation which would criminalize violators or would be subject to effective surveillance.

In this unhappy situation I think it may be useful to add here a note on what has come to be known as a *Consistent Ethic of Life* (henceforth CEL). His Eminence Joseph Cardinal Bernardin, Archbishop of Chicago, and chairman of the Committee for Pro-Life Activities of the U.S.A. National Conference of Catholic Bishops, is not the author of the CEL phrase or concept, but surely its most distinguished proponent.[55]

The Cardinal developed his advocacy of CEL from his involvement in the lengthy elaboration of the two most important pastoral letters written by the U.S. hierarchy, *The Challenge of Peace: God's Promise and Our Response* (1983) and *Economic Justice for All: Catholic Social Teaching and the U.S. Economy* (1986)[56], both of which situated the Church and its social teaching in the very centre of national debates on those subjects. I think that thorough study of CEL and reflection on its implications for the Pro-Life movement — in the widest sense of active advocacy by Christian churches, by other religions and by secular humanists who set a transcendent value on human life, its worth and dignity — will be vitally important, theoretically and practically, in the difficult but essential task of forming a consensus in the shape of their desires. That would be a consensus which will effectively insist on adequate constitutional recognition of the right to life of the unborn — adequate as the best that can be hoped, achieved, in a religiously, philosophically, culturally pluralistic

society. The stakes are awfully — in the root sense — high. How many
hundred thousand abortions annually in our country?

Christian civilization (not alone in this) has always set a transcendent value on human life, appreciated as the gift of God, the
Giver and Lord of life and its sole ultimate arbiter. Sharing in something of this transcendent value are endless other goods, in the
degree that they are necessary for the preservation of life and its high
quality and truly human character. Secular humanists of the west
have entered into this inheritance and appropriated much of it, as
enshrined in philosophy, law and custom, national and international,
the labours of the League of Nations and United Nations Organizations, *The Universal Declaration of Human Rights, The International Bill
of Human Rights, The International Convention on the Elimination of all
Forms of Racial Discrimination, The Convention against Torture* and so
much else.

The web of life issues is very broad indeed, as broad as human
good, and constitutes something of "a seamless robe". The Second
Vatican Council recognized this:

> Whatever is opposed to life itself, such as any type of murder,
> genocide, abortion, euthanasia, or willful self-destruction, wha-
> tever violates the integrity of the human person, such as mutila-
> tion, torments inflicted on body or mind, attemps to coerce the
> will itself; whatever insults human dignity, such as subhuman
> living conditions, arbitrary imprisonment, deportation, slavery,
> prostitution, the selling of women and children as well as dis-
> graceful working conditions, where persons are treated as mere
> tools for profit... all these things and others of their like are infa-
> mies indeed. They poison human society, but they do more harm
> to those who practice them than those who suffer from the
> injury. Moreover they are a supreme dishonour to the Creator.[57]

Recognition of the transcendental value of life requires that one
defend and promote all that makes for *quality of life,* a truly *human* life.

The Cain-Abel story of Genesis (c. 4) is the background of the
divine prohibition "You shall not kill." (Ex. 20:13) Some Christian
sects have made this prohibition absolute, but in a world of sin and
violence, this has not been the central Christian tradition and exceptions have been thought justified, e.g. in legitimate self-defense or
to safeguard or recover very valuable material or other goods, e.g.
liberty from unjust detention, oppression, etc. Killing in a just war
was deemed licit, as well as capital punishment for grave crimes.

The presumption, however, is always against taking life if other less definitive and damaging means can achieve the legitimate defense of the good for which life might be taken.

As armaments became more fearsome, culminating in the possibility of the ruination of earth as a human environment and of the extinction of the human race, individuals and groups have denied the possibility of a just war, at least nuclear. Similarly with regard to the justification of capital punishment as a deterrent, given the possibility of more effective means and the need to affirm and witness to the transcendent value of life. Compare the evolving position of the Canadian Bishops as exemplified in Documents 1, 9, 12, 14 of Section II.

In our One World — and that increasingly post-Christian — it is hard to deny that effective appreciation of the value of human life has suffered a notable decline. Abortion has taken more lives since the second World War than all the wars of this century. Genocide has been frequent and widespread in south east Asia — Cambodia, East Timor — and is not unknown in Latin America. Terrorism as an instrument of political policy, involving the abduction and/or massacre of uninvolved innocents is frequent. The UNO has thought it necessary to publish a *Convention Against Torture* — by governments! — in view of the horrible recrudesence of such barbarity. Euthanasia, generally with the consent of the subject, is advocated and said to be practiced much more frequently than officially admitted.

An integral and effective appreciation of the transcendent value of human life cannot logically or psychologically be maintained apart from a consistent ethical appreciation of the *quality of life*. We are speaking of *human* life, which transcends the purely physical and biological (basically necessary as this is) and includes a spiritual and cultural life, all that makes for a "good life", truly human:

> Every day human interdependence... spreads by degrees over the whole world. As a result the common good, the sum of those conditions of social life... takes on an increasingly universal complexion, involving rights and duties with respect to the whole human race... There is a growing awareness of the exalted dignity of the human person. Therefore there must be made available to all everything necessary for leading a life truly human, such as food, clothing, shelter; the right to choose a state of life freely and to found a family; the right to education, to employment,...

to activity in accord with the upright norm of one's own conscience. [58]

Our world is not evolving in that sense, according to the judgment of many concerned and perceptive analysts. In recent decades the world's poor have become *relatively* poorer and more numerous. The capitalism of the First World has, in many important areas, retreated from the ideal of the Welfare State, and is organizing the socioeconomic order according to market economics, in a world of intense competition for markets and for raw materials. There an enormous advantage is enjoyed by the developed world and the more technologically advanced nations. From the inception of colonialism in the sixteenth century, it has been marked by ruthless exploitation of weaker countries and nations. Transnational corporations have not shown greater justice and compassion, while avoiding a more obvious violence and exploitation.

In developed countries the corporate world of finance-industry-commerce, spurred by the need to be competitive, to survive, strives to carve for itself an increasing share of the national income at the expense of labour and of the poor. TV shows us the terrible human wastage in far places, — results of poverty, disaster, exploitive political and social regimes or of first world investment and development, and we are moved with compassion. It is hard to believe that at home in our consumer society the rich are growing relatively richer, the poor more numerous and poorer.

Many of the Christian Pro-Life tradition do not appreciate the essential integrity, oneness-wholeness, of the Consistent Ethic of Life, strongly opposing abortion, but indifferent to many issues vital to quality of life or even rejecting much social welfare legislation demanded by social and distributive justice. Many of a left-of-centre social philosophy do not appreciate the inconsistency of their strong support for enhancement of the quality of life, while leaving human life itself, the unborn child, without constitutional protection against an exaggerated freedom of the mother "to dispose of her own body as she sees fit". [59] There is grave need of serious reflection and analysis of their ethical consistency by both parties, in the defense of life and of the quality of life in our society and world.

A consistent life ethic of individuals or of a society, supposes a vision of life as a great gift, the first and basic gift, of God or of "Nature". The vision calls the individual to set a transcendent value on life and the quality of life, to labour to communicate such appreciation to as many as possible, to see it enshrined in law, the depositary of social values, as necessary for its preservation. The argument supposes that foetal life is human life. The union of human sperm and human ovum results in a *living being,* unitary in its teleology, moving purposively towards the distant goal of mature, adult, human life. It is a *living human* being.

The central Catholic tradition — shared by many Christian churches since their beginnings — is that *innocent* human life is inviolable, that one may never *directly will or intend* the death of an innocent human being, as an end or as a means to some other end. The limitation is imposed to permit an abortion in cases where the death of the foetus results from some therapeutic procedure, gravely necessary for the health and life of the mother, the death of the foetus not being intended but regretted as an unavoidable concomitant or consequence. This is the so called principle of double effect of classic Catholic moral theology, a principle of wide application and invoked to justify abortion in certain cases where continued pregnancy involves grave danger to the life of the mother. This is hardly the place for further exposition or refinement of the same.[60]

It is with this principle in mind that traditional Catholic moral theology has regarded the *intended* termination of pregnancy (the foetus being inviable) as *always* immoral, the death being intended though for a good end and with sincere regret. And for this traditional position — that of Cardinal Bernardin, of the Sacred Congregation for the Doctrine of the Faith[61] and of most Conferences of Bishops — the prohibition of the *intended* termination of inviable foetal life is absolute, admitting of no exception.

An increasing number of very respectable Catholic theologians, however, judge that the appropriate moral principle of application is not that of double effect. They point to the traditional recognition of the right to kill in self-defense or to protect other very vital values, of capital punishment as a possibly justified deterrent, in certain circumstances and in the case of great crimes, and argue that these are justified *intended* homicides, justified by the *proportional* service of life, since otherwise life itself is at risk, at the mercy of aggressors.

Similarly — it is argued — the proportional and reasonable good served by such termination of pregnancy, justifies the abortion, for instance in the case where refusal to act would predictably result in death of mother and child. Clearly it must be a serious proportional good, to be reasonably weighed against the abortion of an inviable foetus. Richard McCormick, S.J., cites Peter Knauer, Bruno Schuller, Louis Janssens. He writes:

> When the Belgian Bishops were discussing this matter (abortion), they adverted to the direct-indirect distinction but finally concluded: 'The moral principle which ought to govern the intervention can be formulated as follows: since two lives are at stake, one will, while doing everything possible to save both, attempt to save one rather than to allow two to perish.' "[62]

This is the proportionalist argument: that such intervention, to save one life rather than lose two, is a service of life, justified by a proportional good.

It is to be noted that McCormick makes his point not to depreciate the value and need of a CEL, but to indicate an objection to Cardinal Bernardin's principle that the direct intention to abort an inviable fetus is *absolutely and always forbidden* by divine and natural law. Some very good theologians would add the condition, *"if without proportional excusing cause"*.

While the difference in position is not without importance in moral theology and ethics, it hardly touches the practical need to labour for the widest possible acceptance of a CEL, not only by the Roman Catholic and other Christian churches, but by other religious bodies and the not inconsiderable constituency of humanists who deplore the present disarray of Canadian law with regard to the value of foetal life and its effective protection.

It is hard to imagine that a Canadian government could or would pass a law permitting abortion only in the case of a therapeutic abortion, justified by the application of the principle of double effect, i.e. only in the case where the death of the foetus was not intended but resulted unavoidably, from a procedure of last resort to save the life of the mother. Given the religious and ethical pluralism of the Canadian people, such a law would probably not be a "good law", conducive to the common good, public health and the peace and order of the commonwealth. Not conforming to the conscience of a great many, it would be frequently and flagrantly violated, very difficult in application and enforcement, favouring contempt of law and probably detrimental to the health of many.

It might not be too late, however, to rally a coalition of sufficient strength to ensure that foetal life be recognized as human life, from the moment of conception, protected by the Constitutioin and the Canadian Bill of Rights, and not to be sacrificed, by the will of natural guardians or of their qualified medical agents save for seriously proportional cause, e.g. to save the life of the mother or to avoid grave risk of her death or shattered health, adding what other excusing proportional reasons might seem good to legislators to assure the common good. From an ethical or moral perspective, such a law could be a "good law", serving the purposes of public law and order and the common good, even though failing to meet all the demands of a particular religious ethic or to provide absolute or maximal protection to foetal life.

The patient continuing effort to educate in the sense of CEL, if intelligently undertaken, will help build a constituency for amendments and have the effect of strengthening the Pro-Life coalition of those who desire some greater protection for unborn life, enshrined in the Constitution or in the Canadian Bill of Rights or other law.

Lack of consistency in the defence of human life, including foetal life, entails not only a logical incoherence in the defence of quality of life but also, and inevitably, a weakening of *conviction* in the defence of the latter, and vice versa. But consistency costs. As Cardinal Bernardin observed:

> The Catholic position on abortion demands of us and of society that we seek to influence a heroic social ethic.
>
> ... If one contends that the right of every foetus to be born should be protected by civil law and supported by civil consensus, then our moral, political and economic responsibilities do not stop at the moment of birth. Those who defend the right to life... must be equally visible in support of the quality of life of the powerless among us; the old and the young, the hungry and the homeless, the undocumented migrant and the unemployed worker.[63]

Encouraging, inviting, urging the expectant mother to reverence the life she has conceived, the church assumes a serious obligation to aid and support her, single or married, in that resolve, *in every way needed*, materially, psychologically, spiritually, and to throw the full weight of her influence in support of public policy and programs to that end. It is indeed a "heroic social ethic", and not one which will endear her to a society only too ready to have recourse to the easy technological solution of abortion.

CEL is rooted in a vision or faith or perhaps instinct which holds life dear, an inestimable gift, first of a series of gifts culminating in "an endless sharing of a divine life".[64] The vision prompts to the elaboration of a coherent ethic in defense of such a transcendent value, which ethic seeks incarnation in law, all laws protecting life itself and the quality of life, the web or net or "seamless garment" of human rights, finally reduced to practice, *realized*, in the social programs needed to protect those rights, that life, its quality, individual and social. These are moral issues, in a Christian perspective — not exclusively ours — theological issues.

In our country that complex process is realized by the legislative and executive action of democratic government, the responsibility of elected representatives. The churches' persistent education in CEL, in all its breadth and internal coherence, provides some standards or criteria to judge party platforms, public policies and political candidates on a broad spectrum of issues which are fundamentally all *life* issues, issues of social morality. The purpose is not to dictate how a voter should cast a ballot but to help any who would listen to form his/her conscience, thoughtfully and responsibly.

The church legitimately fulfils a public role by articulating a framework for political choices, relating the framework to specific issues and by calling for systematic moral analysis of all areas of public policy. [65]

III — THE DOCUMENTS

It was to illustrate the social teaching of the Canadian Conference of Bishops in the wide sense of social justice noted above, that I undertook to edit this second collection. The variety of topics on which the Conference has undertaken to offer moral and pastoral guidance induced me to divide the material into six sections, in each of which the chronological order is retained.

The section titles are hardly mutually exclusive, and some statements could, with justification, have found a place in two or three categories. I trust that the table of contents and index of subjects will enable the reader to find what is wanted without difficulty.

Section I

Marriage — The Family — Divorce

The Section contains nine documents:
— four on the family in general (1, 2, 6, 7), its social, religious and educational importance;

— in three the bishops speak their mind on divorce legislation (3, 8) and on the Law Reform Commission's *Family Law Report* (4); — two on children, their learning and emotional difficulties (5) and on the need for generously subsidized child care (9).

Section II

Life Issues — Contraception

The section contains nineteen documents:
— four (1, 7, 9, 11) on the death penalty, abolition or readoption;
— five on contraception; on the law governing sales of contraceptives (2); and four (4, 5, 6, 8) on the encyclical of Paul VI, *On Human Life*, its presentation by the Canadian bishops, pastoral messages on marriage preparation and a pastoral instruction on formation of conscience regarding contraception.

— illustrating their concern, no less than ten documents treat of abortion and respect for life, the issue so dividing our country (3, 10, 12 to 19).

Section III

Liturgy — Worship

The Section comprises twelve documents:
— three on Sunday observance (1, 7, 12);
— seven on sacramental liturgical renewal, in general (2), with regard to reconciliation (4, 8, 9, 10), mixed marriages (6), on the Vatican judgment[66] (negative) with regard to the ordination of women to the priesthood (11); two on the penitential discipline of fast and abstinence (3) and on penance in a Christian life (5).

Section IV

Justice — War — Peace

The Section comprises thirteen documents;
— five deal with human rights (1, 2, 5, 6, 12);

— five with economic justice (3, 7, 8, 11, 13);
— two with issues of war and peace (4, 10);
— one on *The Canadian Catholic Organization for Development and Peace* (9), achievements and future.

Section V

Pastoral Messages [67]

There are twelve documents in the section, a selection of spiritual and pastoral messages, addressed either to the whole Roman Catholic congregation or to some particular group. Special messages are: *To Elderly Members of the Church* (3), *To All Priests in Canada* (4), *New Hope in Christ: a Pastoral Message on Sickness and Healing* (6), *Beyond Fear: a Pastoral Message on AIDS* (8). *A Letter to the People of God: on the Ministry of Priests* (Document 12) is addressed to all, but with reference to a critical dearth of priests, their rapidly increasing average age and the pressing need to work and pray for priestly vocations and to develop adequate support systems.

Section VI

At the World Synods [68]

Less known and circulated, the contributions of the Canadian bishops at the Synods may bear some introduction. The Conference enjoys a good reputation for preparation and participation in the Synods, representing the whole Catholic episcopacy, held periodically in Rome. The documentation on the Synod's theme is circulated to all bishops and discussed in the Conference's Plenary Session. The bishop delegates speak in their own names but as presenting the judgment of the Conference and in some degree, the understanding and counsel of the Canadian Church. For this reason I have included a number of their addresses which I thought significant and indicative of the heart and mind of the Canadian bishops, of their openness to the "fresh air" which Pope John XXIII hoped would ventilate the church as a consequence of Vatican II. [69]

The Section comprises sixteen documents, presentations at the Synods of 1971, 1974, 1977, 1980, and 1983. Addresses at the earlier Synods (1967 and 1969) are not available.

I think these documents very illustrative of the broader ecclesial concerns of our bishops, particularly of their pastoral preoccupations. They were not afraid to broach rather sensitive subjects, though in terms suited to the worldwide character of the audience. I thought it might elicit greater interest and be more likely to send readers to the texts presented, if I gave some key thoughts of the speakers, often in their own words. They show themselves very open to development of doctrine, even more so of pastoral practice, adapted to national or regional needs, and concerned for greater collegiality in church government. The proponents of social justice show themselves moved also by social love and a compassion for pastoral needs.

SYNOD OF 1971 *PRIESTHOOD* AND *JUSTICE IN THE WORLD*[70]

Document 1 — Archbishop G. Cardinal Flahiff, CSB, *Orientation of the Synod*: ... Synod must respond not only to the demands of Conferences, but to the proposals of our priests and the suffering of our people — only so will "collegiality be charity".

Doc. 2 — Archbishop Paul Grégoire, *Theology of Priesthood*: ...danger of formulating a definition of the priesthood not taking account of the identity crisis of the priest of today.

Doc. 3 — Archbishop J.-A. Plourde, *Relations of Bishops to Priests*: At stake in this synod is the credibility of leadership... the need for greater freedom of decision by Episcopal Conferences prepared to take greater responsibility.

Doc. 4 — Bishop A. Carter, *Married Priests in the Latin Rite*: Canadian bishops nearly unanimously favour ordaining mature married men... a small majority, even independently of need.

Doc. 5 — Archbishop G. Cardinal Flahiff, CSB., *Ministries of Women*: Recognizing the equality of women and the injustice of discrimination, must we not question if women cannot have place in the sacred ministries of the church?

Doc. 6 — Archbishop P. Grégoire, *Sins of Christians and Injustice*: ... deviations of conscience are frequent, grave sin being limited to certain areas, mostly sexual, though SS. Paul and John teach that love of neighbour is the fulfilling of the law.

SYNOD OF 1974 *EVANGELIZATION*

Doc. 7 — Bishop E. Carter, *Unity and Pluralism in Evangelization*: A church of half a billion has a two-fold need, a strong central authority... but respect for pluralism and local initiative.

Doc. 8 — Archbishop H. Legaré, *Evangelization: Task of the Whole Church*: Not to accept that the whole people of God is missioned to evangelize, is to judge the lay apostolate merely auxiliary, an affront to the dignity of the baptised-confirmed.

SYNOD OF 1977 *CATECHESIS IN OUR TIME*

Doc. 9 — Bishop E. Carter, *The Cultural Context of Catechesis* ... ours is a media culture, ceaselessly forming young and adults to consumerism and secularism, but also to communion, solidarity, authenticity, as light to shadow.

Doc. 10 — Bishop B. Hubert, *Requisites for Education in the Faith* ... a faith environment of liturgy, Word, positive moral *praxis* in groups of human scale: with Bishop, Conference of Bishops, Pope as guarantors of Christian communion.

SYNOD OF 1980 *THE CHRISTIAN FAMILY IN OUR WORLD*

Doc. 11 — Archbishop H. Legaré, *For a Theology of Marriage-Family* Frequency of divorce demands new study of the conditions of valid marriage, of the deepest nature of its indissolubility, of the enormous pastoral problem of the divorced and remarried.

Doc. 12 — CCCB Delegation, *Synthesis for Group Discussion* Need for greater local autonomy in some matters of family life, e.g. spouses of mixed marriages receiving Eucharist together, a pastoral of the divorced-remarried. Need to restudy the theology of marriage in relation to our revolutionary mastery of fertility. Many faithful cannot regard natural birth control methods as definitively the only morally acceptable way. They cannot be dismissed as merely unable to rise above human frailty.

Doc. 13 — Bishop R. Lebel, *Women in Ministry and Church Life* Need that the Church appreciate positively the feminist movement, since we are not responding to the legitimate desires of women to employ all their abilities in the service of the church.

SYNOD OF 1983 *RECONCILIATION AND PENANCE*

Doc. 14 — Archbishop L.-A. Vachon, *Male-Female Reconciliation* We must recognize the ravages of sexism, of male appropriation of privilege in the church and the imperative need to change.

Doc. 15 — Bishop B. Blanchet, *Sacramental Reconciliation*
A plea for re-evaluation and readier use of the third form of reconciliation, i.e. a single group absolution after non-specific confession of sin by the group.
Doc. 16 — Archbishop L.-A. Vachon, *Reconciliation and Non-Believers*
Church must promote dialogue with our secular culture, to humanize it for greater reverence of life, justice, solidarity, the environment and for integral personal development of all.

Somewhat reluctantly — lest this volume be exorbitantly long — I have omitted any of the Canadian addresses at the Synods of 1985 (*Twenty Years Later,* recalling the conclusion of Vatican II) and 1987 (*Vocation and Mission of the Laity in Church and World*).[71] I say reluctantly, because these were events in the history of the Synods, marking, in the first, some modest movement towards a permanent Synodal structure with participation by the laity. The latter was the occasion of the widest ever consultation of the laity in the Canadian Church on an ecclesial theme.[72] Lay speakers and observers also attended the Plenary Sessions of the Bishops Conference in preparation for the Synod and participated in small group discussion. I indicate very summarily some points of concern raised by Canadian delegates at these Synods.

Synod of 1985 — *Twenty Years Later*

The Conference sent three delegates to the Synod.[73] Among their concerns:

— inclusion of the laity in preparation and experience of the Synods.
— the need to clarify, in view of increasing lay participation in church ministries, the meaning and relation of ordained and baptismal ministries, and without *a priori* insistence on two categories of people, but seeking first how best to respond to the mission Christ entrusted to His church.
— the difficulty of educating to a social conscience, transcending a traditional individualistic ethic and of enlisting the laity in action for justice — a challenge to be faced perseveringly;
— renewal of efforts in ecumenism, an area in which progress is possible only "if the authority of the bishop is recognized and he is permitted a certain degree of subsidiarity";

— that the Synod recommend to the Holy Father a Permanent Synod of Bishops, elected by the General Synod, to decide, under the authority of the Pope, questions in the life of the church presently decided by the papal curia, the latter retaining its executive function.

Synod of 1987 — *Vocation and Mission of the Laity*

The Conference sent five delegates to the Synod.[74]

Among the recommendations:

— urgent need to develop the social conscience of the laity, the social order being especially their area of action;

— that without prejudice to the role of the Synod or bishops, care be taken to associate the entire church with the work of the Synods, which look to the good of the whole church. "The bishop is the representative of the local church but can never be separated from *communio* with his people";

— emphasis on the apostolic mission of the entire people of God, without theoretical distinction of what is proper to the laity and what to the ordained. Let there be an end to "dichotomous thinking on the dignity and role of lay people in opposition to or competition with the clergy";

— given the immensely changed status of women in our world and the fact that they are a majority of the laity active in the church, the latter's very credibility demands efforts to assure equitable representation on all levels of ecclesial life;

— need of a sustained effort to effect a synthesis of faith and culture, not only for the salvation of culture, but for faith, since faith which does not become culture is not a mature faith, fully received, lived, proclaimed.

* * *

I have tried to select and include in this second collection all the messages which I thought significant to complete the documentation of the positions taken by the Conference on issues ot social justice and the common good — at least of the Roman Catholic communion.

48 *Introduction*

The endnotes are more numerous and precise than in the originals, to clarify matters which might be obscure to those less familiar with this literature and to indicate more exactly available sources and authorities.

Care has been taken to retain the exact sense of the texts, the editing being principally cosmetic, particularly in the case of texts translated from French or Latin. If anyone is doing studies involving counts of significant words, it would be safer to work from the original texts available from the Documentation Service of the CCCB.

Edward F. Sheridan, S.J.

NOTES

1. Edit. E.F. Sheridan, S.J. (Éditions Paulines, Sherbrooke, Qc, J1E 2B9) 1987.
2. In *Origins* (Washington, 1986) 16, n. 24, p. 409ff.
3. *The Church in the Modern World*, n. 26. Quotations from the Council are generally from *The Documents of Vatican II*, edit. W.M. Abbott, SJ, Guild Press, N.Y. All English editions have the same paragraph numbers.
4. *Ibid.*, n. 27.
5. *Ibid.*, n. 30
6. *Ibid.*, n. 63.
7. *Ibid.*, n. 64; the aim is greater equality, cf. also n. 66.
8. Esp. nn. 12-17 (the dignity of the human person), 23-29 (the community of mankind), 63-72 (and the resultant social ethic). For a very summary outline of the genesis of the *Pastoral Constitution on the Church* and the development of its teaching to John Paul's encyclical *The Priority of Labour* (1981), cf. introduction in *Do Justice!*, (cf. note 1 above) pp. 16-22. Excellent on this, Donal Dorr's *Option for the Poor*, Orbis Books, N.Y., 1983.
9. Homily at Midnight Mass, St. Peter's Square, Rome, Dec. 5, 1975, for the closing of the Holy Year, cf. *Origins* (Washington. 1975-76), V, p. 482, Jn. 15, 1976. He returned to the idea in later audiences and addresses, e.g. Jan. 7, 1976, cf. *Documentation Catholique* (Paris, 1986), 73, p. 101 ff.
10. *Redeemer of Mankind*, n. 16, in *The Papal Encyclicals*, edit. Claudia Carlen, IHM (Wilmington, N.C., McGrath Publishing, 1981) V, n.16/53, p. 258.
11. In C. Carlen, cf. note 10, V, n. 8/32-37, p. 305ff.
12. John Paul II, *Rich in Mercy*, in Carlen, *op. cit.* note 10, V, n. 12/121, p. 290.
13. *Op. cit., l.c.*, V, n. 14/148, p. 293.
John Paul II himself returned to Paul VI's phrase "civilization of love" on more than one occasion. To the Bishops of Germany, Nov. 17, 1980, at Fulda: "Permit me to go back to my appeal to the *Katholikentag* (Catholic Assembly) in Berlin... 'Help me to build a worldwide civilization of love.' " in *Origins* (Washington, 1980) 10, n. 25, p. 389.
Again in his farewell message to Germany, Nov. 19, "All Europe is awaiting the realization of this civilization of love, inspired by the spirit of the Gospel and at the same time profoundly humanist, responding to the deepest needs and aspirations

of men and women, even in the social dimensions of their existence." *Documentation Catholique* (Paris, 1980), p. 1171. Cf. also *Development and the Ideal of Social Love,* to the Pontifical Commission Justice and Peace, Feb. 9, 1980, in *The Pope Speaks* (Washington, 1980) XXV, p. 173.

14. *Op. cit.,* in *Origins* (Washington) 1988, 17, n. 38, p. 654.

15. Cf. *"amare"* in *Indices Auctoritatum etc.,* tome XVI, Leonine Ed., *Opera Omnia,* (Marietti, Torino & Roma), p. 369.

16. *Compassion and Solidarity,* (CBC Enterprises, Montreal, Toronto, N.Y., London, 1987).

17. Cf. *op. cit.* note 1 above, p. 17ff., 2; also Karl Rahner SJ, *Towards a Fundamental Theological Interpretation of Vatican II,* in *Theological Studies,* Washington, 1979, XL, p. 717.

18. On the Medellin Conference, cf. *The Church in the Present Day Transformation of Latin America in the Light of the Council,* 2 vols. (Washington, L-A Bureau of US Catholic Conference, 1973). For brief notes on Medellin and post-Medellin Papal teaching, cf. *op. cit.* note 1, pp. 24-32.

19. *Justice in the World,* Introduction and II , in *The Pope Speaks,* Washington, 1971, XVI, pp. 377 and 382.

20. *Op. cit.,* note 16 above, p. 28f.

21. *The Pope Speaks,* Washington, 1976, XXI, 4, p. 18, n. 30. Cf. nn. 29-33.

22. *Op. cit.,* note 16 above, p. 28f. Cf. John R. Williams, *Canadian Churches and Social Justice* (Toronto, Anglican Book Centre and James Lorimer, 1984), pp. 9, 11.

23. Both instructions in *Origins,* Washington, respectively 14, 1984, 13, p. 193, and 15, 1986, 44, p. 714.

24. In *Origins,* (Washington, 1985), 14, p. 501, nn. 9-11; to Peruvian bishops, *Osservatore Romano,* (Rome) Oct. 5, 1984; and to bishops of Paraguay, in *Documentation Catholique* (Paris) 1984, p. 1159.

25. Congregation for the Doctrine of the Faith, in *Origins* (Washington) 1986, 15, n. 44, p. 722ff.

26. *Op. cit.,* note 16 above, p. 29.

27. *Ethical Reflections on the Economic Crisis,* p. 399 and *Ethical Reflections on Canada's Socio-Economic Order,* p. 417, in *Do Justice!,* cf. note 1 above.

28. *Ibid.,* Documents 58 and 59.

29. Cf. *Do Justice!* (note 1, above), Documents 13, 14, 16, 17, 18, 20, 21-24, 26, 31, 33-46, 49, 51, 55, 56, 58, 59.

30. Various addresses in *The Canadian Catholic Review* (Saskatoon, Sask., S7N 0W6), vol. 2, n. 9; at Flatrock, Nfld, p. 26; Front Mountain Rd., Moncton, N.B., p. 38; St. Paul's Anglican Church, Toronto, p. 46; Namao, Alberta, p. 62.

31. Cf. note 22 above.

32. *Christian Formation for Justice,* p. 218, *op. cit.,* note 1 above.

33. *Justice in the World,* III, in *The Pope Speaks,* Washington, 1971, 16, p. 334.

34. *Op. cit.* in note 32 above, p. 219.

35. *Ibid.,* p. 220.

36. *Ibid.*

37. Robert M. Brown's *Theology in a New Key* (Westminster Press, Philadelphia, 1978) is still a good introduction to liberation theology. Gustavo Gutierrez' *A Theology of Liberation* (Orbis Books, N.Y., 1973) is earlier but classic.

38. Paul VI, *Evangelization* (1975), nn. 6, 9, 30, 39, in *The Pope Speaks* (Washington, 1976) XXI, 17ff.; John Paul II, *The Social Concern of the Church,* 1987, nn. 32, 38-43, in *Origins* (Washington), 17, 1988, nn. 31f, p. 651ff; nn. 38-43, p. 654ff.

39. In *Origins* (Washington) 9, 1979, p. 334, n. 18; and p. 340, n. 43.

40. Cf. *op. cit.* note 30 above, p. 354, nn. 7-9.

41. *Op. cit.* note 39, n. 20, p. 335.

42. Cf. Vatican II, *On the Laity* (1965); also General Synod of Bishops, 1987, *Vocation and Mission of the Laity, Message to the People of God*, in *Origins*, (Washington, 1987) XVII, n. 22, Socio-Political and other secular involvement. n. 11, p. 388. Also in *Synod of Bishops — 1987*, (CCCB Publications Service, Ottawa, K1N 7B1), p. 23, esp. nn. 6, 10, 11, 13.

43. Cf. Sociologist W.E. Hewitt, in *Grail*, (University of St. Jerome's College Press, Waterloo, ON, Canada, N2L 3G3), 4, n. 1, March, 1988) pp. 35, 44ff. Also Gregory Baum, *op. cit.*, note 16 above, p. 23f.; *Puebla and Beyond*, edit. John Eagleson and Philip Scharper (Orbis Books, N.Y., 1979), pp. 19-24, 290 ff., 303f., 317ff., 335-338.

44. *Op. cit.* in note 43, pp. 49f. and 35.

45. In *Twenty Years Later* (CCCB Publications Service, Ottawa, K1N 7B1) p. 27.

46. N. 7, p. 37, *op. cit.* in note 30.

47. *Ibid.* Here he cited Vatican II, *The Church in the Modern World*, n. 39.

48. *Op. cit.* note 45 above, pp. 5 ff.

49. *Ibid.*, p. 43, n. IV.

50. *Ibid.*, D, 1-6, pp. 59-62.

51. Cf. this volume, Section IV, Document 9; on its foundation, cf. *Do Justice!* (note 1 above), Document 17.

52. Often enough the titles of their messages indicate a transcendence of the category of moral virtue and an invitation to love, charity.

Cf. *Do Justice!*, note 1, Documents 14, 18, 20, 23, 31, 33, 36, 38, 42, 43, 44, 46, 49, 55, 56.

In this volume: Section IV, Doc. 1, 2, 3, 5, 11, 12, 13;

Section V, Doc. 3, 6, 8, 9; Section VI, Doc. 8, 10, 13, 14.

Cf. Also the CCCB at the Synods:

— of 1985, Bishop B. Hubert, *Synodal Orientations: Witness of Hope and Truth; Ministries in a Church that is Communion; The Practice of Justice in the World*; and Archbishop James Hayes, *The Church: Communion of Communities*, in *Twenty Years Later*, CCCB Publications Service, Ottawa;

— of 1987, Archbishop James Hayes, *Associating all the Baptized with the Synods*: Archbishop D. Chiasson, *The People Born of Baptism*; Bishop J.-G. Hamelin, *Access of Women to Church Positions*; Bishop J. Sherlock, *The Laity: On the Cutting Edge*, in *Synod of Bishops, Rome, 1987*, CCCB Publications Service, Ottawa.

53. In *Synod of Bishops — 1987*, (CCCB Publications Service, Ottawa, K1N 7B1) p. 10; also in *Origins* (Washington), 17, n. 22, p. 396.

54. Cf. this vol., The Documents, Section II, Doc. 20, Note 1, below.

55. Cf. addresses at Fordham University, N.Y., 1983 (*Origins*, Washington) 13, p. 491; at St. Louis University, St. Louis, Mo., 1984 (*ibid.*) 13, p. 707; at National Right to Life Convention, Kansas City, MO, 1984 (*ibid.*) 14, p. 120; at Loyola University, Chicago, 1985 (*ibid.*), 15, p. 36; at Seattle University, WA, 1986, (*ibid.*), 15, p. 655; at Portland University, OR, 1986, (*ibid.*), 16, p. 345.

Many of these and others of the Cardinal, as well as critiques (and defenses) by some eight theologians, have been gathered in *Consistent Ethic of Life*, edit. T.G. Fuechtmann (Sheed & Ward, Kansas City, MO 64141), an excellent exposition of all facets of CEL, theological, pastoral and political.

56. Cf. *Origins* (Washington) 13, 1983, n. 1, p. 1 and 16, 1986, n. 24, p. 410.

57. *The Church in the Modern World*, n. 27; cf. n. 26. See also *The Church and Human Rights*, The Pontifical Commission Justice and Peace, Dec. 10, 1974, in *Social Justice*, edit. V.P. Mainelli (McGrath Publishing, Wilmington, N.C., 1978), p. 344.

58. In *op. cit.*, note 3 above, n. 26.

59. Cf. Richard A. McCormick, S.J. in *op. cit.* note 55, (edit. T.G. Fuechtmann), pp. 106-108, nn. 4-6.

60. Cf. R. McCormick *ibid.*, pp. 109-120, and bibliography.

61. *Statement on Abortion* approved by Paul VI, June 28, 1974, *Origins* (Washington) IV, n. 25 p. 387 ff., nn. 6, 9, 14; cf. also *On Respect for Human Life, etc. ibid.*, 1987, XIII, p. 695.

62. McCormick, *op. cit.* note 54, p. 112.

63. In *Origins* (Washington 1983), 13, p. 493 also in *op. cit.*, note 55, edit. Fuechtmann, p. 8.

64. *Op. cit.*, note 3 above, n. 18.

65. Cardinal Joseph Bernardin, in *Origins*, (Washington, 1984) 13, n. 43, p. 709; also in *op. cit.*, note 55 above, p. 18.

66. Congregation for the Doctrine of the Faith, *On Ordination of Women to the Priesthood*, in *Origins* (Washington, 1977), VI, n. 33, p. 517 ff.

67. Of these, Documents 1, 2, 4, 7, 8 are available from CCCB Publications Service, Ottawa, K1N 7B1.

68. For brief historical notes on the Synods, and on the participation of the CCCB, cf. *Twenty Years Later,* note 45.

69. Addresses not found here are available from CCCB Publications Service.

70. For other addresses on justice, cf. Documents 27, 28, 29, in *op. cit.* note 1 above.

71. Addresses of the Canadian delegates and other documents are available in *Twenty Years Later* (1985) and *Synod of Bishops — 1987*, CCCB Publications Service, Ottawa, K1N 7B1.

72. *The Great Lay Write-In of 1987,* Janet Somerville and *The Vocation and Mission of Lay People* by Annine Parent-Fortin, one volume; cf. also *Hopes and Concerns of Canadian Lay Catholics*, report on the CCCB Survey of 1986, all from CCCB Publications Service.

73. Their addresses were entitled:
Bishop B. Hubert: *Synodal Orientations: Witness of Hope and Truth; Ministries in a Church that is Communion; The Practice of Justice in the World;* Archbishop James M. Hayes: *The Church: Communion of Communities; Religious Life in Active Communities 20 Years after Vatican II;* Archbishop M. Hermaniuk: *The Dogmatic Constitution on the Church.* Cf. note 71 above.

74. Their addresses were entitled:
Archbishop M. Hermaniuk: *Political Freedom and Responsibility;* Archbishop J.M. Hayes: *Associating the Entire Church with the Synods;* Archbishop D. Chiasson: *The People Born of Baptism;* Bishop J.-G. Hamelin: *Access of Women to Church Positions;* Bishop J. Sherlock: *The Laity: On the Cutting Edge.* Cf. note 71.

Section I

MARRIAGE – THE FAMILY – DIVORCE

Document 1

THE FAMILY IN CANADA

Author — The Administrative Board, Canadian Catholic Conference, Nov. 13, 1958

At a time when Christian teaching on marriage is being assailed and family life undermined, we re-affirm emphatically the Church's constant teaching that marriage was instituted by God. The inclination to marry was implanted in man's nature by his Creator; forthright divine teaching confirmed the inclination of human nature; and Christ not only renewed the original decree of God but raised marriage to the dignity of a sacrament, thereby giving husband and wife the means to attain holiness in the married state. Furthermore, the first man and woman received an explicit divine command that their permanent union should be the natural beginning of the human race. Thus the family has its origin in God, and the begetting of children is both the primary purpose and the first blessing of marriage.

Many consequences flow from this. First, God's plan concerning marriage and the family cannot be changed at the whim or even by the formal decree of individuals or societies. Second, the entire range of human relationships must be ordered to respect the nature of marriage and promote the welfare of the family. The chief reason why the Church is concerned for problems of economic and social life is that disorders in these fields imperil the welfare of the family. To enable the family to attain its destiny, the Church has repeatedly emphasized the need for a program of social reconstruction. History shows that no civilization has long endured without a vigorous family life, and that one of the first symptoms of the decay of a civilization is the disintegration of its family life, marked by a loss of respect for marriage, an increase in divorce and the refusal of married couples to have children.

I — Flagrant Sins against Nature

This refusal too often leads them to prevent conception by artificial means. Such actions are sinful because they interfere with the functioning of a natural faculty. To frustrate these powers of nature is a serious matter; serious, indeed, because the conception of every human being involves the creation of a spiritual, immortal soul. For this reason the Church reaffirms its teaching, based on the law of God and of nature, that artificial birth prevention is sinful under any circumstances. As for divorce, it harms human welfare, being contrary to human nature, which tends towards a permanent union bringing security to husband and wife, children and society as a whole. Proof of this is that divorce, while seeming to solve a marital problem, almost invariably causes a host of new problems and evils, individual and social. Marriage is by nature indissoluble, in the sense that it cannot be dissolved by any merely human authority. Indissolubility is of the essence of marriage and an integral part of its constitution. Divorce, by weakening its foundation, places the whole structure of family life — and therefore of society — in peril of collapse.

Thus, divorce and artificial birth-prevention are flagrant sins against God's plan for marriage and the family. They are also sins against human nature. Men and women are more tempted to sin in these ways as the difficulties of marriage and family life become excessively burdensome. Weak, misguided couples turn from the personal sacrifices required for domestic peace and the proper rearing of families; in divorce and birth-prevention they seek false solutions to their difficulties. All this emphasizes the need for promoting legitimate ways of mitigating or eliminating the difficulties which tempt men and women to sin against God's plan. It makes clear the need for formal programs or pre-marital and marital instruction to teach young couples the true nature of marriage and the family.

II — Housing Shortage

Here in Canada one of the foremost difficulties confronting families is insufficient and inadequate housing. The Federal Minister of Labour has noted that many are living in houses which "no Canadian should be living in".[1] Serious evils follow from this: the family is divided by the fact that many mothers think they are obliged to work outside the home. Poor housing has been identified as a major cause of deliquency on the part of all members of the family. It causes parents to place unnatural curbs on the growth of families. It takes a heavy toll by robbing the family of opportunities for developing and expressing the talents of its members. The real adequacy even of many new houses is open to question. Planners and builders appear to have been caught unprepared by the development in urban settings of larger families with greater need for more space, both in their houses and outside them.

III — Rights and Duties of Mothers

The regrettable spectacle of the mother working outside her home is a consequence of this housing problem and the economic difficulties of families. A recent survey of working women in Canada showed that one in four spoke of working to help pay for her home. This was more than twice the number who mentioned all other specific material objectives combined.[2] Of other reasons given, "the great majority of the women interviewed felt that their families' economic position was such that unless they were prepared to forego all but necessities, they were obliged to work for pay."[3]

Mention of these facts is not intended as indiscriminate criticism of working women because, as Pope Pius XII has noted, it is useless to urge a woman to return to the home "while conditions prevail which constrain her to remain away from it."[4] The attack must be directed against the causes which, by taking mothers out of their

homes, notably contribute to a breakdown of family life. The working mother cannot make her full and proper contribution towards
satisfying the family's many other needs. She cannot be the leader
she should be in the family's physical, spiritual, intellectual and moral
education. Not infrequently her own moral integrity is endangered.
But even in homes where the mother does not go out to work, the
traditional family structure is endangered. Pope Pius XII has observed:

> The daughter of the worldly woman, who sees all housekeeping
> left in the hands of paid help and her mother fussing with
> frivolous occupations and futile amusements, will follow her ex-
> ample, will want to be emancipated as soon as possible and in
> the words of a very tragic phrase 'to live her own life'. How could
> she conceive a desire to become one day a true lady... the mother
> of a happy, prosperous, worthy family.[5]

IV — Rights and Duties of Fathers

We have spoken of the abuses which follow from a neglect or distortion of the true role of motherhood. It must not however, be
thought that women alone are blameworthy. In many instances, the
mother is forced into the circumstances we have deplored. In others,
it is the husband who fails to fulfil his family responsibilities. The
father, as head of the family, has the right and the duty to provide
for his family. Poor wages or unemployment leave many fathers
unable to do this properly. All the resources of private and public
institutions must therefore be directed to the urgent task of guaran-
teeing fathers a wage sufficient to meet adequately the normal
domestic needs of their families as they arise.[6] Beyond this social
aspect of the problem, it is a man's duty to work industriously and
to manage his affairs thriftily, so that all possible opportunities can
be turned to the advantage of his family. Bad management, extrava-
gant habits and irresponsible behaviour on the part of some men
contribute to their families' sufferings.

Another factor undermining the welfare of families is the failure
of many fathers to be leaders in their own homes. The shorter working week should provide opportunity for better mutual knowledge
and familiarity of parents and children. Unfortunately, the opportunities which the shorter work week should provide are often lost

through the second-job practice commonly known as "moonlighting". Whether adopted out of necessity or in a mistaken appreciation of need, this practice not only affects the family adversely but emphasizes defects in the economic structure, as political, industrial and labour leaders have noted. The father should strive to be an understanding guide and friend, a loved and trusted parent to his children, a model of constancy and virtue especially to his sons, an example to be admired and followed. Thus, in harmonious cooperation with the mother, the father must provide leadership in home education.

V — Research Needed

There is evidence of a great need for research into all social factors affecting the Canadian family. Many organizations are looking for something to do. One thing they could do is harness the talent in every community and encourage trained leaders in research projects. Again, universities annually require of their students thousands of term papers and theses. The fact that few students are assigned to study and explore actual social conditions in Canada is reflected in the general lack of research material.

VI — Role of the State

Given the duty of fathers and mothers to improve the way they fulfil their roles, and the need for industry, labour unions, universities and all manner of voluntary and formal associations to do more for families — there remains a great and vital service to be performed by public authority at every level of government. This, however, must be done in a manner consonant with human dignity. Family allowances in Canada are an example of the state's awareness of its duty to aid families. But families should also be assisted indirectly by efforts aimed at stabilizing the economy so that earnings and savings retain their real worth in goods and services, and by other means, the complexities of which cannot be treated here. Trade, monetary and taxation policies, legislative programs and public projects of all kinds have their effects, sooner or later, on the life of every Canadian family.

Since this is so, we urge government at every level to give high priority to the good of the family, in determining or implementing social policy and to recognize and respect the fact that the family has sacred rights prior and superior to any other institution, including the state itself. Thus aided and protected, families will be better able to model themselves according to the Christian ideal, becoming

> ... true centres of holiness, where the Lord is present with His graces; where the members pray together, attend Holy Mass together and receive the sacraments together; where God's law is scrupulously obeyed; where every member works earnestly towards perfection, aided by those means which family life itself provides through the fulfilment of its own duties; where the minds of children worthy of the Church are formed; where love and affection animate parents and children alike; where the eyes of God rest gently, knowing that His Holy and adorable will is constantly fulfilled.[7]

NOTES

1. Cf. *Toronto Star*, Sept. 9, 1958, p. 12.
2. *Married Women Working for Pay*, Dept. of Labour Publication, Ottawa, 1958, p. 40.
3. *Ibid.*, page 76.
4. Pius XII, *The Duties of Women in Social and Political Life*, Address to Italian Women, Rome, Oct. 21, 1945; English version in *Catholic Mind*, N.Y., 1945, vol. 43, p. 711.
5. *Ibid.*, p. 710.
6. Pius XII, *Encyclical Letter on 150th Anniversary of Hierarchy Established in U.S.A.*, Nov. 1, 1939, in *The Papal Encyclicals*, edit. Claudia Carlen, IHM (Wilmington, N.C., McGrath Publishing, 1981), IV, n. 6, p. 184.
7. Pius XII, *Address to Spanish Family Clubs*, Aug. 13, 1958, Osservatore Romano, Vatican, Aug. 14, 1958.

Section I, Document 2

THE CHURCH AND FAMILY LIFE
IN CANADA TODAY

Author — The Canadian Catholic Conference, Sept. 9, 1966

To All the Catholic Faithful, Dearly Beloved:

Christ, the Light of Nations, came among us as a servant. In this first joint message since the close of the Second Vatican Council your Bishops wish to follow his example.

Before the Council was ten days old we joined the Council Fathers from every part of the world, in a first public proclamation to "all peoples and nations." Today we welcome the opportunity of repeating those words:

It is far from true that because we cling to Christ we are diverted from earthly duties and toils. On the contrary, faith, hope and the love of Christ impel us to serve our brothers and sisters, thereby patterning ourselves on the example of the Divine Teacher who came "not to be served but to serve" (Mt. 20:28). Hence the Church too was not born to dominate but to serve. He laid down His life for us and we ought to lay down our lives for our brothers (1 Jn 3:16). [1]

Many of the new challenges we face today in the Church and in the world flow from the active spirit of renewal which marked the progress and outcome of the Council. We ourselves were caught up and moved by that spirit. We have come back with a lively desire to make real and effective in the Canadian Church those fresh insights and initiatives which, under the guidance of the Holy Spirit, found their way into the council documents.

The Present Problem

This message, which is about the family and family life, presents us with an opportunity to realize some of those desires. In Canada today, questions of great concern to the Christian family, such as contraception, abortion and divorce are topics of widespread discussion. Changes in the laws governing these areas connected with family life are now being officially proposed. It is not surprising therefore that an expression of our views is expected by many, nor that we are now responding to that expectation. No member of the Church, indeed no citizen of Canada, can be indifferent to what affects the family's welfare. The individual person of civil as well as Christian society is born, nurtured and formed within the family circle.

For us, it is a clear pastoral duty to do two things: first to speak out and to offer that religious and moral guidance which you have a right to expect; and second, to approach these complex problems in the true spirit of Vatican II, with simplicity, candour and above all with charity for all. In practice this means bearing in mind and using where applicable the Council guidelines on ecumenism, on religious liberty, on the lay apostolate, on the pastoral role of bishops, and especially on the Church in the world today.

We know this is not a simple task since the public debate over these family matters goes on among a great variety of people and institutions. It involves members of all religions and of none. It concerns the role of laity in the Church and in the world, the duties and privileges of legislators, of media persons, of the clergy, of parents. It involves a confrontation of Church with state, of one religious body with another and of all with a variety of public and private welfare institutions.

Contraception is one question, abortion quite a different one and divorce is a third. The issues in each of these questions touch on family life in different ways. We intend for the present, therefore, to deal only with the proposed alteration of the law on contraception. Future statements may deal with abortion and divorce.

Members of parliament in a committee created for that purpose are gathering information about possible changes in Article 150 of the Criminal Code of Canada. According to Article 150 it is a crime to give information, to sell or distribute materials, for any method of birth prevention or of contraception.

No one who looks at the facts can deny that a significantly large proportion of Canadian citizens are strongly opposed to the existing law. According to their own beliefs they consider it is violation of their rights. They wish to see it abolished or at least radically changed.

Changes in Article 150 are being sought even by some who do not favour contraception, for the letter of the law would impede and prohibit various legitimate and acceptable forms of responsible family planning.

The original basis of the law was a fairly common consensus among the citizens that contraception was an offence. That broad consensus no longer exists. Moreover, many citizens do not observe this law. In practice it is unenforceable and attempts to enforce it have been rare. Disrespect and disregard of this law is therefore widespread. But such disrespect for one law, which many violate with impunity, undermines respect for other laws or law in general, harming the common good which civil law is intended to safeguard.

The question, therefore, seen in the context of social fact, civil law and the demands of responsible parenthood, is of concern to every Canadian citizen. Catholic citizens, along with citizens of other persuasions and moral outlook are being asked in effect to discharge their duty to the public good of the whole Canadian society. Like other members of a pluralist society Catholics are therefore judging a civic situation in terms of the *public good.*

In this matter of course, Catholics will be found to differ with some, perhaps many, of their fellow citizens because of a particular morality taught by their Church. In that view the regulation of birth cannot be effected by just any method indiscriminately. For this reason it is important to make clear the general position of Catholics and the issues involved in the proposed changes in Article 150 of the criminal code.

Catholic Teaching on Marriage Today

First of all let us consider the general religious position of Catholics before returning to Article 150.

We believe matrimony has been endowed with certain benefits and purposes by its divine Author. These have a very important bearing on the continuation of the human race, on the personal development and eternal destiny of the individual members of the family, on the dignity, stability, peace and prosperity of the family itself and of human society as a whole. Marriage and conjugal love by their very nature are ordained to the generation and education of children. This is their crown and their glory.

Through the sacrament of matrimony, the Saviour of mankind confers multiple riches on the love of Christian spouses. They are urged by the Word of God to pattern their love on that of Christ for His spouse, the Church (Eph. 5:25). True conjugal love is caught up and merged into the plan of divine love in such a way that a man and woman are led by their mutual self-giving towards God Himself. Their shared love aids and strengthens them in their sublime roles as father and mother.

In the world today we witness a heightened appreciation of the value of a noble and freely given conjugal love. An earlier age found it quite proper and suitable to arrange for marriages by agreement between the heads of families. Such a custom would not be acceptable in this country today.

Characteristic of our present age is a new accent on the enrichment and development of human personality. A decent liberty and an opportunity for the exercise of personal choice and responsibility are more clearly seen as normal requirements for fully human growth.

The Church too has become more conscious of the role of conjugal love in God's decision for the welfare of the spouses no less than of their children. The Fathers of the Second Vatican Council taught this clearly:

> … a man and a woman, who by the marriage covenant of conjugal love "are no longer two but one flesh" (Mt. 19:16) render mutual help and service to each other through an intimate union of their persons and of their actions. Through this union they experience the meaning of their oneness and attain it with growing perfection day by day. [2]

If the transmission of human life to their children is truly a God-given mission for married couples, it must be remembered that the education and nurture of these children is also a sacred part of their responsibility.

Special Difficulties of the Present Time

As everyone knows, the proper education of children is not without its special difficulties in these times. Great changes in cultural and social life have placed new and sometimes heavy demands on the family. At the turn of the century two of three Canadians lived in the country, mostly on farms. Large families were in those days something of an economic asset and the need for advanced education for the average person was not so great. Today two of three Canadians live in the city, and the trend to urban living increases daily. The demands of our technological, urbanized society place new strains on family life. In response to the needs of industry and business, heads of families must move homes and families much more often than in former years. More education and of a higher standard is essential for children if they are to make their way in the specialized, automated economy of the future. The cost of education is mounting, and urban living expensive. Thus it happens that a large family, desirable in a predominately rural world and quite manageable, may be a mixed blessing, if not a clear hazard, for some people in the more difficult conditions of the present time.

Responsible Parenthood

As a result there is now much more concern about family planning or, as it is often called, responsible parenthood. Once again, we can say that the Church recognizes this modern need, accentuated by changed social and economic conditions. The Vatican Council urges parents with docile reverence towards God to come to a right decision about the size of their family through careful consideration and common counsel.

In planning the size of their family, husband and wife should weigh their own welfare as well as that of their children, those born and those yet to be born. To come to a sound judgment they will have to take into account the material and spiritual condition of the times and their own status in life. The needs of the family group, of temporal society and of the Church herself should also be considered.

Parents are thus responsible for making the final decision about how many children they should have. They may not however, make this judgment arbitrarily or on the basis of passing whim. They must accept the responsibility of weighing such concrete factors as health, physical and psychological, economic conditions and obligations to others. Their decision should then be made in the light of the divine law and the authentic interpretation of that law proposed by the teaching office of the Church.

Christian spouses trusting in Divine Providence and cultivating a spirit of sacrifice, glorify the Creator and grow towards perfection in Jesus Christ when they perform their office of procreation, animated by generous responsibility as humans and as Christians. Those parents who are able and who by common consent, with careful thought and generous resolve, assume the task of raising their children suitably, even a large number, are deserving of special commendation.

We cannot deny that married couples are often faced with real hardships in life which make it a matter of prudence that the number of their children should not be increased, at least for a time. Yet not every method of limiting family size can be approved.

Population and Birth Control

Very few of you can be unaware that the whole question of population, family and births is at present being studied in the most thorough manner by a special committee of experts and that more recently Pope Paul VI has set up a special commission of Cardinals and Bishops to prepare a report on this complex and delicate subject.

The Council Fathers did not propose any concrete solutions while this matter was under consideration. They did, however, formulate, an important statement bearing on the whole question.

Therefore when there is a question of harmonizing conjugal love with the responsible transmission of life, the moral aspect of any procedure does not depend solely on sincere intentions or on an evaluation of motives. It must be determined by objective standards. These, based on the nature of the human person and his acts, preserve the full sense of mutual self-giving and human procreation in the context of true love. Such a goal cannot be achieved unless the virtue of conjugal chastity is sincerely practiced. Relying on these principles, sons and daughters of the Church may not undertake methods of regulating procreation which are found blameworthy by the teaching authority of the Church in its unfolding of the Divine Law.

Everyone should be persuaded that human life and the task of transmitting it are not realities bound up with this world alone. Hence they cannot be measured or perceived only in terms of it, but always have a bearing on the eternal destiny of men. [3]

We are by no means indifferent to the worldwide concern over birth control. We share it. But we have no easy readymade or immediate solution.

Recent medical discoveries no less than mounting anxiety over rapid increase in population in some parts of the world have raised new and serious problems. Yet the medical, psychological, social and theological issues are so complex and they go so deeply into the welfare of the family and of society in general that hasty decisions must be avoided at all costs — even at the cost of some present uncertainty and confusion. We are disposed to bear patiently and we ask you to bear patiently this present period of waiting for further clarification.

The Revision of Article 150 of the Criminal Code

There is no need for delay, however, in dealing with the problems connected with the current move to change Article 150 of the Criminal Code of Canada.

Catholics do not seek to impose their morality on the rest of society nor do they expect civil law to be the complete embodiment of that morality. Indeed it should be clear that civil law and morality though having overlapping areas, have distinct purposes, the one aiming at the public good through enforceable law, the other aiming without force or coercion at personal goodness and salvation. Naturally at many points they coincide, but they remin distinct.

This point can hardly be over-emphasized: the question that may come before parliament is not whether the use of contraceptives is morally right or morally wrong. Parliament is not competent to decide such a question. Parliament is not constituted to teach morals but to pass laws for the common good of society. The real question, and this is the business of parliament, centres on whether or not the law of the land should make the sale or distribution of contraceptives or giving information about birth control a legal crime. In answering that question we must remember that a large number of honest Canadians sincerely believe that this law violates their rights of conscience. We must remember too that the law is not in fact enforced; and that it cannot be enforced without creating greater evils than it might prevent.

We do not, therefore, conceive it our duty to oppose appropriate changes in this law. Indeed we could easily envisage an active leadership on the part of lay Catholics to change a law which under present conditions they might well judge to be harmful to public order and the common good. In this connection it should be noted that even to give information about methods of family planning such as the "rhythm" or the "sympto-thermic" technique of the Serena movement, which are definitely not opposed to Catholic teaching, is quite likely a criminal offense according to the present law.

Protecting the Values of Family Life

Now is the time for friendly cooperation of all groups and persons interested in the good estate of the Canadian family. Fundamental differences may appear, for example, in the question of abortion whenever direct destruction of human life is in question. In spite of serious differences, however, nothing should blind us to the fact that there are still many needs of family life on which all can agree to work together.

It would be a great blessing for Canada, therefore, if those who exercise influence over communities or social groups were to join in positive planning through research and beneficial legislation for the support and strengthening of Canadian family life. To this end Christians should be eager to cooperate with all others of good will. Those who are skilled in the sacred sciences as well as those who are expert in medical, biological, social and psychological sciences can by joint labours do a great deal to provide suitably modern counsel for the family. In this way they will not absorb or dominate the family but aid it to perform its role in society with independence and competence. Their research could also make it possible to discover various conditions favouring a proper regulation of births.

Before ending this message we wish to acknowledge once again with gratitude the prayers and support you gave us during the four years of the Second Vatican Council. Thanks is due also to the many who by carefully prepared briefs or by private communications helped us greatly in the arduous work of debate and decision. Christians of other denominations as well as many non-Christians followed our work with genuine interest and sympathy. Not a few of them gave us wise counsel. To these also our warmest gratitude.

We look, forward with hope to a further growth in this fraternal spirit of charity between laity and clergy, Christians and non-Christians. Certainly, no one who is honest with self and with God can compromise on what is sincerely believed to be the truth. We do not ask such false compromises of others and we cannot make them ourselves. Yet the urgencies of the times and the promptings of the Holy Spirit are, we believe, teaching all of us this lesson: we should concentrate less on those things which divide us and more on those which draw us together.

The spiritual turmoil of our day is a part of the profound and total revolution that is affecting the human family in every dimension of its being. The human mind reaches out among the planets and probes ever deeper into the hidden secrets of matter and energy. It explores the mysteries of the mind and body and scrutinizes the dynamic processes of social and cultural life. In doing so men and women are, in a sublime sense, the co-creators with God of the evolving universe in which they live. We remain unsympathetic to this modern world at the risk of losing contact with contemporary humanity. This must not happen for God so loved the world that He sent His only-begotten Son (Jn 3:16).

The presence of Christ in our midst should give us courage. While we struggle to adapt to this new world, perhaps even with some sense of loss and pain, we have no real grounds for discouragement. Faith in Christ and in His power to redeem the world leads us to an unshakeable hope and confidence at all times and in all trials and anguish. Christ, Our Lord, laid down no conditions when He said: "Behold, I am with you all days even to the end of the world" (Mt. 28:20).

NOTES

1. Second Vatican Council, *Message to the Human Family.*
2. Ibid., *The Church in the Modern World*, n. 48.

3. *Ibid.*, n. 51. The translation of the two sentences immediately preceding the note number (3), from the Abbott edition of *The Documents of Vatican II* (Guild Press, N.Y., 1966) is somewhat ambiguous. It separates the obligatory character of "must be determined by objective standards", from the principal verb of the next sentence (only one sentence in the Latin) "These... preserve etc." The Latin combines these in one sentence better translated: "Therefore the moral character of conduct, where there is question of reconciling conjugal love with responsible transmission of life, does not depend only on a sincere intention and evaluation of motives, but *must be determined by objective criteria* drawn from the nature of the person and of his (her) acts, which respect (i.e., must respect) the total meaning (sense, direction) of mutual donation and of human procreation in a context of true love." In *Vatican Council II*, edit. Austin Flannery, O.P. (Daughters of St. Paul Press, Boston, 1975), the sense of the Latin is better preserved: "When it is a question of harmonizing married love with the responsible transmission of life, it is not enough to take only the good intention and the evaluation of the motives into account; the objective criteria must be used, criteria drawn from the nature of the human person and human action, criteria which respect the total meaning of mutual self-giving and human procreation in the context of true love." *op. cit.* p. 955. *Editor's note.*

Section I, Document 3

ON PROPOSED CHANGE OF THE LAW ON DIVORCE: TO THE SPECIAL JOINT COMMITTEE OF THE SENATE AND HOUSE OF COMMONS

Author — The Canadian Catholic Conference, April 6, 1967[1]

The Canadian Catholic Conference is pleased to accept the invitation to present a statement to the Special Joint Committee of the Senate and the House of Commons on Divorce. We offer the following considerations and recommendations regarding proposed changes in Canadian divorce laws.

The Canadian Catholic Conference, the national organization of the Catholic Bishops of Canada, carries on its activities through an administrative board and various elected commissions and committees. The general secretariate of the Conference is in Ottawa.

We have already submitted a statement to the House of Commons Standing Committee on Health and Welfare concerning the changing of federal legislation relative to contraception (September 9, 1966). The principles embodied in that submission are equally essential to a precise understanding of the present submission. For this reason we include the earlier statement as an appendix.[2]

I — THE ROMAN CATHOLIC CHURCH AND THE INDISSOLUBILITY OF MARRIAGE[3]

The Roman Catholic Church maintains that valid marriage is indissoluble. All her members, whatever be the laws of their country, are therefore committed to remain faithful to this sacred law on marriage. When two baptized persons marry, they are united until death by a bond that is both natural and sacramental.

Marriage in Christ is a sacrament of salvation, and the Church received from her Founder the responsibility of providing her members with the means necessary to live their Christian faith. Therefore, in this area the Church has authority to make her own distinctive laws.

It is helpful to recall some of the reasons underlying the Church's position on the indissolubility of the marriage bond. They are rooted in the natural law, namely, the basic obligations arising from the very nature of God's human creatures. But religious reasons transcend the natural law and arise also from the new meaning which Jesus Christ has given to marriage.

The voluntary, permanent and exclusive union of husband and wife becomes, through the grace of the sacrament, the symbol and witness of God's redemptive plan. This is true at several levels.

1 — First, as regards conjugal love: this love, ever faithful and ready to forgive and meet changing circumstances, ever generous, striving to overcome egoism and self-seeking, ever trusting and reverential, sharing joys and sorrows, is at once the manifestation and the extension of the love that God offers to all in Jesus Christ.

2 — Moreover, through the procreation and education of the children, to which marriage is ordained by its very nature, the couple shares intimately in God's work of creation and salvation.

3 — Finally, the Christian home, built on fidelity and the irrevocable gift of husband and wife to each other and to their children, is likewise witness to that profound unity which the Church is called to foster among all. Herein lies a dignity which makes sacred the bond that unites them.

In this new dimension given by Christian marriage to the union of husband and wife, human love finds its true maturity. Conjugal love, when inspired by the Gospel, is able in a special way to foster and develop the potentialities of each spouse, as well as the spiritual riches that they bring to their mutual lives.

Although many married couples may never attain this high ideal of conjugal love and fidelity, nevertheless the Church wishes to encourage and maintain it by her doctrine and laws. In the eyes of the Catholic Church, this ideal corresponds to the deepest longing of mankind, and represents a standard that serves well in times of difficulty.

Nevertheless, in serious and exceptional cases, it can happen that after a number of years a validly married couple may feel obliged to discontinue their common life. This decision may involve the good of the spouses themselves for whom life together may have become unbearable. The decision may look also to the good of the children whose human and religious stability is gravely endangered by the atmosphere of constant disagreement in the home. In these cases, the Church, having seriously examined the facts, permits what is known as "separation". In our view, there should be a civil procedure for a judicial separation upon certain limited grounds which, while not permitting the parties to remarry, would protect the rights of the children and the civil rights of the parties.

When the judicial separation does not provide sufficient safeguards for the rights of the partners and their children, Catholic couples are permitted to seek a civil divorce. They are then freed, before civil law, of all legal responsibility binding them to each other, and are juridically separated. Nevertheless, the Church, while tolerating such a recourse to civil divorce, continues to consider the married couple bound to each other. According to the mind and law of the Church, they remain mutually pledged to each other until one of them dies. Thus they are not free to remarry.

II — THE ROMAN CATHOLIC CHURCH AND PROPOSED CHANGES IN DIVORCE LEGISLATION

So far, we have discussed the teaching of the Church in regard to her own members. The Catholic Church maintains that civil authority has no power whatsoever to dissolve the marriage bond, and many non-Catholics restrict that power to divorce on grounds of adultery. It is possible, however, even for these, out of respect for freedom of conscience, to tolerate a revision of existing divorce legislation, with a view to obviating greater evils.

The Church, when asked her opinion by civil legislators, must look beyond her own legislation to see what best serves the common good of civil society. With this in mind, and given the fact that a divorce law already exists in Canada, we offer the following considerations:

1 — It is alleged that present divorce laws encourage perjury and collusion, if not adultery itself. It can occur too, that the party considered innocent in the eyes of the law may be the more responsible for the marital discord or responsibility may be equal. It is also true that judicial procedure, when carried through in a hurried and superficial manner, can lead to further scandal and even injustice.

This situation, aggravated by the sincere conviction of many citizens that present legislation is defective, contributes to a widespread disrespect for law in general. In view of these considerations, the question arises whether the present law is conducive to the good of society.

2 — Canada is a country of many religious beliefs. Since other citizens, desiring as do we the promotion of the common good, believe that it is less injurious to the individual and to society that divorce be permitted in certain circumstances, we would not object to some revision of Canadian divorce laws that is truly directed to advancing the common good of civil society.

It is not for us to go into detail about grounds for divorce which would be acceptable or not; this, we believe, should be left to the well-informed consciences of our legislators. We cannot, however, over-emphasize that an indiscriminate broadening of the grounds for divorce is not the solution to the problem of unhappy marriages. Such legislation undoubtedly would contribute to destruction of some essential values on which our society is built. In elaborating changes they think should be made in the present law, legislators must never lose sight of the sacred value of the family, the primary and basic cell of society. Their aim should be to avoid anything that might seriously endanger peace, love, frankness, stability and trust that make the home the base and centre of the well-being of the state.

III — PROPOSED PROGRAMS TO STRENGTHEN FAMILY LIFE

Divorce may cause problems more serious than those it seeks to control. Once a family has been disrupted, there arise special difficulties regarding the material, psychological and spiritual welfare of both parents and children. This is particularly true for children of adolescent age.

The best solution is to be found in an extensive rethinking of the entire body of legislation dealing with marriage and the family. An eventual revision of the divorce law makes sense only if it is part of a wide, positive policy for strengthening family values and particularly for ensuring the serious motivation and proper prepration of couples intending marriage.

Social science confirms that the majority of family problems that end in divorce have their roots in the levity and lack of forethought with which many, especially younger people, approach marriage. The subsequent bitter disenchantment and crises should surprise no one.

It is the responsibility of civil authority to seek by appropriate laws to prevent such situations. To this end, we present the following considerations:

1 — We urge your committee to consider how governments can best encourage public support for much more extensive research into all questions concerning marriage and the family.

Adequate research into marriage, its success and its difficulties, is required for any proper revision of legislation, for realistic educational programs to prepare our citizens for lasting marriages, as well as for competent counselling and reconciliation services for marriages that are experiencing difficulties. Your committee might appropriately urge legislators and public authorities at all levels to give serious consideration to opportunities for supporting research into family questions.

2 — We also urge your committee to study seriously ways in which public authorities at all levels, in dialogue and co-operation with religious groups and interested private organizations, may give effective support to programs of education for marriage. Many other groups and Churches appearing before you have made similar proposals. The experience of the Catholic Church in this area lends strength to our conviction concerning the need for these courses.

3 — There is also need for a broad common policy to strengthen family values in existing homes that require help in their difficulties. The basic causes of marital conflicts are often found in the inadequate family training that the partners received, and in the insecurity and discord of the homes in which they were reared. If the young do not learn from the counsel and example of their elders that love requires self-denial and generosity, they are not likely to learn it at all.

4 — Moreover, we earnestly ask that, as a service to couples in difficulty, the civil authority establish agencies to study each case

carefully, and to seek positive remedies, taking account of the religious convictions of each couple. The experience of psychologists, sociologists, social workers and spiritual advisors whom we consulted shows that couples very often can be fully reconciled through the attentive and devoted work of these agencies. Those seeking divorce should first be directed to them. Civil society, and not the Churches, should take an active lead in such attempts at reconciliation.

This calls for important changes in the procedures of divorce courts, where they exist. It is important that these courts include specialists in the social and pastoral sciences as well as in civil law. In this way, each case would be studied thoroughly while taking into account all the human dimensions of the problem.

We are grateful for the opportunity to present our views on this important matter which involves so intimately the future of our country.

NOTES

1. Cf. *Proceedings of the Special Joint Committee of the Senate and House of Commons,* No. 24, April 20, 1967; pp. 1510-1513. Also in *Contraception — Divorce — Abortion,* Publications of CCCB, 90 Parent Ave., Ottawa, K1N 7B1.

The Canadian Catholic Conference was also a signatory of *Statement of Several Canadian Churches to the Minister of Justice on Proposal to Reform the Divorce Laws,* Nov. 8, 1969, cf. Bulletin 200, Feb., 1969, The Anglican Church of Canada, 900 Jarvis St., Toronto, M4Y 2J6.

2. Cf. Section 2, Document 2 of this volume.

3. In this context "Roman Catholic Church" signifies all Catholics in communion with the Holy See.

Section I, Document 4

BRIEF TO THE MINISTER OF JUSTICE ON THE *FAMILY LAW REPORT* OF THE LAW REFORM COMMISSION OF CANADA

Author — The Administrative Board, the CCCB, January 26, 1977

INTRODUCTION

1. The Minister's Request

The Canadian Conference of Catholic Bishops is pleased to respond to the request of the Honourable Ronald Basford, Minister of Justice, for reactions to the report entitled *The Family Law Report*, issued in 1976 by the Law Reform Commission of Canada. Mr. Basford's request for opinions on the report was contained in a speech given in the House of Commons on October 25th last. In the past months the bishops of our conference have studied the report and have consulted with persons experienced in the areas of marriage counselling and of family law. In reacting to the report and offering recommendations, our intention is to foster the well-being of families by advocating measures that will support a healthy family life.

2. Family Well-being

In our time, many factors tend to undermine family well-being. Economic decisions frequently bring families to crowded cities where housing and living conditions are intolerable. Fathers are separated from their families; work often dehumanizes both men and women, and women are still victims of discrimination, with respect to employment and salaries. Advertising too, has very serious effects on family finances, causing many to fall victim to consumerism. Working and living conditions experienced by many parents are often difficult, with the result that husbands and wives frequently need and expect more understanding and support from one another than they receive. Disappointments and serious pressures are the consequences. In turn, families in such difficulties raise a new generation with similar inadequacies, unless conditions change and children are given hope and courage.

3. The Permissive Society

Many attitudes of our permissive society have also influenced marriages and families. When individuals are concerned exclusively with their own real or imaginary needs, and seek to be fulfilled without any concern for the consequences of their actions for others, relations within the home are undermined. Fortunately there are signs that these attitudes are being perceived in a new light. As we become more aware of our interdependence, we are more conscious of the needs and rights of others, and we realize that we cannot exploit one another without damaging ourselves. The search for more human values and an increasing sense of responsibility for one another are hopeful developments that will benefit Canadian families.

4. Religion, the Family and Law

Religion is concerned with the deepest relationships of our lives and the ultimate meaning of life itself. Legislators too, are trusted by the general public to plan programmes and enact laws that will promote and protect those fundamental values and institutions needed not only by the individual person but which are the very cement holding our society together. Leaders of religious communions and our elected legislators have therefore, a common interest in the stability of marriage and in family well-being, since society recognizes marriage and the family to be fundamental values and institutions. For this reason a dialogue is appropriate, to discover what is in the best interests of society. It is in this spirit that our statement has been prepared.

5. Our Basic Position

Our basic position is that marriage stability, which depends upon the voluntary, permanent and exclusive commitment of husband and wife, is both an attainable ideal and the foundation of our society. This ideal "corresponds to the deepest longing of mankind, and represents a standard that serves well in time of difficulty."[1] In such a union, human love finds its maturity and there is mutual enrichment.

Men and women who are courageous enough to make such a promise for life and who believe that God will help them to be true to each other, will have the love and strength to meet the challenges of modern life. Such a love will endure, and it will be a forgiving love.

It is recognized that stable marriages have a beneficial effect on society and that marriage breakdowns cause much pain and hardship.

The Christian Church has a fundamental interest in the establishment and maintenance of wholesome and enduring marriage and family relationships. We are concerned about divorce because of its effects on society and the distress and anguish of persons affected by the breakdown of marriage.[2]

6. Children's Needs

A happy marriage is the foundation of family life. And children will thrive if given the proper home environment.

The family remains the most adequate social structure for bearing and raising children. It constitutes an irreplaceable emotional environment for nurturing the child and for lavishing upon him or her, through all kinds of care, the tenderness and warmth which are necessary for mental equilibrium and psychological development. From one's earliest days, the personality of each is structured positively or negatively...[3]

Recent experiments, such as group marriages, inevitably lead to innumerable human problems among men and women, and the neglect of children. The personal development of parents and children, and the socialization of the latter depend on sound family relationships. From the point of view of an adult, of a child or of the public interest, there is no substitute for such relationships.

7. The Family Law Report

We are pleased that the report states that marriage is the "Major institutional foundation of our society" (Part 2, Dissolution of Marriage, 2.9), and that the family is described as the "basic unit in society" (Part 5, Conclusions, 5.4). It contains recommendations which we support and others which we oppose.

8. The Report's Limitations

We are convinced that some of the perceptions and recommendations of the report should be rejected.

— The report stresses the major importance of marriage and the family but suggests very few measures to strengthen these institutions.

— Marriage appears in the report as a private contract that should be dissolved through simpler procedures than in the past.

— It is more a *Divorce Report* than a *Family Law Report*.

— It suggests measures that may appear humane but which we believe will cause much human suffering.

— Very little is mentioned about the social roots of family problems and society's responsibility to families.

— The report appears to be too optimistic about the value of new legislative machinery for families.

— The power inherent in the law to uphold values is ignored.

— The role of community services and agencies, we believe, should have received more recognition in the report.

I — THE UNIFIED FAMILY COURT

9. General Reaction

Our reaction to this first section of the report is that all the judicial aspects of family matters should be centred in a single court, as the authors recommend. However we do not favour the transfer of the counselling, conciliation and reconciliation dimensions of family questions to the exclusive control of the courts. A court should have a "social arm", but such an arm ought not to embrace all family questions, possessing a near monopoly. The tendency of the report is to favour centralization of all services, while overlooking the need for new initiatives at the community level. While we realize that conditions vary in each of the Canadian provinces, we believe that new coalitions should be encouraged by the courts, various government departments and community and church-related organizations to foster the well-being of families. The situation we are facing today demands such a united effort.

10. Complementary Services

At the present time various community organizations are assisting families through marriag education and a variety of counselling services. On the other hand, neither the above services nor legal aid are available to those in marital or family difficulties in many areas of Canada. Our suggestion is that future legislation take into account what is being done by community and church-related organizations and that such services be encouraged or be organized where they are non-existent. They should be seen as complementry to the courts. Their effectiveness will depend on close liaison with the courts, and the financial aid received.

11. Centralization

When there is too much centralization of services, people often feel less responsible for one another, at the community level. If counselling, for example, were a shared responsibility, a court, when it is first made aware of a family difficulty, could refer the person to a community centre before using its authority or services. Families need such centres, staffed by qualified personnel and recognized by the courts. It will be found that professional, voluntary and religious-oriented persons in such centres will offer new motivations, initiatives and guidance to those in need. Because of the many cultures and faiths in our pluralistic society, and the pressures affecting families, such centres with their many services are urgently needed. Marriage and family life will be strengthened if such centres are encouraged and supported. If, however, the State attempts to do too much, communities will be less responsible and local initiatives smothered.

II — DISSOLUTION OF MARRIAGE

12. Divorce Is a Tragedy

Measures strengthening family values, we suggest, should be the priority for legislators; measures that will *appropriately terminate* marriages which offer no hope of reconciliation are of less importance. In spite of our conviction, however, that the increase of marriage breakdowns could be checked by new initiatives, many couples will still seek civil divorces and legislation for them will be debated. A divorce is a sign of a failure in a human relationship; it is a tragedy, a source of great suffering for adults and children and a serious danger to society. Because it is a result of a marriage breakdown, it is cruel and misleading to claim that a divorce, of itself, is a benefit for anyone.

13. Our Position

It is well known that the Catholic Church opposes the "divorce mentality" so common today. Our opposition is not based on a desire to impose our teachings on others; rather we oppose any philosophy or legislation that could undermine family life and be contrary to the best interests of society. We believe that a validly married couple remain pledged to each other until one of them dies. And while we acknowledge that in some circumstances the civil effects of a divorce may provide necessary protection or support to members of a family, when common life is unbearable or the welfare of children is an issue, such a divorce should be sought only when all other approaches have failed. Validly married Catholics who may be given a divorce in such circumstances are not free to remarry. In stating our position in this way, we of course realize that many divorced persons are victims of another's irresponsibility. We wish to support the victims of such marriages, while working with others to take preventive measures that will lessen marriage breakdowns.

14. Positive Elements of Report

In this section of the report, we wish to acknowledge the efforts made to avoid vindictiveness during a marriage breakdown, and to promote assistance from the court, when circumstances warrant it. We believe, too, that the "collusion and connivance" aspect of the present legislation could be eliminated (mentioned in recommendation 2), since there are situations in which both spouses might agree to present a petition to the court. We also support the suggestion that separation need not be a requirement during the dissolutiion process (recommendation 6). We further acknowledge the importance of the special provisions for a spouse and children in times of difficulty, as outlined in recommendations 8, 9, 10, 11, and 12. Finally, we endorse recommendation 15, since a minimum amount of time is necessary when a petition has been presented, to allow for reflection and counselling.

15. Recommendations Unacceptable

With respect, we oppose the central recommendations of this section; i.e. that the only basis for the dissolution of marriage should be the failure of the personal relationship between husband and wife, and that the concept of "matrimonial fault" be inapplicable (recommendations 1, 2). Earlier in this section (2.19) it is recommended that the dissolution process in the court be a ministerial and not a judicial process. We also oppose this recommendation.

16. Destruction of Values

Such recommendations, if implemented, would contribute significantly to the devaluing of marriage in our Canadian society. In 1967, our Conference adopted this position in respect to divorce:

> We cannot over-emphasize that an indiscriminate broadening of the grounds for divorce is not the solution to the problem of unhappy marriages. Such legislation undoubtedly would contribute to destruction of the essential values on which our society is built. [4]

17. The Role of Law

Family law, and all law, should aid us to understand our responsibilities to one another by affirming society's fundamental values. Good laws should be normative and should educate us about our values. They ought to support our fundamental institutions. They should assist us to be just in our relationships.

The Law Reform Commissions's Report entitled *Our Criminal Law* provides a general philosophy of law:

> ... The Criminal Law is fundamentally a *moral* system... basically it is a system of applied morality and justice. It serves to underline those values necessary, or else important, to society. When acts occur that seriously transgress essential values, like the sanctity of life, society must speak out and reaffirm those values. [5]

We suggest that this philosophy ought to inspire legislation dealing with marriage and the family. It is lacking in *The Family Law Report.*

18. Basis for Dissolution

The report recommends that the only basis for dissolution of marriage should be the failure of the personal relationship between husband and wife (referred to as "marriage breakdown"). We find this recommendation inconsistent with a statement earlier in the report, that marriage is the "major institutional foundation of society".

A contract with society is involved and it should not be terminated as if it were a private contract only. The word "failure" permits various interpretations. It should be rejected as a concept for family law. Further, failure, whether real or imaginary, is caused by many factors. Should not a court be concerned with the causes of the "failure" in order to reach a just settlement? Marriage loses much of its significance if we profess that it is the foundation of our society and yet terminate it, almost casually. Such a law would negate the principle we profess.

19. Matrimonial Fault

The present legislation, which includes the concept of fault, is portrayed in the report as the cause of much pain. No doubt some reform is needed. The question should be asked: is the legislation inadequate, or is it the manner in which opponents in court use the law for their own purposes?

Were it possible, we would be happy to eliminate all vindictiveness and pain in the courts and advocate forgiveness and reconciliation. We believe, however, that when a court is concerned with such a profound and intimate relationship, some pain, bitterness and disappointment are inevitable.

In the past, animosity has often arisen in cases involving maintenance and custody. As other sections of *The Family Law Report* deal with these matters, it is reasonable to hope that there will be less animosity in the future, assuming that such suggestions will be implemented. It seems unreasonable therefore, to sweep away the concept of fault, since it concerns conduct and human actions, which are truly relevant considerations for a court. As mentioned above, animosity will be decreased through other measures advocated in the report. We believe therefore, that this concept has a place in family law. Perhaps the phrase "matrimonial fault" could be altered, and the concept expressed in more appropriate language.

20. Accepting Responsibility

We believe too, that lawyers should be asked to co-operate in such cases. There are ways of establishing facts that will contribute to a person's self-understanding and healing. Ideally, this should at times be experienced in a court.

The world-famous psychiatrist, Dr. Karl Menninger, in a recent book wrote that when no one is responsible or guilty, and no moral questions are asked, people feel helpless and give in to despair. He stated as well that hope would return to the world if we learned to accept responsibility for our actions and were answerable for ourselves and for others. [6] We suspect that many judges would agree with Dr. Menninger, and we believe that the fault concept should play a more creative role in family law.

21. The Dissolution Process

In recommendations 3 and 5, the report suggests that a breakdown may be established by the evidence of one spouse and that the function of the court, in the dissolution process, should be ministerial, not judicial. We are convinced that the first recommendation, if implemented, would be a cause of injustice and hardships. It would facilitate hasty decisions in a time of difficulty, while the law should inspire reflection on our responsibilities and values. Insecurity and injustice would be the results of such a law, which would often favour the person with the greater earning capacity and economic independence, who may lack a sense of responsibility for the spouse. For these reasons we oppose this recommendation.

We are convinced too, that the dissolution process should be judicial, not ministerial, for otherwise, the grant of a divorce would be merely a formality. When a court is concerned with society's major institution, it should make a judgment, and not reduce the procedure to the level of a minor incident. To make a fair judgment, a judge must have access to all relevant information.

22. Grounds for Divorce

In this section (2.2) it is suggested that churches invented the concept of matrimonial fault. This is inaccurate. Recognition of mutual responsibility in marriage, and of the serious consequences of failure to accept such responsibility, are prevalent in many cultures and predate Christianity.

We also question the allegation that a woman's economic needs are primary factors in the concept of fault grounds (2.4). Promises to one's marriage partner and responsibility assumed, have been taken most seriously by civilized societies everywhere, independently of economic considerations.

23. The Needy Spouse

Financial provision for a needy spouse (and children) is also recommended (8a). We urge that this be reviewed and be made more precise. We are concerned, for example, about a wife and mother who, following a marriage breakdown, considers it her duty to remain at home with her children rather than to work outside the home. She should be encouraged to do so and financial provision should be made, regardless of the fact that she may be capable of earning a good income. This could also apply to a father who has complete responsibility for his children.

24. Other Reactions

We urge caution in respect to the need of a child for legal counsel (9b). We would hope that judges and court officials would involve agencies and representatives of the child's faith in such circumstances. What is most important is that a child be free to speak to a person in whom he or she has confidence. Except in unusual circumstances, we suggest that a legal counsel would not be required and recommend that a child not be asked to choose one parent in preference to the other.

The report uses the word "enable" to describe the court's role in encouraging a couple to seek reconciliation (13a). While there will be couples for whom little can be done, there will also be many who could be counselled and reconciled. Because of the possibility of such a reconciliation, and because these first relationships with the court are so critical, we recommend that it be mandatory for a couple to seek reconciliation. They owe this to one another and to society.

III — OTHER COMMENTS ON THE FAMILY LAW REPORT

25. Economic Support

In section 3 (*Economic Readjustment*) we commend the members of the Commission for their sense of justice, in the formulation of recommendations that would protect the interests of spouses and children. In particular we support the suggestion that the family unit be considered a joint venture, with the spouses being equal (3.6) and having equal responsibility regarding finances and child care (3.9).

26. Children's Rights

In section 4 (*Children and the Dissolution of Marriage*), we commend the Commission for its concern for the rights of children and the many suggestions relating to the care and custody of children.

27. Maintenance

In its conclusions, we share the concern of the Commission in its recommendation that measures are urgently needed to enforce maintenance obligations for spouses and children (5.2). The consequences of non-support are well documented. Elementary justice demands that support be obligatory.

IV — FAMILY POLICY AND FAMILY LAW

28. The Family

In our introduction (#5), we expressed our conviction about the objective value of a stable and happy marriage. The good of children, of communities of persons and of our nation depend on the stability of marriage. If this stability is threatened, then if we are to be consistent, we must all be concerned, become better informed, and collaborate to strengthen family life. Since marriage, by its nature, is ordained to the procreation and education of children, a couple shares intimately in God's work of creation and salvation. This gives them a special dignity and a right to society's support.

In this context, true progress for families would consist in the increasingly clear recognition of the nature of married love, the meaning of mutual responsibility, the dignity of marriage, the duty of families to society and the duty of society to families.

29. Family Policy

The family exists for the full development of its members. Such development evidently contributes to a healthy society. We suggest that policies at any level of government which touch family life require a criterion, and that it should be the effectiveness of the policy to contribute to the authentic development of all members of families. Such a criterion would give society a reference point.

One test of how we value the family is our willingness to foster, in government and business, in our social and cultural environment, and in all our planning, those moral values which nourish the primary relationships of husbands, wives and children. Another test is our willingness to develop policies and programmes that will attack and eliminate the causes of marriage breakdowns.

30. Responsibilities of Governments

Families have frequently been considered by governments to be a part of the "social problem". Should families not be considered, rather, the institutions that determine the quality of life in Canada? Often positive measures have not been introduced because of this limited perception, and because of the division of responsibility, in the British North America Act, between federal and provincial governments. It is urgent that roles be clarified and co-ordination in family policies be given a high priority, between the levels of government and among the various departments at each level.[7]

31. Family Law

Family policies should be expressed in new legislation. Society will be strengthened if its basic unit is strengthened by an overall family policy and family laws developed through the co-ordination of governments. Examples are laws touching the protection and support of parents and children, health care, education, housing, living conditions, social assistance, working conditions, income, pensions, taxation, advertising, consumer affairs and laws concerned with the unique situation of new Canadians.

V — CONCLUSIONS AND RECOMMENDATIONS

32. Consultations

The Minister of Justice spoke in Parliament last year (October 25, 1976) of his intention to carry on formal consultations on the recommendations of *The Family Law Report* with interested groups in Canada. We welcome this prospect and are prepared to participate in this and any other initiative that could lead to the strengthening of family relationships.

33. Policies and Legislation

As several of the central recommendations of *The Family Law Report* cannot be implemented until agreements are concluded between the federal and provincial governments, we suggest that, since these questions concern important family needs, governments give priority to family law questions, so that responsibilities may be clarified and new policies and legislation prepared. We refer to such issues as the care and custody of children, maintenance obligations, economic readjustmens and family courts. In the case of the latter, we believe that consultations are of special importance at the community level and with the churches, as was outlined in #9, 10 and 11 of this statement. We suggest too, that consultations are a pressing need in respect to the policies and legislation recommended in #29, 30 and 31 of this statement.

34. Marriage Education

It is obvious that marriage breakdowns are related to such factors as insufficient preparation, low income, lack of job opportunities, absence of personal values and the ages at which couples marry. The necessity of preparation for marriage was contained in the Joint Church Statement on Divorce presented to the Minister of Justice in 1967:

> Lifelong marriage is the ideal for which those intending marriage should be adequately prepared in their parental home and through educational programmes in schools and various other agencies. These agencies should have support from the public purse to aid and augment private initiative. [8]

Churches and agencies are attempting to assist couples, but a concerted effort is needed in this urgent matter.

We recommend therefore, that public authorities at all levels, in dialogue with religious groups and other interested organizations, begin at once to give more effective support to programmes of education for marriage, and that they consider the possibility that a basic knowledge about marriage be a necessary condition for marriage. Legislation already exists concerning conditions for marriage, such as the proper age, health requirements, etc. This is truly a critical question. Inaction is unpardonable.

35. Values and the Law

We are living in an age in which values are questioned. In some respects, this can be a healthy exercise. Our society however, is built on certain fundamental values which we ignore or reject at our peril. At a time of transition, when there is a certain blindness to values, it is essential that our fundamental values be clearly affirmed. Our position in this statement is that marriage stability and the well-being of families are fundamental values. And we believe that our laws should be normative and should therefore uphold our values.

It is also relevant to recall our common perceptions about law. We perceive law to be concerned with what is just. Many would phrase their perceptions this way: "If it is legal it must be just, and if it is just it must be moral."

For this reason, and others already stated, we believe that the concept of mutual responsibility in marriage is necessarily related to marriage legislation.

36. The Increase in Divorce

In Canada, divorces increased from 8,623 (1964) to 26,093 (1970) to 45,019 (1974). [9] We recommend that research be undertaken concerning the increase in divorce and marital instability, and we suggest that legislators have a serious responsibility to obtain such information before considering new legislation relative to grounds for divorce.

37. The Foundation of Society

For our part, we will continue to reflect on the implications of *The Family Law Report* and will support those recommendations which we have identified in this statement. The authors of the report deserve our gratitude for placing before us such crucial and challenging questions.

As an alternative to the report's recommendations regarding the dissolution of marriage, we suggest that legislation be studied that would enshrine in law the Canadian value that "marriage is the major institutional foundation of our society."

We offer our own support to the reservation expressed by Claire Barrette-Joncas, Q.C., a part-time member of the Commission, regarding conditions for divorce. Her statement is attached.

APPENDIX: RESERVATION OF CLAIRE BARETTE-JONCAS, Q.C. MEMBER OF THE LAW REFORM COMMISSION OF CANADA [10]

I agree with my colleagues with respect to the position of the children and the economic adjustments on divorce but I cannot endorse their recommendations regarding the conditions under which divorce should be obtained.

One cannot end a marriage in the same way as a mere contract. Marriage is the very basis of society. There is a public interest in the perpetuation and reinforcement of the institution of marriage.

If a spouse can obtain a divorce on a simple motion, merely because that spouse does not want to remain married any longer, marriage then loses all its significance. People will no longer enter marriage, convinced that it is for life and that it is the best way to secure their own fulfillment and that of their children to be born. It would be only a phase. A society wishing to survive and produce emotionally sound children cannot encourage its citizens to entertain such a concept of marriage.

Furthermore — and statistical data seem to prove it — any broadening of divorce laws means a considerable increase in the number of divorces. The states of the United States with more liberal divorce laws have a far greater proportion of divorces and separated people than the states having stricter laws.

For these reasons, I cannot subscribe for the moment to the broadening of divorce laws and in particular to unilateral divorce on a simple motion.

NOTES

1. Canadian Catholic Conference, *Statement on Proposed Change of Canadian Law on Divorce*, cf. Document 3 of this Section, I, 2.

2. Introduction, *Marriage Breakdown: a Statement of Several Canadian Churches to the Minister of Justice on Proposals to Reform the Divorce Laws*, November 8, 1967. The Statement was prepared by the competent bureaus or secretariats of the Anglican Church of Canada, the Canadian Catholic Conference, The Lutheran Council in Canada, the Mennonite Central Committee (Canada), the Presbyterian Church in Canada, the United Church of Canada. In Bulletin 200, *Recent Statements of the Anglican Church* (Toronto, February, 1969), p. 11.

3. *Lettre de l'Épiscopat du Québec sur la Famille*, April 3, 1975, I (3), in *Documentation Catholique*, Paris, 1975, LXXII, p. 518.

4. Cf. Statement of note 1, above, II, 2.

5. *Our Criminal Law*, a report submitted to the Minister of Justice, by the Law Reform Commission of Canada (Ottawa, K1A 0L6), March, 1976, VI, 2.

6. Karl Menninger, M.D., *Whatever Became of Sin?* (New York), Hawthorn Books, 1975), chap. 9, esp. pp. 180-88.

7. Dr. Philippe Garigue, *Famille, Science et Politique* (Éditions Lemeac, Ottawa, 1973), chap. IV; a study prepared at request of Law Reform Commission of Canada, Ottawa, K1A 0L6.

8. Cf. note 2, above, n. 27, p. 17.

9. *Vital Statistics*, Vol. II, Marriages and Divorces, 1974, p. 26 (Statistics Canada, Ottawa, K1A 0T6).

10. Claire Barette-Joncas, Q.C., *Divorce, Working Paper 13*, Law Reform Commission of Canada (Ottawa, K1A 0L6), 1975, pp. 69f.

Section I, Document 5

THE INTERNATIONAL YEAR OF THE CHILD

Author — Archbishop Gilles Ouellet, President, the CCCB,
        January 22, 1979

The United Nations General Assembly has proclaimed 1979 the International Year of the Child. The event will not be marked by a world conference, as is often the case. Instead, governments and people in each country are being urged "to take permanent, practical measures that will benefit children everywhere." As President of the Canadian Conference of Catholic Bishops, I want to add my voice to those who are stressing the importance of such projects. For, as the resolution of the United Nations General Assembly said:

> ... in spite of all efforts, far too many children, especially in developing countries, are undernourished, without access to adequate health services, missing the basic educational preparation for their future and deprived of the elementary amenities of life.

In speaking especially to Catholics about the Year of the Child, I want to emphasize that if deprived children are to be found "especially in developing countries," they are also to be found elsewhere, and even in our own country. This year will mark the 10th anniversary of publication of the report of a study of *Canadian* children with emotional and learning disorders. Have we forgotten that the study was entitled *One Million Children* to sum up the finding, at that time, "that between 840,000 and 1,260,000 children and youth have emotional and learning disorders."[1] More recently, in a 1975 report on children in poverty in Canada, the National Council of Welfare gave us the following scandalous picture of ourselves: of 6,759,373 Canadian children under 16 years of age, 1,657,017 of them — 24.5 percent — were living in poverty as defined by Statistics Canada.[2] In short, at least one child in every four in this country is seriously disadvantaged by poverty, by emotional and learning disorders, or by other handicaps.

There is no need, then, to stress that the Year of the Child can be a time for increased efforts to help assure "A Future for Every Child" in this country and throughout the world. It is up to people at every level to become actively involved in researching what needs to be done, evaluating what is already done, and undertaking new projects as they are needed. In particular, we invite parents to reflect on their responsibilities to their own children. Are the things you do with your children truly educational for them, leading them to become responsible persons, in a context of liberty and creativity with your constant support? And all groups and organizations that serve children should ask themselves the same sort of question.

In recommending in a special way that members of the Church unite, and join others, in projects for the Year of the Child, I wish to paraphrase the teaching of a recent Synod of Bishops: action on behalf of justice for children is a constitutive dimension of the preaching of the Gospel. [3] It is our mission to liberate children in this country and everywhere from every oppressive situation. We owe each child the best we have to give.

NOTES

1. *One Million Children*, Report for the Commission on Emotional and Learning Disorders in Children, 1970, published by L. Crainford, Toronto.

2. *Poor Kids, Report by the National Council of Welfare on Children in Poverty in Canada*, 1975, Nat. Council of Welfare, Ottawa, K1A 0K9.

3. Cf. Third International Synod of Bishops, Rome, 1971, *Justice in the World*, Introduction, n. 6; in *The Pope Speaks*, Washington, 1971, XVI, 377.

Section I, Document 6

FAMILIES ON THE PATH OF FAITH [1]

Author — Joint Committee of the Canadian Conference of Catholic
    Bishops and the Canadian Religious Conference,
    Pentecost, 1981

Pentecost — the Church celebrates!
The Spirit of Jesus and of the Father
unceasingly creates and renews the People of God.
The Spirit is present in our world
and in every woman and man...
helping us read the signs of the times
and giving meaning to the events of life...
The Spirit calls us to celebrate,
to brotherhood, to sisterhood...
trusting each of us, sending all
to accept each other in mutual love.

Faith Challenges the Family

Raising children and helping them to mature is an important
ongoing challenge families face. Is it possible to introduce children
to the Gospel, community and sacramental life and invite them to
live their faith while we ourselves still search, doubt and struggle?

All families, believing families as well as others, are facing the
fragility of marital bonds and a questioning and even reversal of traditional moral values. They also face geographic and professional
mobility, a redefinition of traditional male and female roles, and
new parent-child relationships.

It is not easy to want "to create family" when marital life itself faces complex questions in the midst of a society based on power and consumerism and an economy based on disposables or throw aways. Yet we believe that in our fragmented and changing society the Christian family remains a special source of life, of awakening, of learning faith and of experience of the Gospel.

A PLACE WHERE FAITH IS AWAKENED

In the Day to Day

It is through daily realities, the experience of human love, the affection of parents that we are gradually introduced to the mystery of God — a mystery of dialogue not isolation, of respect not domination, of differences not uniformity.

If the family tries to be loving in its everyday life the children will discover themselves and grow as persons. The family needs to be flexible enough to let the adolescent experience a measure of autonomy, yet firm enough to give support and happy enough to help in bearing divisions and crises.

God Lives in the Child

Modern educational theories try to develop all the child's potential and possibilities. Should we not do the same in the area of growth in faith? From the very beginning children are "formed in the image and likeness of God" (Gen.1:26f.). God already lives with them. The Church proclaims this when a newborn child is baptized. God's love, God's presence surround and fill the child long before adults begin to teach. God lives within the child, speaks to the child, acts in the child, takes possession of the child. Are we consciously aware of this? Is it enough to leave everything up to God? How can we help sensitize the child to God's active presence within him or her?

Respecting this Presence

We need to believe in and respect this presence of God within the child. This is the first way to awaken the child to this reality. We need to give children and adolescents our time and our attention. Being watchful and accessible, listening rather than avoiding their questions, remembering that God also speaks to them, all these help to awaken the child to the faith-life. This must be accompanied by respect for the child's freedom, rhythm of growth, doubts, insights and uncertainties. We don't have to be perfect or wait until we have arrived before we invite children to join us on the path of faith. Often, simply our own searching for God will be enough to encourage a child to come along with us, following or perhaps even leading us.

If children sense that their parents are really trying to live their daily lives with reference to God, from time to time turning to Him, speaking to Him, open to Him, gradually the children themselves will awaken to the One who lives within them and their parents. They will want to know God and to talk to Him.

It is for each family to invent, experiment and search for the climate and conditions that are most favourable to the faith growth of its members. "Seek and you will find" Jesus tells us (Mt. 7:7). Faith is a gift, but it must germinate, take root and grow. This growth takes place most naturally and often most lovingly within the family.

A PLACE WHERE FAITH GROWS THROUGH LIVING

Communicating Values

The family is not the only place where human and Christian values are communicated nor the only place where the child receives social formation. Christian adults and adolescents have a role to play in updating the content of faith. They can live and act in such a way as to show that the Word of God is not locked away in books, but rather that the Gospel message is still alive and challenging.

At times discussion and dialogue within the family and with others will be necessary to discover what is best for a particular family or group. Often it is through questioning, challenging, negotiating priorities that parents, children and adolescents discover how to work together. This process helps them to create a new Christian culture while at the same time trying to discern what the Resurrection teaches and what its meaning is today.

The young are sometimes not attracted to rituals and structures which have little significance for them. Nevertheless, they are sensitive to calls to action inspired by the Gospel. Encouragement to oppose injustice and dehumanizing situations, to help the under-privileged can elicit their profound response and prompt them to participate in a living Christian community.

Not Just Handing Out Knowledge

Teaching a person to know God requires more than handing out information about Him. Faith is not the result of knowledge nor the fruit of extensive learning. Faith is above all a life, a relationship with another Person — God. Helping children grow in faith means introducing them and gradually letting them become familiar with the Mystery of God. This must always be rooted in their own lives and real experiences.

Of course children need to be told about God, Jesus' life and what Jesus tells us about His Father. But we don't have to say everything about God, as if we know all about Him. Rather than give long speeches, we should day by day point out what we see, explain what we are living and join children in their own searching and questioning. Parents should not hesitate to speak of their own longing for God or of their own difficulties in relating to Him. Perhaps the best way of introducing children to the reality of God's love is to let them see that we love God ourselves and to help them realize that Jesus loves and respects each of them. The children will spontaneously come to express their own relationship with God by actions, words and attitudes.

Children Help Us to Know God

If we pay attention and are open to children, they will reveal God to us, teaching us the freedom, spontaneity and newness of the Gospel. Openness to their children will help parents nourish their own faith. It often leads parents to live more fully their own commitment as children of God and active members of the Church.

Together with children we can draw near to Christ who said "Let the children come to me; do not stop them; for it is to such as these that the Kingdom of God belongs." (Mk. 10:14) It is not always easy to be the kind of family that brings "little children to Him for Him to touch them" (Mk. 10:13), but children need adults to introduce them to the world of the divine and to help them grow in it.

A PLACE FOR EVANGELIZATION

A Gospel Model

The Gospel provides no developed model of family relationships. It proposes no road map nor ready-made patterns for the transmission of faith or education in faith. Instead, the Gospel is a call to go further. It calls us to live to the full all the challenges and tasks which confront the family and each of its members.

Jesus truly believed in the profound value of family life experience. He chose to spend the first thirty years of His life in a family setting. He drew on His observations of family life and on His own family heritage to help us understand the meaning of the Kingdom. He revealed to us the new type of relationship with God that we are called to live. God is our Father, we are His sons and daughters and together we form a family of brothers and sisters.

New Horizons for the Family

Jesus was not afraid to say that the commonly accepted horizons for the family could be extended and transcended for the sake of the Kingdom. All our endeavours must be seen in light of a Kingdom in growth, the rule of the Father in His world. The realities of family life keep their full importance but are seen in a new way and situated within a more fundamental searching that will lead us to become part of the family of Jesus. "Anyone who does the will of God, that person is my brother and sister and mother" (Mk. 3:35).

The Call of the Gospel

According to Jesus' plan the family, in respect and trust, permits each of its members to grow in freedom, to discover personal gifts, and above all to become aware of each individual as a person who is oriented to others and to God.

The Gospel gives us some concrete directives: Do not judge. Blessed are the peacemakers. Love one another. Love your enemies. It is, however, primarily the way in which a family lives the Gospel that leads children to discover the human face of God — His mercy, tenderness, pardon, generosity, service of all and endless welcome — the image of a Father who loves each and everyone.

HOME OF SERVICE

Jesus at the Service of Mankind

In order to proclaim the Good News, Jesus did not limit himself to preaching and speaking to crowds. He acted. He was present to the little ones. He was attentive to people. He healed the sick, brought life to people, humanized their existence. His actions in the Gospels help us to learn what His message of love really involves. In the same way, children can see their parents praying, questioning, celebrating with other Christians. If they realize their parents are seeking the best ways of serving people, of living Jesus' message, searching for God and a more human world, and doing this in a community, in collaboration with others, then children will also want to be involved in this movement.

Believers Serving the World

It is within the family that children learn how to be open to the world. To fully understand faith and translate it into daily living, the child must go beyond the family circle and benefit from other resources. The family however, will remain the primary and indispensable reference point. Each family member must make the family a stimulating milieu which always reaches out to the needs and urgencies of the broader community. They join with those seeking the advent of a more human and loving world. Working this way to promote a better quality of life means the family is responding to its true vocation. The family is to be the leaven and an agent of resurrection in a world that is seeking new paths of life.

NOTE

1. CCCB Publications Service, 90 Parent Ave., Ottawa, K1N 7B1.

Section I, Document 7

THE FAMILY:
A COMMUNITY OF LIFE AND LOVE[1]

Author — The Pastoral Team, Canadian Conference
of Catholic Bishops, 1983

In 1981, Pope John Paul II addressed a message to the Church on
the Role of the Christian Family in the Modern World.[2] In it he
stressed two very rich concepts.

— The family symbolizes the community of life and love which exists within the Holy Trinity.
— The family shares in the community of life and love existing
within the Holy Trinity.

Symbols of Love

Sometimes a simple event can convey deep meaning. For example, a father discovers a bunch of wild flowers on the breakfast
table. He is surprised at first. Then his five-year-old daughter runs
to him, kisses him and says "Happy birthday, Daddy." Those flowers now have new meaning. They are a symbol of love, "My little
girl loves me; she remembered my birthday. I am her friend, not just
her father. Not every father is loved like that." For this father, the
little bouquet has become the most beautiful thing in the world.
Our Christian family can be compared to that gift of wild flowers: it may be humble, seem very ordinary, but it is full of meaning.
It is a symbol of love.

As John Paul says, the family is "a sign of the community of life and love that exists in God."[3] Many events help us to come to a deeper understanding of this reality. The birth of a child, a baby's first smile, the process of growing up, long talks with a teenager, discussions on the choice of a career, et cetera. Ordinary everyday life with its misunderstandings, its worries and its routines can be full of love, and communicating this love to others, or proclaiming it to the world. Is not the cross the humblest and yet greatest symbol of love?

God's Love

The source of love is God our Father whose life is unity and love. The Father loves the Son, the Son loves the Father, and the love which unites them is the Holy Spirit. Each of the three divine Persons lives in an outpouring of love for the other. The family, parents and children together reflect this beauty and love in many ways. God invites us to share in this reality. Just as we might welcome someone to our table or lovingly bring a child into our home, so God invites our family to His table and brings us into His community of life and love.

When parents look at their children they are happy to recognize some of their own characteristics in their children's features or behaviour. A mother and father can say to each other, "This child is a symbol of my love for you, a proof of how much I care for you." A child is the most beautiful gift, the most convincing proof of love that parents can give each other.

However, God too can say, "This child is a symbol of my love for you, made in my image, sharing my life." A child is always a manifestation of God's life and God's love. It has been said that every child born is a symbol of God's eternal hope for our world.

The dawning awareness of all that our parents do for us leads us to a first understanding of tenderness and affection. And when we realize that our parents love us in spite of our faults and failings, we begin to appreciate what love really is and something of God's love for us. Parents are "the visible sign of the very love of God".

We may not have understood the family's vocation quite this way before, but if we believe that God is love and that, in creating human beings in His own image, He implants within their souls and

bodies the vocation to love and be united, then we begin to understand why we are a family (no. 11). [4] Because we are made in God's
likeness, we are able to mirror His love. It is part of our nature.
In speaking of the family's duties the Pope is simply inviting the
family to *"become* what you *are"*, [5] namely a deeply rooted community of life and love.

Symbol of God's Faithfulness

At the heart of the couple and of the family is a mysterious and
holy reality: their fidelity to each other. This is a symbol of God's
faithfulness to His people, God's unchanging love. This is why
divorce is a heartache for all concerned: for God, for the couple who
separate, for the children and the friends of the family. All of us therefore must pray to be open to the gift of fidelity to others, a sharing
in the Lord's fidelity to us.

By "serving life in many ways" the family proclaims that God is
the Source of life, promoting life in countless ways. We co-operate
with God's creative and saving love which increases and enriches
our own lives and the whole human race.

Those who are unable to have children of their own can be fulfilled by adopting children or by helping others in need of love and
care. By widening our vision of fatherhood and motherhood we can
discover many ways of witnessing to the loving fidelity of God for
our world.

The Family as Church

The values of unity and love which are lived in our families are
the very ones most needed by society and by the Church.

No governmental policy, no diocesan pastoral program can ever
replace a family life founded on human and Christian values. There
is no substitute for real family life. The family living its fulness is
a "small" Church which symbolizes the "big" Church, an eloquent
sign of unity in our world, a home which "manifests to all peoples
the Saviour's living presence in the world". [6]

Such a mission makes heavy demands and at times these may
even appear overwhelming. Never forget though, that because of

the sacrament of marriage the Holy Spirit, the Spirit of love, is the soul of your conjugal and family life. The Spirit is always ready to renew and revitalize us. Whenever your family draws nourishment from the word of God and from the sacraments, the Spirit is there. The sacrament of forgiveness and the Eucharist are always available, and are indispensable aids to help people live together. Through them we build life, strength, unity. A family grows by living together, working together, eating together and forgiving whenever there is need, but in their togetherness they are still open to the world.

Let our lives echo the Holy Father's call to love our families, for the family helps us to penetrate a little deeper into the mystery of God and of His presence in our world.

NOTES

1. A simple summary of the teaching of John Paul II, on the *Role of the Christian Family in the Modern World*, 1981, CCCB Publications Service, 90 Parent Ave., Ottawa, K1N 7B1.
2. In *Origins*, Washington, 1981, XI, 437.
3. *Op. cit., l.c.*, n. 17, p. 443.
4. *Ibid.*, n. 11, p. 441, f.
5. *Ibid.*, n. 17 ff., p. 443 ff.
6. *Ibid.*, n. 49 ff., p. 453 ff.; cf. Second Vatican Council, *The Church in the Modern World*, n. 48.

Section I, Document 8

BRIEF TO THE HOUSE OF COMMONS COMMITTEE ON JUSTICE ON BILL C-47: *AN ACT RESPECTING DIVORCE*

Author — The Canadian Conference of Catholic Bishops, June 18, 1985

INTRODUCTION

Over the last decade, we have seen a dramatic rise in the number of divorces in this country and its consequences have brought considerable change to Canadian society. As the recent Statistics Canada Report, *Divorce: Law and the Family in Canada* (henceforth, Statistics Canada Report) argues, it is therefore "clearly time to assess the phenomenon of divorce in Canada in those years subsequent to the passage of the 1968 Act".[1]

In our view, this review should focus on how we can collectively foster the well-being of families and prevent marriage breakdown. Measures that strengthen family values should have priority for the government, whereas measures that will facilitate the dissolution of marriages are of less importance. At the very least, these latter measures should be adopted only if they are placed within the context of firm government commitments to strengthen marriages and the role of the family in our society.

We are conscious of the fact that all three parties have expressed agreement with the principles of the present proposals. Nevertheless, we trust that your committee will still consider seriously our reflections before submitting its final recommendations to Parliament. For the most part, our concerns have already been expressed in our 1977 Brief to the Honourable Ronald Basford and again in Bishop

Sherlock's December 19, 1983 letter to the Honourable Mark Mac-Guigan. [2]

1 — Marriage and Family Stability as the Foundation of Happiness in Personal and Social Life

Most Canadians recognize that stable marriages and families contribute greatly to their personal well-being and that marriage breakdown causes much pain and hardship for the people involved. Thus, even from the limited perspective of individuals' personal interests, we can argue strongly for wholesome and enduring marriages and family relationships.

The suffering brought about by marriage breakdown, however, extends not only to the marriage partners and their children but to society at large. Marriage is "the major institutional foundation of our society" and the family is "the basic unit in society". [3] Its widespread dissolution poses serious problems for society. The authors of the Statistics Canada Report fail to draw the appropriate conclusions from their own premises but they nevertheless recognize this vital relationship between divorce and social development when they acknowledge that "divorce is a significant social event with many economic and social consequences for society". [4]

We cannot accept therefore, any reform proposals that would seem to regard marriage as no more than a private contract between two individuals that could be dissolved at will. Marriage is by no means a private affair but an eminently social event and undertaking. There is a serious public interest in the perpetuation and reinforcement of the institution of marriage. Neither at the beginning of marriage nor at its end can the state be simply "gatekeeper", as the Statistics Canada Report would have it. [5]

In view of these considerations, we cannot accept the frequently voiced statement that the purpose of divorce reform is "to follow the evolution of social realities". As all law enacted by Parliament, divorce law should help us understand and live our responsibilities to one another by affirming society's fundamental values. Good laws should support our fundamental institutions, educate us about our values and assist us to be just in our relationships.

The Law Reform Commission's *Report on Criminal Law* supports this philosophy where law serves "to underline those values necessary, or else important, to society". "When acts occur that seriously transgress essential values, like the sanctity of life, society must speak out and reaffirm those values".[6] This general philosophy of law, we strongly suggest, should inspire all legislation dealing with marriage and the family.

2. Easy Divorce no Magic Formula for Personal and Social Well-Being

So far, we have argued for the state's inherent interest in marriage stability and therefore also in its dissolution. We willl now consider how this concern may be expressed within the legal process of divorce.

Speedier divorce proceedings, so the argument goes, will eliminate much of the suffering that comes from the present adversarial approach. We would be happy, as we have stated in 1977,[7] to eliminate all vindictiveness and pain in the courts and advocate forgiveness and reconciliation, were it possible. It seems reasonable, however, to assume that the dissolution of such a profound and intimate relationship as marriage will always bring about a measure of pain, bitterness and disappointment. In this regard, it is important to note that introducing "no fault divorce" and "divorce on demand" does not appear to have proven, in other jurisdictions, to be the magic formula for "humanizing" divorces. It would seem that there are still horrendous battles over child custody, including increasing numbers of kidnappings, and the battles over property continue also with even greater negative impact for women than before.

Simplified access to divorce without an equal commitment to marriage support measures will do little in the long run to diminish personal anguish. In our considered opinion, it will in fact add to people's suffering as it will further erode respect for permanence in marriage, encourage people to seek divorce rather than trying to improve their marital relationship and let them hasten into second marriages without serious reflection on their own life history.

In view of these considerations, we strongly urge you to retain for all divorce cases, a court hearing presided over by a judge. Marriage will be seriously endangered if we profess it to be the foundation of our society and yet make it possible to terminate it by a simple administrative *fiat*. A contract with society is involved and marriage should not be terminated as if it were only a private contract.

3. Suggestions for Reform

Before we go on to propose certain avenues for reform of the present divorce laws, we wish to reiterate our primary concern for strengthening marriage and family life.

First of all, it is obvious that marriage breakdowns are related to such factors as insufficient preparation and the age at which couples marry.

The need for more marriage preparation was already expressed in the Joint Church Statement on Divorce presented to the Minister of Justice in 1967:

> Life-long marriage is the ideal for which those intending marriage should be adequately prepared in their parental home and through educational programmes in schools and various other agencies. These agencies should have support from the public purse to aid and augment private initiative. [8]

Churches and various service agencies are attempting to assist couples but a greater concerted effort is needed in this urgent matter. We ask therefore, that public authorities at all levels, in dialogue with religious groups and other interested organizations, give more effective support to marriage education programmes.

Another reason for marriage breakdown is the stress placed on people by low income and lack of job opportunities. Our collective willingness to develop policies and programmes that will attack and remove the socio-economic roots of marriage breakdowns will be a further test of how we value family life in Canada.

Finally, we are all asked to foster, in government and business, in our social and cultural environment and in all our planning, those moral values which nourish the primary relationships of husbands, wives and children.

With regard to the specific legislative proposals at hand, we agree with the Statistics Canada Report that the legal process should "serve positive social ends more clearly and effectively" (p. 235). This praiseworthy objective, however, will not be achieved by simply designing a procedure "that would more fully match the already difficult social process of transition from the married state to the unmarried state". [9]

Divorce procedures should first of all be directed towards establishing in an impartial manner whether the marriage in question is indeed irreparably broken. We should take very seriously the contention that many people rush into divorce before putting a special effort into making their marriages work. In our view, it should therefore be mandatory for the partners in question to have recourse to qualified marriage counsellors before any court proceedings could be initiated. Indeed, consideration might be given to judges concluding irreparable marriage breakdown only after hearing evidence of qualified and possibly licenced marriage counsellors.

The help of these professionals should also be sought for establishing the reasons for marriage breakdown, a positive responsibility quite different from the present fault finding requirement. If the court were to establish, as far as humanly possible, the objective reasons for marriage breakdown, the couple could be helped to analyze past conduct, assume their responsibilities and avoid similar suffering in the future. As the Manitoba Catholic Women's League said in a 1977 brief to the provincial government:

> What the legal procedure should do is to assist people to understand the 'why' of their marital breakdown, and hopefully discover certain realities about themselves which will encourage a sense of responsibility enabling them to enter into more meaningful, realistic personal unions, if and when they occur.

Such an innovative vision of the role of divorce procedures would not only reduce the traumatic effects of the adversarial process but would make the legal process serve positive social ends more clearly and effectively. Experience in our own communities and general statistics tell us that second marriages fail more often than first marriages. Society should therefore do everything in its power to help people learn from their life experiences and not rush into second marriages, likely to become increasingly frequent, if divorce be granted after only one year of separation.

CONCLUSION

In concluding, we would urge you, in your unique responsibilities as members of the House Committee on Justice and Legal Affairs, to resist attempts further to privatize marriage and its dissolution. Instead we ask you to use the shortcoming of the present divorce procedures as an opportunity for government to strengthen family life in Canada and to take the time needed to design divorce procedures that will emphasize conciliation, reconciliation and personal renewal.

Specifically, we would recommend:

1. THAT all three political parties commit equal efforts in time and human resources to protect the family bond as were devoted to changing the present divorce proceedings;

2. THAT together with the new divorce laws, strong government programs be adopted to strengthen marriage and family life in Canada, such as increased support for adequate marriage preparation and counselling (especially for the divorced who are planning to remarry), better provisions for child care for parents working within or outside the home and improved family allowances;

3. THAT these policy commitments be expressed in major additions to the present legislation or through the introduction of corollary legislation;

4. THAT the establishment of unified family courts be encouraged in all jurisdictions;

5. THAT recourse to marriage counselling be made mandatory before a divorce be granted;

6. THAT a formal hearing by a specially qualified judge be retained for all divorce cases;

7. THAT the presiding judge, in consultation with qualified resource persons, attempt to establish the reasons for marriage breakdown with a view to helping the couple make a fresh start in life together, as singles, or in a future second marriage.

NOTES

1. Statistics Canada Report, *Divorce: Law and the Family in Canada*, (Statistics Canada, Ottawa, 1983), p. 4.

2. Cf. Section I, Document 4 above for the 1977 brief to the Minister of Justice. Bishop Sherlock's letter of 1983 to the Hon. Mark MacGuigan, also Min. of Justice, has been omitted. In it he promised a fuller presentation of the Conference: that promise is fulfilled in this document covering all the points of Bishop Sherlock's letter, at greater length.

3. Cf. *Family Law Report* (Canadian Law Reform Commission, Ottawa, K1A 0L6), pp. 16 & 70.

4. *Statistics Canada Report* (Canadian Law Reform Commission, as in note 3, above), n. 5.

5. *Ibid., p. 13.*

6. *Criminal Law Report* (Canadian Law Reform Commission, as in note 3, above), n. 5.

7. Section I, Document 4, above, n. 19.

8. Cf. *Marriage Breakdown, Joint Statement of Several Canadian Churches to the Minister of Justice* (Nov. 8, 1967) *Bulletin 200,* The Anglican Church of Canada, Church House, 600 Jarvis St., Toronto, M4Y 2J6); also in *Contraception — Divorce — Abortion,* Publication Services, CCCB, 90 Parent Ave., Ottawa, K1N 7B1.

9. *Statistics Canada Report* (cf. note 1, above), p. 235.

Section I, Document 9

SUBMISSION TO THE
FEDERAL PARLIAMENTARY TASK FORCE
ON CHILD CARE

Author — The Episcopal Commission for Social Affairs, the CCCB,
June 10, 1986

INTRODUCTION

We welcome the opportunity to address one of the most fundamental and pressing issues of our times. Few other matters have such a profound or immediate impact on the day to day lives of so many. Child care is not just another political issue or of interest only to special interest groups. It concerns the basic values and priorities of our society. Indeed your recommendations and the government's response will be a litmus test of Canada's commitment to children, the advancement of women and the stability of the family.

We speak to you as members of the Catholic Bishops' Social Affairs Commission. Yet we do not speak for ourselves. As pastors we speak for children, the most powerless and voiceless among us. They have the *social right* to quality care and all Canadians have the *social obligation* to provide it. We also speak for women who, despite the increasing involvement of fathers, are still assuming the primary responsibility for the upbringing of children. In speaking most particularly for women we are conscious of the recommendation passed by the Canadian bishops at the 1984 Plenary Assembly "to speak out clearly and courageously against the injustices which are still being perpetrated against women throughout society."

Our study of the situation has led us to the inescapable conclusion that Canadians are facing a monumental child care crisis and that concerted government action is urgently required. We join with many other groups and individuals in endorsing a publicly funded, non-compulsory, quality, comprehensive child care system.

MODELS OF FAMILY

Our comments are not an exhaustive review of Catholic teaching on the family, but limited to those aspects which pertain to your mandate.

The family is the most important unit in our society. It is however, as stated in the Vatican *Charter of Rights of the Family,* "much more than a mere juridical, social, and economic unit". It is

> ... a community of love and solidarity which is uniquely suited to teach and transmit cultural, ethical, social, spiritual and religious values, essential for the development and well being of its own members and of society. [1]

The structure or particular model of the family is therefore of less significance than the community, love and commitment of its members.

Families take many forms. At the risk of over-simplification, we mention the extended and blended families and those households which have (a) two parents only one of whom (usually the father) is the wage earner; (b) two parents both of whom are wage earners; and (c) only one parent who may or may not be employed outside the home. Each of these models has limitations but it must be assumed that whichever model is adopted, either by choice or force of circumstances, parents are striving to do what is best for their children. Regardless of the model, families are entitled to the support of the whole community and a government policy which responds to their diverse needs and expectations.

While diversity in family structures is not new, cultural and economic forces have contributed to the predominance of one or more models at different points in our history. For example, the Industrial Revolution was the catalyst for the emergence of the wage earner/ homemaker model. In the last twenty-five years, the economic climate, women's movement and high incidence of divorce and separation have been influential factors in the dramatic increase in two-earner and single-parent families. You are no doubt inundated with statistics, but it is worth repeating some of the statistics presented in the Cooke Task Force on Child Care. [2]

1. a) In 1961 the husband was the only income earner in 65% of all married couples whether or not they had children. In 1981 this figure was 16%.

b) In 1961 both spouses were income earners in 14% of all married couples whether or not they had children. In 1981 this figure was 49%.

c) In 1961 families with but one parent (earner or non-earner) were 6% of all families. In 1981 this figure was 11%.

d) In 1961 16% of married couples either had no income earner or more than two earners. In 1981 this figure was 24%.

2. a) In 1976 32% of mothers with a child under three worked outside the home. In 1984 this figure was 52%.

b) In 1976 41% of mothers whose youngest child was between three and five worked outside the home. In 1984 this figure was 57%.

c) In 1976 50% of mothers with children in school worked outside the home. In 1984 this figure was 64%, 70% of whom worked full-time.

These statistics indicate that the majority of mothers, even those with very young children, are employed. They are in the work force essentially for the same reasons as men — financial necessity and personal satisfaction. One fact, however, affects women in particular: the frequency of women left alone with children to raise but with no marketable job experience and outdated or inadequate skills or education. It is indeed chilling to note that one-half of single-parent families headed by women are living below the poverty line.

You have no doubt heard submissions from people who sincerely and genuinely believe that except in cases of strict economic necessity, a mother's place is the home. The Catholic Church has always recognized and continues to recognize with particular gratitude the important and valuable contribution of mothers and vigorously supports their choice to remain at home with their children. It is however, their choice, if indeed their financial situation or the availability of quality child care allows them to choose.

Since the Second Vatican Council, the Church has increasingly recognized and supported the advancement of women, acknowledging their increasing involvement in public and cultural life and condemning discrimination based on sex. So while the Church steadfastly affirms motherhood, it does not preclude other options for women. More recently, Cardinal Vachon, speaking on behalf of the Canadian bishops at the 1983 International Synod of Bishops on Reconciliation, said, in a presentation on Male-Female Reconciliation.[3]

> In our society and in our Church, men have come to think of themselves as the sole possessors of rationality, authority and active initiative, relegating women to the private sector and dependent tasks. Our recognition, as Church, of our own cultural deformation will allow us to overcome the archaic concepts of womanhood which have been inculcated in us for centuries.
>
> The history of our country and our Church has already shown our ability to place proper value on the ingenious creativity and inventive participation of women in collective endeavours. Today women are more and more numerous in all areas of public life. They are experiencing a remarkable qualitative upsurge, indicating a notable change in our way of conceiving humanity. This should encourage us to live out with them, as Church, the relationships of equality demanded by our fundamental identity as persons and our life as sons and daughters of God.

The statistics indicate that the entry of mothers into the labour force is increasing, even in the face of inadequate child care, and is unlikely to slow down. Given this reality, the work of your committee ought not to be distracted by a debate on the appropriateness of mothers working outside the home.

Current Child Care System

The Cooke Task Force has done an extensive review of the situation.[4] We now know that:

1) almost two million children require care;

2) fewer than 9% of those needing care are in licensed facilities;

3) a disturbing number of children under 12 (including pre-school children) are left to care for themselves;

4) over 80% of children receiving care are in a variety of unsupervised, unregulated, informal arrangements of uneven quality and reliability;

5) the special needs of shift workers, mothers seeking employment, full-time homemakers, rural children and disabled children are not met;

6) traditional surrogate care givers (neighbours, family members) are usually not available because most have other jobs;

7) the cost of child care today is prohibitive except for the wealthy or the poor, the latter qualifying for subsidies only after undergoing demeaning needs tests;

8) child care workers are among the most underpaid and exploited members of the work force;

9) full-time homemakers require child care on a periodic basis.

The findings of the Task Force and the compelling personal witness of those who appeared before it and your committee call seriously in question Canada's social policy. Few quarrel with the truism that "children are our best resource". That, however, has not been translated into programmes and reflected in priorities. Quality child care has become either a privilege for the rich or a component of the welfare system rather than a social right. Those who assume the care of children are expected to shoulder the bulk of the costs, be they surrogate care workers (usually women) who are paid the minimum wage with few benefits, or full-time homemakers who receive no pay or other tangible recognition for their work. In our consumer society we value what we pay for and value most highly what costs the most. Canada fails this value test miserably when it comes to child care just as it failed it when family allowances were de-indexed and fails it when pensions for homemakers are opposed.

THE COSTS OF AN INADEQUATE CHILD CARE SYSTEM

1 — The Costs to Children

Experts agree that the early childhood years are the most critical. From the research done for the Cooke Task Force, it would appear that the experts also agree that *quality* surrogate care has no harmful effects and in fact benefits disadvantaged children. The emphasis is therefore on the quality of care, not the identity of the care giver.

Poor care has detrimental effects on the emotional, intellectual and social development of the child.

2 — The Costs to Mothers

While we support the principle that child care is the responsibility of both parents and of society as a whole, it would be a grievous error to ignore the fact that at present it impacts most particularly on women. For women, the uncertainty, unavailability, inaccessibility or unsuitability of child care means:

a) the denial of freedom to enter the labour force, especially for single mothers;

b) work interruptions with resulting loss of pension benefits and seniority;

c) accepting jobs for which they are over-qualified;

d) or part-time work often at low wages and with no benefits;

e) absenteeism and stress affecting job performance and opportunity for promotion.

Women who choose to enter the work force have a right to do so with opportunities equal to those of men. We agree with the Abella Report that "Child care is the ramp that provides equal access to the work force for women".[5] There will never be true equality between men and women until men accept that they are co-responsible for parenting and society accepts that it has a social and moral duty to assist in the care of children when parents cannot be there.

3 — Costs to the Family

The anxiety and frustrations resulting from unavailable or inadequate child care create intense pressures within the family that affect its very stability and weaken the ability of its members to contribute to the community.

4 — Costs to Society

If society is not prepared to pay now it will pay a much higher price later in terms of juvenile crime and increased costs for remedial education and health care. There will also be increasing numbers of women dependent on unemployment insurance and welfare. It will be difficult for these women to break the poverty cycle and there will be attendant health and other costs because of inevitable loss of self-esteem and dignity.

TOWARDS A PUBLICLY FUNDED CHILD CARE SYSTEM

1 — Community Responsibility

We reiterate the traditional position of our Church that parents are *primarily* responsible for the health, education, care and upbringing of their children. They are not, however, expected to do it all alone, nor can they. While the state must not and cannot replace parents, it must provide assistance in an ancillary way to enable them more fully to perform their own pivotal role. We see the proper care of children, when their parents cannot be with them because of job commitments, as an *essential service* comparable to health care and education. If we truly believe that children are the hope of our future, we must accept that their health, education and care is the collective responsibility of all sectors of the community. We agree with what was stated in the Abella Report:

> Child care is a social investment in the future. It is not, therefore, the exclusive financial responsibility of an employer, or a union, or a worker, or a parent. It is a public expense that should ultimately be borne by all taxpayers, much as education is. Child care should be seen as a public service to which every child has a right.[6]

2 — Sources and Application of Funds

We applaud the vision of the Cooke Task Force in recommending the eventual creation of a comprehensive child care system totally supported by public funds. We recognize that the programme will have to be phased in and do not propose to get into any details about how that should be done because there are others more competent to advise. It is however, readily apparent to us that it will not be enough to tinker with the range of deductions, exemptions and credits available under the Income Tax Act. We submit that what is needed is new money. We say this for the following reasons:

1) most of the tax provisions are regressive, benefitting those with higher incomes and of no benefit to those with insufficient income to pay tax;

2) some tax payers are unable to take advantage of child care deductions because they are unable to obtain receipts;

3) tax breaks come at the end of the year and do not supply money when it is most needed;

4) most importantly, it is the service rather than the users that must be funded. A quality system cannot be built on the basis of tax breaks or vouchers.

While we do not expect a publicly funded system to be compulsory or to prevent parents from choosing alternative care, we suggest that all government child care funds be directed to non-profit facilities. We feel compelled to make this suggestion because of the disturbing trend toward privatization of social services. It is abundantly clear that child care is a social necessity and not a commodity to be subjected to the fluctuations of market forces. In fact it is fundamentally repugnant to use market analysis in planning child care or to consider parents consumers of child care.

Although parental contributions will be required until the programme is phased in, we ultimately oppose all user fees because they will inevitably exclude some children.

There is no question that the economic cost of providing publicly funded child care will be considerable. There are however, as stated by the Cooke Task Force, not inconsiderable benefits in terms of reduced unemployment (for those entering the child care field or involved in the construction industry) and increased tax revenue from their earnings.

The real issue is not whether the money is available, but whether the government has the political will to make children a priority. It is time Canada caught up with most of the other western nations, whose child care programmes give significant witness to the high value they place on children and expose Canada's lack of correspond-ing commitment as a scandal that can no longer continue.

Recommendations

A. We recommend that the federal government, in cooperation with the provinces, implement a fully funded child care system which will include the following features as essential components:

1) respect and support for the primary role of parents as care givers by providing mechanisms for frequent and meaningful consultation on all aspects of the programme;

2) highly competent staff whose salaries and benefits reflect their training and serious responsibility. Support should be provided (including income replacement) for those attending early childhood education programmes;

3) small child/staff ratio;

4) universal accessibility so that no child will be denied access because of family income, disability, or the location of his or her home be it rural or urban;

5) flexible, comprehensive services which will accommodate the var-iety of needs of infants, pre-schoolers and school age children and parents including shift workers, full-time homemakers, and those looking for employment;

6) enriching, stimulating, programmes designed not only to meet needs of children, but to enhance their development;

7) non compulsory;

8) strict regulation and accountability to parents and the community;

9) the funded services must not be operated for profit.

B. Society, and all levels of government, must soon come to grips with the fact that more substantial support must be given for the socially valuable contribution of parents who remain at home to care for their children.

Conclusion

Members of the committee, you have before you the comprehensive and convincing reports of the Cooke Task Force and the Abella Royal Commission. Both recommend a quality, publicly funded, universally accessible child care system. Each has povided a valuable service in collecting and analyzing the pertinent data and consulting the public. Surely the fact should now be recognized and the principle accepted that proper care is an essential service to which our children are entitled. If you do not act now the many groups who have testified before your committee, the Task Force and the Royal Commission will find it difficult not to feel betrayed. Frankly, Canadians are tired of being consulted but not heard. Having been consulted, they expect some action. We urge you to seize this rare opportunity to make a meaningful difference in the lives of many and, in so doing, to provide the moral vision and leadership so needed in our world today.

In our introduction we said that we appeared not in our own interests but for the social needs and rights of our country's children. We wish to conclude as we concluded our 1983 Statement on the Economy:

> We believe that the cries of the poor and the powerless are the voice of Christ, the Lord of history, in our midst. As Christians, we are called to involvement in the struggle for economic justice and to participate in building a new society sensitive to Gospel principles. In so doing, we fulfill our vocation as a pilgrim people on earth, participating in Creation and preparing for the coming Kingdom.[7]

NOTES

1. *Charter of the Rights of the Family,* "presented by the Holy See, central and supreme organ of government of the Catholic Church", Nov. 24, 1983, Preamble E, in *Origins* (Washington, 1983), n. 27, p. 462.

2. *Report of the Task Force on Child Care in Canada* (Cooke Task Force), co-authors Katie Cooke and Minister responsible for Status of Women Canada (1986, Ottawa, K1A 1C3).

3. Cf. Section VI, Document 14 of this volume.

4. *Report of the Cooke Task Force* (cf. note 2, above), *passim.*

5. *Report of the Commission on Equality in Employment* (Abella Commission), Judge Rosalie Silberman Abella, 1984 (Supply & Services Canada, Ottawa, K1A 0S5), p. 178.

6. *Ibid.*, p. 192.

7. *Ethical Reflections on the Economic Crisis,* CCCB Commission for Social Affairs, in *Do Justice!*, edit. E.F. Sheridan, SJ (Éditions Paulines, Sherbrooke, QC, J1E 2B9), p. 407f.

Section II

ABORTION — CAPITAL PUNISHMENT CONTRACEPTION

Document 1

STATEMENT ON CAPITAL PUNISHMENT

The Social Action Department, the CCC, February 17, 1960

Capital punishment is being discussed from many points of view. Questions are asked about the right of the state to inflict capital punishment, its effectiveness in safeguarding the common good by deterring from serious crimes and about the propriety of this or that form of capital punishment. We will deal here only with the first of these questions, for the answers to the other questions assume that the state has the right to inflict capital punishment.

Catholic teaching has always maintained that three types of killing not forbidden by the Fifth Commandment are capital punishment for serious crime, waging a just war and legitimate self-defence.

According to this teaching, the state has the right — indeed, the duty and the obligation from God — to protect its citizens from harm and to take all moral means needed to maintain the common good of all. When a criminal gravely endangers the common good by evildoing, the state has the right to put him to death, if that be necessary.

This was the right to which Pope Pius XI alluded when he wrote that the right to take life " has regard only to the guilty."[1] This right is based on the precedents of the Old Testament, in which capital punishment was incorporated by God in the Mosaic Law; on the New Testament, which takes for granted that the state, whose authority is the authority of God for the welfare of all the people, is "God's minister" (Rom. 13:6) in punishing great crimes in this way; and on Christian ethics, which teaches that the state has the right to self-defence against internal enemies, by means of capital punishment and against external enemies, by means of war.

While defending the state's right to inflict capital punishment for the reasons noted, the Catholic Church has never either demanded nor urged capital punishment as the only means of punishing criminals or preventing crime. It is for the state to decide whether capital punishment is opportune or necessary in a given case, or in a general situation.

NOTE

1. Pius XI, *On Christian Marriage*, 1930, in *The Papal Encyclicals*, edit. Claudia Carlen, IHM (Wilmington, N.C., McGrath Publishing, 1981), VI, p. 401, n. 64.

Section II, Document 2

TO THE HOUSE OF COMMONS' STANDING COMMITTEE ON HEALTH AND WELFARE: ON CHANGE IN THE LAW ON CONTRACEPTIVES

Author — The Canadian Catholic Cnference, Sept. 9, 1966[1]

The Canadian Catholic Conference (CCC) thanks the House of Commons Standing Committee on Health and Welfare for the invitation to testify on the subject matter of Bills C-22, C-40, C-64 and C-71.

The CCC is the national organization of the Catholic Bishops of Canada. At present there are 101 episcopal members of the CCC, which carries on its activities through an administrative board and various elected commissions and committees. The general secretariate of the Conference with its offices in Ottawa carries out the national policy of the CCC through various departments, e.g., for ecumenism, liturgy, lay apostolate, social action.

The invitation to give evidence before this committee is welcome for two reasons in particular.

First of all, it presents an opportunity for the Conference to make its views known on proposed legislation affecting marriage and the family, an area of great concern to the Church as well as to society at large.

Secondly, it provides an opportunity for the Conference to situate its particular observations on these bills in the broader perspectives of pertinent teachings of the Second Vatican Council.

Our comments are now being asked on proposed changes in Article 150 of the Criminal Code which would make it no longer a crime punishable at law to give information about or to distribute the means of preventing conception.

Because of the lively interest evoked by the hearings before this Committee, legislators in general and Catholic legislators in particular want to know our position.

Two questions may arise. First, how should one conceive the role of a Christian legislator faced with any controversial moral issues? Second, what are our views on the proposed changes in the Criminal Code?

The first and more general question might be put in this way. Are legislators who are loyal to their Church bound to vote for laws prohibiting what the Church declares to be wrong? Are they obliged by their allegiance to the Church to work for the repeal of laws which allow what the Church holds to be wrong?

These questions could touch the legislative attitudes of a number of persons in public life. We think therefore that they are quite properly presented before this committee, which is necessarily concerned with anything that might be an obstacle or aid to the legislative process in the question of the proposed changes of Article 150 of the Criminal Code.

To put our remarks on the role of the legislator in proper perspective, and to avoid as far as possible all misunderstanding, we will refer at some length to the teachings of the Second Vatican Council. The Council has given all of us deeper insights into the nature of the Church, the relationship of her official teaching authorities to her other members and of all of them to the political community. [2]

A simple and evident truth is proposed by this Constitution. The same persons are members of the religious community which is the Church and of the political community which is the State. The two institutions "serve the personal and social vocation of the same human beings". The obvious ideal, then, should be "wholesome mutual co-operation" for the benefit of human persons. [3]

The political community, says the Constitution,

> ... exists for that common good in which the community finds its full justification and meaning, and from which it derives its pristine and proper right. Now the common good embraces the sum of those conditions of social life by which individuals, families and groups can achieve their own fulfilment in a relatively thorough and ready way... [4]

The Church for her part

> ... has also the right to pass moral judgments, even on matters touching the political order, whenever basic personal rights or the salvation of souls make such judgments necessary. In so doing, she may use only those helps which accord with the gospel and with the general welfare as it changes according to time and circumstances... [5]

The Church recognizes that her role and competence are not to be confused with the role and competence of the political community. Thus

> ... the faithful will be able to make a clear distinction between what a Christian conscience leads them to do in their own name as citizens, whether as individuals or in association, and what they do in the name of the Church and in union with her shepherds... [6]

It is significant for our present purpose to note the Council teaching that within the political community Christians act "... in their own name as citizens".[7] Their actions, to be sure, should be guided by a well formed Christian conscience since, "... even in secular affairs there is no human activity which can be withdrawn from God's dominion".[8]. But the fact remains that their decisions and actions in the political sphere must be their own. Their rights and duties as citizens do not flow from the fact that they belong to the Church.

Thus in the same *Dogmatic Constitution on the Church*, which is held by many to be the most basic document emanating from the Council, we read:

> Because the very plan of salvation requires it, the faithful should learn to distinguish carefully between those rights and duties which are theirs as members of the Church, and those which they have as members of society. Let them strive to harmonize the two, remembering that in every temporal affair they must be guided by a Christian conscience... In our time it is most urgent that this distinction and also this harmony should shine forth as radiantly as possible in the practice of the faithful, so that the mission of the Church may correspond more adequately to the special conditions of the world today.[9]

The same truth is explicitly taught again by the Council in its *Decree on the Apostolate of the Laity*. The laity are told that they must take on the renewal of the temporal order as their own special obligation. They must be guided by the light of the gospel, the mind of the Church and Christian love, yet in the temporal sphere they are exhorted to act on their own responsibility: "As citizens they must co-operate with other citizens, using their own particular skills and acting on their own responsibility". [10]

The Christian legislator then has a Christian conscience and if it is truly formed it will be thoroughly imbued with Christian principles. But it remains *his or her* conscience. The Church may play a major role in the formation of that conscience through her teachings on the social order and the moral aspects of the political order. But these teachings do not properly extend to the technical areas of social or political questions. It will be up to the legislator to apply the principles to the concrete and often complicated realities of social and political life and to find a way to make these principles operative for the common good. They should not stand idly by waiting for the Church to tell them what to do in the political order. The ultimate responsible conclusions are their own as they fulfil the task they have along with all other legislators. That task is the promotion of the common good through the provision of wise and just laws.

At this point we are now able to return to the questions asked earlier, the answers to which we said were important in view of the legislative proposals before this committee.

Are Christian legislators bound to vote for laws which forbid what the Church forbids? Are they bound to oppose laws which permit what the Church forbids?

Perhaps we can see now that the questions answer themselves in the light of the principles of the Second Vatican Council which we have just cited.

The Christian legislator must make his or her own decision. The norm of action of a legislator is not primarily the good of any religious group but the good of society. Religious and moral values are certainly of great importance for good government. But these values enter into political decisions only in so far as they affect the common good. Members of parliament are charged with a temporal task. They may, and in fact often will, vote in line with what the Church forbids or approves because what the Church forbids or approves may be closely connected with the common good. Their standard always lies in this question: is it for or against the common good?

A willingness to honour this truth stressed by the Council and to trust Christian legislators to fulfil their function in the light of

Christian conscience and technical competence is the surest pledge of our desire to join with all persons of good will in building a truly human world open to supernatural and Christian values.

And now, applying the foregoing arguments, we may approach more directly the matter of Article 150 of the Criminal Code.

In our minds it is of the utmost importance to make it clear that our not opposing a change in the present law does not imply approval of contraception or of all methods of regulation of births. This is an entirely different question and we are not dealing with it in this statement.

Civil law (we use the term in the broad sense which includes criminal law) and morality are different in important respects, yet they have areas in common, too. Civil law and moral law are neither completely distinct nor completely one. Not every evil deed calls for a civil law to forbid it. Those wrong deeds that can do notable harm to the common good constitute, in certain circumstances to be described below, proper subject matter for criminal laws of the political community. Other wrong deeds are in truth forbidden by God's law and the wrongdoer will have to answer to God for his transgressions. It could be alleged that any genuinely immoral act is at least indirectly and remotely prejudicial to the common good. Yet there has to be a reasonable proportion between the wrongdoing and the means taken to suppress it. The comparatively slight harm to the common good that might be caused by certain types of private or hidden delinquency has to be weighed against a much greater potential damage. Clearly, the common good would not be served by a hopeless attempt of public authority to supervise the smallest details of moral behaviour through a vast and oppressive network of criminal laws and punishments.

The first condition then, for making a moral offence into a legal or criminal offence is that it be notably contrary to the common good. But that is only the first condition. Certain other conditions must also be fulfilled before a law should be passed to turn the wrongful act into a statutory crime punishable at law:

1) it should first of all be clear, as indicated already, that the wrongful act notably injures the common good;

2) the law forbidding the wrongful act should be capable of enforcement, because it is not in the interest of the common good to pass a law which cannot be enforced;

3) the law should be equitable in its incidence — i.e., its burden should not fall on one group in society alone;

4) it should not give rise to evils greater than those it was designed to suppress.

In the light of these conditions we consider Article 150, which forbids giving information about contraception as well as the sale or distribution of contraceptives, an inadequate law today. We consider it so quite independently of the morality or immorality of various methods of birth prevention. We believe it a deficient law because it does not meet all the conditions outlined above.

The law is not in fact enforced, and the good of public peace might well be lost by attempts to enforce it. A large number of our fellow citizens believe that this law violates their rights to be informed and helped towards responsible parenthood in accordance with their personal beliefs.

It is our clear understanding, of course, that the modification of the law in question is not to extend to that part of it which has to do with abortion. For our conclusions would be quite different were there question of such direct destruction of human life.

We have noted with satisfaction the number of witnesses before this committee who have called for safeguards to protect juveniles and the public in general from the dangers inherent in uncontrolled advertising and uninhibited display or sale of contraceptives. It is admittedly difficult to frame protective laws. But since it is possible to have a law that is at least partially effective against irresponsible advertising or sale of contraceptives, such safeguards should somehow be built into law.

If it seems likely that such safeguards would not immediately be operative but might have to wait for new legislation even in provincial jurisdictions, then it would seem to us to be unwise to remove the existing protection provided by Article 150 of the Criminal Code until such safeguards are by one means or another assured.

Although the proposed legislation makes no provision for governmental programs in regulation of births, it would, if passed, remove a legal barrier to them. We feel bound to express grave concern for the privacy and effective freedom of the individual within such possible programs. The fields of financial help to the needy and of information on regulation of births should be so separated that acceptance of contraceptive devices or information is never in reality made a condition or necessary concomitant of welfare assistance.

While the state has a legitimate interest in health, education and poverty as social problem areas, it would be intolerable that the state should enter into the business of dictating to married couples how many children they may or should have, or what methods of regulation of births they should adopt. That should be the free decision of the individual couples. Psychological pressures or persuasions that violate their rights and freedom would, if permitted, be a grave abuse. Any governmental program would be strictly bound to protect the freedom and the human rights of family and conscience.

We are not suggesting that such abuse would necessarily be the official policy of any major governmental agency. But it does not take too much imagination to see how such subtle violence to individual rights could creep into actual practice.

Protection to prevent coercive tactics can and should be provided. We do not question the capacity of persons of good will working together to provide such safeguards, perhaps through the provision of a board of review and control, or in some other effective way. What is necessary is to take positive steps at the outset by studying the potential dangers of governmental involvement in regulation of births. Otherwise changing Article 150 of the Criminal Code could result in avoidable moral damage and social discord.

Provided, then, that safeguards against irresponsible sales and advertising are built into the law and that protection of personal freedom is ensured, we do not conceive it to be our duty to oppose appropriate changes in Article 150 of the Criminal Code. Indeed, we could easily envisage an active co-operation and even leadership on the part of lay Catholics to change a law which under present conditions they might well judge to be harmful to public order and the common good.

At the same time we would urge continuing research into and public review of the effects that any changes in the law would have on individuals, families and the common good of Canadian society as a whole.

NOTES

1. Cf. Proceedings of the House of Commons Standing Committee on Health and Welfare; No. 18, October 11, 1966; pp. 576-581.

2. Here the brief mentioned as an appendix of special relevance, Part II, chap. 4, of the *Pastoral Constitution on the Church in the Modern World.* The appendix is omitted here.

3. Second Vatican Council, *The Church in the Modern World,* n. 76.

4. *Op. cit., l.c.,* n. 74.

5. *Op. cit., l.c.,* n. 76

6. *Ibid.*

7. *Ibid.*

8. Second Vatican Concil, *Dogmatic Constitution on the Church,* n. 36.

9. *Ibid.*

10. Second Vatican Council, *On the Apostolate of the Laity,* n. 9.

Section II, Document 3

PASTORAL STATEMENT ON PROPOSED CHANGE OF CANADIAN LAW ON ABORTION[1]

Author — The Canadian Catholic Conference, February 7, 1968

About a month ago, draft amendments to the Criminal Code were introduced in the Canadian House of Commons. One amendment would so change the law on abortion that a medical doctor, with the approval of a hospital committee, would be permitted to perform an abortion when continuation of pregnancy "would endanger, or would be likely to endanger, the life or the health of the mother".

With parliament about to discuss a law of such serious consequences, careful study of the question is a duty of conscience for everyone, especially for doctors, lawyers, politicians and all who influence public opinion. Therefore we, too, must try to set before you as clearly as possible what we believe to be in harmony with Christian faith, moral norms worthy of humanity and the requirements of civilized life. Our concern for the common good compels us to do this. While speaking primarily to Catholics, we hope to receive sympathetic hearing from all who want to serve the best interests of the Canadian people in the study of this grave and complex problem.

I — ABORTION AND RESPECT FOR LIFE

The Mind of the Church

Although it did not deal at a length with abortion, the recent Vatican Council repeated in general yet forceful terms the traditional teaching of the Church.

> God, the Lord of life has conferred on men and women the surpassing ministry of safeguarding life — a ministry which must be fulfilled in a manner which is worthy of humankind. Therefore, from the moment of its conception, life must be guarded with the greatest care, while abortion and infanticide are unspeakable crimes. [2]

The Council's teaching, it is clear, condemns the direct taking of foetal life, but not treatments needed to save a mother's life even if they sometimes result in the unwanted and unsought death of the foetus.

No one should be surprised that the Church takes so firm a position on this question. Her words in this case are but a faithful echo of God's solemn and grave commandment, "Thou shalt not kill." They also give witness to the great law of Christian love (Rom. 13:8-10). These words touch on something that is fundamental for any true civilization or real progress — respect for life and for the human person.

It is clear that this commandment of God obliges in conscience, no matter what legislation may be in force in a country.

Must Respect for Human Life apply to the Foetus?

"The Church's principles," it is sometimes said, "are noble in themselves but do not take into account the basic difference between life in the womb and life after birth." This prompts us to make the following points which will clarify the Church's position on abortion.

First, we note that science has not established a fundamental difference between life in the womb and the child's life after birth. Instead, scientific findings lead us to look upon the whole development that begins with conception as the slow, complex maturing process of a distinct individual, an autonomous biological reality progressing towards full human stature. Scientists even affirm that this individuality is already perceptible in the fertilized ovum itself; that is, from the time of conception. To be sure, it is difficult to determine the exact moment when we can be certain that the foetus is human. At least in the latter stages of its development there can be no doubt. A mother knows her little one has become her partner in a secret dialogue of awakening human love. Mothers are not misled in this basic insight; they know that they bear not mere vegetable or animal life but a human offspring with the right to be recognized as such.

Moreover, for those who think they have good reasons to doubt the human character of the foetus in the early stages of its development, and therefore argue that abortion is legitimate in certain cases, we have a question: since you too consider human life sacred, can you justify even the risk of taking a human life?

Borderline Cases

The question is sometimes asked: the Church advocates that the unborn be regarded as human and invites us to respect human life in its very origins. In so doing, does not the Church treat too lightly the very serious dangers that sometimes threaten the mother because of the new life within her? The question is asked as if the concern for the human person expressed and fostered by the Church were accompanied by an inability to grasp concrete situations and provide satisfactory answers to them.

We know the anguish felt by mother, husband and doctor when two equally innocent lives are in a mysterious conflict that involves risk of death for the mother, or at least danger of serious or permanent effects on her physical or mental health. When such cases occur, they are always difficult and sometimes tragic. But resort to abortion, because it involves the taking of innocent life, does not render the situation less tragic.

When the mother's life is truly in danger, we understand that there may be a temptation to consider abortion, even direct abortion, justifiable. Nevertheless, we must point out that this view is contrary to a persistent Judeo-Christian tradition that life is sacred. Likewise, to advocate abortion in order to protect something other than the very life of the mother, even if it be her physical or mental health, is to disregard the sacred right of the foetus to life; also, it is to sacrifice a greater value for a lesser.

Besides, abortion itself often has harmful effects on the physical, mental and moral well-being of the mother. And it is also relevant that advances in medicine and psychiatry now make it possible to find positive solutions that respect life in many borderline cases.

Medical opinion is virtually unanimous that cases where a direct abortion is necessary to save the mother's life are fortunately so rare these days that their existence is becoming merely theoretical. Less rare, to be sure, is the case where a pregnancy may seriously endanger the mother's physical or mental health. At any rate, it certainly would be a false approach to think that solution of such borderline cases calls for legislative changes of the kind proposed.

II — ABORTION AND THE LAW

A bill to amend the law on abortion has been presented in the House of Commons. The issue is now something more than the morality of abortion. We must also consider what the state's role in this matter should be and, more precisely still, what one should think of the proposed amendments.

The State, Protector of Life

Effective protection of human life, especially of the weakest, is always a foremost duty of the state. Considering the complexity of modern living and the new and often hidden dangers that threaten life, this protective function of the state is today more important than ever. Through criminal law, police forces, control of public health and drugs, protection for children, social legislation and many other means, the state must strive today, even more than in the past, to fulfill effectively its role as protector of life. We note here, for example, the government's recent praiseworthy measures to assure greater traffic safety and better control over possession and use of firearms.

Everyone speaks of progress, and there is surely no one unwilling to promote it. But do we automatically have to accept as progress every measure made out to be — sometimes in a rather peculiar way — a "liberalization" or a "broadening" of the law. When it is a matter of respect for and protection of human life, progress does not lie in laxity but in ever more attentive and effective concern and vigilence. Progress in civilization, we say without hesitation, consists in the increasingly clear recognition of the dignity, sacredness and absolute inviolability of the human person, on both the theoretical and practical levels.

Consequences of the Proposed Amendments

The proposed amendments on abortion are well known. According to the bill, those who procure an abortion would be liable, as in the past, to life imprisonment; but a qualified doctor would be allowed to perform an abortion if pregnancy endangered, or was likely to endanger, the life or health of the mother, provided the abortion was performed in an accredited hospital and a written certificate obtained from the hospital's therapeutic abortion committee. This brings us to the following considerations.

This amendment of the law not only allows the direct and voluntary taking of an innocent life, but opens the door to the broadest interpretations. Through the press, radio and television we are already familiar with expressions of public opinion that show a clear and alarming decline in respect for the life of the unborn. Some, for example, see the amendment proposed in the House of Commons as only the first step towards official recognition of "abortion on demand". Others believe that the amendment, as it stands, already provides the possibility for abortion in a very large number of cases.

Such reactions are not at all reassuring. When we consider also what has happened in countries where similar legislation has been adopted, we can easily foresee what will happen here.

On this point, it should be noted that the parliamentary committee looking into the question acknowledged in its first report last December that there had not been sufficient study and investigation. We must ask, therefore, whether the Canadian people really have before them all the necessary information. Secondly, is it right for Parliament, without measuring through appropriate research the moral, psychological and sociological implications, to venture into new legislation on a problem of such grave consequences for humanity and for civilization itself?

Illicit Abortions

Many who find the very idea of abortion repugnant still see some merit in the amendment proposed by the government. They think that the new law would significantly reduce the number of illicit abortions and their disastrous consequences.

With regard to illicit abortions, arbitrary unverifiable figures are produced which catch public attention simply by being repeated. To be sure, such abortions are too common, and they have serious consequences. Every effort must be made to eliminate them. But the real question is what means should be used to bring about the desired result.

There is good evidence that it is only an illusion to expect that the proposed amendment will succeed in reducing the number of illicit abortions. Judging by the experience of countries with laws similar to the one proposed for Canada, we may justly fear the very opposite result. In fact, could it be otherwise? A law that lessens the right of the foetus to life by the exceptions it allows leads to a lax attitude that abortion is no longer a real crime. Lawmakers should never underestimate the educational value of law. Men are all too ready to consider as morally permissable whatever the law itself permits.

True Reform

Progress, especially in human affairs, is rarely achieved by easy solutions. The proposed amendment is just that — a too-simple solution to a serious and complex problem. We have in mind a completely different approach. Respect for human life at all stages of development should be fostered through education and through laws that teach respect for life. A serious study of the frequency of illicit abortions and of means to eliminate them should be undertaken. Medical research should be encouraged. Real efforts should be made to provide mothers in distress with the medical and psychiatric care they need. There should be a more humane understanding of unwed mothers and their children and we should provide them with real help. Greater effort must go into the care of those afflicted by mental illness. More adequate social and family policies should be planned and developed with all seriousness and great generosity.

The state must devote itself to a program of this kind. For our part, we call on the Catholic people to become active leaders and ardent collaborators in this common undertaking.

This is the way of real social progress and true freedom. For us only one approach is worthy of mankind, of civilization and of Canada's spiritual mission in the world. That approach calls for creative imagination, not the all-too-easy imitation of other countries. It calls for ever-increasing respect for all human life, including the defenceless and most dependent.

During the recent parliamentary debate on capital punishment, this was said: "We can set an example of our respect for the sanctity of human life to a world that is sorely in need of a higher regard for human life and a higher standard of human conduct". These words, you will agree, touch the heart of the matter. They throw light on the present debate. May they also be its inspiration!

NOTES

1. Canadian Catholic Conference witnesses appeared before the House of Commons standing Committee on Health and Welfare, March 5, 1968. Proceedings of the House of Commons Standing Committee on Health and Welfare; No. 24, March 5, 1968; pp. 860-863.

2. Second Vatican Council, *The Church in the Modern World*, n. 51.

Section II, Document 4

STATEMENT ON THE ENCYCLICAL
HUMANAE VITAE [1]

Author — The Plenary Assembly, Canadian Catholic Conference,
September 27, 1968

1. Pope Paul VI in his recent encyclical *On Human Life* has spoken on a profound human problem as is clearly evidenced by the immediate and universal reaction to his message. It is evident that he has written out of concern and love, and in a spirit of service to all humanity. Conscious of the current controversy and deep differences of opinion as to how to harmonize married love and the responsible transmission of life, we, the Canadian bishops, offer our help to our priests and Catholic people, believing it to be our pastoral duty.

I — SOLIDARITY WITH THE POPE

2. We are in accord with the teaching of the Holy Father concerning the dignity of married life and the necessity of a truly Christian relationship between conjugal love and responsible parenthood. We share the pastoral concern which has led him to offer counsel and direction in an area which, while controverted, could hardly be more important to human happiness.

3. By divine commission, clarification of these difficult problems of morality is required from the teaching authority of the Church.[2] The Canadian Bishops will endeavour to discharge their obligation to the best of their ability. In this pursuit we are acting consistently with our recent submissions to the federal government on contraception, divorce and abortion, nor is there anything in those submissions which does not harmonize with the encyclical.

II — SOLIDARITY WITH THE FAITHFUL

4. In the same spirit of solidarity we declare ourselves one with the People of God in the difficulties they experience in understanding, making their own and living this teaching.

5. In accord with the teaching of the Second Vatican Council, the recent encyclical[3] recognizes the nobility of conjugal love which is "uniquely expressed and perfected through the marital act".[4] Many married people experience a truly agonizing difficulty in reconciling the need to express conjugal love with the responsible transmission of human life.[5]

6. This difficulty is recognized in deep sympathy and is shared by bishops and priests as counsellors and confessors in their service of the faithful. We know that we are unable to provide easy answers to this difficult problem, a problem made more acute by the great variety of solutions proposed in an open society.

7. A clearer understanding of these problems and progress toward their solution will result from a common effort in dialogue, research and study on the part of all, laity, priests and bishops, guided by faith and sustained by grace. To this undertaking the Canadian bishops pledge themselves.

III — CHRISTIAN CONSCIENCE AND DIVINE LAW

8. Of recent years many have entertained doubts about the validity of arguments proposed to forbid any positive intervention which would prevent the transmission of human life. As a result there have arisen opinions and practices contrary to traditional moral theology. Because of this many had been expecting official confirmation of their views. This helps to explain the negative reaction the encyclical received in many quarters. Many Catholics face a grave problem of conscience.

9. Christian theology regarding conscience has its roots in the teaching of St. Paul (Rom. 14:23 and 1 Cor. 10). This has been echoed in our day by the Second Vatican Council: "Conscience is the most secret core and sanctuary of a man. There he is alone with God, whose voice echoes in his depths".[6] "On his part, man perceives and acknowledges the imperatives of the divine law through the

mediation of conscience. In all activity a person is bound to follow conscience faithfully, to come to God, the final end of each."[7] The dignity of the person consists precisely in this ability to achieve fulfillment in God through the exercise of a knowing and free choice.
10. This does not however, exempt one from the responsibility of forming conscience according to truly Christian values and principles. This implies a spirit of openness to the teaching of the Church which is an essential aspect of the Christian's baptismal vocation. It likewise implies sound personal motivation free from selfishness and undue external pressure which are incompatible with the spirit of Christ. Nor can one succeed in this difficult task without the help of God. We are all prone to sin and evil and unless we humbly ask and gratefully receive the grace of God this basic freedom will inevitably lead to abuse.

IV — TEACHING OFFICE OF THE CHURCH

11. Belief in the Church which is the prolongation of Christ in the world, belief in the Incarnation, demands a cheerful readiness to hear that Church to whose first apostles Christ said: "He who hears you hears me" (Lk. 10:16).
12. True freedom of conscience does not consist, then, in the freedom to do as one likes, but rather to do as a responsible conscience directs. The Second Vatican Council applies this concept forcefully. Christians therefore:

> … must always be governed according to a conscience dutifully conformed to the divine law itself, and should be submissive towards the Church's teaching office, which authentically interprets that law in the light of the gospel. That divine law reveals and protects the integral meaning of conjugal love, and impels it towards truly human fulfillment.[8]

13. Today, the Holy Father has spoken on the question of morally acceptable means to harmonize conjugal love and responsible parenthood. Christians must examine in all honesty their reaction to what he has said.
14. The Church is competent to hand on the truth contained in the revealed word of God and to interpret its meaning. But its role is not limited to this function. In our pilgrimage to salvation, we achieve

final happiness by all our responsible conduct and whole moral life. Since the Church is our guide in this pilgrimage, she is called upon to exercise her role as teacher, even in those matters which do not demand the absolute assent of faith.

15. Of this sort of teaching Vatican II wrote:

> This religious submission of will and of mind must be shown in a special way to the authentic teaching authority of the Roman Pontiff, even when he is not speaking *ex cathedra*. That is, it must be shown in such a way that his supreme teaching authority is acknowledged with reverence, the judgments made by him are sincerely adhered to, according to his manifest mind and will. [9]

16. It follows that those who have been commissioned by the Church to teach in her name will recognize their responsibility to refrain from public opposition to the encyclical; to do otherwise would compound confusion and be a source of scandal to God's people. This must not be interpreted however, as a restriction on the legitimate and recognized freedom of theologians to pursue loyally and conscientiously their research with a view to greater depth and clarity in the teaching of the Church.

17. It is a fact that a certain number of Catholics, although admittedly subject to the teaching of the encyclical, find it either extremely difficult or even impossible to make their own all elements of this doctrine. In particular, the argumentation and rational foundation of the encyclical, which are only briefly indicated, have failed in some cases to win the assent of scientists, or indeed of some people of culture and education who share in the contemporary empirical and scientific mode of thought. We must appreciate the difficulty experienced by contemporary minds in understanding and appropriating some of the points of this encyclical, and must make every effort to learn from the insights of Catholic scientists and intellectuals, who are of undoubted loyalty to Christian truth, to the Church and to the authority of the Holy See. Since they are not denying any point of divine and Catholic faith nor rejecting the teaching authority of the Church, these Catholics should not be considered, or consider themselves, shut off from the body of the faithful. But they should remember that their good faith will be dependent on a sincere self-examination to determine the true motives and grounds for such suspension of assent and on continued effort to understand and deepen their knowledge of the teaching of the Church.

18. The difficulties of this situation have been felt by the priests of the Church, and by many others. We have been requested to provide guidelines to assist them. This we will endeavour to do in a subsequent document. We are conscious that continuing dialogue, study and reflection will be required by all members of the Church in order to meet as best we can the complexities and exigencies of the problem.

19. We point out that the particular norms which we may offer will prove of little value unless they are placed in the context of our human and Christian vocations and of all the values of Christian marriage. This formation of conscience and this education in true love will be achieved only by a well balanced pastoral insistence upon the primary importance of a love which is human, total, faithful and exclusive as well as generously fruitful. [10]

V — PRELIMINARY PASTORAL GUIDANCE

20. For the moment, in conformity with traditional Christian morality, we request priests and all who may be called to guide or counsel the consciences of others to give their attention to the following considerations.

21. The pastoral directives given by Pope Paul VI in the encyclical are inspired by a positive sacramental approach. The Eucharist is always the great expression of Christian love and union. Married couples will always find in this celebration a meeting place with the Lord which will never fail to strengthen their own mutual love. With regard to the sacrament of penance the spirit is one of encouragement both for penitents and confessors and avoids both extremes of laxity and rigorism.

22. The encyclical suggests an attitude towards the sacrament of penance which is at once less juridical, more pastoral and more respectful of persons. There is real concern for their growth, however slow at times, and for the hope of the future.

23. Confession should never be envisaged under the cloud of agonizing fear of severity. It should be an exercise in confidence and respect of consciences. Paul VI invited married couples to "... have recourse with humble perseverance to the mercy of God, which is poured forth in the Sacrament of Penance". [11] Confession is a meeting between a sincere conscience and Christ Our Lord who was "... indeed intransigent with evil, but merciful towards individuals". [12]

24. Such is the general atmosphere in which the confessor and counsellor must work. We complete the concept with a few more particular applications.

25. In the situation we described earlier in this statement (n. 17) the confessor or counsellor must show sympathetic understanding and reverence for the sincere good faith of those who fail in their effort to accept some point of the encyclical.

26. Counsellors may meet others who, accepting the teaching of the Holy Father, find that because of particular circumstances, they are involved in what seems to them a clear conflict of duties; e.g., the reconciling of conjugal love and responsible parenthood with the education of children already born or with the health of the mother. In accord with the accepted principles of moral theology, if these persons have tried sincerely but without success to pursue a line of conduct in keeping with the given directives, they may be safely assured that whoever honestly chooses that course which seems right does so in good conscience.

27. Good pastoral practice for other and perhaps more difficult cases will be developed in continuing communication among bishops, priests and laity, and in particular in the document we have promised to prepare. In the meantime we earnestly solicit the help of medical scientists and biologists in their research into human fertility. While it would be an illusion to hope for the solution of all human problems through scientific technology, such research can bring effective help to the alleviation and solution of problems of conscience in this area.

VI — INVITATION TO SOCIAL PASTORAL ACTION

28. The whole world is increasingly preoccupied with the social impact of people's thoughts, words and actions. Sexuality in all its aspects is obviously an area of the greatest human and social impact. The norms and values which govern this so vital human concern merit the attention and reflection of all. Our world evolves at a frightening rate, creating at once a vivid sense of unity and a set of conflicting forces which could destroy us.

29. This concern will be fruitful only if it leads all of us to recognize our true human worth in the possession of our inner powers by which we are distinctively ourselves with the full recognition of our

complementary sexual differences on the physical, the psychological and the spiritual plane. Only in this manner will we achieve marriages that are truly unions of love in the service of life.

30. To this end there must be a mobilization of all the positive energies of the family, the school, the state, the Church. No one may stand aloof, nor are there really national boundaries in a matter of such universal application. With this in mind we call on all members of the Church to realize the importance of the process of education for marriage on every level from the very youngest to the various possibilities of adult education.

31. Without wishing to specify in detail we single out for special mention a few aspects which may have richer possibilities. We place first the dialogue and cooperation, which have been so encouraging, among all members of the Church and, through the ecumenical movement, with other Churches.

32. We note with deep satisfaction the spread and strength of so many activities calculated to prepare for marriage or to deepen the appreciation by married persons of this sublime state. For example, marriage preparation courses, family apostolates, discussion groups, etc.

33. Educators, too, are to be commended for their growing attention to the question. Everywhere the problems of sex education and family life are being studied. And this education is happily being deepened by scientific research and diffused through the creative use of mass media. Nothing less than this mobilization of all human forces will suffice to meet the challenge of divisive and destructive forces which begin deep in willful human selfishness and inhibit the true expression of human love. We pledge ourselves to the pastoral priority of encouraging and promoting these programs whenever and wherever possible.

34. We conclude by asking all to pray fervently that the Holy Spirit will continue to guide His Church through all darkness and suffering. We, the People of God, cannot escape this hour of crisis but there is no reason to believe that it will create division and despair. The unity of the Church does not consist in a bland conformity in all ideas, but rather in a union of faith and love, in submission to God's will and in a humble but honest and ongoing search for the truth. That unity of love and faith is founded in Christ and as long as we are true to Him nothing can separate us. We stand in union with the Bishop of Rome, the successor of Peter, the sign and con-

tributing cause of our unity with Christ and with one another. This very union postulates such a love of the Church that we can do no less than to place all our love and intelligence at her service. If this sometimes means that in our desire to make the Church more intelligible and more beautiful we must, as pilgrims do, falter in the way or differ as to the way, no one should conclude that our common faith is lost or our loving purpose blunted. It was the great theologian, John Henry Cardinal Newman, who penned the comforting lines of the well known "Lead kindly light amid the encircling gloom". We believe that the kindly Light will lead us to a greater understanding of God and of human love.

NOTES

1. The initial Latin words of Pope Paul IV's encyclical letter, variously named *On Human Life* or *On the Regulation of Birth*, July 5, 1968, cf. *The Papal Encyclicals*, edit. Claudia Carlen, IHM (Wilmington, N.C., McGrath Publishing, 1981), V, 223.

2. Vatican II, *The Church in the Modern World*, nn. 4 and 18.

3. *On Human Life*, n. 8, cf. note 1.

4. Vatican II, *The Church in the Modern World*, n. 49.

5. *Ibid.*, n. 51.

6. *Ibid.*, n. 16.

7. Vatican II, *Declaration on Religious Freedom*, n. 3; *The Church in the Modern World*, nn. 16f.

8. Vatican II, *The Church in the Modern World*, n. 50.

9. Vatican II, *Dogmatic Constitution on the Church*, 1964, n. 25. The Holy Father speaks *ex cathedra* — "from the chair" (of Peter) — when he intends to teach authoritatively, revealed truth demanding the assent of faith.

10. *On Human Life*, n. 9; cf. note 1.

11. *Ibid.*, n. 25.

12. *Ibid.*, n. 29.

Section II, Document 5

ON COLLABORATION WITH THE MEDIA AND ON DELIBERATIONS OF THE PLENARY ASSEMBLY IN THEIR STATEMENT ON *HUMANAE VITAE*[1]

Author — The Administrative Board, Canadian Catholic Conference, November, 1968

The aftermath of the statement of the Canadian Bishops on the Papal Encyclical, *On Human Life,* has, in many respects, been almost as interesting as the original event. Perhaps the answer to this phenomenon is found in the insight of Father Julien Harvey, S.J., who writes concerning our statement,

> Events which bear the impression of the Holy Spirit have this constant characteristic of being more weighty than they seem. And their breadth is revealed only in their impact and in the profound transformation which they cause within us.[2]

In all humility, even after such a short period of reflection, we seem justified in stating that the Spirit was with us.

One of the practical decisions made by the Assembly at the request of the president was that no minutes of the open discussion be kept. The reason governing this decision is obvious. If, indeed, the Holy Spirit were to manifest Himself, it would have to be through the human condition of reflection, of agony and of honest debate. The bishops must necessarily feel free to express their total opinion without worrying about how it would look on the record with or without context. Such an absence of record also allows for growth in opinion, and what one may say today one may willingly change tomorrow if he is not bound to a previous position.

But we may not fail to note the danger in the absence of record. Above all, we cannot permit commentators or observers who were necessarily on the outside of our deliberations to formulate a record which lacks accuracy.

The main thrust of this document is twofold. First, we wish to record our immense satisfaction with the professional sense of responsibility which characterized almost the totality of the representatives of the press and other communications media during our Winnipeg meeting. Secondly, we wish to point out certain concomitant conditions of human relationships which now in retrospect give us a great sense of human achievement and an even greater hope for true unity in the Church in Canada. Let us take each of these in turn.

From all sides we have received heartening tributes from the representatives of the communications media of Canada, and even of the United States. The role of those who represent the public in this important function is to record events as they take place and to make sure that the public is aware of their total dimension. No one will accuse this profession of not using every possible means to fulfill this role! Some have admitted to us either directly or through our representatives that they came to Winnipeg with the anticipation of having to break an unfair blockade of secrecy if not of hostility. We take pleasure and pride in noting that, with only the rarest of exceptions, those who came to harass remained to cooperate.

In the attempt which was manifestly being made to arrive at an honest and clear statement of a difficult and important pastoral problem, it was evidently necessary for the bishops to work in closed surroundings until the consensus was achieved. But all through this process relationships were so warm and so human with the representatives of the media that they soon became aware that here was no desire for an authoritarian or dictatorial conspiracy of silence or obfuscation but a necessity not to be pressed into saying things which would have to be adjusted or even corrected at a later date.

We ourselves soon felt a lessening of the pressures upon us and we express with all sincerity and deep appreciation our gratitude to the men and women who gathered around us on this occasion and who so rapidly became not only our collaborators but our friends.

We note in passing that since the event so few attempts have been made to write up a cloak-and-dagger, liberal-versus-conservative background of hostility and opposition that it constitutes a minor miracle in these days where the spectacular sometimes leads the reporter astray. This was not a failure on the part of the media people present but evidence of their honesty and efficiency. Because the fact must be entered into the record with all precision and force. There was no such atmosphere.

Many of us have been asked in various circumstances how we could have achieved the kind of unity and consensus in honesty which were the hallmark of our meeting in Winnipeg and of our statement on *On Human Life*. Looking at our hierarchy from the outside, it could hardly be anticipated. We have approximately one hundred bishops in Canada. These follow the usual spectrum of human reaction, personality, temperament and age. Ours is a large and diversified country, where regional conditions vary and points of view are necessarily and, indeed, richly variegated.

An obvious condition exists in the Canadian hierarchy which, to the unwary, might easily be envisaged as a divisive factor. We refer to the natural condition of a bilingual country in which the Church is presided over by bishops of French or English linguistic background. Such a hierarchy in these days of contradicting currents of opinion, of political and ecclesial conflicts, would appear to be unmanageable if not explosive. And yet what happened was an extraordinary feat of unity and consensus.

To pretend that there was no difference of opinion at any point in the Winnipeg deliberations would not only be dishonest and naive but a calculated insult. The men who were present are all men of strong and intelligent views, with passionate loyalties to the Church and to all that it stands for, including those mysterious facets which are constantly evolving and which are not always understood by all in the same light. In the formulation of those loyalties and the expression of our pastoral concern for a profoundly difficult problem, it was not likely that we would discover ready to hand an easy solution to the formulation of our positions.

Yet the fact remains that, despite one "background" article — the only one we are aware of — there was no cloak-and-dagger atmosphere, there were no camps, and there was no tension of any proportion. Hard work there was and honest disagreement in abundance until an acceptable formula was found, but no confrontations and no "taking-to-the-floor" of positions, no "block" separations. These are the simple facts.

Even here it is not our intentionn to make any attempt to write a record. But we must note that on the various votes taken concerning the substance of this document, votes which were based upon the various sections, each was unanimous with the exception of one vote in which there were six dissenting voices against approximately seventy in favour. There was one close vote, a matter of a majority of one, and that concerned a procedural matter allowing the Drafting Committee to use its discretion about the retention or the removal of the words "the teaching of" (the Holy Father) in Section I, n. 2 of the Declaration. The interesting part of this matter is that the Drafting Committee found it possible to retain the words and when the formula was presented it was unanimously approved by the Assembly.

Consequently, we repeat that the backstairs divisions and the dramatic "appeals to the floor" so dear to the seeker of the spectacular were not there. In this connection it was very different from many of the dramatic struggles that took place in Vatican II. We could sum up our position by saying that there was a constant basic unity in the Theological Commission; we achieved unity — not without some small difficulty — between ourselves and our consultors; the Bishops themselves arrived at a consensus that was about as close to unanimity as can be achieved in this world.

We write this partly as a correction, partly as a tribute to the whole team which worked together in Winnipeg. On that team we take the liberty of placing not only the bishops themselves with their competent and devoted secretarial staff, but also the theologians and *periti* (experts) and, not least, the men and women of the communications media. Any one of these groups could have created a divisive atmosphere. That no one did is a source of deep and abiding satisfaction for all of us.

We look forward to devoting a large proportion of our future plenary assemblies to the consideration of the more profound aspects of the role of the Church in the present world. We believe that it is the will of the bishops to delegate more of routine matters to its Board and Executive in an attempt to find again the movement of the Spirit. In this Spirit we will always have the same kind of unity and consensus which characterized the work done and the results achieved by all of us in the Canadian statement concerning *On Human Life*.

NOTES

1. Cf. previous Document 4 of this Section II, note 1.
2. In *Relations* (Montreal, Nov. 1968), p. 309.

Section II, Document 6

STATEMENT ON FAMILY LIFE AND RELATED MATTERS

Author — The Plenary Assembly, April 18, 1969

The bishops of Canada in plenary assembly take cognizance of the report of the special committee appointed to discuss what steps should follow the statement of the Canadian Catholic Conference in Winnipeg, September 27, 1968, concerning Pope Paul VI's encyclical letter, *On Human Life*[1]

This committee, composed of two bishops, a number of priests, religious and lay persons, after serious study and deliberation have summarized their recommendations as follows:

1. that the Canadian Catholic Conference give its utmost support and encouragement to marriage preparation programs — short of recommending that they be compulsory for Church marriages;

2. that the Canadian Catholic Conference recommend to priests, family movements and other interested Church members the possibility of an "apostolate to new parents";

3. that the Canadian Catholic Conference initiate a study of the theology of marriage in today's world;

4. that the Canadian Catholic Conference strongly support family life education in the school as a supplement to parental efforts, with particular stress on the need for adequate preparation of teachers for such classroom courses.

We are pleased to accept these resolutions and to make them our own. We request our Administrative Board and Executive Committee to see to their implementation.

In this context we wish to express our conviction that the present concern and preoccupation with the problems of marriage can best be met by the positive approach recommended by our committee.

At the same time we cannot close our eyes or our minds to the reactions of a certain segment of the public, both within our communion and outside it, which appears to have distorted to some degree our pastoral application of the encyclical *On Human Life.*

Nothing could be gained and much lost by any attempt to rephrase our Winnipeg statement. We stand squarely behind that position but we feel it our duty to insist on a proper interpretation of the same.

In particular we feel that our teaching on freedom of conscience and the role of the *magisterium,* the authentic teaching authority of the Church, has not always been accurately reflected.

Consequently we wish to reiterate our positive conviction that a Catholic Christian is not free to form his conscience without consideration of the teaching of the *magisterium,* in the particular instance exercised by the Holy Father in an encyclical letter. It is false and dangerous to maintain that because this encyclical has not demanded "the absolute assent of faith",[2] any Catholic may put it aside as if it had never appeared. On the contrary, such teaching in some ways imposes a great burden of responsibility on the individual conscience.

The Catholic knows that he or she may not dissent from teaching proposed as infallible. With regard to such teaching one may seek only to understand, to appreciate, to deepen one's insights.

In the presence of other authoritative teaching, exercised either by the Holy Father or by the collectivity of the bishops one must listen with respect, with openness and with the firm conviction that a personal opinion, or even the opinion of a number of theologians, ranks very much below the level of such teaching. The attitude must be one of desire to assent, a respectful acceptance of truth which bears the seal of God's Church.

In order that this matter of the Christian attitude to the transmission of life be not further distorted, we believe that this whole question will best be studied and situated in the larger context of the formation of responsible conscience in general. We recommend that studies along these lines be initiated as soon as possible by the Canadian Catholic Conference.

NOTES

1. Cf. Document 4 of this section.
2. *Ibid.,* n. 14.

Section II, Document 7

CAPITAL PUNISHMENT: TO THE HONOURABLE MEMBERS OF THE SENATE AND THE HOUSE OF COMMONS

Author — The Administrative Board, the CCC, January 26, 1973

The Question of Capital Punishment

Canada has still to face a whole complex of questions about reform of corrections, parole and rehabilitation. The Bill soon to come before Parliament, to extend the suspension of the death penalty, treats in an isolated way a problem which has connections with these many other problems. We would rather wait until we had time to explore the whole field and take a broadly based position. In the current debate on the death penalty however, many persons have adduced varying understandings of Christian teaching to support this conclusion or that. In these circumstances, even though we do not have a final solution for the question, we believe it our duty to make some comment.

1. We consider it an illegitimate use of Scripture, especially of the Old Testament, to quote texts for the retention of the death penalty in our time. Each biblical text supporting the death penalty must be studied in the light of its historical context and not simply applied to contemporary Canada. Further, each such Old Testament text must be weighed against many passages in the New Testament where Jesus constantly rejects the normal human tendency to redress injury by injury and calls instead for generosity. He established the norm that violence and hostility are not corrected by countermeasures of violence and hostility.

2. The question of the death penalty, in our opinion, ought not to focus on whether a convicted murderer, no matter how wanton his crime, "deserves" to die. The focus should be on us: should Canadians as a community try to break the escalating spiral of violence by refraining from violence even as a deterrent?

3. To a Christian, whose starting point is reverence for the sanctity of life, the death penalty can surely be only a desperate last resort. A Christian must be utterly convinced of its social necessity before supporting it. Our society, it is true, has traditionally exacted the death penalty. But this ought not to mean, as often seems taken, that those who favour suspension must bear the burden of proof. On the contrary, those who favour retention should be required to convince a Christian of its necessity.

4. There is also a pragmatic, statistical question whether the death penalty is an effective deterrent. We will not enter this debate. Our question is not whether the death penalty is an effective deterrent; our question is whether it is an *absolutely necessary* deterrent, required by good order in Canada today. Unless you are convinced that it is, then we feel that the presumption should be for suspension. Furthermore, in our opinion, the case for retention of the death penalty has not been proven.

5. We would hope that, during a possible second period of suspension, research committees would study, exhaustively all the ramifications of this complex problem and publish their reports within a specified period. We might note the need for study of the effects of violent crime on the families of both the criminal and the victim.

The Administrative Board of the Canadian Catholic Conference in a spirit of collaboration offers the cooperation of the staff of its Social Life Department.

Section II, Document 8

STATEMENT ON
THE FORMATION OF CONSCIENCE

Author — The Canadian Catholic Conference, December 1, 1973

PROLOGUE

1. In all the earth, we humans alone are called by God to accept responsibility for our actions. But God has not abandoned us in a world of mystery, where good and evil are often interwoven and frequently filled with complexities. We who are Christians believe that not only did God give us His guidance "engraved on our hearts" (Rom. 2:15), showing us in the very depth of our being the things which are for our good, He also intervened in history to reveal Himself in His Son, our Lord Jesus. Henceforth, Jesus and the Spirit He was to send from the Father, would be the focal point of our lives and of our doing, "I am the way, the truth and the life. No one comes to the Father except through me" (Jn. 14:6).

2. We have then, God's clear teaching to guide us, found in Scripture and tradition, protected and authenticated by the teaching Church. God speaks to us also through concrete situations, the providential framework of our existence, our times, our vicissitudes, events, happenings, circumstances. "The People of God believes that it is led by the Spirit of the Lord, who fills the earth".[1]

3. Above all, we believe that we live now in the time of the fullness of Christ, of the law of love. Our Christian responsibility is not only to fight against our sinful nature, in which we are assisted by our obedience to all legitimate laws. It is also to respond to God's call

to conversion in a movement towards Christ and His Spirit, the realization of what it is to be a Christian, a child of God. "Christian, acknowledge your dignity. It is God's own nature that you share."[2]

4. It is in this context that we wish to present these considerations on conscience. We must of necessity at times leave this high ground because we are frail and readily lose our way. We journey always however, with the serenity and joy of those who know we have already triumphed in our risen Lord.

PART ONE

I — THE MEANING OF CONSCIENCE

The Basic Concept

5. The signs of the times have much to tell us, even when they point to negative and harmful dimensions. The most optimistic person could hardly deny that our time is characterized by a frightening confusion in regard to moral life and the understanding of values which for many centuries were taken for granted. It is to this confusion of mind that we would like to address ourselves in order to provide certain pastoral guidelines which are meant primarily for our Catholic people, but to which we invite the attention of all people of good will interested in preserving the best elements of our civilization and culture. We appeal in a special manner to those who share with us our faith in Christ as Redeemer and as guide of our lives.

6. To be consistent, since we openly admit the existence of confusion, we cannot even take the idea of "conscience" for granted. It has always been a somewhat ambiguous term and has frequently been presented with more poetry than clarity. Conscience is not simply some "still small voice" which is evoked by a mysterious mechanism within us, when we are faced with a practical decision as to whether a given course of action is acceptable or not. Conscience is that ultimate judgment that each is called to make as to whether this or that action is acceptable without violating the principles which one is prepared to admit as governing human life. To act against these principles is to act "against conscience".

Different Connotations

7. It follows that conscience has different connotations for different persons. We will develop this point further in the following section on the formation of conscience. For the moment it suffices to point out that for some, the very existence of conscience will be denied. These are the men and women who refuse to accept that we are subject to any laws outside ourselves; in a word, they maintain that the individual person is Lord and Master. In strict logic they are consistent, even though it is hard to understand their premise that each is supreme in a universe not of our making.

8. To accept the idea of conscience, as we here present it, one must begin by agreeing that one is not Lord of the universe and that humanity is subject to a Law-giver greater than ourselves. In a word, we must begin with that very first basis of any moral life and of any question of responsible judgment in our actions, the acceptance of God. And not a God who is remote and unconcerned but a God who is our Father, who made the universe, made each one of us and who has lovingly cast our lives in a certain framework (Gen. 1:26-7).

9. Out of that same love, God has made us, not automata moved by the blind forces of the universe, but free intelligent beings, adoptive sons and daughters, challenged to adapt our conduct to our dignity. We must appreciate fully that dignity and its consequences in terms of responsible conduct.

II — THE FORMATION OF CONSCIENCE

10. This never-ending search which each must undertake to discover what is worthy and what is not worthy of a human person is what we call the "formation" of conscience. And this quest will be qualified by various assumptions which a person makes at any period in life. The formation of conscience of one who believes no more than that God is, will be different from that of one who accepts that God has intervened in history. And different again if one believes that God has sent us a Saviour in the Person of the Lord Jesus, incarnate in our human nature, to rehabilitate our race, giving it a new life, illumined by revealed truth, and prescribing our path of return to God (Jn. 3:16; 8:12; 1 Jn. 2:3-6).

11. Further, a Christian who is also an adherent of the Catholic faith and a member of the Catholic Church must probe deeper in the refinement of what God has revealed as our norm of conduct. As Catholics we accept that Jesus committed to His apostles His own authority. "As the Father has sent Me, now also I send you..." (Jn. 20:21), "Whatever you bind on earth shall be considered bound in heaven; what you loose on earth shall be considered loosed in heaven" (Mt. 18:18). We believe that this power transmitted to His apostles was meant to endure in the Church and now resides in the College of Bishops under the presiding direction of the successor of Peter. This is what we call the *magisterium* or teaching service of the Church and, in the guidance of our conduct, a binding rule for those who call themselves Catholic (Cf. Mt. 28:18-20 and Jn. 14:25-6).

12. Nor is this to be considered some sort of inhibiting or limiting force. It would be wrong to think that the persons most free are those who do not believe at all and that we go in a descending scale of freedom till we meet the Catholic. We believe that the reverse is true. We believe that knowing what God has established for the fulfillment of humanity is a freeing principle, not a principle of enslavement. The more we know about God's will for us, the more fully human we be, the surer that we will not harm ourselves, wandering into paths which will not enhance our liberty but destroy it. "The truth will make you free" (Jn. 8:32; Cf. Ps. 1).

13. This is the basic context in which we would like to situate some of the problems of our times.

Part Two

PROBLEMS OF OUR TIMES

Confusion in the Church

14. Although we admit that it would be wrong to think that changes within the Church during the past quarter century have been unrelated to the even greater upheavals in the world, for the sake of clarity, we distinguish between the two areas.

15. Faithful Catholics have been disturbed and sometimes confused in recent years by multiple and rapid changes unparalleled in modern history. These changes have often had implications for day to day conduct and consequently appear at least to affect the very norms of that conduct. A few years ago, the Catholic was largely distinguished by external practices, such as abstinence on Fridays, fasting and various penitential disciplines, a number of holy days of obligation, etc. The liturgy was an unchnging structure which had remained the same for hundreds of years. Devotions of various sorts seemed also to be unchangeable and irreplaceable and a necessary part of the practice of the faithful. The priest seemed almost the conscience of the community and interpreted the teaching of the Church with a voice that was considered authoritative and usually unchallengeable.

16. Today much of this has changed. Many of the penitential disciplines such as fasting and abstinence are left to individual judgment, the emphasis on the liturgy is one of participation and commitment, and a biblical renewal has moved some traditional devotions into the background. As far as the priest is concerned, his role is not less important but his person is less overwhelming. He still has the duty of teaching his community the way of God and of morality, but he understands better that this judgment must ultimately be made by the individual Catholic, as we will try to describe later.

Confusion in the World

17. It is rare that changes take place in the world without influencing the Church or that changes take place in the Church without influencing the Christian world. During this period of confusion, popular morality has been shaken to its foundations. There is a general attitude that "I can do pretty much anything which doesn't hurt somebody else". Permissiveness dominates our society. Practices which previously would have been repudiated as absolutely unacceptable are becoming common. We have only to look at the practice of abortion, at a growing pressure for euthanasia and the other manifestations against life itself to see the truth of the statement. In the midst of this, legislators rightly make the distinction between that which is legal and that which may or may not be evil

in the mind of an individual. Even Catholic legislators take the position that legislation cannot be guided absolutely by principles deriving from religious conviction. Many Christians are influenced by this and falll into the trap of thinking that what is legal must be morally acceptable.

18. Another factor is the widespread propaganda which makes all aspects of family planning and sexual activity a matter of private concern and individualistic ethics. The idea is abroad that since "everybody is doing it", it must be acceptable. Finally, the economic and political conditions of our society are tending to depress our moral sensitivity. The calm acceptance by some of material inequality — a few having so much, so many having so little — contributes to the depersonalization of society and the exploitation of others. All these and other factors have tended to bring about a reversal of traditional morality or at least a widespread questioning of moral values.

Reaction to Confusion: Types of Conscience

19. From these factors has stemmed the confusion of conscience to which we alluded in the first lines of this statement. Although it may entail some over-simplification, we feel that something can be gained by dividing reactions to the general situation into three categories. These are not mutually exclusive but they sum up quite well the possible attitudes of the Catholic today.

20. (a) In the first category are those who have developed a static or complacent conscience. These are persons who have not accepted the dynamics behind the changes in the Church and in society, and have not seen the positive value inherent in personal acceptance of moral responsibility. They insist that the Church must spell out for them every obligation down to the last detail. This attitude of conscience is of course a denial of responsibility and can result in negating the whole positive value of the movement of the Spirit at the present time.

21. (b) At the opposite extreme we have the excessively dynamic and revolutionary conscience. This characterizes the person who has totally misread the idea that each must ultimately and before God be the judge of one's actions and that in the ultimate decision each must form one's own judgment. The persons in this category have distorted any appeal for intelligent personal decision into a destruc-

tion of law and of objective morality, and have arrived at the conclusion that no one can tell them what to do, including the Church. It is seldom stated this way but it is where this type of exaggerated subjectivism necessarily leads.

22. (c) In the middle position is what we consider to be the proper attitude of any human being in today's society, and particularly of the Catholic Christian. We can qualify this as the dynamic Christian conscience. This is the conscience which leads to the adoption of a responsible attitude to someone, to Jesus, to the community, to the Church, etc. Persons in this category feel a responsibility for a progressive search and striving to live out a life ideal according to the mind of Christ (Phil. 2:5).

Part Three

FUNDAMENTAL BASIS FOR MATURE CONSCIENCE

23. In support of this type of conscience, we offer the following considerations.

Human Dignity

24. In the first place, this category represents a truly acceptable and dignified human position. The Second Vatican Council has clearly placed great emphasis upon the basic dignity and value of the human person and on one's responsibility as the ultimate judge under God of the moral value of one's action.

> For its part, authentic freedom is an exceptional sign of the divine image within us. For God has willed that we be left 'in the hand of our own counsel' (Ec. 15:14) so that we can seek our Creator spontaneously, and come freely to utter and blissful perfection through loyalty to Him. Hence our dignity demands that we act according to a knowing and free choice. Such a choice is personally motivated and prompted from within. It does not result from blind internal impulse nor from mere external pressure.[3]

Consequently, it is the proper dignity of every human being to assume the responsibility conferred by God Himself in His creation of our free, intelligent persons. This is the basis for the argument St. Paul presents in his letter to the Romans, where he so clearly enunciates that every human being, in coming into the world, has God's law in his or her heart. By this he means two things. First, that we are responsible for our acts, and second, that we cannot take it upon ourselves to act according to the whims of the moment without reference to our Creator, to our fellow human beings and the dignity of our nature (Cf. Rom. 2:14-16).

Responsibility

25. In our time we welcome the growing maturity of people who understand this first element, but would remind them that so to judge does not dispense them from the second element of referring to God's presence, variously but truly manifested in their lives and guiding their judgments.

26. In the depths of conscience, we detect a law which we do not impose upon ourselves, but which holds us to obedience. Always summoning us to love good and to avoid evil, the voice of conscience can, when necessary, speak to our hearts more specifically: do this, shun that. For we have in our hearts a law written by God. To obey it is the very dignity of the person. It is according to this obedience we shall be judged. [4]

Antidote to the Denial of Sin

27. We feel that this type of mature conscience will be the greatest antidote to the growing attack, both explicit and implicit, on the idea of human sinfulness. An exaggerated and false human autonomy has led us to an attitude of mind which depreciates the concepts of sin and redemption. We have deliberately turned from the clear teaching of God and of our Lord Jesus Christ that while God is a loving Father, He cannot be mocked (Cf. Gal. 6:9). This truth does not depend on the ancient error that God is something of a tyrant, seeking an opportunity to punish. On the other hand, the very gift

of freedom indicates that when we misuse it, we ourselves suffer loss. In this sense, possible punishment is the necessary concomitant of the law of love. Love cannot be forced upon anyone, but as a modern writer has put it, "He who rejects love is in turn rejected by it and lies howling at the threshold".

The "howling at the threshold" could hardly be blamed on the Person Who has offered love and has been rejected. The suffering of those who reject God's norms of life is of their own causing. Hence, we feel that a dynamic Christian conscience is one which recognizes all these facts and is freed thereby, freed from the need to pretend that sin is not and that there is no consequence of sin.

Faith Dimension

28. We have already pointed out that the basic responsibility of every human being lies in the fact that each is God's creature and that, as a result, each must assume responsibility for actions over which God has given direct stewardship. But we have also pointed out that for the Christian and for the Catholic Christian, in particular, there are guides freely accepted which are meant to help discern the light of God's guidance within.

29. In this context, we necessarily insist first and foremost upon the working of the Spirit in the hearts of men and women (Jn. 14:26; 16:7-13; and Cf. Rom. c.8). The Second Vatican Council brought us from a somewhat widespread opinion that the Catholic Church constituted a monolithic institution in which the very voice of the Spirit was controlled and channelled. Everything was supposed to come from the above, with the faithful, as it were, the ultimate recipients of the filtering of the Spirit by the upper echelons. It is obvious that nothing so crass was ever officially taught by the Church, but impressions are sometimes more lasting and more universal than teachings. The insistence of the Council on the importance of the people of God and of their personal and direct relationship to the Spirit is a clarification which must never be lost to sight.[5]

30. It is under this heading that we recognize the need for the personal conversion and acceptance of salvation by every human being. The Council[6] has explicitly upheld the scriptural teaching that God wills the salvation of all. There is always however, the second movement to this symphony of love and that is that we cannot be

saved without our acceptance. Each must turn freely to God. For us who believe in an order over and above that of the temporal and the temporary, this turning to God and the acceptance of His loving will for us, even though He has revealed Himself in the obscurity of mystery, is called an act of faith. It is the free decision to accept as true that God has spoken to us"... in former times... in fragmentary and varied fashions through the prophets. But in this the final age He has spoken to us in the Son..." (Heb. 1:1-2). The guidance of the Church is a part of that revelation.

Part Four

GUIDES FOR CHRISTIAN CONSCIENCE

31. We are now in a position to lay down certain norms for the guidance of the conscience of the Catholic Christian. If our positions to this point have been accepted, it follows that an act of conscience is an individual judgment but must be based upon certain accepted principles and positions. It becomes, therefore, the duty of the individual to acquire the information and attitude necessary to make the right decision.

Human Balance

32. Certain human conditions undoubtedly aid in the balanced judgment of conscience which is desired in a mature Christian. Emotional stability, developed self-knowledge and clear objective judgment, even education itself, will undoubtedly help, although we must not fall into an elitism which would expect only the better educated to have sound conscience. Sound communal attitudes and wholesome cultural and social influences — all of these are helpful contributions to the development of moral sensitivity and the formation of correct moral judgments.

33. But these fall far short of the total necessary conditions for the formation of conscience and its ultimate application in life situations.

Presence of Christ

34. For one who has a vital religious faith, the prime factor in the formation of conscience and moral judgment is the place and role of Christ in one's life (Jn. 14:6-8; 12:46). Who wishes to have and preserve a true Christian conscience must be perseveringly in communion with God, our Lord, particularly in prayer and the prayer of the Church. Indeed, properly understood, the vital presence of Christ in one's life, the God-Man loved and revered, is paramount (Cf. 1 Jn. 2:5-6). All other aspects of conscience formation are based on this and stem from it. This does not make them unnecessary or superfluous, but simply puts them in their place (1 Jn. 4:1).

Scripture and Tradition

35. With this in mind, persons of faith draw inspiration from the Scripture, the very Word of God in which we find revealed not only the designs of the Father in the historical context of the world, but a refined series of ideals, precepts and examples given to us by the same Lord Jesus. This is communicated to us not only in the words of scripture but in the Spirit of Jesus which continues to live with us and which makes us "a chosen race and a royal priesthood, a consecrated nation and a people set apart" (1 Pet. 2:9).

The *Magisterium* or Teaching Service of the Church

36. It is in this context that the teaching of the Church finds its full force. We have seen through sad historical example, the kind of conclusion that can arise from an unguided and overly subjective reading of scripture and interpretation of tradition. The Church has been given to us to make sure that the Word of God contained in scripture and illustrated to us in the Spirit can be authenticated in the community of believers.

37. In this one Spirit of which we speak, we have the service of the apostles and of their successors, the college of bishops, united with their head, the Pope. The role of the apostles and their successors was and is to bear witness to Christ, the revelation of the Father and

His will (Cf. Heb. 1:1-3). It was and is the duty of the latter to trans-
mit the testimony of the original apostles concerning Christ, to
celebrate the New Covenant and to guide the people of God in living our new creation in Christ (Mt. 28:18-20; Mk. 16:15-16). Guided
by the Spirit, the Church has sought to do precisely this in the past
and continues to do so in the present world while awaiting the second coming of Christ. The doctrinal service of the successors of the
apostles includes the interpretation of scripture and tradition as
described above. In the fulfillment of this task, they do not seek to
suppress the other gifts of the Spirit but encourage all to test the
gifts according to the criteria found in scripture and tradition.

38. For a believer, this *magisterium* or authoritative teaching of the
Church, as outlined above cannot be just one element among others
in the formation of conscience. It is the definitive cornerstone upon
which the whole edifice of conscientious judgment must be built.
"You are built upon the foundation laid by the apostles and prophets,
and Christ Jesus Himself is the foundation stone" (Eph. 2:20). "You
are Peter and upon this rock I will build my Church" (Mt. 16:18).
What must be kept in mind is that we are in the dimension of faith.
And we should be encouraged and hopeful because we can count
on the continued assistance of the Holy Spirit in a manner which
pure reason could never give.

39. The responsible person, as described above, must weigh all the
facts, the total situation, before acting. This is far from saying that
one may act in accordance with whim and wish. A believer has the
absolute obligation of conforming conduct first and foremost to what
the Church teaches, because first and foremost for the believer is
the fact that Christ, through His Spirit, is ever present in His Church,
in the whole Church to be sure, but particularly with those who exercise services within the Church and for the Church, the first of
which services is that of the apostles.

40. Even in matters which have not been defined *ex cathedra*, i.e.,
infallibly, as of faith, the believer has the obligation to give full priority to the teaching of the Church in favour of a given position, to
pray for the light of the Spirit, to refer to Scripture and tradition and
to maintain a dialogue with the whole Church, possible only through
the source of unity which is the collectivity of the bishops. The reality itself, for example, sex, marriage, economics, politics, war, must
be studied in detail. In this study, one should make an effort to
become aware of one's own inevitable presuppositions and cultural

background which lead one to act for or react against any given position. If the ultimate practical judgment to do this or avoid that does not take into full account the teaching of the Church, an account based not only on reason but on the faith dimension, one is deceiving oneself in pretending to act as a true Catholic should.

41. For a Catholic, "to follow one's conscience" is not, then, simply to act as unguided reason dictates. "To follow one's conscience" and to be a Catholic, one must take into account first and foremost the teaching of the *magisterium*. When doubt arises due to a conflict of "my views and those of the *magisterium*", the presumption of truth lies on the side of the *magisterium*.

> In matters of faith and morals, the bishops speak in the name of Christ and the faithful are to accept their teaching and adhere to it with a religious assent of soul. This religious submission of will and of mind must be shown in a special way to the authentic teaching authority of the Roman Pontiff, even when he is not speaking *ex cathedra*. [7]

And this must be carefully distinguished from the teaching of individual theologians or priests, however intelligent or persuasive.

Part Five

LAW AND CONSCIENCE

42. These positions serve to introduce the delicate question of law, which is a regulating force in human and Christian action. The word itself is frequently used in various senses and we recognize the complexity of the subject.

Distinction of Law as Spirit and as Precept

43. Any Christian reflection on law must take into consideration the crucial distinction between law as precept and law as the dynamic structure of personal being.

44. With regard to the latter concept of law, the passage of St. Paul to the Romans quoted above (Rom. 2:12-15) illustrates this distinction by contrasting the impotence of the precepts of the Mosaic Law with the fundamental belief of Christians that sinful rebellion has been radically — though not completely — healed. All forms of preceptive law stand under the Spirit of love released when Christ, by suffering in Himself the consequences of the law, passed from death to life. As already stated (Rom. 8:1-5), any law is ultimately subject to that influx of the Spirit by which the redeemed are transformed into brothers and sisters of Christ enjoying the freedom of the children of God in His Spirit (Rom. 8:15-17). This operation of the indwelling Spirit of Christ, this conformity of our nature to Christ's word in our hearts, is the New Law. It is discipleship to this word which makes us free (Jn. 8:31-32).

45. This note of the freedom of the children of God is crucial because it establishes the ultimate priority of personal conscience informed by the Spirit of Christ in the case of possible conflict with extrinsic law. God had promised that the New Law would be written in the person's heart, not on tablets of stone (Jer. 31:31; Ez. 36:25). Jesus teaches that the spirit of God's laws takes priority over the letter (Mt. 5:20-48). The great teachers of the Christian tradition have re-echoed this centrality of the interior law of grace. "There on Sinai the finger of God wrote on stone tablets, here, in our hearts, with the sending of the Spirit and Pentecost".[8] The whole strength of the New Law and its specifically Christian meaning consists in its being written in the hearts of people by the Spirit which is given through faith in Christ".[9] In our day the supremacy of the voice of God making Himself heard in the depths of the personal conscience has been reaffirmed, as already stated, by the Second Vatican Council.[10]

Preceptive Law

46. Having established this as a fundamental principle, we can ask how preceptive laws are to be judged by the conscience conformed to the indwelling Spirit which gives life. The new life of Christ in us is not yet perfectly dominant. The preceptive law of legitimate authority must be taken into account in every moral decision because it has the right to command our assent and stands as a constant reminder of our sinfulness and of our dependence upon a source

of life which transcends our individual selves. Moreover, it would be unthinkable that the Spirit, speaking in the heart of the redeemed Christian, would be in opposition to Himself teaching in the authority established by Jesus.

47. It is in this context that we offer some considerations on preceptive "law" in our lives.

48. In a society which finds it extremely difficult to accept any limitations upon even the grossest perversions of freedom, law has become a sort of whipping boy. Yet it can be said that the law is nothing more or less than the expression of conditions which must exist if we are to be free. Scripture has told us, "The truth shall make you free" (Jn. 8:32). This idea could be extended to law when it is a good law since we are thus led to our best, fully liberating conduct.

49. In particular, the presence of evil within us and the ability we have to explain away our most bizarre actions easily incline us to ignore facts and adopt a false sense of values. It is precisely as an antidote to this soft deception that laws are formulated. In a statement of this necessarily limited scope, it is impossible for us to make all the necessary distinctions between divine law and natural law, civil and ecclesiastical law. We limit ourselves to saying that any law promulgated by legitimate authority and in conformity with divine law must be taken into account in every moral action.

50. Some, established by God in the very nature in which He has created us and the universe, are immutable and not subject to any exception. Such are the prohibitions against killing the innocent, adultery, theft, etc. Nor has basic morality changed over the years. The fundamental points of the ten commandments are as valid today as they were when Moses received them on Mount Sinai. Others are established by legitimate human authority to regulate and regularize our human relationships and to govern society whether civil or ecclesiastical. These presume the great laws of God and take them for granted as a basis for their obligatory nature.

51. In the same context, laws made for the proper government of the Church are required for the inter-relationships of the people of God and for the guidance of believers. In every case, they should suppose the law of love and be designed to assist us in its realization. A totally mature and saintly people would require a minimum of laws. But the Church is a pilgrim Church and a Church sent precisely to redeem sinners. The laws it promulgates are specifically

to guide us away from the traps set by our sinfulness and our own tendencies to sin.

The Use of Exceptions

52. In particular, we warn our faithful people against the abuse of seeking exceptions to law in particular cases (a procedure legitimate in itself — the *epikeia* of scholastic moralists — when there is proportionate reason excusing from observance of human law, civil or ecclesiastical), an abuse which has now become so widespread as to threaten the whole structure of our moral lives. This abuse is akin to the situation described above, where some feel exempt from being told anything by anybody, an exaggeration and flagrant abuse of "I must form my own conscience".

53. It is understood that every law is for the general condition and there may be situations in which a person not only is not bound to observe the law but may be unable to do so. (We refer, of course, to matters which are covered by ecclesiastical law, by positive law, not to the great moral laws that have been given to us by God and, as stated, are without exception.) In such exceptional circumstances, the true believer, understanding the law of love, has no feelings of guilt, but a certain regret in not being able to fulfill the law in this particular instance.

54. But the moral use of exceptions has its requirements. And, as we have already intimated, the truly sincere person uses such excusing cause only when absolutely necessary, regretting the need to make exception in the community in this particular case. One who understands that the law originates from love will respond in love and will not be a seeker of exceptions.

CONCLUSION

55. Such, we feel to be the major points upon which our present concern should bear. There is, of course, a great deal more that could be said about conscience. Much, indeed, has been said and we refer our faithful people to the various pronouncements of the Pope, particularly in recent years, to the statements of a number of national

hierarchies, and to the teaching of reliable theologians. In the present text we have striven only to place the problem of the formation of conscience in the contemporary situation and to deal with the major problems facing our people here.

56. We have tried to avoid legalism and to make the Person of Christ, His teachings and His Spirit the basis of our considerations. The true Catholic will generously transcend a minimal observance and go deep into that country whose guide is the Spirit and whose sole law is love. But he or she will not venture there contrary to the mind of the Catholic Church but only in accord with it and freed by it for the journey ahead (1 Jn. 4:16).

NOTES

1. Vatican II, *The Church in the Modern World*, n. 11.
2. St. Leo the Great, *First Christmas Sermon,* in *The Nicene and Post-Nicene Fathers* (Grand Rapids, Michigan, Eerdmans Publishing, 1964), Second Series, Vol. XII, p. 129.
3. Vatican II, *l.c.*, n. 17.
4. *Ibid.*, n. 16
5. Vatican II, *Dogmatic Constitution on the Church,* 1964, nn. 4 and 12.
6. *Ibid.*, nn. 13 and 48.
7. *Ibid.*, n. 25.
8. St. Augustine, *On the Spirit and the Letter,* in *The Nicene and Post-Nicene Fathers* (Grand Rapids, Michigan, Eerdmans Publishing, 1971), First Series, vol. V, p. 95.
9. St. Thomas Aquinas, *Summa Theologica,* I-II, q. 106, aa. 1 and 2; cf. Gal. 3:21f.
10. Vatican II, *The Church in the Modern World,* n. 16; *Declaration on Religious Freedom,* n. 3.

Section II, Document 9

CAPITAL PUNISHMENT

Author — The Administrative Board, the CCC, February 26, 1976

At its meeting of February 26, 1976, the members of the Administrative Board of the Canadian Catholic Conference took cognizance of the presence and acuity of the question of capital punishment, both in parliament and in common discussion. As a result, the following motion was adopted by the Board by a vote of 16 to 2:

Given that:

— abolition of capital punishment in Canada would witness to a profound respect for life in our society;

— a society which so respects the right to life that it does not wish to make use of capital punishment even for its own protection, creates by such attitude a premise favourable to respect for other human rights;

— it is not licit to take human life except in legitimate self-defence, personal or collective, so that capital punishment is acceptable only in a society not sufficiently established to defend itself in any other way, against elements which jeopardize the life of its citizens, which is clearly not the case in Canada;

— violence breeds violence and capital punishment is a violent act;

— studies have not shown that the suspension of capital punishment in Canada has of itself occasioned an increase of criminal activity, any such increase being attributable to many other causes of an economic, social and moral order;

— a considerable number of countries have abolished capital punishment;

— the spirit of the Gospel calls us to forgiveness, clemency and reconciliation, not vengeance or such punishments as the death penalty;

in view of the consideration that:

— the vote of the death penalty will be taken not according to party divisions but according to the personal convictions of the members; in which context a statement by the bishops remains apolitical;

— a declaration by the Administrative Board of the Canadian Catholic Conference would have considerable impact on public opinion and would make clear the leadership of the bishops in a moral question of great importance;

— serious criticism is leveled at conditions prevailing in our penal institutions;

— it is moved by Bishop Jean-Guy Hamelin, seconded by Archbishop Donat Chiasson:

THAT the Administrative Board of the Canadian Catholic Conference state that it favours the abolition of the death penalty in Canada, at the same time urgently requesting the government to initiate effectively the just reform required in our penal system and in the whole area of justice.

Section II, Document 10

ETHICAL REFLECTIONS
ON RESPECT FOR LIFE

Author — The Administrative Board, the CCCB, August 8, 1983

INTRODUCTION

Never before in history has human life been so menaced on our planet, in its growth and in its very existence. All of us live under the shadow of fear cast by the spectre of a nuclear war. Governments of both left and right — in the name of national security — strip their own citizens of basic human rights. Economic policies on both the national and international levels create social injustice destructive of the dignity of both individual and family life. In our own country however, the most flagrant attack upon life, because it is a direct attack upon the most defenceless, is seen in the flood of abortions in recent years.

As a Conference of bishops we have spoken out against all such attacks upon human life. We believe they are interrelated. To be silent in the face of any attack upon human life is ultimately to weaken respect for all human life. Affirming our respect for life from its very beginning, and reaffirming the position of the Church on abortion, we are deeply conscious of the radical anti-life position which abortion represents.

We call the ecclesial community and our whole society to a true dialogue on this question which is both delicate and complex. With this in mind, we reflect first on the sacred character of human life and on the right to conditions which allow the full development of every life. As Pope John XXIII affirmed: "Every human being has a right to life, to physical integrity and to the necessary and suffi-cient means for a decent living".[1] These reflections are followed by suggestions for positive action by both the Christian community and society in general.

THE SACRED CHARACTER OF HUMAN LIFE

The Right to Life is Inviolate

The great Charters of Human Rights recognize that certain rights are proper to the human being by the very fact that one is human and that one's value goes beyond criteria of production, corporal or physical usefulness, etc., by which the dignity of the person is often dismissed. Among these rights, the first and the most fundamental is the right to life, since it is this right which makes all others pos-sible and gives them their rationale.

The unborn child is a human being from its very conception. This fact has been established in biological science:

> Genetics show us that the characteristics of each being, particu-lar traits, the shape of one's face, the colour of one's skin and hair are very precisely defined by the primitive writing contained in the fertilized egg.[2]

At conception there begins the slow and complex process of matu-ration of a being distinct from its mother, growing to full human sta-ture. From the very beginning until the end of life, it is the same human being who is called to a continuous evolution. "A mother knows very well that the child she carries becomes, well before its birth, the partner in a secret dialogue, the attraction of a love already begun."[3]

To desire to find solutions for the dilemma of abortion only at the technical level or according to economic or legal considerations is to dismiss the eminently spiritual nature of human being. Life comes from God and can find its full meaning only in Him.

For believers in the Judeo-Christian tradition human life has a sacred character. "Created in the image of God" (Gen. 1:27), each of us shares in that creating love which loved us into being. This divine love is operative from the very beginning of life: "It was you who created my inmost self and put me together in my mother's womb" (Ps. 139:13). Thus every human being is willed by God and loved for him or herself: "Does a women forget her baby at the breast, and fail to cherish the child of her womb? Yet, even if these forget, I will never forget you. See, I have branded you on the palms of my hands" (Is. 49:15-16).

It was to reveal to us the ultimate significance of human destiny that Jesus, Son of God, Himself became one of us. "Perfect man, He entered world history, taking that history into Himself and recapitulating it."[4] In accepting the human condition in all its dimensions, except sin, the Word of God testifies that nothing human is foreign to Him. Therein lies the determining reason why, for His disciples, human life has an inestimable value: it is sacred. Moreover, the Gospel encourages us to care for our neighbour, in particular, the poorest and those most in need: "Insofar as you did this to one of the least of these, you did it to me" (Mt. 25:40). In this perspective unborn children demand all our solicitude, precisely because they are weak and voiceless.

In this light abortion constitutes a radical attack on human life. It is the destruction of an innocent and defenceless living being, loved by God, an offense to God the Creator. No individual nor any collectivity can usurp the right of life or death over any innocent human being, however small or helpless it might be: "Thou shalt not kill". Doing so would be to assume a power which belongs to God, alone the Master of life and death.

Nor can we neglect the consequences of an abortion: for the mother, whose bodily integrity is attacked, with risk of sterility and other physical and psychological disorders; for children in subsequent pregnancies, the possibility of premature birth, of mental or physical defect; for the family, in interpersonal relations between spouses as well as between parents and children, compromised in so many ways; for the medical personnel involved, anguish, nightmares, guilt, depression, etc.

For these reasons, the Church is strongly opposed to abortion:

> God, the Lord of life, has entrusted to humanity the noble mission of safeguarding life, and we must carry it out in a manner worthy of ourselves. Life must be protected with the utmost care from the moment of conception: abortion and infanticide are abominable crimes.[5]

Medical research and techniques which allow illness in the child to be detected before birth, if undertaken with a view to possible healing, are a hope for humanity. On the other hand:

It is clear that endouterine research tending to the early identification of defective embryos or fetuses in order to eliminate them quickly through abortion are to be considered corrupt at their origin and, as such, morally inadmissable. Equally unacceptable is every form of experimentation on the fetus which may damage its integrity or worsen its condition, unless it is a matter of a last resort attempt to save it from certain death... Medicine will scrupulously refrain from any kind of treatment which could be considered a disguised form of induced abortion... It is necessary for all responsible persons to be in agreement in reaffirming the priority of ethics over technology, the primacy of the person over things, the superiority of the spirit over matter. [6]

The Right to a Decent Standard of Living

Human life is menaced today in many ways besides abortion. One need only recall the arms race and the danger of nuclear holocaust, the pollution of the atmosphere, land and water by industrial waste, the social injustices generated by economic systems based on having rather than on being, the increase of suicide, particularly among youth, of violence in all its forms, and of the various ways the dignity of women is attacked.

We cannot remain indifferent when any aspect of respect for life is threatened. "We are convinced," wrote Pope Paul VI, "that any efforts made to safeguard the rights of the person effectively serve all human life." [7] That is why in recent years, the Canadian bishops have raised questions dealing with a number of fundamental human rights, the right to food, to decent lodging, to work, to culture and self-determination, the rights of native peoples, of the aged, of workers, invalids or the handicapped.

When we have intervened in areas such as peace and disarmament, the economic crisis or capital punishment, one sole motive moved us: to serve human life in all its forms and at all the successive steps of its evolution. Pope John Paul II described it in this manner:

When the rights of minorities are fostered, when the mentally or physically handicapped are assisted, when those on the margin of society are given a voice — in all these instances the dignity of life, and the sacredness of human life are furthered...[8]

When, in the name of "quality of life", individual freedom, egoistic satisfaction or the fear of a changed life style become idols to which we sacrifice even human life, particularly that of the unborn child, we must cry out a very resolute "No!" Life itself is a value always superior to some quality of its social environment or living standard. Here we are dealing with the meaning of human existence. A procured abortion confronts us with a fundamental choice: "The option for 'quality of life' to the point of suppressing life or the option for 'respect for life' to the point of accepting sacrifice and suffering."[9]

That is why, while realizing the pain lived by women who see themselves with no choice but an abortion, we still have the duty to affirm that such is a mistaken solution. The Church, to be faithful to her mission, must find new means and solutions which give people hope and lead to forgiveness and reconciliation.

SOME OUTLINES FOR ACTION

Demand Laws which Respect Life

As pressures mount to liberalize the law and to make abortion more easily accessible, we reaffirm all human rights and the specific right of a child to be born.

We repeat the message addressed to Christian families in the world of today by Pope John Paul II in *The Role of the Christian Family in the Modern World*:

> ... the Church condemns as a grave offence against human dignity and justice all those activities of governments or other public authorities which attempt to limit in any way the freedom of couples in deciding about children. Consequently, any violence applied by such authorities in favour of contraception or, still worse, of sterilization and procured abortion, must be altogether condemned and forcefully rejected. Likewise to be denounced

as gravely unjust are cases where, in international relations, economic help given for the advancement of peoples is made conditional on programs of contraception, sterilization and procured abortion. [10]

To governments we recall that the state has as its mission the preservation of the rights of every person, of protecting the weakest and most disfavoured. Human law cannot contradict laws written by the Creator in the heart of every human being, even if social consensus contradicts them. The state "cannot declare to be right what would be opposed to the natural law, for this opposition suffices to give the assurance that a law is not a law at all." [11] In this regard, it is important not to underestimate the educative value of law. Certain behaviour often comes to be considered moral because civil law allows or tolerates it. But a law which allows abortion is radically immoral. A Christian cannot accept such law either in its concept nor in its application:

> Nor can a Christian take part in a propaganda campaign in favour of such a law, or vote for it. Moreover, a Christian may not collaborate in its application. It is, for instance, inadmissible that doctors or nurses should find themselves obliged to co-operate closely in abortions and have to choose between the Christian law and their professional situation. [12]

Social conduct must be responsibly ordered within the framework of the moral order and with a view to the common good, assuring all citizens the effective enjoyment of their rights as persons, be this from the very beginning of life within the womb or at any other stage of development. In this regard, we give our support to all citizens who struggle for respect for life and who are engaged in trying to change laws which attack the dignity of the person and imperil the very meaning of human life.

Create Structures Which Welcome Life

Services need to be organized to aid the pregnant woman in difficulty, the pregnant adolescent, the unwed mother and her child, the adolescent father and their families. Help is also needed for battered women and those despised or abandoned; for the victims of sexual exploitation through pornography or prostitution, to help them rediscover their dignity and to develop, knowing that they are loved and respected.

We also recommend that each diocese bring together health professionals of various competences and Christian aid agencies to meet the needs of those who find themselves in difficult situations, particularly the pregnant woman, her partner and her family, helping them to live through this suffering and to grow as persons, couple and family. This work must take into account all the dimensions of the human person. In a Christian perspective, complete development is possible only when the human being is reconciled with self, with others and with God. We encourage parents, educators and Christian communities to promote these organizations and to support their projects.

The young should be encouraged to prepare themselves for the roles that they must assume in the near future in order to construct a society truly respectful of human life and dignity. We must be sensitive to the anguish and the despair which haunt them as they face life and their future. With Pope John Paul II, we wish to say to youth:

> Your thirst for the absolute cannot be quenched with ideological substitutes that lead to hatred, violence and despair... With the vitality that is characteristic of your age, with the generous enthusiasm of your young hearts, walk towards Christ. He alone is the solution to all your problems. He alone is the way, the truth, and the life; He alone is the real salvation of the world; He alone is the hope of mankind. [13]

The contemporary mentality suffers from an unjustifiable dualism which separates the realm of human nature from the realm of the spirit. We strongly encourage all educational institutions, universities and schools in the human and medical sciences, to help their students acquire an integrated vision of the human being and not to reduce their teaching to technical and biological mechanisms. "The spiritual dimension of man is indispensable for a true harmony which is personal, familial and social." [14]

Education in Respect for Life

Any initiative to promote respect for life must find its roots in convictions and insights that appreciate the profound value of human life. Thus, attitudes of justice and equity on which society must be based can develop only through an education which envisages the human person in its totality and in all its relations to others. Parents have the primary duty of raising their children in a warm family atmosphere which favours a total personal and social education of their childlren.

We believe that sexual education plays a particularly important role in teaching respect for life.

> Education in love as selfgiving is also the indispensable premise for parents called to give their children a clear and delicate sex education. Faced with a culture that largely reduces human sexuality to the level of something commonplace, since it interprets and lives it in a reductive and impoverished way by linking it solely with the body and with selfish pleasure, the educational service of parents must aim firmly at a training in the area of sex that is truly and fully personal; for sexuality is an enrichment of the whole person — body, emotions and soul — and it manifests its inmost meaning in leading the person to the gift of self in love. [15]

Those collaborating with parents, be they day care centres, nurseries or schools, have the same responsibilities towards the children confided to their care. Sex education in schools must reflect the same values as parental education and deserves careful scrutiny by parents. This education must not neglect education to chastity, the virtue which elevates instinct to the service of love:

> In the Christian view, chastity by no means signifies rejection of human sexuality or lack of esteem for it: rather it signifies spiritual energy capable of defending love from the perils of selfishness and agressiveness, and able to advance it towards its full realization. [16]

When sex education in our schools is reduced to imparting technical and biological information, directed too often towards the exploitation of erotic pleasure and justifying the use of contraceptives, there is a tragic reduction of the meaning of sexuality to mere genital satisfaction. Instead of developing a responsible attitude towards life, it disposes youth to favour abortion. We firmly oppose this sort of biased education. It is a flagrant injustice to our children.

Responsibility of the Media

The influence of the media on both private and public life imposes a responsibility to form a healthy public opinion respectful of life so that society can develop in reciprocal respect for all its members. We wish to draw the attention of producers, writers, performers and others in responsible positions, to the importance of their role as influential educators of individuals and groups. The use of these means of communication demands that the information given respects the moral law and the dignity of the human person. Careful attention must be given to the content to avoid weakening these values.

Support for Pro-life Groups

We note with joy that many Christians have dedicated themselves to the cause of respect for life, working for the defense of the rights of the unborn child. We encourage respect for persons, self-control and all initiatives that contribute to the growth of love and guarantee the freedom of partners called to a responsible participation in the mystery of the creative love of God. Our support also goes to the health workers and those in the social services who assume their responsibilities and who are opposed in conscience to any attack on the life of the innocent; to those who are working for a redirection of society in justice and peace thus favouring an ever deeper respect for every human life including that of the weakest and most dependent.

CONCLUSION

It seems that to counter the anti-life mentality which is prevalent in our society, we need to rediscover and recommit ourselves to the full meaning of life and to demand laws that respect human life. Each one of us must personally and collectively work to renew society and to promote an education which takes into account all dimensions of the human person.

In coming to the assistance of the little ones and the weak, the Church stands for life against the pessimism and selfishness which casts a shadow over our world, since "in each human life, we see the splendour of that 'yes', that 'Amen' who is Christ Himself". [17]

NOTES

1. John XXIII, *Peace on Earth*, 1963, in *The Papal Encyclicals*, edit. Claudia Carlen, IHM (Wilmington, N.C., McGrath Publishing, 1981), V, 108, n. 11.

2. Dr. J. Lejeune, Conference at Notre Dame de Paris, Oct. 10, 1982, in *L'homme nouveau* (Paris, Dec. 19, 1982).

3. *Declaration of the Canadian Conference of Catholic Bishops on Abortion*, Feb. 7, 1968, cf. Document, 3, above.

4. Vatican II, *The Church in the Modern World*, n. 38.

5. *Ibid.*, n. 51.

6. John Paul II, *Address to Pro-Life Movement Congress*, Dec. 5, 1982, *Osservatore Romano*, English edit., Vatican, Jan. 3-10, 1983, p. 19.

7. John Paul II, *Homily*, Washington, Oct. 7, 1979, in *The Pope Speaks*, Washington, 1979, XXIV, 370. The Pope was quoting predecessor Paul VI, Address to Several U.S. Bishops, May 26, 1978, in *Origins*, Washington, 1978-79, VIII, 42.

8. John Paul II, *op. cit.*, note 7 above.

9. P.E. Chabot, *L'avortement*, in *Revue Notre Dame* (Paris, Juin, 1983), p. 5.

10. John Paul II, *Apostolic Exhortation on the Christian Family in the Modern World*, 1981, in *Origins*, Washington, 1982, XI, n. 30, p. 447.

11. S. Congregation for the Doctrine of the Faith, *Declaration on Procured Abortion*, 1974, in *Origins*, Washington, 1974, IV, 390, n. 21.

12. *Ibid.*, n. 22.

13. John Paul II, *Address to Students*, Feb., 11, 1979, *Osservatore Romano*, Vatican, Feb. 12, 1979, p. 8.

14. Dr. M. Copti, Conference, Fifth Assembly of Health Workers, in *Lumière et Paix*, vol. 6, n. 6, Nov.-Dec., 1986.

15. John Paul II, *op. cit.*, note 10, above, n. 37, p. 449.

16. *Ibid.*, n. 33, p. 440.

17. *Ibid.*, n. 30, p. 447.

Section II, Document 11

A SPIRAL OF VIOLENCE: CAPITAL PUNISHMENT

Author — The Administrative Board, the CCCB, March 25, 1986

A Step Backward

The debate on capital punishment has been revived recently with full vigour. Following a series of murders which have re-awakened deep emotions, indignation and fear, politicians are under great pressure to re-establish capital punishment. Yet, in 1976, when the Canadian Government voted for abolition, we hoped, together with many other citizens in this country, that our country had entered a new era of increased civility and humanity. It would be difficult for our society to take a step backward now and return to a system that tries to overcome one evil by doing another, without weakening the very basis of our moral unity: respect for the life of every human being, which is itself the first foundation of all our human rights.

Indeed, this was the hope expressed by our Administrative Board members in 1976 as they said:

> ... a society which so respects the right to life that it does not wish to make use of capital punishment even for its own protection, creates by such attitude a premise favourable to respect for other human rights... It is not permissible to take human life except in legitimate self-defence, personal or collective, so that capital punishment is acceptable only in a society not sufficiently established to defend itself in any other way against elements which would jeopardize the life of its citizens; which is clearly not the case in Canada... Violence breeds violence and capital punishment is a violent act. [1]

Eight years after the abolition of capital punishment we still hold these convictions. If, as a society, we respect each human life as sacred and inviolable, recognizing the rights of each person as primary, we ourselves advance in humanity and contribute to its growth worldwide, even if that progress seems slow and not always evident. This conviction, confirmed by Pope John Paul during his recent visit,[2] is based on the Gospel message itself. At its core, this message affirms that sinful humanity finds reconciliation with God through the forgiveness of Jesus. Innocent Himself but considered a criminal and condemned to death, He showed us the path of total forgiveness: "Father, forgive them; they do not know what they are doing" (Lk. 23:34).

A Problem from the Past

The debate on capital punishment has its roots in a problem that we have inherited from the past. In early and traditional societies, such punishment was applied without hesitation and almost instinctively as an obvious way to punish the guilty. Just as martial law was readily applied in war time, there was rigorous enforcement of the ancient principle of "eye for eye, and tooth for tooth". Four reasons — which really only served to conceal the act of collective revenge — were given to justify capital punishment: retribution for the crime committed, example to society, deterrence of future criminals and protection of society. It is now recognized that these reasons are problematic and cannot serve as bases for a moral judgment. Moreover, the argument that capital punishment is a deterrent does not hold, especially when one takes into account the fact that aggravating or attenuating circumstances vary from crime to crime: crimes committed with or without premeditation; crimes committed in panic, passion, anger, resentment, or under the influence of alcohol, drugs, etc.

The urge to punish is strong when we feel threatened. There is a powerful instinct within us not only to defend ourselves but also to seek revenge. If not carefully controlled, limited and guided by the virtues of love and justice, this instinct can become destructive and murderous. Throughout history we see it at work, in wars, deliberate torture, duelling, slavery, as well as in racial, ethnic and sexual discrimination against both individuals and groups. Though some traces of such cruel and barbarous conduct and customs survive, in recent centuries and especially since World War II, we have witnessed the slow growth of a deeper appreciation of the transcendent worth of each human being. Correspondingly, we reject ever more strongly all actions that attack the human person. Sanctions once considered natural, just and even necessary for social order, have come to be appreciated as radically unjust and inhuman.

Who is without Sin?

Jesus himself revoked the ancient law of Moses on stoning. To the pharisees and scribes ready to condemn the woman taken in adultery, Jesus replied: "Let him among you who is without sin throw the first stone!" (Jn. 8:7) We cannot justify capital punishment today on the basis of its historical acceptance. No longer is it possible to assert that legal homicides are necessary to atone for illegal ones. That would be only violence in reply to violence, without any repair of the broken social order. Capital punishment puts an end to the criminal without thought of possible reform. It is throwing the first stone, rejecting any belief in forgiveness or that the murderer's personal and social reintegration is possible. Who among us, or what society, is without sin and completely innocent? What person or society can disclaim all responsibility, personal or collective, for delinquency? Certainly, criminals cannot be lightly freed from responsibility for their offences, but in all justice and truth must not society seriously address all the social factors that spawn deliquency and crime, such as unemployment, family breakdown, exploitation of the poor, discrimination, the spread of dehumanizing ideologies, pornography and drugs, the exhaltation of money as the supreme value, etc.? It is not enough to do away with criminals or to imprison them for life, if society provides occasions and incentives to crime and continues begetting new criminals. We must undertake to break the spiral of violence against any person, innocent or guilty. It is not necessary to take a life for a life, or to try to end violence by violence. Rather, we must turn to more humane and civilized endeavours to build a just society.

The Master of Life

But there is more! There is this basic question that no one can brush aside: Who is master of life? If as citizens we recognize the sacredness of human life and the imperative necessity to protect it totally, if as Christians we believe that we are created in the image and likeness of God, the sole Master of life, we must understand that we really cannot take life. Given today's continuing violence and ferocity — think of wars, guerrilla movements, the summary execution of political rivals in many countries, the brutal actions of "death squads" — the Church cannot yield to a timorous silence. To fulfill its prophetic mission, it must constantly proclaim that life is sacred, a gift from God, and that no one has the right to mutilate or destroy it. No authority, no society may claim this primordial right, even though it may restrict the exercise of other rights flowing from it. That is the message and meaning of Jesus' life: by His resurrection He conquered death and gave us life in abundance, annihilating forever humanity's ultimate enemy.

The execution of a murderer cannot make good the suffering caused by crime as it destroys lives, ruins families and crushes the hopes of innocent people. The care and support we must give to the victims of crime and to their families will be the measure of our ability to be more human and to ensure the victory of good over evil. Even more, we must establish adequate measures for the protection of all citizens, especially those who ensure order in our country or who guard prisoners. What our police and prison guards need and desire is to be able to carry out their often thankless and dangerous duties under conditions of security, which offer them real protection. They too want to go on living. In its constant vigilance to enhance the valuation of and respect for life, our society must investigate and clarify the social causes or factors that favour criminal activity. Finally, as a mark of our humanity, we must try to improve the correctional system so that it may make a positive contribution to rehabilitating criminals and reintegrating them into society.

Life, a Divine Gift

Pope John Paul II's act of pardoning his attacker helps us to understand better that in our society there must always be room for forgiveness. Such forgiveness, far from interfering with the necessary course of human justice, shows us that, in God's view, "love and truth meet, justice and peace embrace" (Ps. 85:11). How often the Holy Father told us during his visit that human life is a divine gift that we must reverence from its inception to its close. In this way, by defending the rights of every person and recognizing the value of life as created by God, the Church stands against anything that diminishes life. In opposing abortion, euthanasia or any other destruction or manipulation of life, it demands respect for life and security for all humanity, the born and the unborn. In our times, there is no better news to proclaim than this Gospel of God's love for every person, even the sinner, the criminal, the assassin.

NOTES

1. *Capital Punishment,* Declaration of the CCCB Administrative Board, February 27, 1976. Cf. Document 9, above.

2. Repeatedly, during the course of his visit, John Paul II celebrated life and recalled the fundamental dignity of the human person, pointing out that the quality of a society is measured by the respect it shows the most vulnerable of its members: for example, at the François-Charron Centre in Quebec, at the Izaak Walton Killam Hospital in Halifax, at B.C. Place in Vancouver, etc. Cf. *The Canadian Catholic Review,* Saskatoon, vol. 2, n. 9 (*The Papal Visit*), pp. 10f.; 41f.

Section II, Document 12

ON AN INSTRUCTION
OF THE CONGREGATION
FOR THE DOCTRINE OF THE FAITH
ON RESPECT FOR HUMAN LIFE
IN ITS ORIGINS AND ON THE DIGNITY
OF PROCREATION[1]

Author — The Permanent Council, the CCCB, May 8, 1987

The Canadian Conference of Catholic Bishops welcomes the *Instruction on Respect for Human Life in its Origins and on the Dignity of Procreation* from the Congregation for the Doctrine of the Faith. It is a timely and authoritative intervention in the debate on how to integrate science within an authentically human culture. This debate concerns everyone, believers and non-believers alike.

The Church is not alone in insisting that there are limits to human activity. Indeed, at one level of reflection, the *Instruction* must be seen as joining the voices of eminent scientists, jurists, political leaders and ordinary people. Many are calling for controls and guidelines for experimentation on the origins of human life, as well as on nuclear power and developments that threaten the natural environment.

The *Instruction* is not intended to be a complete exposition of the Church's teaching in regard to procreation and the beginnings of human life. Similarly, this brief statement does not review the whole *Instruction*, but emphasizes some of its main points.

The *Instruction* is not anti-science. Science and technology, it says, are valuable resources when they serve humanity and are directed to full human development for the benefit of all.[2] Nor are procedures that touch human procreation to be rejected on the grounds that they are artificial. "As such, they bear witness to the possibilities of the art of medicine. But they must be given a moral evaluation in reference to the dignity of the human person."[3] This because the worth of each human person demands unconditional respect. Such is the central principle of the *Instruction*.

The value of each person requires that from the moment of conception human life is to be respected and safeguarded as a gift from God. This fundamental moral principle is central both to the questions addressed in the *Instruction* and to the continuing debate in this country about abortion. Those who are struggling so hard to safeguard this principle, in parliament and at all levels of our society, will find fresh insight and encouragement in the *Instruction*.

Similarly, all those who are dedicated to promoting the value of marriage and the privileged place of sexual intimacy inside marriage will be heartened by the *Instruction*. Scientific techniques for fertilization, it says, are subject to the moral demand that human procreation be effected as the fruit of conjugal intimacy specific to the love of spouses in the context of marriage. This is of importance to parents, pastoral agents, teachers and the members of various movements dedicated to informing young people about the meaning and responsibilities of human sexuality, marriage and parenthood.

The powerful natural desire to have a child does not confer an absolute right to have one by any means, the *Instruction* insists. "The child is not an object to which one has a right."[4] Rather, a child is a gift, the supreme and most gratuitous gift of marriage, and is a living testimony of the mutual self-giving of the parents.

It must be acknowledged that the *Instruction* raises particular problems in our affluent, North American society. Wealth can lead people to think that they may licitly procure what they want, when they can pay for it. This sense of power is coupled with a pervading cultural ethos of independent individualism. An awareness that there are some duties of social relationships is too often missing. For instance, there is little evidence of any genuine solidarity with the poor. Further, in such a society, sexual activity is seen by many as having only that moral meaning individuals choose to give it. The *Instruction* points towards a much more responsible, organic and social attitude in interpersonal relations, both between parents and their children and between richer and poorer nations.

This, then, is a text that calls for careful and open-minded reading and study. Anyone who does not go beyond media accounts, which are inevitably short summaries, will be missing an important opportunity. We make our own the confident invitation of the Congregation in the *Instruction* itself. In particular, we invite moral, medical and other researchers, as well as all Christian couples, to study the *Instruction* and to reflect deeply about the relevance of its basic principles for the development of an authentically human view of sexuality.

NOTES

1. In *Origins*, Washington, 1987, XVI, 697.
2. *Op. cit.*, n. 2.
3. *Op. cit.*, n. 3.
4. *Op. cit.*, n. 8.

Section II, Document 13

ON THE SUPREME COURT DECISION STRIKING DOWN THE ABORTION LAW

Author — Archbishop James M. Hayes, President, the CCCB,
          January 28, 1988

The Supreme Court decision striking down the abortion law is a dramatic challenge to all lay members of the Church and to us, their pastors.

The need for responsible political action was never more urgent, for God's law condemning abortion is not changed by the Supreme Court decision.

In the process of writing a new law that protects human life from the moment of conception, Christians as voters or legislators have the first responsibility.

The situation on legal "abortion on demand" that follows from the Court's decision must be corrected legislatively as soon as possible. This is now our common task and our future as a humane and moral society depends on how soon and how well it is done.

In the process of working for new legislation, all Christians must also apply themselves to the continuing pastoral work of evangelizing modern culture regarding the God-given values and rights of every human life, and the need to safeguard and respect that life in all circumstances.

Abortion is the destruction of human life. The challenge is to change our society's attitude toward life and to channel the energies and strong emotions involved in this debate toward correcting mentalities and situations that lead to abortion. We must create a society that supports life and permits children to be raised with dignity, a society that places rights and needs of others before personal comfort and gain, a society that respects human life at every stage of its development.

The vision and hope that lead us forward flow from our faith conviction that every human life is sacred. Today's Supreme Court decision leaves us in a situation where the sacredness of life is legally violated. It is urgently imperative that we work together with all Canadians for legislation that will indeed safeguard the life, liberty and security of every person, including the unborn.

Section II, Document 14

ON POLICY GUIDELINES
FOR THE CANADIAN CONFERENCE
OF CATHOLIC BISHOPS
ON ABORTION LEGISLATION

Author — The Permanent Council, the CCCB, March 17, 1988

1. Each human life begins with conception. From conception, a separate and unique human life is present, with all the chromosomes and genes necessary for a human life.

2. Respect for the sanctity of all human life is not just a Catholic tenet, nor even peculiarly Christian. Now is the time for all persons of good will to work to build a society hospitable to all life.

3. The debate about an abortion law is part of a larger question that includes the matter of experimentation on foetal tissue. An abortion law that puts the foetus entirely at risk during the first trimester would open a Pandora's box of problems. Abortion cannot be dealt with in isolation from these other profound and complex bioethical issues.

4. There is no question of depriving women of rights. What an eventual law must deal with is how to handle conflicts of rights of mother and child. In this, the right to life itself is primary.

5. Canada's legal tradition has been to defend life from conception to natural death. This tradition calls all law to respect unborn life, in the context of a general social policy aimed at building a society hospitable to life. All levels of government are challenged to this end. Services and programmes to enhance human life are a particular challenge to provincial and local governments under the Canadian Constitution.

6. There can be no quick and easy solution for this complex issue. What is at stake is the country's whole future. Just as the natural resources must be protected for future generations, so members of the coming generation must have full, life-enhancing protection and support. Our common future depends on our respect for all nature.

7. The bishops wish to praise and support those working to protect life and to enhance the quality and civility of society. Dialogue with pro-life groups is particularly important.

8. Regarding Direct Political Action

a) Until a new law is passed:

— it is the duty of all to work for the best possible law to protect all life;

— morality supersedes law: civil law must always try to reflect morality. In a pluralistic society, what civil law can do may be limited;

— parliamentarians must keep in mind the whole issue of life, and the extending implications of any abortion law. It is not just a matter of replacing Section 251, [1] important as that is.

b) After a new law:

— it is to be expected that efforts to put in place a better law, and many programmes to promote life, will have to continue. We may have to live with a law we find defective, but will continue to try to improve it.

NOTE

1. Section 251 of the *Criminal Code* (Protection of the Unborn).

Section II, Document 15

FAITHFUL TO THE FUTURE: A STATEMENT ON ABORTION

Author — Archbishop James M. Hayes, President, the CCCB, April 7, 1988

Dear Sisters and Brothers in Christ:

The recent decision of Canada's Supreme Court, striking down the law regulating abortions, has left the unborn with no legal protection whatsoever. This lawless interval presents us with a crisis and an opportunity. It is now both necessary and possible to create new legislation which will recognize the right to life of the most voiceless and vulnerable in our society.

Since the Court's decision on January 28, there have been many public statements by individuals and groups within the church, and there will be more. My purpose in writing to you, the people of God, is to call forth the faith and hope that we all need at this time.

Our best energies are required for this challenging task which we face together. Let us draw on those energies which arise from the deep reservoir of our faith. This is a moment to recall not only what we are against but also what we are for, whom we are for.

Our rejection of abortion flows from our affirmation of faith in God who is the Creator of all life. We believe in a God Who is a God of beginnings — the mysterious beginning of the world and of each human person. The first words of scripture proclaim this mystery: "In the beginning God created..." (Gen. 1:1).

Each human is a whole new creation struggling to be born and to grow into the fullness of life. Because each of us begins in God from the moment of conception, every life possesses infinite value at every point along the way. What has begun in God is not ours to end. What has been created by God is not ours to destroy.

In the coming months, there will be those in our country who will dare to debate at what point human life begins in order to decide at what point the life of an unborn can be ended. There are those who will presume to discuss which of the unborn are fit to live and which ones fail to measure up to some arbitrary standard of performance. We will not join this debate: we will not play God. Human life begins in God at conception and struggles to realize the promise of this beginning.

We cannot play God but we can live our humanity more fully. We can participate with others in the creative process of transforming the world into a place where the promise of life can be better realized for all. We can play our part in helping to liberate human beings from whatever denies or diminishes the mystery of creation which has begun in each person.

This vision of our vocation as Christians reveals how short-sighted is the view that the Supreme Court decision is a step forward for women, for anyone. It is, in fact, a step backwards for all of us because it reasserts a social situation which women have so justly been struggling against — a situation in which persons are treated as objects, in which the rights of the weaker are defined by the stronger, a win-lose situation. We must resist adapting to such a social situation through practices such as abortion. We must commit ourselves to working towards a more inclusive and interdependent society, the kind of society longed for by so many women for generations. It would be a tragedy if the longings of so many stopped short of including the right of the unborn, female and male, to belong to the human community.

For us to accept abortion would be to deny our belief in the value of human life. That life has a right to continue to the end of its natural course. Neither individuals nor governments may make an arbitrary decision to end that life at any point.

We dare to hold out such a hope, not because we ourselves are always a sign of its realization but because we believe in Jesus Christ in Whom the power of redeeming love is stronger than the forces of discrimination and destruction.

We desire to hold out such a hope in Canada, particularly at this time. There are signs that our country is consumed by the present and is losing faith in its future. How we treat our youngest and the beginners in our midst is a significant measure of our commitment to the future.

The issue of abortion is often narrowly construed as a question of the rights of a woman versus the rights of the unborn. Yet, it would be more appropriate to say that the issue is whether the wants and needs of the women and men of the present will be allowed to predominate over the basic needs of the women and men of future generations. The society which accepts abortion as a solution to present problems (whether personal or social) is also a society which abuses its children, lays waste the environment, risks nuclear war and implements economic policies in which the immediate benefits to some now will be dearly paid for by many in the future.

All of us are tempted to live as if there were no tomorrow. Persons who are still in the process of coming to birth are a real reminder to us of the fact that, for some, the future is just beginning. These beginners are holdouts for humanity, our humanity.

We hold out hope for a future in which the relationships between men and women, adults and children, can be transformed. We have reason to hope that we can move beyond the individualism of this culture to become a more inclusive, human community in which each person is treated with ultimate respect. Changes in male attitudes and behaviour are central to this hope. Irresponsibility, neglect and violence towards women willl not end if men do not grow in respect, solidarity and concern for every human life.

We hold out this hope, not because we have arrived but because we believe in the Holy Spirit present among us, moving us beyond where we ourselves could go.

We should all take heart in the many signs of fidelity to the future which are so obviously present in our country. Since the Supreme Court decision on January 28, there has been a surge of concern on the part of Catholics, other Christians and many people of good will. Many Canadians feel that their basic sense of decency has been deeply offended by the present situation of abortion on request.

We are encouraged by the continuing witness of those married couples whose marital fidelity bears the promise of new life, a promise which is received with joy. We are equally encouraged by those couples and single parents who bear the burden of difficult pregnancies or who commit themselves to raising children in difficult economic and social circumstances. The courage and care of parents who commit themselves to raising a child with disabilities is deeply inspiring for all of us. In joy or in suffering, parents call all of us to become more co-responsible in providing a community of real support for parents and children.

We are inspired by those who have worked long and hard to make pregnancy and child care more possible and desirable than abortion. Their efforts sometimes take the shape of simple personal support or of involvement in various social projects and programs, such as providing pre-natal counselling, accessible child care, economic assistance for parents who wish to be at home with their children, shelters for battered women, affordable housing, pay equity, affirmative action, medical research into the causes and treatment of disabilities, etc. Of course, such services are far from adequate. Our commitment to build a society hospitable to all life must include increased efforts to expand and improve aid and care for all family members.

We are urged on by those who are educating and acting in order to transform the world into a place where life is respected at every stage. We stand with those who work for greater economic and political equality, who work against capital punishment, war, poverty and euthanasia.

All of these signs of fidelity to the future give us energy to begin the task of procuring the passage of legislation which recognizes the right to life of the unborn from the moment of conception.

There is something for each one of us to do at this creative moment. In order to encourage informed and effective action, the Canadian Conference of Catholic Bishops has prepared an animation leaflet called *The Gift of Life — The Right to Life*. It is to be used by study groups and individuals. It draws on the experiences of ordinary people, the wisdom of the tradition of the church, current theological thinking, the findings of modern science and the legal tradition of our country which has always enshrined principles of public morality in laws that value and protect human life at every stage. The leaflet suggests practical responses which can be made by each Catholic.

We must share our faith in the future and our commitment to the unborn with the parliamentarians of Canada and with all Canadians. We must be signs of that redeeming love and hope which come to us through Jesus Christ, Who calls us to respect and love all our neighbours, especially the least among us.

Section II, Document 16

STATEMENT TO THE HONOURABLE MEMBERS OF THE SENATE AND OF THE HOUSE OF COMMONS ON ABORTION

Author — Archbishop James M. Hayes, President of the CCCB, June 23, 1988

In reply to a number of inquiries about the difficult matter of abortion legislation, I wish to offer the following in the name of the Canadian Conference of Catholic Bishops.

The teaching of the Catholic Church, as well as of other churches and groups opposing any attack on human life after conception, is meant to help form the consciences of all people, including lawmakers who must strive to find ways to enshrine that teaching as best they can in the actual process of legislation. In this process, efforts along the lines of Senator Haidasz's bill are to be encouraged. [1]

The three options for new abortion legislation which are presented in the Government's motion on the Order Paper are all objectionable from the standpoint of Catholic teaching. [2] Amendment A, however, is the least censurable.

In forming their consciences, legislators should take serious account of the concern expressed by many pro-life Members of Parliament that to abstain from voting because the perfect law has not been presented, may indirectly contribute to the passage of the Government's main motion which allows for the totally unacceptable gestational approach. [3]

We call on all people of good will to continue to work and pray for the best possible law. No matter what law is passed, we will continue to teach the moral obligation to respect and safeguard life from conception to natural death.

These points were approved by the Permanent Council of the Canadian Conference of Catholic Bishops meeting June 15-16, 1988.

Appendix

POLICY GUIDELINES FOR THE ABORTION DEBATE

Approved by the CCCB Permanent Council, June 16, 1988

1. The March 17, 1988, Notes of the Permanent Council are confirmed as policy guidelines for any discussion of specific legislative proposals. [4]

2. The President's May 9, 1988, telex to the Prime Minister is confirmed, as indicating the CCCB's determined opposition to the gestational approach in any specific law. [5]

3. The teaching of the Church opposing any attack on human life after conception is meant to help form the consciences, including those of lawmakers, who must strive to enshrine that teaching as best they can in our legislation.

4. Of the three options suggested in the Government's motion now on the Order Paper, Amendment A is the least objectionable.

5. Efforts along the lines of Senator Haidasz's Bill are to be encouraged.

6. No matter what law is passed, we will continue to teach the moral obligation to respect and safeguard life from conception to natural death.

NOTES

1. Bill S-16, *An Act to amend the Criminal Code* (protection of the unborn), introduced by the Honourable Senator Stanley Haidasz, PC, MD, Toronto-Parkdale. The text follows.

Explanatory Note

A vacuity now exists in the criminal law of Canada as a result of a recent decision of the Supreme Court of Canada. For the first time in its history, Canada has no enforceable law to protect the most helpless of human beings, the unborn child.

The purpose of this Bill is to reassert society's vital interest in its unborn children. That interest is as fundamental to the continued existence of our society as it is to the existence of the human race.

An Act to Amend the Criminal Code
(protection of the unborn)
Section 251 of the *Criminal Code* and the heading preceding it are repealed and
the following substituted therefor:
Protection of the Unborn
251. (1) Every one who, with intent to cause the death of an unborn human being,
uses any means to carry out that intent is guilty of an indictable offence and is liable
to imprisonment for life.

(2) Everyone who, in doing anything, or in omitting to do anything that is the
duty of that person to do, shows wanton or reckless disregard for the life or safety
of an unborn human being and thereby causes the death of that unborn human
being is guilty of an indictable offence and is liable to imprisonment for five years.

(3) Every pregnant female person who, with intent to cause the death of an
unborn human being within her, uses any means to carry out that intent is guilty
of an indictable offence and is liable to imprisonment for two years.

(4) No one is guilty of an offence under subsection (1) if the life of the unborn
human being was ended as a result of medical treatment necessary to prevent the
death of the mother of the unborn human being or to remedy a condition that, if
left untreated, would cause the death of that mother.

(5) In this section,
"any means" includes
  (a) the administration of a drug or other noxious thing,
  (b) the use of an instrument, and
  (c) manipulation of any kind;
"unborn human being" means a human life from the moment of conception until
birth, whether conceived naturally or otherwise.

Haidasz made a cogent defense of his bill at Second Reading, May 25, 1988, cf.
Debates of the Senate, Second Session, 33rd Parliament, Vol. 131, n. 150, p. 3476 ff.

2. In June, 1988, the government offered members of parliament three voting
options in the coming debate and division on abortion: a virtual ban on abortion,
abortion on demand, a law in which abortions in later stages of pregnancy would
be restricted. Because of the House of Commons procedures, Amendment B (below),
the pro-choice option, would be voted on first. Next, Amendment A, the pro-life
option, would be voted on. Finally, the main motion — which would permit abortion
"during the earlier stages of pregnancy" — would be voted on. Cf. *Catholic New Times*,
Toronto, June 26, 1988; *Maclean's*, Toronto, Aug. 8, 1988. The text follows:
MOTION
That, in the opinion of this House, the Supreme Court of Canada having declared
that the provisions of the *Criminal Code* (Section 251) relating to abortion are inconsistent with the provisions of the *Canadian Charter of Rights and Freedoms* and are therefore of no force or effect, the government should prepare and introduce legislation,
consistent with the *Constitution of Canada,* including the *Charter of Rights and Freedoms,*
which reflects the fundamental value and inherent dignity of each human being and
the inherent worth of human life, and which achieves a balance between the right
of a woman to liberty and security of her person and the responsibility of society
to protect the unborn; and
Such legislation should prohibit the performance of an abortion, subject to the
following exceptions:

When, during the earlier stages of pregnancy: a qualified medical practicioner is of the opinion that the continuation of the pregnancy of a woman would, or would be likely to, threaten her physical or mental well-being; when the woman in consultation with a qualified medical practicioner decides to terminate her pregnancy; and when the termination is performed by a qualified medical practicioner;

When, during the subsequent stages of pregnancy: the termination of the pregnancy satisfies further conditions, including a condition that after a certain point in time, the termination would only be permitted where, in the opinion of two qualified medical practicioners, the continuation of the pregnancy would, or would be likely to, endanger the woman's life or seriously endanger her health.

AMENDMENT A

That all of the words in the motion after the words "to protect the unborn; and" be deleted and the following be substituted therefor:

Such legislation, giving pre-eminence to the protection of the foetus, should prohibit the performance of an abortion except when:

— two independent qualified medical practicioners have, in good faith and on reasonable grounds, stated that in their opinion the continuation of the pregnancy would, or would be likely to, endanger the life of the pregnant woman or seriously and substantially endanger her health and there is no other commonly accepted medical procedure for effectively treating the health risk; but grounds for such opinion are not to include:

(I) the effects of stress or anxiety which may accompany an unexpected or unwanted pregnancy,

or

(II) social or economic considerations.

AMENDMENT B

That all of the words in the motion after the words "to protect the unborn, and" be deleted and the following substituted therefor:

Such legislation, giving pre-eminence to a woman's freedom to choose, should permit the performance of an abortion under the following conditions:

(I) When the woman in consultation with a qualified medical practicioner decides to terminate her pregnancy; and

(II) When the termination of the pregnancy is performed by a qualified medical practicioner.

The procedural debate was postponed in July, due to widespread dissatisfaction among members of parliament.

3. The gestational approach to the problem of *legal* abortion would determine *legality* according to the estimated age of the foetus, the elapsed time since conception.

4. Cf. Section II, Document 14 above.

5. Archbishop James M. Hayes, President of the Bishops' Conference had sent the following telex to the Prime Minister, copied to the leaders of the opposition parties and several members of the cabinet.

May 9, 1988

The Right Honourable Brian Mulroney

Anticipating that your cabinet will soon — perhaps as early as Wednesday this week — discuss abortion law options, I wish to insist once again that human life be legally recognized and protected from the moment of conception. I wish to leave you with no doubt whatsoever that the gestational approach which provides no protection to the unborn child in the early weeks of life is totally unacceptable and will be vigorously opposed by the Canadian Conference of Catholic Bishops.

Section II, Document 17

STATEMENT TO THE HONOURABLE MEMBERS OF THE SENATE AND OF THE HOUSE OF COMMONS ON ABORTION

Author — Archbishop James M. Hayes, President, the CCCB,
        July 25, 1988

The Government has introduced a Motion that proposes the totally unacceptable gestational approach for a new Canadian abortion law. [1]

The position of the Catholic Church is that human life begins at conception and must be valued, respected and safeguarded from the beginning.

The gestational approach is scientifically and ethically indefensible since it draws an arbitrary dividing line between life which is worthy of protection and life which is not.

The government's Motion abandons a primary function of the law: the protection of human life. Furthermore, it does not achieve the socially imperative balance between the rights and interests of women and the equally important rights and interests of unborn children.

We count on the good will of everyone who values human life to work and pray for legislation which recognizes, values, respects and protects human life from conception to natural death.

To this end, a new abortion law must be developed in the context of other laws and social policies which together will make this a society ever more hospitable to all human life at all stages of development.

We assure you that the Canadian Conference of Catholic Bishops will continue without interruption to pursue and support programs and policies that protect, enhance and celebrate life.

NOTE

1. The motion was presented to the Clerk of the House, July 22, 1988, in the name of the Hon. Doug Lewis, P.C., M.P., Minister of State (Treasury Board). It is identical with the motion in note 2, Document 16 of this section, immediately above, *but without Amendments A and B*.

The gestational criterion was no more acceptable to many other church leaders, witness the following letter, dated Sept. 23, in *Catholic New Times*, Toronto, Oct. 8, 1989.

Prime Minister Brian Mulroney
House of Commons, Ottawa, Canada

Dear Mr. Mulroney:

As you and your caucus explore options for a new abortion law, we want you to know that, as church leaders, we *unequivocally* oppose a gestational approach.

We have legal advice that constitutionally the unborn child can be given legal protection at all stages of development. We urge you to take a wholistic approach that respects the rights and the needs of both women and unborn children.

Your government must not do less than this.

Respectfully submitted,

Signatories were leaders of the Canadian Conference of Catholic Bishops, the Presbyterian Church in Canada, the Anglican Church of Canada, the Salvation Army, the Council of Christian Reformed Churches, the Mennonite Central Committee of Canada, and the Evangelical Fellowship of Canada (on behalf of 23 groups).

Section II, Document 18

TO THE LAW REFORM COMMISSION OF CANADA, ON WORKING PAPER 58: *CRIMES AGAINST THE FOETUS*[1]

Author — Archbishop James M. Hayes, President, the CCCB, for the Permanent Council, June 5, 1989

On behalf of the Permanent Council of the Canadian Conference of Catholic Bishops (hereinafter "the Council"), I would like to thank the Commission for inviting members of the public to respond to your Working Paper 58. I would also like to express our appreciation for the considerable time and effort the Commission has devoted to this important topic.

The position of the Catholic Church is that all human life must be valued, respected and protected from conception until natural death. The Church's consistent and strong opposition to abortion is rooted in the profound belief that life is a gift from God and all human beings are created in the image of God. All human life without exception is sacred, irreplaceable and inherently worthy of protection and respect.

The Commission's recommendations that allow abortion are therefore totally unacceptable to the Council. These recommendations are all the more disappointing and unacceptable coming, as they do, as conclusions to a line of reasoning that defines the foetus as a human being having life through all stages of development from conception to birth. The Commission's decision to accept abortion after positing such a view of the foetus is a complete break in logic. It is also disappointing, in view of what it said about the life of the foetus, to find in the Commission's majority paper an underlying value judgment that discriminates between individual lives as to their relative worth. In any other context, the Commission would surely resist such arbitrariness.

Before returning in more detail to our points of disagreement, the Council would like, however, to commend the following positive elements which are found in the Working Paper:

1. The fact that the word 'life' is understood and "used in its usual sense in medical contexts to mean life from conception to death". At no point is the unborn child referred to as "potential life".

2. The definition of "foetus" to include all stages of development from conception to birth.

3. The acknowledgement that a foetus is a human being. The following statement in the Working Paper is particularly welcome:

> True, the present Criminal Code has a curious provision in section 206 to the effect that a child doesn't become a human being until it has proceeded completely from its mother's body. This, far from being a proper definition of the term, runs counter to the general consensus that the product of human conception, in the womb or outside, is a human being. (p. 50)

4. The recognition that the foetus has intrinsic value and that abortion is not simply a private matter of concern only to the mother. The Council notes that in declining to accept a proposal explicitly permitting abortion on request in the first trimester the Commission said:

> … in our view neither maternal autonomy nor foetal life should be allowed in the early trimester to completely outweigh each other — one may prevail in this case, another in that, but neither should ever be extinguished from consideration. The law should recognize the foetus as having at all stages some *intrinsic* value. So, while the termination of a woman's pregnancy should be primarily a matter between her and her doctor, it should never be a purely private matter — *there is a public interest in the unborn at all stages.* (p. 43, emphasis added)

5. The Commission's refusal to regard abortion as simply another medical problem. The Council notes the following comment by the Commission:

> … the process of human procreation is trivialized by equating the foetus with a tumour and abortion with other surgical procedures. Like it or not, abortion destroys a being with the full potential

to become a living, breathing person. This distinguishes abortions from other surgical procedures, raises ethical and moral considerations not at issue in other clinical contexts and results in potential psychological complications quite different from those present in most other operations. (p. 55)

6. The Commission's recognition that protection of the unborn child is an important moral and social question.

7. The Commission's designation of foetal harm or destruction as a crime.

8. The Commission's conclusion that criminal law can contribute to the solution of the problem of abortion. Particular reference is made to the following comment by the Commission:

> Criminal law, however, can still contribute symbolically by upholding respect for human life, stressing the value of the unborn human life and emphasizing that pregnancy termination has to be — not least for the sake of the mother's own health — a medical matter. In short, the prohibition itself may well achieve as much as its enforcement. (p. 47)

9. The Commission's endorsement of the need for social programmes to address the reasons why a pregnancy is unwanted.

Regrettably, these positive elements in the Commission's report do not deliver what they promise. In the end there is no concrete protection for the life of the unborn child. In particular, the Council wishes to underline the following *negative aspects* of the Working Paper:

1. The significance of the Commission's conclusion that the foetus merits criminal law protection is seriously undermined by the exception for abortion — the most common form of foetal destruction. As noted earlier, this exception can be arrived at only by a break in the logic of the Commission's reasoning, that the foetus is a human being from conception to birth.

2. Although the Commission decided that abortions are lawful only if done for medical reasons, rejecting rape, incest and socioeconomic reasons as specific grounds for abortion, the practical result is abortion on request. Some reasons for this are:

a) The proposed health standard prior to viability (when most abortions are done) is very weak — i.e., *protect* the mother's physical or psychological health.

b) The word 'health' is too vague and subjective, notwithstanding the addition of the words "physical or psychological".

c) Prior to viability, there is no independent means of confirming that the health standard has been met. In the *Morgentaler* case, Mr. Justice Beetz found that Parliament was "justified in requiring a reliable, independent and medically sound opinion in order to protect the state's interest in the foetus" and "I do not believe it to be unreasonable to seek independent medical confirmation of the threat to the woman's life or health when such an important and distinct interest hangs in the balance." [2]

3. When the general section on foetal destruction is read in conjunction with the exception for lawful abortion, it is seen that foetuses are afforded more protection from third parties than from their mothers. For example, a drunken driver who kills or seriously harms a foetus will be held criminally responsible, whereas a mother who meets the rather loose conditions for a lawful abortion will not. The existence of a crime appears to depend on *who* harms or destroys the foetus.

4. The designation of a *separate* crime of foetal destruction distinguishes foetuses from persons and perpetuates a distinction between unborn and born human life.

5. The gestational approach is unacceptable in principle because it arbitrarily determines that human life is more worthy of respect at some stages than at others. It is in this sense, and also with regard to 4, immediately above, that, as noted earlier (paragraph 3), the Commission makes a value judgment that discriminates between the worth of individual lives.

6. The Council questions the Commission's proposition that the balancing of maternal and foetal interests requires not only an examination of the qualitative difference among the interests of life, security of the person, liberty or autonomy, but also a consideration of whether the interests are those of the foetus or the mother. The Commission's opinion that in some cases the foetus' higher interest in life may be tempered by the higher "status" of the mother is theologically unacceptable, philosophically dubious, and legally tentative given that the foetus may be found to have the constitutional right to life.

7. The Commission makes an interesting presentation concerning the social and moral uncertainty of the status of the foetus and the

difficulty of discerning *how* to reach agreement on this status. Mention is made of the fact that some regard the foetus as a person, others as a non-person, and still others as a potential person. It is also noted that people choose different stages of foetal development as deserving of protection on the basis of philosophical, religious or scientific reasons. The Commission believes that market research, religious doctrine and "common sense morality" are of little help in resolving the uncertainty.

The Commission uses the uncertainty to justify its own view that the criminal law should be used with caution and not to impose one conscientiously held view over another. In the end, however, the Commission does what it purports not to do. It chooses one sincerely held position over another and seems to do so on the basis of bald assertions about foetal, maternal and third party interests. Having rejected "market research," it nevertheless depends on market-like assumptions concerning "what we take to be a general consensus" (p. 51) about what is acceptable. The Commission assumes rather than persuades that the protection of foetal life is qualitatively different from the protection of persons already born and qualitatively different, depending on their stage of development.

8. The Commission states that the debate is no longer about scientific facts but how to evaluate them. Moral and philosophical principles are central in such an evaluation. It is not simply a legal question.

For the Commission, a human being is not automatically a person for legal purposes. For the Catholic Church, a human being is a person for all purposes. "The human being is to be respected and treated as a person from the moment of conception." [3]

9. The Council is aware of the Commission's sensitivity to the fact that we live in a pluralistic society. Choices, however, still have to be made and it is unrealistic to suppose that a law on abortion can be morally neutral. A decision not to legislate on abortion and the Commission's own recommendations inescapably involve moral judgments.

The Council wishes to express particular gratitude to Commissioner Maingot for his *cogent dissent* wherein he refuses to make distinctions between persons and human beings, or between the born and the unborn. [4] He argues forcefully for what he considers to be the best available legal protection for the unborn child. In his view:

> ... abortion should be available where necessary to save the mother's life or to protect her against serious and substantial

danger to her health where there is no other commonly accepted medical procedure for effectively treating this health risk. I would point out, first, that 'health' must be carefully defined and, second, that with the current state of medical science and practice such situations arise rarely today. In most cases doctors, true to the spirit of the Hippocratic oath, try to save both of their patients, the mother and her unborn child. (p. 88)

It should be reiterated that according to Catholic teaching, causing the death of the unborn child is acceptable only if it is the *indirect result* of medical attempts to save the lives of both the mother and the child. In this respect, Commissioner Maingot's recommendation does not go far enough.

Commissioner Maingot should also be commended for his eloquent plea for legislation which addresses the social, economic and psychological reasons why women have abortions. In the following comment he makes a convincing case that the abortion question cannot be solved exclusively by either restricting or liberalizing abortion:

Truly equitable measures have to extend equal protection to the unborn not merely by restricting access to abortion but also, and primarily, by increasing the protection of pregnant women. Even if regulated access to abortion remains a regrettable necessity, new legislation must go beyond this and try to reduce the factors in women's lives that force them to reject pregnancy, and lead them to choose abortion as a deceptively simple escape from economic, social and cultural dilemmas.

To offer access to abortion shows a callous failure of responsibility to protect life. To outlaw it without proposing positive measures to remedy the situations encountered by pregnant women would also amount to a failure of responsibility. A coherent and effective family policy requires a coordinated effort from all levels of the state. Measures have to be taken in various fields, such as labour, revenue, family life, housing and education. (pp. 102-103)

In closing, I would like to reiterate that there is much that is good in your report, particulalrly at the level of language and symbol, both of which are important in shaping attitudes. Our Council urges you to go further and provide a final report which will substantively and effectively protect the right to life of the unborn child without distinction as to stage of development. Yours is an important task because the legislation you recommend will be seen as a statement of the value which Canadians place on human life.

Once again, thank you for the opportunity to comment on the Working Paper and the concern with which you have approached this serious topic.

NOTES

1. *Crimes Against the Foetus,* Law Reform Commission of Canada (130 Albert St., Ottawa, K1A 0L6), 1989. Available free of charge.

2. Cf. *op. cit.* in note 1, pp. 93f.

3. *Instruction on Respect for Human Life, etc.,* Congregation for the Doctrine of the Faith, Vatican City, 1987, in *Origins,* Washington, 1987, XVI, p. 695.

4. Commissioner Joseph Maingot, Q.C., *op. cit.,* in note 1, above, *ll. cc.*

Section II, Document 19

SUBMISSION TO THE PARLIAMENTARY COMMITTEE ON ABORTION

Author — The Permanent Council, the CCCB, January 31, 1990

This brief is submitted on behalf of the Permanent Council[1] of the Canadian Conference of Catholic Bishops. The Council would like to thank the Committee for the invitation to present our position on abortion and to address the particular legislative proposal contained in Bill C-43.

Abortion is a complex and sensitive issue. There are scientific, legal, social, philosophical, moral, political and other aspects to be considered. It affects individuals in a very personal and painful manner but also concerns the common good.

Abortion is a controversial issue and divisions run deep. There is, however, wide agreement that it is an individual and collective tragedy and a false solution to social and economic problems.

As legislators, you have the difficult but significant opportunity to decide a matter of profound importance to the human community. The quality of debate in the house of Commons on this Bill has been high. May you continue this thoughtful approach as you listen to the submissions of Canadians and try to discern what is best for those who are already born and those who are yet to be born.

Legislation cannot be considered in isolation from the underlying causes of abortion and its impact on women, or from social and religious values. This brief, therefore, considers the legislative proposal in the more global context of these other aspects.

ABORTION IS NO SOLUTION

Numerous social and economic problems have been identified by Members of Parliament and others as contributing to abortions. Those most often cited are: poverty, rape, incest, family violence and the inequality of women. Abortion, however, is a false solution because it does not and cannot address the underlying causes of why the pregnancy is unwanted.

Abortion may not stop the incest and may even permit it to continue. Rather than eliminating poverty, it eliminates those who might be born poor. Instead of encouraging men to be more responsible, abortion reinforces the notion that pregnancy and child care are the private concern of women. If abortions are readily available, employers might have less incentive to modify their practices so that women are not penalized for having children. Far from attacking the causes, abortion lets society in general and men in particular off the hook.

While there may not be consensus on how best to protect the unborn child, there is some basic agreement on how to protect women and families from social and economic conditions which discourage having children. Every sector of society is implicated.

Governments at all levels must introduce policies and programs which are truly hospitable to life. Obvious places to do more include child care, parental leaves, shelters and second stage housing for battered women, assistance for parents who wish to be home with their children, affordable housing, affirmative action and pay equity. These measures cannot be realized, however, without the educational efforts required to motivate such social change.

Government reforms are not sufficient. They must be accompanied by social changes throughout society. Communities must be more responsive to families and women in need. Adoption needs to be promoted as a solution to an unwanted pregnancy but with greater compassion for the agony of giving up a child. Educational, cultural and other institutions, including the Catholic Church, must be more active in promoting the equality of women and respect for them as persons. Some male attitudes and behaviours have to change radically if there is to be an end to violence against women, more co-responsibility in parenting and more respectful inter-personal relationships.

IMPACT ON WOMEN

Although it is our belief that abortion is a societal issue, it has a profound impact on women's lives. The experience of women is not uniform but it is clear that they have always paid a disproportionately high price for unexpected pregnancies.

Many women have been left to face unwanted pregnancies without the support of their partners, friends, employers, families or church communities. Their anger, bitterness and distrust are real and understandable. Other women have been supported during their pregnancies and enabled to pursue life-giving options. Efforts should be directed to ensuring that there can be similar positive solutions for all women.

Reliance on abortion may impede efforts for personal and social reforms. Moreover, it is giving up on the human spirit and on the capacity of people to transform attitudes and structures.

Personal experience has made us aware of the anguish of women faced with unexpected pregnancy and our own need to be more sensitive to women's experience and to promote a more inclusive church community. Although we cannot fully share the pain experienced by women in these difficult situations, we can express our solidarity with them. At the same time, we reiterate our commitment to the unborn child who is the weakest and most defenceless member of the human family.

CATHOLIC TEACHING ON ABORTION

Catholic teaching on abortion is clear and unequivocal. Abortion is a moral evil because it involves the destruction of human life. Direct killing of an unborn child is never justified.

The induced termination of a pregnancy is permissible, however, if it is the indirect result of efforts to prevent the death of the mother. Examples of these situations are ectopic pregnancies and cancer of the uterus. The death of the unborn child in these cases is not commonly said to be an abortion.

Catholics are not the only Canadians who take this position. Others do so because of the indisputable scientific evidence that life begins at conception; others because they see abortion as an issue of fundamental human rights and justice or because they value the potential of the unborn human being. While we feel supported by the views of others, our own position is particularly rooted in the unshakable belief that life is a gift from God and that all human beings are created in the image of God. As Pope John Paul II said:

> ... the Church firmly believes that human life, even if weak and suffering, is always a splendid gift of God's goodness. Against the pessimism and selfishness which cast a shadow over the world, the Church stands for life: in each human life she sees the splendour of that "Yes", that "Amen". who is Christ himself. (Cf. 2 Cor. 1:20) To the "No" which assails and afflicts the world, she replies with this living "Yes", thus defending the human person and the world from all who plot against and harm life. [2]

In discussions about abortion, some people use the words human being and person interchangeably. Others make careful distinctions because, in law, only persons have rights and duties. On the one hand, it is argued that the unborn child is a person because science has established that he or she is a human being. On the other hand, it is said that even though the unborn child is a human being, he or she is only a potential person. The teaching of the Catholic Church is that "the human being is to be respected and treated as a person from the moment of conception". [3]

Irrespective of the present state of the law, it is our view that all human beings should be treated and respected as persons at all stages of life.

PLURALISM

We recognize that there are strongly held views which differ from ours. This is understandable because the basic values of life and freedom are at stake. It is also part of the reality of living in a pluralistic society.

Authentic pluralism is enriching and challenging. On the one hand, it means that no one group has the right to impose its particular point of view. On the other hand, there is the freedom to inform and persuade public opinion and room for both religious and secular values. Tensions between individual and social rights and competing values are inevitable and part of the creative process of living in a pluralistic society.

The state has a key role to play in the formation of a collective conscience within the framework of a climate of social peace and respect for people who hold differing views. Recent legislation on smoking and drinking are good examples of how the law shapes as well as reflects consensus.

The diversity of the views on abortion and the commitment of those who hold them, make your task more difficult. It would be tempting to act simply as an arbitrator and select the lowest common denominator as the basis for legislation. But genuine pluralism does not relieve you of your duty to legislate for the common good. The Second Vatican Council in speaking of the common good said:

> Because of the closer bonds of human interdependence and their spread over the whole world, we are today witnessing a widening of the role of the common good, which is the sum total of social conditions which allow people, either as groups or as individuals, to reach their fulfillment more fully and more easily. The whole human race is consequently involved with regard to the rights and obligations which result. Every group must take into account the needs and legitimate aspirations of every other group, and still more of the human family as a whole... The social order requires constant improvement: it must be founded in truth, built on justice and enlivened by love: it should grow in freedom towards a more humane equilibrium. If these objectives are to be attained there will first have to be a renewal of attitudes and far-reaching social changes. [4]

THE LEGISLATIVE PROPOSAL — BILL C-43

Prior to examining the bill in detail, we would like to thank the government for responding to numerous requests from all over the country that there be a law. The fact of legislation confirms that abortion is a matter of public morality and not solely a private concern.

Positive Elements

1) We are particularly relieved that the gestational approach has been rejected. The concept is offensive and unprincipled because it presumes that human life is more worthy of protection at one stage than another. This bill accepts that human life has intrinsic value from the beginning.

2) The requirement that there be grounds is significant because it affirms that abortion is more than a matter of choice and reinforces the state's interest in protecting the unborn child.

As Canadians we value freedom because it enhances human dignity and autonomy. Yet freedom is more than individualism or unfettered choice. It is also relational and as such limited by the demands of social responsibility. Sometimes it is necessary to restrict freedom to avoid harming others or to benefit them. Laws directed against violent and degrading pornography or favouring affirmative action are other examples of moral choices and freedom being curtailed in the interests of the common good.

3) The use of the criminal law power is welcome because of its powerful message. As Law Reform Commissioner Joseph Maingot said:

> The criminal law can make a significant contribution by addressing the issue of abortion. Criminal prohibitions of abortion are desirable for both functional and symbolic reasons. Functional, because criminal prohibitions will reduce, although not eliminate, abortions. Since foetal life deserves legal protection, it follows that a reduction in abortions is a new social benefit. The symbolic function of the criminal law is not less important. The criminal law is our nations's fundamental statement of public policy. It is the instrument by which the community draws a line between the tolerable and the intolerable. Criminal law defines those whose interests are worthy of respect and protection, and in my view this should include all members of the human family. Ultimately, the criminal law is a mirror of what we are; it reflects our commitment, or lack of commitment, to human dignity and equality. [5]

Negative Elements

At the level of principle then, the bill is encouraging. It is seriously flawed, however, because in practical application it will not sufficiently protect the unborn child.

The major deficiencies are the weak definition of health and the failure to provide any means for confirming that the health standard has been met.

Proposed Amendments

Amendments are required to protect the unborn child not only in principle but also in fact. The following proposals are offered to strengthen the bill.

1) Definition of Health:

A more restrictive definition of health is needed because for some doctors abortion is a first response rather than a last resort.

The health risk must be substantial, serious and permanent. Moreover, it should be such that it cannot be treated by any other commonly accepted medical procedure. This amendment is critical to ensure that all therapeutic alternatives are explored and that abortion is not used to remedy other problems or the stress and anxiety which may ordinarily accompany an unexpected or undesired pregnancy.

For all these reasons, social and economic considerations should be explicitly excluded from the definition of health and the word "psychological" dropped.

2. Accountability

In order to prevent abuses, procedures are needed to ensure that the health standard is respected. Sanctions play a role but they apply only after the death of the child.

There is reason to believe that there will be greater compliance if a second independent medical opinion is required and both doctors are obliged to furnish written reasons for their opinions. Mr Justice Beetz and Mr. Justice Estey in the Morgentaler case held that a second medical opinion was justified, given the state's interest in the unborn child. In particular, they stated:

"Parliament is justified in requiring a reliable, independent and medically sound opinion in order to protect the state interest in the foetus" and later, "I do not believe it to be unreasonable to seek independent medical confirmation of the threat to the woman's life or health when such an important and distinct interest hangs in the balance." [6]

3. Informed Consent

Some women have said they felt pressured into having an abortion without time for adequate reflection. Others have indicated that they might have made a different decision had they been provided with more information as to foetal development or existing support systems for pregnant women. In addition, the psychological effects and physical complications of abortions are beginning to be documented.

In light of these factors, your Committee may wish to consider including a waiting period and mandatory counselling.

4) Sanctions

The Committee should give some thought to differentiating between the sanctions for the persons who perform abortions and those for the pregnant woman involved. While women are moral agents and responsible for their actions, women faced with an unexpected and undesired pregnancy are under more pressure than those who do the abortions. We recommend that penalties other than jail terms (e.g. community service) be considered for these women. As has been observed, "The legal system should reflect both the justice and mercy of God — God who is just, because we have the capacity to be responsible, God who is merciful, because we are weak." [7]

5) Conscience Clause

It is shocking that some health care workers are required to participate in abortion procedures when this is contrary to their personal consciences. Since the Bill does not impose a positive duty to perform abortions, we are unsure if a conscience clause can be included. We wish to indicate, however, our strong support for legislation which would prohibit anyone from being compelled to assist at an abortion contrary to his or her religious or moral views.

THE BEST POSSIBLE LAW

We urge your Committee to draft a law which will protect the unborn child to the maximum degree possible. It is understood, however, that as bishops, it is not our role to suggest in detail the best possible legislative solution. As we wrote to your predecessors in 1966, Christian legislators must make their own decisions. The norm of their actions as legislators is not chiefly the good of any religious group but the good of society.

Religious and moral values are certainly of great importance for good government. But these values enter into political decisions only in so far as they affect the common good. They may, and in fact often will, vote in line with what the Church forbids or approves because what the Church forbids or approves may be closely connected with the common good. Their standard always lies in this question: is it for or against the common good?[8]

During the difficult debate of the last two years around legislative options, some have said that Catholics can support only a law which completely accords with Church teaching. This opinion may have been occasioned by failure to distinguish between the moral law and the civil law or to appreciate the special problems of balancing conflicting claims in a pluralistic society.

While Catholics may not dissent from the Church teaching that abortion is morally wrong, they may differ as to the most effective approach for achieving legal protection of the unborn child. In selecting particular approaches, Catholics are guided by their consciences, informed by Church teaching from which certain general principles can be drawn.

In particular, Catholics may not favour abortion or any proposal which seeks to weaken existing legal protection of the unborn child. Nor may they advocate that there be no legal protection. However, when it is the only available or feasible option, support may be given to legislation which attempts, if only imperfectly, to restore protection or strengthen existing protection and to express publicly their opposition to abortion.

Questions as to feasibility and whether the legislation improves or weakens the legal position of the unborn child, are always matters of prudential judgment where certitude is not possible.

In a country as diversified as ours, in matters of religion and ideology, Catholic politicians must assess the legal and political realities they face and work for the law which will provide the maximum possible protection for unborn children.

CONCLUSION

In closing, we again thank members of the Committee for the opportunity to participate in this debate in the public forum.

You have the responsibility of drafting legislation which will profoundly affect future generations. Your recommendations will be a statement about the value Canadians place on human life. Yours is not an easy task but we are confident that you have the ability, humanity and integrity to make a difference.

For our part, the Canadian Catholic bishops shall continue to teach reverence for human life from conception to natural death and to work for greater social and economic justice. We shall also renew our efforts to educate about positive life-giving solutions to unwanted pregnancies and to increase our support for those individuals and agencies who are providing much needed services (e.g. adoption, support for young mothers, parenting classes, affordable housing and child care).

No civil law will alter our moral teaching on abortion or affect our commitment to a comprehensive and respectful attitude to life at all stages.

NOTES

1. Members of the Permanent Council: Most RR. A. Ambrozic, B. Blanchet, His Em. G. Emmett Cardinal Carter; Most RR. N. Delaquis, G. Drainville, R. Ebacher, A. Exner, T. Fulton; His. Em. Paul Cardinal Gregoire; Most RR. C. A. Halpin, J-G. Hamelin, M. Hermaniuk, R. Lebel, J.H. MacDonald, J.A. O'Mara, His Em. Louis-Albert Cardinal Vachon.

2. John Paul II, *The Christian Family in the Modern World,* in *Origins* (Washington), XI, 1981, n. 28-29, n. 30, p. 447.

3. *Instruction on Respect for Human Life in its Origins etc.,* Congregation for the Doctrine of the Faith, in *Origins,* (Washington), XVI, n. 5, pp. 700f.

4. Vatican II, *The Church in the Modern World,* n. 26.

5. *Crimes against the Foetus* (Law Reform Commission of Canada, 1989, Ottawa, ON, K1A 0L6), p. 100.

6. In Maingot, *Op. cit.*, note 5 above, p. 94.

7. *Catholic New Times* (Toronto, Oct. 8, 1898), editorial.

8. Cf. CCC *Statement on Proposed Change in Canadian Law on Contraceptives,* in this volume, Section II, Document 2.

Section III

LITURGY — WORSHIP

Document 1

A STATEMENT ON SUNDAY OBSERVANCE

Author — The Plenary Assembly, the CCC, October 13, 1960

The Cardinals, Archbishops and Bishops of Canada, meeting in Plenary Session in Ottawa, give thanks to Divine Providence which has inspired the leaders of our country to take a firm stand in defence of world peace, to make generous plans for helping the under-developed countries and to propose measures which, we hope, will prove effective in wiping out the scourge of unemployment. However, the Canadian Catholic Conference observes with grave anxiety the growing tendency on the part of commerce and industry to consider Sunday as an ordinary working day.

If this tendency should one day be confirmed by legislation or, by increasing toleration, should come to be accepted as normal in our society, then all who proudly profess the doctrine of Christ would witness the disappearance of institutions which were established through the unceasing efforts of many generations.

The Sovereign Pontiffs, particularly from the time of Leo XIII to our present Pope John XXIII, have reminded us time and again that the observance of Sunday is a clear indication of a sane economic and social order. In his encyclical *On the Condition of the Working Classes*, 1891, Leo XIII taught that:

Rest (combined with religious observances) disposes us to forget for a while the business of everyday life, to turn our thoughts to things heavenly, and to the worship which we so strictly owe to the Eternal Godhead. It is this, above all, which is the reason and motive of Sunday rest; a rest sanctioned by God's great law of the Ancient Covenant, "Remember thou keep holy the Sabbath Day," and taught the world by His own mysterious "rest" after the creation of humanity, "He rested on the seventh day from all His work which He had done." [1]

He also reminded us, "It can never be right or just to require on the one side or promise on the other, the giving up of those duties which one owes to one's God and to oneself." [2]

Pope Pius XII saw Sunday observance as one prize at stake in the battle against the forces of materialism. "In fact, the outcome of the battle between faith and unbelief will depend in large part on the way in which the opposing camps regard Sunday", advising all people of good will: "Set bravely to work and do your part to give Sunday back to God, to Christ, to the Church, for the peace and happiness of families". [3] Our Canadian legislators recognized the wisdom in this teaching, by enacting the *Lord's Day Act*. [4]

Today, when militant materialism is attacking the forces of good, are we to yield to the pressure exerted by the power of money against our sane and democratic institutions? Will Sunday work eliminate unemployment? Will the abolition of the Lord's Day call down upon our country that protection of Divine Providence which we all know to be so urgently necessary?

The Canadian hierarchy believes that our federal and provincial leaders will, in their wisdom, find ways to solve our present difficulties, and even to ancitipate possible future economic fluctuations in such a way as to uphold the sanctity of the Lord's Day in years to come. "Techniques, economies and societies demonstrate the degree of their moral health by the way in which they promote or thwart the sanctification of Sunday." [5]

NOTES

1. *The Papal Encyclicals,* edit. Claudia Carlen, IHM (Wilmington, N.C., McGrath Publishing, 1981), IV, 251, n. 4.

2. *Op. cit.,* n. 42.

3. *To Men of Catholic Action,* Rome, Sept. 7, 1947, in *Catholic Mind* (New York, 1947), XLV, 643 f.

4. *Revised Statutes,* 1952, c. 171, and c. 123, Art. 4.

5. Pius XII, *To Italian Catholic Workers' Association* (Rome, May 14, 1953) in *Catholic Mind* (New York, 1954), L11, 373F.

Section III, Document 2

ON LITURGICAL RENEWAL:
A PASTORAL LETTER

Author — The Canadian Catholic Conference, December 21, 1964

PART ONE: GENERAL NORMS

I — Preparation for Liturgical Renewal

Only history will be able to measure adequately the effect of the Second Vatican Council on the people of the world both Catholic and non-Catholic. We, who have been closely involved in this great movement of the Holy Spirit, can count various facets of achievement which have already characterized this great Council.

There can be no doubt, however, that on the practical level and in terms of immediate impact on the spiritual lives of our faithful, nothing surpasses the liturgical renewal, for which we are preparing, and which will reach full application on the First Sunday of Lent, March 7, 1965.

As in many movements in the Church, although we like to feel confident that its success has been the first fruit of the operation of the Spirit in our midst, human instrumentality has been cooperating with care and devotedness for a long time. Theologians, liturgists and, above all, a whole series of saintly and learned Popes have prepared our minds for this renewal of our worship.

In particular, the two latest Pontiffs have seen the need for better participation and communion in our worship of God, and it was under our present Holy Father, Pope Paul VI, that the Council's *Constitution on the Sacred Liturgy,* begun in the time of his predecessor,

John XXIII, was promulgated at the conclusion of the second Session of the Council. On the 25th of January, 1964, Pope Paul VI published his *Apostolic Letter on Implementing the Constitution on the Liturgy,* [1] setting forth the rules governing the application of the *Constitution.*

The *Consilium* and its Work

Later, he established a body called the *Consilium* to apply the *Constitution on the Liturgy,* and this international body of bishops and experts from all over the world has since been working with great care and deliberate speed to help in an organized presentation of the liturgical renewal.

Thanks to the work of the *Consilium* we now have the basic rules governing a host of changes in the Liturgy which are calculated to make worship a more personal, shared, vibrant and dynamic community exercise of communication with God.

The work of the *Consilium* is not done. Although we are happy to be able to inform our faithful that the changes which will take effect either on the first of January or on the seventh of March will be definitive, inasmuch as they represent a ground work for liturgical renewal, there are still a number of matters to be settled. For example, the rite of concelebration, which is now in an experimental stage, has to be perfected before its normal use can be made universal. The same applies to the rite of the reception of Holy Communion under both species, which will be permitted on certain occasions. And perhaps the most important work of the *Consilium* at the present time is a complete revision of the liturgical books. In this way the Missal, the Pontifical, the Ritual and the Breviary will be completely re-examined and reformed.

In all this the *Consilium,* in union with the Bishops of the world, has set as its final goal an orderly development of liturgical participation so that the people of God may join with its clergy in celebrating the glories of the Most High and in uniting to invoke the blessings of a loving Father.

The bishops of Canada, in union with the Holy Father and the other bishops of the world, who decreed the *Constitution on the Sacred Liturgy,* are filled with an earnest desire that this liturgical renewal be brought to our people in the simplest yet most effective way. It is our hope that the enthusiasm of our priests will be matched by the understanding of our people and that the glory of God and the good of souls will be served thereby.

II — The Development of Renewal

We have already begun to implement the spirit of the liturgy and we are currently engaged in trying to present it to all our dioceses and parishes in accord with the needs of our times and the liturgical rules.

It was with this in mind that we promulgated the rules governing the reading of the Epistle and the Gospel in the vernacular. We were then very conscious of the fact that the ministry of the Word, the message of God, particularly as found in the words and deeds of Our Lord in the New Testament, should be made accessible to the minds and the hearts of our people. In this manner, we have prepared our people for the sound of their own language in the liturgy, particularly in the mystery of the Holy Sacrifice.

Latin

We recognize that the departure from Latin represents a loss to many people. It is true that few actually understood the words of the Latin, but there was a familiar ring to them, a sense of mystery and awe which we attached to the mass from our earliest childhood. Moreover, there was a certain easy recognition which helped us no matter where we were or under what circumstances.

Common Prayer

All this justifies a legitimate attachment to the use of Latin in the rites of the Holy Sacrifice and we point out that Latin will not disappear during the mass and will be used almost exclusively during the Canon. At the same time, the fact that the celebrant and the ministers at the altar spoke a language which was unfamiliar, did constitute a very real obstacle for the participation of the faithful.

For many, in the past, partly because of the difficulty of a foreign language, the mass has constituted something of an opportunity for personal and private devotion. Even in the introduction of the Epistle and the Gospel in English, some have found a difficulty in what they call "concentration". In countries where wider use of the vernacular has already been introduced, the main objection is stated in terms of a feeling that it is no longer the mass "as we knew it" and that, as people say, "we cannot pray properly". This represents an unfortunate misunderstanding of the nature of the Holy Sacrifice itself, which is a corporate action, an action of the whole People of God offering Our Lord in sacrifice to His heavenly Father. It is not primarily a time for pious private prayer, however beautiful this may be on other occasions.

Thus, it has become imperative — and recognized so by bishops everywhere — for the people of God to unite in common prayer, and particularly to join the celebrant, in the offering of the Holy Sacrifice in all the phases of the Mystery. This is the real meaning of the liturgical reform.

III — The Profound Inspiration

Let us now examine further this simplification of the rites of the mass and the sacraments and in particular the introduction of a living language.

There can be no doubt that these steps facilitate understanding and will be a boon to those who must teach the faithful the deep significance of these acts and words.

The reasons, however, go much deeper than this. This renewal is primarily calculated to help us penetrate more deeply the great sanctifying action which God accomplishes in our midst through the words, the actions and the sacred signs of our liturgy. Indeed, as the *Constitution on the Liturgy* teaches, God continues in the mass and in the sacraments to fulfill what He did in the Old Testament for His chosen people and what He brought to its high point of achievement in Christ. [2]

In the death and resurrection of His Son, God destroyed death and gave us life. He made us His children, filled us with His Spirit.

Henceforth we can live a new life, dead to sin and selfishness, and we must open our hearts and our minds to God and to our brothers and sisters to work out our salvation, in union with them.

Faith

But none of this can be achieved simply by our personal or human efforts. We must be united in the death of Christ and in His resurrection. God has come to save us, to reconcile us to Himself since He has brought us back from the slavery of sin and wishes us to enter into contact and communion with Himself. This cannot be accomplished except through faith and the sacraments.

God's Intervention

We must not then consider the liturgy as only our act of homage rendered to God in song, in prayer and in action. It is, above all, the intervention of God Himself in order to destroy our sin, to combat our selfish tendencies and to bring us to the true life which lasts forever.

The deep sense of the liturgy is the sense of the people of God. St. Peter calls us "a chosen race, a royal priesthood, a holy nation" (1 Peter 2:5). The people of God so qualified cannot stand mutely by as simple spectators or attendants at the great action of God's intervention in our human drama and our return and response to Him. There must be a sense of belonging, of fulfilling, of acting. The sacred liturgy is not essentially a time of quiet devotion, but of participation and of communal prayer in which we storm heaven and in which the very action of God in our midst becomes tangible and perceptible.

These are the reasons why the Church is renewing its liturgy. The external forms must become more accessible, more penetrating, more understandable and, above all, more active.

IV — Divisions of the Mass

As will be shown in the documents which are now accessible to the clergy and the faithful, this will be clearly and distinctly visible in the celebration of the mass in its new form, since its various parts are now more carefully marked.

In the first part, which is called the Mystery of the Word, the role of the faithful is to listen with care to the words of Holy Scripture as proclaimed by the celebrant or by an authorized herald, and to reply by the acclamations and responses indicated.

During the Offertory the people must have a vivid sense of bringing to God not only the matter of the sacrifice but themselves, their lives, all that concerns them, above all their minds and hearts in union with the action of Christ in His self-offering and sacrifice.

The Canon, which begins with the dialogue preceding the Preface and which ends with the great Amen after the second elevation, is the heart of the Eucharistic action and in it the people, although represented by their priest at the altar, are anything but remote spectators. Theirs is the Sacrifice, theirs is the Victim. Not only are they active in mind and heart, but united with the Priest and the Victim on the altar.

After the great Amen, the Our Father is recited by all together, that we may set our minds on our heavenly Father whence all blessings flow, and prepare our souls for Holy Communion, not only in an attitude of adoration and respect, but, above all, as freely dedicated, so that Christ entering our lives may be reflected in all our thought and conduct.

The final rites, although simplified, are filled with symbolism and beauty. Their very brevity now indicates that we carry with us into the world the Christ whom we have received, adored, offered, and that God must be the dominant reality of our lives in all our concerns.

Liturgical reform, therefore, is much more than external change, but must penetrate the most intimate life of Christians.

PART TWO: PRACTICAL RULES GOVERNING THE LITURGICAL RENEWAL

It is our fervent hope that this liturgical renewal will effect in all of us a more profound Christian life and a more intimate union with Christ in the life of grace. This hope can be realized only if our priests and faithful accept our decisions in a spirit of faith and begin immediately to put them to work with understanding and diligence.

Let us keep always before our eyes the main aim. It is simply the full and active participation of all the people in liturgical celebrations. The introduction of the vernacular, however important it may be,

however it may contribute to this participation, is not in itself sufficient to produce what we have in mind.

Responsibility of the Clergy

"Pastors themselves must become thoroughly imbued with the
spirit and power of the liturgy and undertake to give instruction
about it."[3]

The success or failure of the renewal rests largely with the priests, both secular and religious, engaged in pastoral ministry. They
must labour to acquire a greater comprehension and deeper appreciation of the sacred functions that they fulfill, that they may live true
liturgical lives, communicating their faith and their love of the liturgy to the faithful whose souls are confided to their care.

"To promote this active participation, the people should be encouraged to take part by acclamations, responses, singing of hymns
and psalms, antiphons and canticles".[4] This general prescription is
applicable to all liturgical celebrations, whatever the language used.

On the other hand, it is most important that all priests refrain
from unauthorized experiments. They must accept the direction and
guidance towards renewal which will be furnished by the Episcopal
Commission on Liturgy and by their respective Diocesan Commissions.

The right to make reforms or to promote experiments in this field
is reserved strictly to the Holy See and the bishops.[5] This applies
to all matters, but particularly to liturgical music and singing in the
vernacular. We are pursuing research in this domain with all possible diligence but a great deal remains to be done.

Liturgical Education

Nothing will be achieved in the liturgical renewal without the education of the faithful in the rites and mysteries of the faith. It would
be a serious dereliction of duty for any priest to neglect to instruct
his people in these changes and simply to introduce the changes
without warning. Indeed, the proper preparation of the faithful in
the matter of liturgical reform is one of the most solemn and pressing duties of the priest today. This is true in general and it is espe-

cially true of the preparation of readings and chants. Pastoral Institutes for priests and study groups for the laity are urgently needed to help prepare both for the implementation of the bishops' decrees. In this way both can study the difficulties inherent in the introduction of the vernacular into the liturgy, the sacred nature of liturgical celebrations and the necessity of an understanding of the sacred rites. Without this serious preparation, both in theory and in practice, the confusion which will arise from the changes will tend rather to harm our people than to benefit them.

Rules

The *Constitution on the Sacred Liturgy* lays down clear and unmistakable rules governing the use of the vernacular. We point out that only translations of the Latin texts that have been approved by the bishops may be used.[6] The Episcopal Commission on the Liturgy has prepared, in some cases, and, in other cases, is preparing vernacular editions of the liturgical books which will be in use. No other translations should be used, even as an interim measure.

Final Wishes

There is no doubt that the implementation of the *Constitution on the Sacred Liturgy* is a difficult and delicate and urgently needed task. It cannot be successful without the cooperation of all, a true understanding in faith of the Church's wishes and an awareness of present pastoral needs.

Although the guidance of this renewal is the responsibility of the Holy See and the bishops, it is quite clear that the success of the whole process will depend on the priests and on the faithful. This is a living movement which must pervade the entire Church.

We conclude with the prayer that all will have the grace to give to the directives of the Holy See and of their bishops their generous and sincere cooperation. We beg you to be patient in the case of delay, to avoid unauthorized and ill-considered innovations and to put the fullest trust in the operation of the Holy Spirit in the Church which is leading us to this liturgical renewal in the spirit of the Second Vatican Council.

Notes

1. *The Pope Speaks* (Washington, 1964), IX, 299.
2. Vatican II, *Constitution on the Sacred Liturgy,* nn. 5-13; 47-56.
3. *Op. cit.,* n. 14.
4. *Ibid.,* n. 30.
5. *Ibid.,* n. 22.
6. *Ibid.,* n. 36.

Section III, Document 3

STATEMENT ON PENITENTIAL DISCIPLINE IN CANADA

Author — The General Assembly, the CCC, October 14, 1966

The General Assembly has decided:

1. To give new emphasis, by an intensive and well-coordinated catechesis, to the evangelical law of penance and to recall its obligatory character.

2. To maintain the penitential character of Lent and of all Fridays of the year, with particular insistence on Fridays of Lent and especially Good Friday. On these days, penance should be considered an important requirement of the Christian life, but the manner of fulfilling this duty is left to the discretion of the faithful.[2]

3. To remind parents and educators, on the occasion of this legislation which is directed especially to adults, of their duty to introduce children gradually to the practice of penance.

4. To recommend to the faithful certain forms of penance, privileged either by reason of their evangelical authority (e.g., fasting, almsgiving, prayer, works of mercy), or of their traditional commendation (e.g., abstinence).

This decision is to take effect immediately.

NOTES

1. Although this is a pastoral rather than a liturgical declaration, it seemed good to include it here, with the subsequent decrees on the Sacrament of Penance.

2. But cf. Document 5, this section, more strictly preceptive with regard to Good Friday.

Section III, Document 4

STATEMENT ON THE LITURGY OF PENANCE

Author — The General Assembly, the CCC, October 14, 1966

God does not will the death of sinners, but that they be converted and live. Moreover He calls everyone to a life of union with Him through faith in His Son Jesus and through Baptism in water and in the Holy Spirit.

Stamped with the sign of Christ, we nevertheless remain sinners because of the weakness of our human condition. God however, in His mercy, never ceases to call us to repentance, and, when necessary, offers us in the sacrament of penance a sign and a means of reconciliation.

The ministry of reconciliation has been given to the Church. In the current liturgical renewal, this ministry of reconciliation often takes a new form called the community celebration of the sacrament of penance. This seeks to manifest more clearly the ecclesial dimension of the sacrament and to emphasize the fact that conversion has its source in the word of God. It brings together two fundamental values set forth in the Conciliar *Constitution on the Liturgy,* which recommends that communal forms of celebration are more perfect, and strongly urges that greater prominence be given to the Word of God in the liturgy.[1]

1. Individual or private celebration of the sacrament of penance still retains all of its value: through personal conversation and the ministry of the priest, the penitent can better experience the mercy of God;
2. Sacramental absolution must not be given in a communal way. During community celebrations of the sacrament of penance, the private and individual confession of sins by each penitent, as well as individual absolution must be assured.

3. A pastoral approach that takes advantage of these various forms of penance (celebration of the Word on a penitential theme, penitential formulas in the eucharistic liturgy, etc.) will help the faithful to a greater appreciation of the sacrament itself. [2]

NOTES

1. Vatican II, *Constitution on the Sacred Liturgy,* nn. 24, 26-27.
2. It is appropriate to cite here a brief explanation given later by the General Assembly of the Canadian Catholic Conference, during their meeting of Nov. 24-28, 1969, on *The Penitential Rite and Absolution.*
Questions are sometimes asked concerning the meaning of the words "confession" and "absolution" at the beginning of the Mass in the new *Order of Mass.*
The Canadian Catholic Bishops state that these words have no other meaning than that which they conveyed in the former *Order of Mass.* The penitential rite at the beginning of Mass is not a sacramental absolution. (It is not a celebration of the sacrament of penance. Editor's note)

Section III, Document 5

A PASTORAL LETTER ON PENANCE FOR CATHOLICS OF THE LATIN RITE

Author — The General Assembly, the CCC, February 5, 1967

Beloved Brothers and Sisters in Christ:

The Season of Lent invites us again to reflect together on the practice of penance by the renewed church in modern times. Christ the Lord calls us all to make the Church a more dynamic and effective sign of His saving presence in the world.

This, our time of salvation, offers a challenge both terrible and wonderful: terrible, because now humanity has the power to effect instant disaster; wonderful, because, while we are keenly aware of the agony of our brothers and sisters everywhere, we know that we have greater resources than ever to relieve their sufferings. Countless men and women all over the world are attempting to solve the problems of our day. We Christians must be counted among them. The gospel of peace which Christ has given us should make us leaders in working for justice and order.

If our efforts are to bear fruit, however, they must rest on peace with God and our neighbours. Peace will be achieved only if we humble ourselves and remove that which is offensive in us. We are all sinners; we have need of repentance. We need to accept again the urgent demand of Christ: "Be converted and believe in the gospel" (Mk. 1:15).

As we begin this Lent of 1967, what do these words say to us? They tell us to turn away from anything damaging to mind and heart and turn to the greatness of Christ Jesus our Lord. We have been united to Him by baptism; we have accepted to share in the mystery of His death and resurrection. Therefore, daily with Him we die and rise: die to sin, selfishness and pride and rise to a new life of goodness, love and humility. Christ calls to a personal conversion. This begins with a humble admission of our sins and failings and ends with a faith and love which hears and answers the call of Christ in the suffering cry of humanity (Mt. 25:40).

We have been united to Him by baptism. We must go on to accept our share in the mystery of His death and resurrection. Through Him, with Him and in Him, we suffer and die, as He suffered and died on the Cross; through Him, with Him and in Him, we will then rise again, in the greatest of His mysteries, His Resurrection.

From the beginning, Christians have adopted certain practices as particularly helpful in promoting and sustaining this conversion, this change of heart to the Lord. These practices are specially fitting in the season of Lent.

The most important is prayer. In the privacy of our hearts and in union with others we pray for the forgiveness of sins and for a serious desire to live the gospel. We gratefully accept God's pardon offered to us in the sacrament of penance. During Lent we should often participate in the Eucharist, daily if possible. At mass we are united with Christ in the mystery of His death and resurrection — the source of the strength needed to cooperate with the grace of conversion.

Self-denial is another means which helps us turn to God with sincerity. It can bring us an awareness of sin and of the pain our sins have caused others. Bodily penance can help us appreciate the sufferings of our Lord for the sins of humanity, our sins. Fasting gives us some slight experience of the hunger and thirst of millions of our brothers and sisters. In our land of abundance fasting is particularly needed to awaken our minds to the glaring injustices both at home and abroad. This should help us to be doers of the word and not hearers only (cf. James 1:23).

Although the Council has been extraordinarily positive in most of its pronouncements, self-denial is an important part of Christian living. Your bishops have altered the regulations governing the practice of penance in Canada; but the need for self-denial remains. The new law still obliges us to choose some form of penance during Lent and on Fridays of the year. Let us here recall the words of the Council's *Constitution on the Sacred Liturgy*:

> ... let the paschal fast be kept sacred. It should be observed everywhere on Good Friday and, where possible, prolonged through-

out Holy Saturday, so that the joys of the Sunday of the Resurrection may be visited on uplifted and responsive spirits.[1]

Adopted in union with the suffering and death of our Lord on the
cross, this fast is a most fitting preparation for the celebration of the
feast of the Resurrection.

Almsgiving is also a practice which helps us live the gospel. The
unselfish giving of our time and money is love, and love is the goal
of conversion.

Prayer, self-denial and almsgiving not only dispose us to sincere
conversion, they are signs of conversion begun. In fact, if one does
none of these, it is doubtful if the call of Christ is being taken seriously. Let us remember, however, that if we adopt such practices to
impress others, we are not pleasing God.

If we enter into the spirit of Lent, participating in the sorrowful
mystery of Good Friday, we will be prepared to celebrate the greatest
mystery, the resurrection of the Lord. In celebrating the death and
resurrection of our Lord, especially at the Easter Vigil when we renew
the promises of our baptism, we open ourselves best to the grace
of conversion, for it is through Him, with Him and in Him that we
die and rise again.

We are not to think that conversion is something dramatic and
exciting. No, it usually begins very humbly in our daily effort "to
walk in the same way in which Jesus walked" (1 Jn. 2:6). Against
the background of the problems of the world, the conversion of one,
or even of several persons, seems a very small thing. Small as it may
appear, it is the only true beginning of a happier world. The lively
faith and active love of one person exercised in the service of the
world is like a little bit of yeast in several measures of flour. It works
until the whole is leavened (Mt. 13:33). It is not pride but faith that
leads us to say that the hope of the world lies in Christians on fire
with the Spirit of Jesus. This boast is not vain, for the Lord is with
us to the end of time (Mt. 28:20).

With strong faith we will be able to read the signs of the times
and to adjust as necessary to change; with a mature love we can and
will meet the challenges of our day. Determined to follow the Son
of God, we will listen and respond to His words: "Be converted
and believe in the gospel" (Mk. 1:15). Together we will pray for the
courage to be in action what we are in fact, children of God.

May the good gifts of the Father and of the Son and of the Holy
Spirit be given you in abundance during this Lent, and may the peace
and joy of our risen Lord be with you always.

NOTE

1. Vatican II, *Constitution on the Sacred Liturgy,* n. 110.
   Current discipline is resumed in *Liturgical Calendar,* 1989-90 (CCCB Publications Service, Ottawa, K1N 7B1), Note 29, p. 47.
   c) Lent... The Paschal fast for Good Friday and Holy Saturday is described in the notes for Passion Sunday*.
   * Paschal fast: pastors should remind the people of the special fast. The paschal fast should be observed everywhere on Good Friday and continued where possible on Holy Saturday. Cf. Vatican II, *Constitution on The Sacred Liturgy, n. 110.*
   The *New Code of Canon Law,* cc. 1249-53, *On Days of Penance,* does not mention prolonging the Good Friday fast into Holy Saturday. Editor's note.

Section III, Document 6

MIXED MARRIAGE LEGISLATION FOR CANADA

Author — The Plenary Assembly, the CCC, September, 1971

On March 31, 1970, after consultation with the Episcopal Conference of the Catholic Church, Pope Paul VI issued an Apostolic Letter on Mixed Marriages. [1] The substance of this letter opens up new and welcome pastoral approaches to be adapted and implemented by national and territorial conferences. Accordingly, the Bishops of Canada, after sufficient experience of provisional regulations, now present to the Catholic clergy and people under their jurisdiction the following preamble and definitive norms for the application of the Apostolic Letter.

PREAMBLE

1. Within the Church there has been a constant solicitude for the stability and harmony of family life, not only when Catholics are involved, but also when others, whether Christians or non-Christians, are united in matrimony. This concern has been well expressed in the Pastoral Constitution, *The Church in the Modern World.*

The well-being of the individual person and of human and Christian society is intimately linked with the healthy condition of that community produced by marriage and the family. Hence Christians and all who hold this community in high esteem sincerely rejoice in the various ways by which people today find help in fostering this community of love and perfecting its life, and by which spouses and parents are assisted in their lofty calling.[2]

2. Since religious differences are obstacles to full sharing within the family, even though they do not necessarily threaten its peace and tranquility, it is normally desirable that those who enter into marriage belong to the same religious community. Therefore, the Apostolic Letter, which is directed to Catholics, encourages Catholic marriages.

3. Nevertheless, it recognizes as a primary principle the natural right to marry and have children.[3] For this reason the Church is prepared to make pastoral provisions for those marriages in which a Catholic is united with another Christian or non-Christian.

4. In Catholic teaching the natural contract of marriage was established by God in the creation of the human race and is, consequently, good and holy in its own order. It is also true, however, that the contract receives the added dignity of a sacrament when it is entered by baptized persons and it becomes a sign of the union of Christ and His Church (cf. Eph. 5:25-33).

5. Furthermore, in such a marriage, despite the disunity of Churches within the context of Christian faith, there is a greater sharing in religious convictions flowing from a common belief in Jesus Christ as Lord and Saviour. Therefore, the Apostolic Letter says:

> Undoubtedly, there exists in a mariage between baptized persons, since such a marriage is a true sacrament, a certain communion of spiritual benefits which is lacking in a marriage entered by a baptized person and one who is not baptized.[4]

6. Nevertheless, even in a mixed marriage which is a sacrament, the Church has a duty to proclaim the obligations in conscience devolving upon the Catholic partner. The first of these is that the Catholic party must remain faithful to his or her own faith as professed in the Catholic Church.

7. The second is that the Catholic "as far as is possible" must "see to it that the children be baptized and brought up in that same faith and receive all those aids to eternal salvation which the Catholic Church provides for her sons and daughters."[5]

8. This, as the Apostolic Letter acknowledges, is particularly difficult "in view of the fact that both husband and wife are bound by that responsibility and may by no means ignore it or any of the obligations connected with it."[6]

9. For the good of the marriage it is advisable that this question of the Baptism and education of the children be settled before the marriage takes place. It cannot be a unilateral decision. It must be one in which the consciences of both parties are respected. As the Declaration on Religious Freedom says:

> In the exercise of their rights, individuals and social groups are bound by the moral law to have respect both for the rights of others and for their own duties towards others and for the common welfare of all.[7]

10. When the couple can achieve no agreement on this most important matter, they should seriously consider dropping their marriage plans. Failure to resolve this issue would constitute a major obstacle to harmonious living.

11. When, however, this matter is resolved without violence to conscience, neither parent should be divorced from the religious education of the children. Both parents should share in forming the religious values of their children and neither should view this responsibility as fulfilled by mere passive "non-interference". Not only from a pastoral but also from a pedogogical viewpoint, the combined religious influence of both parents is important for the children.

12. This co-operative spirit implies that the couple strive valiantly for religious understanding in their home. In calm dialogue, in reading common prayer, in occasional attendance at each other's services, they can discover what they truly share in belief, and grow in esteem and respect for both communities of faith which have shaped their positive values.

13. The formation of this religious atmosphere, in turn, will call upon increased pastoral and ecumenical care by the communities to which the couple belongs. Clergy and counsellors are invited to act together as far as possible both to prepare the man and woman for marriage and to provide such aftercare as is necessary.

14. The Apostolic Letter also addresses itself to another area of tension, the celebration of marriage. It envisages that Catholics will normally be married in the canonical and appropriate liturgical form of the Catholic Church. It takes into account, however, special circumstances in which an Ordinary may dispense from the canonical form, which binds a Catholic of the Latin Rite for validity.

15. This authority to dispense makes it possible to consider the good of the couple as a primary pastoral concern. The Church stands

before them, not as a legal institution, but as a friend to assist them in the very beginning of their married life. There is a breadth of understanding which encompasses religious, traditional, cultural and familial ties which surpasses the logic of law alone and is rooted in a total humanity.

16. Here, indeed, is the whole thrust of the Apostolic Letter. It is concerned with people. Nowhere does it express this more succinctly than towards the end of its own preamble, where it states:

> No one will be really surprised to find that even the canonical discipline on mixed marriages cannot be uniform and that it must be adapted to the various cases in what pertains to the juridical form of contracting marriage, its liturgical celebration, and, finally, the pastoral care to be given to married people and to children of the marriage, according to the distinct circumstances of the married couple and the differing degrees of their ecclesiastical communion. [8]

NORMS

Preparation for Marriage

1. Couples preparing to enter marriage require adequate preparation for this state of life. The individual priest must be aware of his role and responsibility in this important pastoral function. This is even more necessary in the case of a marriage between persons of different religious affiliations. In this latter instance, the ministers of both parties should seek to cooperate in exercising this responsibility, both ministers where possible jointly undertaking the spiritual preparation of the couple, guiding them in the preparation of their marriage ceremony and preparing them for their future life as an interfaith couple.

2. The couple shall be instructed on the purposes and essential properties of marriage which are not to be excluded by either party. [9]

Promises

3. The Catholic party will declare his/her intention of observing the laws of the Church, of living according to them, and of bearing witness to his or her faith. The Catholic partner promises to respect the religious convictions of his or her partner, and to allow complete freedom in living that faith and bearing witness to it.

4. The Catholic party, after having discussed the matter with the other party, will promise to do his/her utmost to see that children to be born of the marriage receive Catholic baptism and education, while respecting the religious convictions of the non-Catholic partner and without placing their conjugal life in jeopardy.

5. "To do one's utmost" in the particular circumstances of this marriage means that the parties should arrive at a decision agreeable to both, after sincere discussions which take place with due respect for the religious convictions of the partner. No one can dispense the Catholic party from this obligation of conscience which lasts for life. Whenever the religious convictions of one are irreconcilable with the other's, serious consideration should be given to abandoning their plans for marriage.

6. The promises to be made by the Catholic party will be made orally, and the presence of a witness is not necessary; the priest who prepares the couple for their marriage will inform the Ordinary that these promises were sincerely made and that he is morally certain that the Catholic party will do his/her best to be faithful to the obligations.

   The celebration of a mixed marriage cannot be authorized in those cases where it is clearly evident that the Catholic party is not sincere in making the promises or when the Catholic party refuses to promise to be faithful to the Catholic faith and to see to the Catholic baptism and education of children born of the marriage.

7. The priest who prepares the couple for marriage will inform the non-Catholic party of the obligations of the Catholic party and will notify the Ordinary that this has been done.

Marriage Banns

8. In order to ensure greater cooperation between the ministers of both Churches, it is recommended that the practice be introduced

of publishing the Marriage Banns in both churches (Catholic and non-Catholic); this applies in places where it is customary to have such publications.

Canonical Form

9. A Catholic must normally contract marriage in and before the Catholic Church.

10. The Ordinary of the Catholic party, or the Ordinary of the place where the marriage is to be celebrated, may dispense from the canonical form.

11. Reasons for granting dispensations from canonical form should concern in some important way the good of the parties, especially their spiritual well-being, the tranquillity and peace of their personal or family relationships, or be based on some special relationship to a non-Catholic minister or place of worship.

12. If the Ordinary of the Catholic party grants a dispensation from form for a marriage which is to take place in another diocese, the Ordinary of that diocese must be informed beforehand.

Celebration

13. It is fitting that only the Catholic priests and non-Catholic ministers preside only over those particular marriages which take place in their respective churches.

14. It is desirable that the non-Catholic minister be invited to take an active part in the Catholic ceremony, for example, by reading a Scripture lesson, by giving an address or by offering prayer. It is equally desirable on the occasion of a mixed marriage celebrated outside the Catholic Church with a dispensation from canonical form, that the Catholic priest accept a similar invitation to take part in the ceremony.

15. Authorization is not given for a second religious ceremony in which the exchange of consent is renewed either before or after the Catholic ceremony.

16. Authorization is not given for a marriage to be celebrated before a Catholic priest and a non-Catholic minister when both ministers accomplish their respective marriage rites.

17. For all marriages celebrated in the Catholic Church the exchange of consent normally should be accompanied by sacred rites which help the couple to turn their minds and hearts to God, to discover God's love in their love for each other and to give Him thanks.

18. Regardless of how profound our desire may be to share with non-Catholics the Church's means of grace, participation in the same sacred actions must always be in accord with the truth as well as the convictions of the persons involved. The words and actions in the celebration of a marriage must therefore correspond to the religious beliefs of both parties.

19. The marriage may, in some circumstances, take place during mass and, in other circumstances, should be accompanied by a celebration of the Word. In each case, it will be the priest's responsibility, after discussion with the parties, to decide which sacred rites should accompany the exchange of consent.

20. Because of the differences in doctrine and sacramental life that exist between the Catholic Church and the other Christian Churches and communities of the West, it is generally more opportune that a marriage between a Catholic and a non-Catholic be celebrated without mass.

Nevertheless, it may sometimes be desirable that such a marriage be celebrated with mass. If such is the case the prescriptions of general law with regard to Eucharistic Communion would be observed. [10]

Witnesses

21. Non-Catholics may be invited to act as witnesses at mixed marriages or to assist the spouses in some other capacity.

Registration of the Marriage and of the Dispensation

22. A marriage celebrated with dispensation from the canonical form will be recorded at the place where the marriage was celebrated (e.g., church, courthouse, etc.).

23. The priest who prepared the couple for marriage and registered the dispensation from form must see to it that a marginal notation, indicating the date and place of marriage as well as the dispensation from form, will be made in the baptismal records of the church or chapel where the Catholic party was baptized.

24. Record of the grant of dispensation from the canonical form will be kept in the Chancery Office of the Ordinary granting the dispensation.

In order to locate documents readily in the future, the priest petitioning the dispensation from form will indicate in the petition which parish archives will receive the marriage file following the ceremony.

After the Marriage

25. Pastors shall see to it that the Catholic husband or wife and the children born of a mixed marriage receive spiritual assistance. They shall encourage them ever to cherish the gift of Catholic faith which they have received and to bear witness to it "with gentleness and reverence" as suggested in Holy Scripture (1 Peter 3:15). They shall assist the couple in strengthening the unity of their conjugal and family life which, for Christians, is based also on their baptism.

To this end, pastors should establish with ministers of other religions relationships, sincere openness and judicious confidence.

NOTES

1. *Acta Apostolicæ Sedis* (Vatican, 1970), LXII, 257; English version, *The Pope Speaks* (Washington, 1970), XV, 134 ss.

2. Vatican II, *The Church in the Modern World*, n. 47.

3. *Op. cit.*, note 1, above, p. 134.

4. *Ibid.*, p. 135.

5. *Ibid.*, p. 136.

6. *Ibid.*, p. 136.

7. Vatican II, *Declaration on Religious Freedom*, n. 7.

8. *Op. cit.*, note 1, above, p. 136.

9. *Ibid.*, p. 138, n. 6.

10. *Ibid.*, p. 139, n. 12.

Section III, Document 7

STATEMENT ON SUNDAY OBSERVANCE

Author — The Plenary Assembly, the CCC, April 21, 1972

The question is being raised, even in Christian circles, concerning the value of the Sunday celebration. Some appear to entertain a doubt, as if, in the post-Conciliar period, this tradition had become outmoded and no longer deserved a place in the life of Christians.

The fact is that, as in the past, the Christian community will always come together to honour God in this highest form of prayer; to celebrate the life, the death and the resurrection of Christ; to listen to His Word and to find therein life and light; to share in the communion of His Body and Blood; to discover with one another how the Lord prepares, for them and with them, "a new heaven and a new earth" (Is. 65:17, Rev. 21:1).

It is impossible to deny the need of the individual Christian and of the believing community to meet from time to time in united assembly, to give new life to their faith in this communion with Christ and new dedication to their hope in the service of the world it has pleased God to give them to transform.

It is precisely in the Sunday celebration of the parish that the universality of the Church is manifested. The Church becomes visible to us in this reunion of Christians of all social classes, rich and poor alike, of all ages and of all conditions.

Far from disappearing as an outdated obligation after the Second Vatican Council, the Sunday celebration takes on greater importance in the light of the Council. The Council has brought new values and new facilities to Christians to enrich their lives through a Christian Sunday. At a time strongly marked by individualism and a thirst for freedom in all its forms, the sense of community achieved in the Sunday celebration is of great value in the fulfillment of these new needs.

As a sign of God among us, as a road leading in the direction of "the new earth" so ardently desired, as a strength for the long and difficult quest, the meeting of the Christian community is a bonding of the utmost importance and a true privilege.

We conclude that the Sunday celebration cannot be separated from its context of the gospel law of love. This is an obligation which, in the full sense, must be "taken to heart". Indeed the mature Christian will honour it as a valid and primary obligation of one's life. It remains a precept of the Church to be reaffirmed in our times because of its basic value and validity.

Today's parish should be open to all legitimate modes of expression, of inspiration and of community. The need is to build a true Christian family, an articulate prayer life and an ever-growing sense of the Church as the gathering of God's people. For this, all must be involved, all must work together for the development of the larger human community. Various particular groupings and other legitimate human initiatives may well serve as valuable instruments in this evolution.

We invite all Christians to a collective effort to achieve greater understanding of this mystery of Christian Eucharistic community.

Section III, Document 8

NORMS FOR THE ADMINISTRATION OF SACRAMENTAL ABSOLUTION

Author — The Administrative Board, Canadian Catholic Conference,
September 1, 1972

1. On July 13, 1972, the Sacred Congregation for the Doctrine of the Faith published a document entitled *Pastoral Norms for the Administration of Sacramental Absolution.* [1] This text was specially approved by the Holy Father, Pope Paul VI.

The bishops of Canada wish to underline the interpretation of this text given by Pope Paul, on July 19,[2] which is in accord with the pastoral concerns we have striven to promote since the inception of our study of this question. It is important that the authentic idea of sin be clearly present to the hearts and minds of all Christians, and that a genuine moral responsibility be appreciated in accord with human and Christian dignity.

In the same vein, we wish to emphasize the sacrament of penance as the manifest sign of the mercy of the Father to us. Finally, we would like to see expressed in this sacrament, our joyful reconciliation with Christ, in Whom we find our own resurrection.

2. The *Norms* (above, n. 1) clearly establish that individual confession is the ordinary means available to all for sacramental absolution. This individual confession must remain accessible at all times in accord with the age-old tradition of the Church.[3]

The *Norms* provide for the possibility of collective absolution in the cases defined in paragraphs II and III. This innovation, according to the explanation of Pope Paul VI, deals with certain cases outside the danger of death.[4]

It is our intention to present an interpretation and application of the directives concerning collective absolution during our Plenary Assembly in October. In particular we will comment on paragraph 5 of the *Norms,* which deals with the case in which general absolution is permitted subject to the decision of the local bishop.

3. This is an opportunity for us to inform the local churches that we are now studying the possibility of a statement on the pastoral orientation we feel should be given to the sacrament of penance in the life of Christians.

4. Finally, we intend also to publish a letter concerning the formation of moral conscience in order to respond to the expectation of priests, religious and laity. The purpose of this letter will be to enlighten the conscience of the Christian of today, so often harassed by the confusion and questioning of these latter years.[5]

NOTES

1. In *Origins* (Washington, 1972), II, p. 125.
2. Paul VI, in a general audience, *On the Importance of the Individual Confession,* in *The Pope Speaks* (Washington, 1972), XVII, p. 272.
3. *Op. cit.,* note 1, above, p. 126.
4. Paul VI, *op. cit.,* note 2, above, p. 273.
5. Cf. Section II, Document 8, n. 14ff.

Section III, Document 9

STATEMENT ON THE ADMINISTRATION OF GENERAL SACRAMENTAL ABSOLUTION

Author — The Plenary Assembly, the CCC, October 13, 1972

God's mercy toward us, made manifest in Jesus Christ, has been mediated by the Church in an uninterrupted way throughout the ages, in the ministry of Penance which the Lord confided to her on Easter morning.

The history of this sacrament shows that the Church has always recognized its power to remit sins in the name of God, although it has exercised this ministry in different ways throughout the course of time, according to the needs of the faithful. Different ways of celebrating the sacrament have emphasized now one, now another aspect of the whole, such as sin or divine mercy. Together they express the richness of the sacrament, but sometimes particular emphasis on one aspect may obscure certain others also important. In our times the ecclesial dimension of sin and pardon has sometimes suffered eclipse, diminishing the appreciation of many for so great a benefit.

The Sacred Congregation for the Doctrine of the Faith has expressed concern over certain developments in current penitential practice. Among these is a general decline in the use of the sacrament of Penance, as well as misunderstandings regarding the practice of communal sacramental absolution. Another area of concern has been the difficulty in confessing individually which the faithful of some regions have sometimes experienced because of the shortage of priests. Accordingly, the Congregation has published, with the approval of the Holy Father, some pastoral norms for the administration of the sacrament of Penance, with particular attention to the use of communal sacramental absolution. [1]

This document restates the present discipline regarding individual confession:

Individual and integral confession and absolution remain the only ordinary way for the faithful to be reconciled to God and the Church unless excused by physical or moral impossibility from such confession. [2]

Something new, however, is added regarding communal sacramental absolution in cases other than danger of death:

Apart from the cases of danger of death, it is lawful to give sacramental absolution collectively to a number of faithful who have confessed only generically but have been suitably exhorted to repent, provided that there is serious necessity, namely, when in view of the number of penitents there are not enough confessors at hand to hear properly the confession of each within an appropriate time, with the result that the penitents through no fault of their own would be forced to do without sacramental grace or Holy Communion for a long time. This can happen especially in mission lands but in other places also and within groups where it is clear that this need exists.

This is not lawful, however, when confessors are able to be at hand, merely because of a great concourse of penitents such as can occur, for example, on a great feast or pilgrimage. [3]

The application of this norm is reserved to each local bishop. Accordingly, the bishops of Canada provide the following directives:

a) We are conscious of the confusion and even the suffering of many Catholics concerning individual confession and we feel strongly that as pastors we have a primary duty to help our people to understand and accept this sacramental practice which remains the privileged means of obtaining pardon for sin. In this light we urge all priests, parents, educators and catechists to do everything possible to establish and maintain among the faithful a sound practice of confession. They should be instructed on the value and necessity of individual confession, and should be taught to confess well in advance of great feasts and solemnities. Good pastoral practice can all but eliminate the crowding that sometimes takes place on these occasions to the detriment of the sacrament.

b) Communal sacramental absolution is linked, as the document from the Congregation specifies, to cases of real necessity. These cases must be specified by the local bishop in accord with the norms set down by the Sacred Congregation for the Doctrine of the Faith. Then, on the basis of these specifications, the priest may consider the possibility of communal sacramental absolution. Apart from those cases, if a serious need arises, the priest is obliged, whenever it is possible, to have previous recourse to the local bishop in order to grant the absolution lawfully: if this is not possible, he is to inform the bishop as soon as possible of the need and of the granting of the absolution.

We wish to recall to pastors the insistence of the *Norms* on certain points which affect the faithful. First, individual confession remains the general rule. When, by reason of exceptional circumstance, recourse is had to communal absolution, it is imperative that the faithful be suitably disposed, having true sorrow for sin, firm purpose of amendment and the intention of repairing any scandal or loss caused by sin. The faithful are also required to confess in due time (at least within the year, unless prevented by moral impossibility, and before a second communal absolution, unless a just cause prevents them) each serious sin for which the communal absolution was desired. This last point must be well explained to avoid encouraging the opinion that general absolution now takes the place of individual confession.

The faithful should likewise be instructed on the reasons which underlie the obligation of confessing serious sins individually to the priest: to signify the personal reception of reconciliation at the heart of the Christian community, to assure the firmness of their conversion, to specify the concrete steps that must be taken, to find in this fraternal dialogue with the priest the light of the Gospel as it applies to their particular situation, to assist them to repair any damage or scandal they may have caused, and so on.

These present directives will have to be part of an improved pastoral catechesis of the sacrament of penance.

Since we are dealing with the mode of administering this sacrament, it will be important that those responsible for this pastoral ministry evaluate the results, particularly the various effects among the faithful, and communicate their findings to the bishops of the diocese.

For its part, the Canadian Catholic Conference intends to follow attentively the application of these directives and will continue, in communion with the other episcopal conferences of the universal Church, to dialogue with the Holy See to facilitate whatever adaptations may be called for in the pastoral needs of our country. We therefore intend to publish a pastoral directory on penance and a document on the formation of conscience.

We take this opportunity to recommend once again the practice of holding communal penitential celebrations, with private confession of sin and individual absolution. We are happy to see an increase in this type of service, because it brings with it a strong sense of celebration, the celebration of joyful reconciliation with the risen Lord, and gives us a renewed sense of the Lord's pardon. These communal rites also underline the social dimensions of sin and pardon in the Church, and illustrate the common lot of our human family in evil and in return to God. This penitential style corresponds to the desire of the Second Vatican Council, which sought to strengthen the ecclesial role in the penitential action and emphasize the intercessory power of the prayer of the entire Church on behalf of sinners. [4]

We hope that priests and faithful alike will welcome the norms approved by the Holy Father "after considering with a sense of responsibility and pastoral insight the real welfare of the Church and of each of the faithful." [5]

Above all, we count on priests to give these directives wide circulation in a program of reeducation of consciences in the meaning of sin and in the importance of the sacrament of pardon. We appeal to their love for souls and to their apostolic zeal as confessors to accept willingly the self-denial required for the assiduous exercise of this holy ministry, and to make themselves available to the faithful, not only in special periods of the liturgical year, but as often as possible, especially before the celebration of the Holy Sacrifice of the Mass.

NOTES

1. June 16, 1972, in *Origins* (Washington, 1972), p. 125, n. II.

2. *Op. cit.*, p. 126, n. I.

3. *Ibid.*, p. 126, n. III.

4. Vatican II, *Dogmatic Constitution on the Church*, n. 11; *Constitution on the Sacred Liturgy*, nn. 26, 27, 72.

5. Paul VI, in a general audience, *On the Importance of Individual Confession*, in *The Pope Speaks* (Washington, 1972), p. 273, n. XVII.

Section III, Document 10

A NEW COMMANDMENT?
A LENTEN EXHORTATION[1]

Author — The Administrative Board, the CCC, January 21-22, 1976

I — ARE WE FAIR TO EACH OTHER?

1. *Lent and Reconciliation*

As Canadians, we live in a specific social situation that should mark our Lenten reflections on penance and reconciliation. We should also try somehow to penetrate and shape that situation by our concerns for forgiveness and fraternal solidarity.

2. *Ethical Questions for Canadians*

The most striking aspect of the situation in which we live may be what we have come to know as the battle against inflation. Many political and economic questions are involved, but the following ethical dimension is central to the total problem.

As individuals and through our institutions, are we seeking more for ourselves than a fair proportion of our country's resources? Seeking to maximize our share of the national riches and of the products of human labour, are we demanding more than our share?

Are we thereby accepting and promoting the goals of an economic system that urges us to over-consume and waste and thus create shortages that are expressed in increasing prices and wages? By constantly striving for more material goods and services, are we contributing to the social disorder that is called inflation?

3. *Personal and Social Sin*

When a society commonly pursues selfish ends, the common sin becomes institutionalized, so that one can speak of sinful social structures. The name given to this persistent state of injustice and resultant suffering is "social sin".

In many specific ways, are we guilty of personal and social sin — that is, the guilt of self-seeking both as individuals and as groups? Greed and waste cause inequalities and divisions. By seeking more for ourselves, are we deepening divisions among people and increasing the powerlessness of an ever-growing number? Are we using what corporate power we have to respond to the needs of others, or are we abusing our power to harm the weak?

4. *Examining our Attitudes*

No one living in this country should fail to apply these questions in a personal way. They have particular import during Lent, when we are called to reflect on our sins, our need for forgiveness and the meaning of Christian love. We Christians are asked to examine, openly and rigorously, our attitudes and activities, in light both of the basic principles that we draw from our reading of Holy Scripture and of our understanding of our duties to each other.

In the present social context, then, questions about our individual and collective participation in injustice and in the abuse of natural resources, manufactured goods and human services, should form part of our self-examination as we take note of our failings as individuals and as community.

5. *Labour Day Messages*

The recent Labour Day messages of the Canadian Catholic Conference have dealt in depth with these questions. Lent is an excellent time to review them in our homes and parishes.[2]

II — COMMITMENT TO LOVE, JUSTICE, RECONCILIATION

6. *God's Love*

The call to love and to be just is the call of God, Our Father, to His children. His love is personal and ever active. It is given freely.

It is a love that is made visible in Jesus. Through our union with Jesus and with one another, we are given the power to love by the Holy Spirit, so that the love Jesus has for us is the love with which we love one another.

Love Demands Justice

Because love requires that we recognize and respect the dignity and rights of our neighbour, Christians are called to be just to one another.[3] Our love "is not to be just words or mere talk, but something real and active." (1 Jn. 3:18) Such an active love necessarily involves a daily effort to be just in all that we say and do. Justice also involves a genuine concern for persons who are the victims of injustice. These victims, our neighbours, are to be found in every city and community in Canada. We can discover their discouragement and their need of support by being with them.

7. Ways of Reconciling

Christians are called to be reconcilers. For some this may mean taking those first steps toward forgiving a person or a group. It may require us to accept forgiveness. Often it involves joining with Christians and other citizens to take a stand with people whose rights are ignored and violated.

8. Opportunities for Restraint

The daily experiences of life offer each of us many opportunities for the renewal and reconciliation to which we constantly are called, and especially during the Lenten season. We have not far to seek for the changes that would bring us closer to God and our neighbours in that spirit of love our faith calls us to express. Indeed, opportunities are daily present in precisely the restraints on acquisition which is a cause of the hardships and shortages that are part of life for many under what is termed runaway inflation.

9. Concern for Ethics not Politics

To invite Canadians to a genuine spirit of caring about how much of this world's goods each is consuming; to call for a greater sharing of goods and services; to insist that each of us must be much more sparing in personal consumption as well as in striving for more benefits for any group to which we belong — to invite, to call, to insist on the Gospel demands of justice and love, does not mean we are endorsing particular economic or political proposals for a solution of the social problems we know exist. Rather what we are calling for is an examination of our attitudes and activities and a reflection on the requirements of our faith and its obligations.

10. *Spiritual Growth and the Cross*

Our life-long task is to become Christ-like. Actions inspired by love make this growth possible, just as selfish actions prevent it. Periods of reflection are necessary and especially helpful during Lent. At such times our awareness of our responsibilities to our families, to our communities, to those with whom we work, are often seen much more clearly. We also realize more fully the meaning of the Cross in our lives. Challenging ourselves in this way and raising questions of injustice with others, often leads us to arrive at a decision on a critical question: will we continue the struggle and face misunderstanding and apparent failure, or will we abandon it because progress seems impossible? Praying with Jesus will help us to see our "Good Fridays" as only apparent defeats, to be turned into victories.

11. *Opportunities to be Merciful*

In Lent, we recall the appeal of Jesus to be merciful. We have in our midst the poor, the weak and the oppressed. By reaching out to them, we develop our ability to love and become reconcilers among very neglected persons. In His description of the Last Judgment, Jesus tells us that, at that time, power and possessions will not matter but love and mercy will (Mt. 25:31-46).

III — SACRAMENT OF RECONCILIATION

12. *We Belong to a Family*

Our growing appreciation of the injustice in our world should not discourage us. While we need to confront and oppose injustice, we must look to God for courage and strength. God always meets our deepest needs. He forgives us when we sin; He is present to us as we attempt to be reconciled with one another; He unites us in a family where true solidarity is experienced.

13. *A Church of Sinners*

We are sinners. We are called to a life of love, yet so often we refuse. We act selfishly. With St. Paul we cry out: "My own actions
bewilder me; what I do is not what I want to do; I do the very things
I hate." (Rom. 7:14-16) Do we not perceive ourselves as such? Are
we not often unforgiving? Callous at times and insensitive to our
injury of others? Are we not unfair, untruthful and unfaithful?
Repeatedly wasteful and greedy? Every sin involves a refusal to love
— a turning away from God's call and the commandment of Jesus.
Besides violating our neighbours' rights, sin includes the will to act
independently of God. It is a decision to satisfy a real or imaginary
need, regardless of the consequences. It leads to alienation from God
and others.

14. *A Father's Love*

Our very awareness of our sinfulness is coupled with faith that
Our Father is merciful and patient. We recall the parable of the prod-
igal son, and hope fills our hearts as we come face to face with the
Father's love and mercy. If we but turn to Him, He reaches out to
touch us and re-integrate us into His living family (Lk. 15:11-22).

15. *The Sacrament of Forgiveness*

Jesus offers the forgiveness of the Father to those who believe in
Him. Jesus is our reconciliation through His life, death and resurrection. The Church is a paradox. Her glory is to be holy while at
the same time embracing sinners. In the Church we celebrate God's
forgiving love and are enabled to turn from sin and return to a life
of love (Jn. 20:20-23). The Sacrament of Reconciliation (Penance),
while celebrated in a variety of ways throughout the centuries,
has always been understood as God's gift of forgiveness for sins
committed after baptism.

16. *Social Dimension of Sin*

A revised rite of the Sacrament is being introduced, which emphasizes aspects often overlooked in recent years. Our reflections
on suffering and injustice illustrate our inter-relatedness one with
another. The social dimension of sin is now given more prominence
in the new rite for the Sacrament through communal celebrations.

We are reminded that, just as we fail to recognize the good we do by being believing and forgiving members of our parishes and communities, we fail also to realize the social effect of our sins, especially those related to injustice. Further, when we are separated from our brothers and sisters through sin, we weaken the entire human family. The Church is now with us — for we together are the Church — to pray with us so that we will return to God.

17. *Prayer, Reflection*

Essential here is a heartfelt acceptance that we are powerless without God's grace. Prayer is a vital part then of our preparation to pardon and be pardoned in the sacrament. Our hard hearts are softened in prayer. The revised rite calls for reflection on God's Word — the Word that enlightens, judges and heals. Reflection and prayer from the heart will lead us to conversion.

18. *The Meaning of Conversion*

Conversion involves a return to a life of love, as well as a recognition of our personal and social sins. We need to pray for this change of heart, and be convinced that some of our attitudes are contrary to the Gospel. God's grace will bring about an interior renewal and make possible a new beginning. It is important to pray that we will forgive others from our hearts, when possible, and actually to be reconciled with them before celebrating. Finally, let us remember that achieving full conversion is our life-long task.

19. *Absolution*

The new rite suggests that a special place be set aside for the celebration of the sacrament, to facilitate discussion and prayer with the priest. Guidance is important in matters of conscience, since, without it, we may be either too severe or too lenient with ourselves. [4] Absolution is bestowed after the confession of our sins. It is the culmination of the actions of the penitent and of the believing community. To absolve from sin is an integral part of the ministry of the Church. Through it, the Church testifies that we are forgiven and the remission of sin is effected by the power of the Holy Spirit. Through the ministry of the priest, God restores us to peace with Himself and His people. We are reconciled. We experience the reality described by St. Paul: "It was God Who reconciled us to Himself

through Christ and gave us the work of handing on this reconciliation." (2 Cor. 5::18-20)

20. *Options for Sacrament*

It is in God's plan for us that we assist each other to be reconciled. Much can be done in parishes to facilitate this by providing
motivation and guidance. As pastors, we hope that our people will
look upon the celebration of this sacrament as a joyful event, and
will share in it more frequently. We trust, too, that more time will
be taken to prepare for it. All of us must work together to become
more aware of the social dimension of the sacrament. While absolution is normally not given to a group, except under conditions
approved by the bishop of the diocese, the first part of the celebration may take place in a group, to be followed by individual confession. Participating in this way will deepen our understanding of our
life in the Church and of our need one for another shared. There
is also a new rite for absolution for the individual penitent which
will bring new meaning to the sacrament. Parishes and dioceses now
have several options in Canada for such celebration.[5]

21. *The Family*

Parents and children, husband and wife, will grow together by
celebrating the sacrament together. In the *Come to the Father* catechetical program, children are made aware of the need to forgive and
to be forgiven. At each level of growth, they grow more ready to
experience the gift of forgiveness in richer ways. In the first three
years of the program, they are guided through their first experience
of the sacrament. In later grades, the meaning and importance of
moral choices are explained.

IV — CONCLUSION

22. *The Eucharist*

In celebrating the Eucharist, we rejoice in the Good News that
we are a community of forgiven sinners. In Lent, particularly, this
celebration should focus on our gratitude to God for His goodness
and, in a special way, for the gift of baptism and union with Jesus
and with one another. The Eucharist expresses and effects our recon-

ciliation and unity. May we celebrate in such a way that they become realities visible in our lives.

23. *Love at the Service of People*

God has taken the initiative to love us — sinners though we are (1 Jn. 4:9-10). Let us respond to His love and enter into the process of our conversion to a life of love and a commitment to justice. His grace makes this possible for those living their Christian faith. May we become a truly loving community of brothers and sisters. As the bishops expressed it in the 1974 Synod in Rome:

Let us nurture the hope that the Church, in more faithfully ful- filling the work of evangelization, will announce the total salva- tion of all, or rather our complete liberation, and from now on will start to bring this about. ... The Church, as a truly poor, pray- ing and loving community, can do much to promote the integral salvation or the full liberation of humanity. She can draw from the gospel the most profound reasons and ever new motivation to encourage generous dedication to the service of all — the poor especially, the weak and the oppressed — and to eliminate the social consequences of sin which are translated into unjust social and political structures. [6]

NOTES

1. Since this exhortation contains a lengthy reflection on the sacrament of recon- ciliation, it seems to find an appropriate insertion in this Third Section.

2. Cf. CCC Labour Day Messages, in *Do Justice!*, edit. E.F. Sheridan, SJ (Sher- brooke, QC, 1987, Éditions Paulines), *Simplicity and Sharing*, 1972; *Inequality Divides, Justice Reconciles*, 1973; *Sharing Daily Bread*, 1974; *Northern Development, at What Cost?*, 1975, Documents 33, 35, 36, 40.

3. General Synod of Bishops, Rome, 1971, *Justice in the World*, Part II, in Philip Land, SJ, *An Overview*, Pontifical Commission Justice and Peace, Vatican City, 1975.

4. Cf. CCC *Statement on the Formation of Conscience*, Section II, Document 8, above, reprinted in *National Bulletin on Liturgy*, n. 52, Jan.-Feb., 1976, CCCB Publication Serv- ices, Ottawa, K1N 7B1.

5. Cf. *The Rite of Penance*, CCC, 1975, reprinted in *National Bulletin on Liturgy*, n. 52, cf. note 4, above. Also Section III, Doc. 9, above.

6. Declaration of the Synod, Oct. 25, 1974, in *Origins* (Washington), IV, p. 308, n. 20.

Section III, Document 11

ON THE ADMISSION OF WOMEN
TO THE MINISTERIAL PRIESTHOOD

Author — The Administrative Board, the CCCB, January 26, 1977

With the approval of Pope Paul VI the Congregation for the Doctrine of the Faith has published a *Declaration* containing the official position of the Catholic Church on the Ordination of Women to the Ministerial Priesthood.[1] The main thrust of the document is to reaffirm the traditional position on the subject.

In view of the interest shown in this topic since the mid-fifties there can be no denying the significance of this *Declaration* and the interest that it will arouse. It will also arouse considerable controversy and not all will accept its findings with equanimity. The document itself mentions the "pain" which it will inflict.

In this context of importance it is of the utmost necessity that the document be read and that it be read carefully. It is the fruit of several years of study, specifically on the issues raised, and at least deserves a hearing.

The first point to which we should advert is the key declaration itself which is to be found in the last paragraph of the Introduction.

> ... the Church, in fidelity to the example of the Lord, does not consider herself authorized to admit women to Priestly Ordination... it is a position which will perhaps cause pain but whose positive value will become apparent in the long run, since it can be of help in deepening the understanding of the respective roles of men and women.[2]

This is obviously a very carefully phrased statement. Its effect is cumulative. It reflects the responsibility felt by the Church to remain faithful to the teaching and example of the Lord. Hence the negative formulation "does not consider herself authorized". In turn, this is an insistence upon the tradition in the Church dating from the beginning and never changed nor even challenged until recent times. It implies that it is not simply a decision to be made by the present leaders of the Church. To these custodians of the teaching of Christ and of the tradition of His Church the way does not appear to be open to change.

Careful persual of the document strips away much of what might be considered a rejection of the aspirations of some very devoted women and which could be interpreted as a depreciation of women in general. We do not consider that such is the case and the document opens up many horizons which need to be explored, in terms of recognizing the true equality of women without, at the same time, denying that men and women have different roles to play.

Perhaps the most frequently asserted basis for demanding ordination to the ministerial priesthood for women is that they have "a right to it". The document meets this objection directly and points out that no one has a right to the priesthood which is the decision of the Lord and a call from Him authenticated by the Church. Not all men have this "call" and no one can say, whether man or woman, that he or she has a "right".[3]

It also rejects the assumption that the priesthood is some sort of superior position. It clearly underlines the teaching that the priesthood is a service, not a promotion to superiority. A most revealing phrase comes at the very end of the document in which it is written, "The greatest in the Kingdom of Heaven are not the ministers but the saints."[4]

Finally we wish to state that the Canadian Bishops will pursue their study of the role of women in the Church with even greater interest. Already many ministerial and other roles are opening to women in our midst. Our attempt will be to emphasize and promote the true equality of women, to encourage their positive and special gifts in the leadership of the Church and in spreading the Kingdom without necessarily postulating an identity of roles.

NOTES

1. Sacred Congregation for the Doctrine of the Faith, *Declaration on the Admission of Women to the Ministerial Priesthood,* in *Origins* (Washington, 1977), VI, n. 33, p. 517.
2. *Op. cit.,* Introduction, p. 519.
3. *Ibid.,* n. 6, p. 523.
4. *Ibid.,* n. 6, p. 523.

Section III, Document 12

THE MEANING OF SUNDAY IN A PLURALISTIC SOCIETY

Author — The Canadian Conference of Catholic Bishops, September, 1986

INTRODUCTION

1. Recent court challenges to Sunday closing laws have renewed the debate across Canada on whether to maintain Sunday as a day free of commerce. In a pluralistic and multi-cultural society, can we continue to keep Sunday special without binding all to a "sectarian Christian ideal"?[1] By opening stores on Sunday to provide better service to busy customers, are we helping Canadians, as many business people argue, or does this impose significant social costs on everyone.

2. The debate in the courts makes these questions particularly urgent, but their implications reach far beyond the specific legal cases in hand. They affect the very understanding we have of Canadian society and culture. In other words, they involve value choices about the kind of society we want to build in the future. Our desire to share our own thoughts as bishops on these questions is therefore in direct continuity with our other statements on the social and economic structures of this country.[2]

3. The reflections that follow are meant, first of all, to help our Catholic sisters and brothers to appreciate better the link between the Christian Lord's Day and Sunday as a common day of rest and renewal in a secular society. Our message may also be helpful for other Christians and anyone interested in this question, as the Sunday shopping debate invites all Canadians to discuss and shape the future direction of our society and culture. We hope this deepened

understanding of the issues will help Catholics, and others as well, to participate with greater clarity in public policy debates on the place of Sunday in our society and, at the same time, to live the full meaning of this day with greater commitment.

4. We will begin by reviewing the relationship between the Lord's Day and Sunday in a pluralistic society. In a second and third step, we will explore the need for all Canadians to enjoy a common day of rest, a day when we reflect on the ultimate purpose in our individual and collective lives. We will then try to explain why, even in our pluralistic country, Sunday can still be this day of common rest and renewal. Finally, we will show how the Christian celebration of Sunday as the Lord's Day strengthens the secular vision of this day, and we will close by suggesting practical actions that flow from this perspective for Catholic people and groups.

THE NEED TO REVIEW THE MEANING OF SUNDAY
IN A SECULAR SOCIETY

5. Most Christians celebrate the first day of the week as the day on which Christ rose from the dead. On this day, we acknowledge our continued dependence on God Who created all things and profess in a special way the lordship of Christ in our daily lives. On Sunday, our original feast day, we come together to hear the Word of God and to offer thanksgiving and praise. We celebrate our salvation in Christ and await in joyful anticipation the fullness of life in God's eternal glory.

6. Many Canadians share this outlook. They would like the laws of the land to reflect this vision, especially the Christian desire to worship and to refrain from work on this day. However, in our multicultural and pluralistic society there are others who do not share this belief. They honour a different day of the week as their day of worship and see no need at all for setting aside Sunday as a day of praise and thanksgiving to God. Given the changed nature of our society, it is no longer appropriate to protect Sunday closing laws on the basis that most Christians hold it to be the Day of the Lord. However, this does not mean that Sunday should become less special, for Canadians in general of for Christians in particular.

7. There are several other profoundly human reasons why one day of the week should remain free of commerce. These considerations

arise from a vision of society that people can share whether or not they believe in the lordship of Jesus. They relate to our common desire to organize and adapt the whole labour process in such a way "as to respect the requirements of the person and his or her forms of life".[3] Our own view of Sunday as the Lord's Day confirms and strengthens this secular vision but does not replace it. In other words, keeping Sunday special is more than a "sectarian Christian concern". It is an important step in our efforts to build social and economic structures that respect "the social, economic, cultural and spiritual needs of the whole person."[4]

A COMMON DAY OF REST

8. Most people will readily admit that in our hectic, competitive society, we need at least one day a week to rest from the hardships of daily work. Indeed, as Pope John Paul II states in his encyclical *On Human Work*, we have a *right* to rest.[5] This right includes at least one regular weekly day of rest and also a longer period of holidays once a year. As individuals, we need time to renew and restore our spent physical and mental energies.

9. While it is necessary in the first place to be able to enjoy a day of rest, it is equally important to hold this day in common. As social beings we need in our lives the experience of community and communication with others for our growth and development. A common day of rest helps us maintain these relationships and strengthen interpersonal communication. For each to select a day off at random would further increase the dangers of the widespread privatization and individualism in our society.

10. This opportunity to experience and build community is especially important for families. Sunday has come to be the only day on which family members and friends can be certain of being together. If days off are scattered throughout the week, working mothers and fathers, especially in the retail business, will not be able to be together with children on the weekend. Removing this opportunity would place a further strain on the family as the basic institution of our society. Families need a common day of rest to help them strengthen the bonds of the couple and the communication between parents and their children. As the Union of Ontario Retail Workers said some time ago: "Sure, we might get another day off

during the week, but we all know that Monday, Tuesday or Wednesday can seldom be a family day. And since our friends or relatives are usually working anyway, our days off during the week are no real substitute for week-ends."[6]

A DAY OF INNER RENEWAL

11. A common day of rest does more than restore our physical and mental energies. True rest, repose, leisure, or as our Jewish sisters and brothers would say, shalom, renews us in our whole being. It puts us at peace with God, with ourselves and with our fellow human beings. Thus our day of rest is a time for reviewing the basic values in our lives. It lets us stand back from our daily preoccupations to focus on our highest goals and to follow the call of our conscience with renewed commitment. It becomes a concrete sign and symbol for what is most important or holy for us. In this sense, we can continue to speak of the sanctity of Sunday, of its holiness or sacredness for all Canadians.

12. Such distance from everyday life does not mean that on Sunday we should flee the world for some private sphere of undisturbed, inner peace. Rather, it is a precious moment of recollection to help us serve others during the week with even greater commitment and courage. It helps us to make adjustments in our daily lives and to become whole again. It is truly a time for re-creation, for making a fresh start in all our actions.

13. Through our common day of rest, we also affirm the values that are constituent of our society. It spells out our personal and collective vision of humanity and the world. At present, economic interests tend to dominate our society. Wealth and commercial success are seen as the keys to happiness and to a good society. The move to permit shopping on all days of the week seems to reflect this emphasis on material prosperity. It can be seen as another sign of the exaggerated importance we give to trade and commercial activity. Even many leisure and sports events have become heavily commercialized and fail to encourage human growth by their emhasis on consumption rather than active participation. In this way, more freedom to buy and sell can mean less freedom to develop deep and lasting human relationships that reach beyond superficial economic interests.

14. In limiting commercial activity on this day, we give witness to our belief that as a society we value people as more than cogs in the production process. We affirm that fullness of life means more than efficiency and profit-making. We signify that true human life goes far beyond economic considerations and is open to transcendence, that is to higher and ultimate meaning for all human beings. As Cardinal Hume said so well in the recent British debate on Sunday shopping:

> Our principle is that there is more to being human than supply and demand; there is more to social life than trading and commerce. For all its shortcomings, the regulated Sunday is a sign which points society beyond itself and affords people the opportunity of standing back, of renewing themselves. That is the meaning of recreation without which human beings are not truly human — they are drudges. Genuine humanism requires such a perspective.[7]

15. Sunday's emphasis on the human person also points to life as gift rather than as ongoing challenge. In our industrial or post-industrial society, we face enormous pressures from the surrounding culture to build, to improve, to be active and constantly "on the go". As a people's day, Sunday can be a day without the push to achieve, to produce, to be "useful" and efficient. It can be a day of playfulness and simplicity, of contemplation and wonder, of praise and enjoyment of life. Rather than doing different things on Sunday, we should consider *doing* less so as to *be* more. On Sunday, we should rest from our day-to-day efforts to change the imperfections of our own world and should, instead, rejoice in the beauty and splendour of creation.

SUNDAY AS OUR COMMON DAY OF REST AND RENEWAL

16. Many Canadians will accept the need for a common day of rest from work and commercial activity. They may even support the need for a common day of reflection and renewal. It is less obvious why this day should be Sunday.

17. In our pluralistic society, the choice of Sunday as the day of renewl for all is rooted more in tradition than in religious conviction. Many groups, especially in the labour movement, have emphasized repeatedly that Sundays are our traditional days of pause. In

our society, the observance of Sunday as a holiday is more firmly entrenched in people's habits than any other day of the week. Sundays off are part of our culture, a culture that Christians have shaped in the past and in which they continue to take their rightful place in full and free cooperation with people from other religious and world views.

18. Maintaining Sunday as our common day of rest does not exclude special respect and consideration for people who wish to celebrate another day as their day of spiritual and physical renewal. We should be able to devise laws that will not penalize people with different beliefs as long as these laws protect the shared experience of leisure and rest for the majority. It should also be possible to devise shopping regulations that permit the purchase of basic necessities without destroying Sunday's emphasis on people and playfulness.

19. Finally, it is clear that there will always be some members of the work force who will have to work on Sunday to provide essential services for the public. They deserve our understanding and appreciation for their contribution to the common good. Even for these workers, however, we should carefully protect and respect their right to enjoy the full benefit of Sundays, at least on an alternating basis.

THE CHRISTIAN CELEBRATION OF SUNDAY

20. In the long run, Sunday will retain its character as a special day not through the force of law but because people wish it to remain so. Until recently, we have tended to take the special place of this day for granted. All too often — and for too long — we have simply gone with the tide. Our own willingness to shop on Sunday, when the opportunity has arisen, has helped to make Sunday more profit-oriented and less human.

21. As Christians, we are called in a special way to live the full meaning of Sunday.[8] To begin, we will continue to honour Sunday as the Lord's Day whether commercial activity is permitted or not. Following the example of the early Church, we will always come together on this day to remember and celebrate the death and resurrection of Jesus. It will remain for all Christians a day of extra time to spend with God in prayer, spiritual reading and Christian conversation. In the name of all creation, we will continue to give thanks to God for His blessings, and to pray for the welfare and salvation of all human beings.

22. For Catholics, Sunday's Eucharistic celebration is the highest form of praise and prayer. There, the whole community comes together

> ... to celebrate the life, the death and the resurrection of Christ; to listen to His Word and to find therein life and light; to share in the communion of His body and His blood; to discover with one another the manner in which the Lord prepares for them and with them a new heaven and a new earth. [9]

This celebration of the Eucharist on Sunday is the centre and culmination of the whole life of the Catholic community, especially the parish community. In the words of the General Instruction of the Roman Missal: "Mass celebrated by any community is important, but especially for the parish community which represents the universal Church at a given time and place. This is particularly true of Mass on the Lord's day." [10]

23. Our participation in Sunday's liturgy does not end at the church door. We would seriously misunderstand our Christian Sunday obligation if we were to see it exclusively as a duty to attend church service. Going to church on Sunday is the highlight and source of a changed outlook on life throughout the week, but especially on this day.

24. Strengthened by our celebration of God's new creation in Christ, we will unite with our brothers and sisters from other faiths in renewing, in recreating, especially on Sunday, all our mental and physical energies. Moreover, our belief in the dignity of the human person as the image of God calls us to make a special effort on this day to identify areas where we have let material aspirations replace human values in our personal lives or in the life of society around us. As followers of Christ Who calls all people by name, we should try, especially on Sunday, to be more fully ourselves as persons and to pursue those activities which make society more human.

25. Sunday is also the day when we celebrate our adoption as God's children and our membership in His holy people, the Church. Especially on Sunday we are called to carry this new togetherness in Christ into all our relationships, be they the bonds of our family, our neighbourhood or of the community at large. Sunday should be the day when we do not count the minutes, when we visit others, when we take time to listen to each other and to talk with others.

26. Finally, our belief in God's saving action helps us to step back on Sunday from our daily concerns and responsibilities. Before our

own doing, Christ sends us His grace to meet the challenges of the week with confidence and joy. For this gift and the many blessings of creation, we praise God in contemplation and playful rest.

SOME SUGGESTIONS TO HELP KEEP SUNDAY SPECIAL

27. Obviously, our first priority as Christians will be our own personal respect for the true meaning of Sunday. The reflections we have shared in this message are meant, above all, to inspire and encourage our own personal commitment to this day.

28. As an expression and extension of this commitment, we see a special responsibility for Catholic lay people and other Christians to participate in the public debates about Sunday shopping. One may think here of letters and phone calls to the press and the electronic media. Catholic lay organizations especially may present briefs to political leaders when the opportunity arises. Whenever possible we should try to work with other Christian churches and religious or secular groups who share the same or similar aspirations for Canadian society. Such actions will ensure that the views and expectations of Christians as citizens and as Canadian consumers are considered in political and economic decision-making.

29. Not only politicians but business people, too, should learn about our vision for Canadian society. Here again, letter writing and phone calls by individuals and groups will be very important. More than that, we should not hesitate to give our practical business support to those employers and employees who respect a common day of rest and renewal. Finally, there is a special responsibility and challenge for Catholic and Christian business leaders to respect Sunday in their own business practices and to work for similar goals within their professional associations and relationships.

CONCLUSION

30. Sunday closing is a deep social concern which affects the very fabric of our society. Far from being a "religious" issue, in the narrow sense of the word, it has profound implications for all Canadians whether they be Christians or not. Surely, whatever the final

outcome of the present debate on Sunday closing, it should make our society more people-oriented, more human and less stressful for individuals, families and the community at large. As citizens of this country, Christians have an important role to play in achieving this goal.

NOTES

1. In April, 1985, the Supreme Court ruled that the federal *Lord's Day Act* "to the extent that it binds all to a sectarian Christian ideal, works a form of coercion inimical to the spirit of the Charter".

2. Cf. *Ethical Choices and Political Challenges,* and many other statements prepared for the Bishops' Conference by the Episcopal Commission for Social Affairs, in *Do Justice!,* edit. E.F. Sheridan, SJ (Sherbrooke, P.Q., Éditions Paulines, 1987), p. 411.

3. John Paul II, *On Human Work,* in *The Papal Encyclicals,* edit. Claudia Carlen, IHM (Wilmington, N.C., McGrath Publishing), V, 318, n. 92.

4. *Op. cit.,* in note 2, above, n. 13, p. 416.

5. *Op. cit.,* in note 3, above, *loc. cit.* n. 93, p. 318.

6. *Ontario Retail Council Newsletter,* Winter 1980, p. 2. Diligent search has failed to locate such Council or Newsletter. *Editor's note.*

7. Basil Cardinal Hume, *Sunday Trading,* in *Briefing* (Newsletter of Bishops' Conference of England and Wales, 39 Eccleston Sq., London, SW1 PD), March 14, 1986, p. 90.

8. Issue #43 of the *National Bulletin on Liturgy, Sunday Belongs to the Lord,* takes a complete look at the celebration of Sunday, with special emphasis on the parish community. The National Office for Liturgy has also prepared a one-sheet leaflet to highlight the meaning of Sunday for Catholics. Both available from Publications Service, CCCB, 90 Parent Ave., Ottawa, K1N 7B1.

9. CCCB Plenary *Statement On Sunday Observance,* April 27, 1972, in Section III, Document 9, above.

10. In *The Sacramentary,* CCCB Publications Service, cf. note 8, above.

Section IV

JUSTICE – WAR – PEACE

Document 1

STRANGERS IN OUR MIDST[1]

Author — The Episcopal Commission for Migrants and Tourism,
the CCCB, September 27, 1977

Now that Canada has a new Immigration Act,[2] we, as pastors,
wish to share with fellow members of the Roman Catholic Church
some thoughts about the spirit that should prevail between citizens
of this land and strangers in our midst. We believe it particularly
necessary in this regard to recall some basic values that come to us
through revelation and the Church's teaching and experience. These
should influence our attitudes and policies with regard to all immigrants, and shape our pastoral programs for immigrants who share
our religious faith.

Under the new Act, this country will continue to receive immigrants and refugees. One aim of the Act is to make their entry
ever more fair and efficient. It also provides, however, for greater
control and limitation of numbers, to be decided year by year.
Furthermore, government officials are given broad power to make
regulations whose effects will need careful watching.

We say this because in Parliament and outside it the argument
has been heard that, for our economic good, this country should

reduce the number of immigrants, as if they were to blame for current economic difficulties or would aggravate them. In addition, a number of local incidents have revealed tensions over the arrival of newcomers whose presence challenges us to think and act differently. Many Canadians, it seems, are far from open-minded about the numbers and kinds of immigrants and refugees we will admit in the future.

It is important to understand that people uproot themselves and move mainly because of a sense of relative deprivation. They emigrate, or flee as refugees, because they perceive that their life chances would be better elsewhere. Because ours is seen as a rich and pleasant country, people want to come here and we risk being extremely selfish in our efforts to control their entry or to exclude them.

This is not the first time that, as pastors, we have spoken of the current anti-immigrant mood. We are in fact returning to a theme developed by our Episcopal Commission for Social Affairs. In July, 1975, they wrote:

> Fear of people seems to lie at the root of this willingness to limit or exclude newcomers. They are seen as competitors for jobs, goods and services, and so as threats to our present life styles and future aspirations. Our reflex, therefore, is to try to protect and maintain what we have by excluding others. [3]

We return to these reflections for one main reason. There is a heightening of tensions among our people, and an increasing need for Christians in this country to reflect on the need for harmony among different peoples and on the role of Christians in promoting that harmony.

We begin by asking what specific contribution Christians can make in such a situation. We would like to describe that contribution as a particular vision. It deals with the kind of society we believe we should be seeking. It also indicates the attitudes individuals should strive to make their own in their daily actions and interactions.

Christians are called to build on earth a society that foreshadows and is itself a sign of the promised New Jerusalem, the city of God's kingdom come. We have been told that this New Jerusalem will be an open city, with gates on every side to receive a multitude coming from every nation (Rev. 21:12-14).

The image illustrates the spirit in which we should be open and hospitable to newcomers. In this, we are heirs to the ancient admonition of Yahweh: "If a stranger lives with you in your land, do not molest him. You must count him as one of your own countrymen and love him as yourself — for you were once strangers yourselves in the land of Egypt" (Lev. 19:33-34).

Some might say that such ideals are dated or unrealistic. It is evident, however, that as life is going, we are more and more called to become a single people, without boundaries. Our view of the world expands; our awareness takes in the entire planet. No longer should we think of strangers, but only of sisters and brothers. That is just what the Church aspires to. In the words of the Second Vatican Council: "Christ and the Church... transcend every particularity of race or nation and therefore cannot be considered foreign anywhere or to anybody".[4]

This movement towards universal brotherhood stems from the Gospel and the apostolic writings. In the Old Testament, God is presented as "defender of the stranger," and what is prefigured in the Old Testament is explicitly taught in the New, in terms of the universality of mutual love.

Jesus, despite established custom, speaks to a Samaritan woman and asks her for help (Jn. 4:7). He praises the faith of a Roman centurion (Mt. 8:10-12) and of a Canaanite women (Mt. 15:28). He contrasts the attitude of a priest and levite to that of a Samaritan who "proved himself a neighbour to the man who fell into the brigands' hands" (Lk. 10:32-37). He asks His disciples to love everyone, even their enemies (Mt. 5:43-48; Lk. 6:27-36). Finally, at the Last Judgment, He will say: "I was a stranger and you made me welcome", or "I was a stranger and you never welcomed me." (Mt. 25:35-43).

Without denying human diversity, St. Paul points to the unity of all in Christ. "There is neither Jew nor Greek, neither slave nor free, neither male nor female; for you are all one in Christ Jesus." (Gal. 3:28 and cf. Col. 3:11)

What, then, will be our response to people who wish to migrate to escape deprivation and to better their life chances among us?

We should ask the Lord to help us overcome fear of newcomers and strangers, whether from outside Canada or within. Let us pray that the kind of society we build may be less scarred by greed and self-seeking and marked rather by solidarity and sharing, by openness, hope and love.

As one step in building a just world, we must share with our sisters and brothers who are in greater need. That God's love may abide in all of us, Let us not fear to change our own life styles and our use and control of resources, so that created goods may be justly redistributed.

When strangers arrive in our midst, a great spirit of openness and welcome is required of the Church. Canadian Church members have given commendable example in this regard but more can always be done. A conversion of love is called for. People are really welcomed only to the extent that they are made to feel loved, with all their own cultural values, their history and the hopes they bring with them.

To rise to this love, prayer is the first requisite, for love is a gift from God, and love for our migrant sisters and brothers is a particular gift. At the same time, this kind of love will enrich us, moving us to specific acts of thoughtfulness and self-sacrifice, to think first of those whom we should welcome and assist.

Let us avoid anything of a domineering or patronizing attitude. Rather, let everything be done with them, for them, to enable them. Often they are constrained to a humiliating conformity in their work and social life. Let them feel the Church's respect for their freedom and dignity.

Account must be taken of their roots in their homelands; from them we can all draw riches. But migrants must also be helped to adapt to their new country. Here again, love comes first: migrants should fall in love with their new home. If there are mutual bonds of friendship, trust and respect, everything will be possible.

We must realize that racism and exploitation of migrants will disappear only to the extent that all feel themselves really sisters and brothers in one human family. If there is a climate of conversion and reconciliation, it will be easier to discover what to do to overcome racism and exploitation of migrants and to help them in everyday life.

This must be a continuing effort, in parishes, in various social groups. Particular attention should be paid to events that have special meaning in the lives of migrants themselves.

Our deepening social awareness has led us to see the need for something more than individual conversion. Personal renewal willl not be truly effective unless it is accompanied by structural transformations. For our attitudes not only shape our institutions; they are in turn molded by these same institutions. There will continue to be masked racism and exploitation of immigrants unless there are changes in social policies and structures touching such matters as housing, jobs and job security, wages and credit. Labour unions, credit unions and other co-operatives have much to do in this regard, as do voluntary and local organizations.

Some particularly important new public policy matters have been opened up by the new Act. Once each year the Minister of Immigration will have to tell Parliament "the number of immigrants that the government of Canada deems it appropriate to admit during any specified period of time." To arrive at that figure, the provincial governments are to be consulted. It therefore becomes imperative for Christians to be constantly aware of and involved in this new decision-making process, at both federal and provincial levels. Christians, to be generous and openhearted as they should, have genuine responsibilities to be vigilant regarding the regulations under the new Act, and informed of their effects on the dignity and rights of immigrants and refugees.

In these and other ways, in fidelity to Our Lord's command that we love one another, we must work together so that the rights and needs of every person may be more fully recognized, the demands of justice and love more fully realized.

NOTES

1. Cf. other related statements of the Canadian Conference of Catholic Bishops in *Do Justice!*, edit. E.F. Sheridan, SJ (Éditions Paulines, Sherbrooke, P.Q., 1987), Documents 8, 13, 39, 41.

2. Bill C-24, 1977.

3. *On Immigration and Population Policies, op. cit.,* note 1, above, p. 272.

4. Second Vatican Council, *Decree on the Missionary Activity of the Church,* n. 8.

Section IV, Document 2

SUBMISSION TO THE COMMITTEE ON PORNOGRAPHY AND PROSTITUTION APPOINTED BY THE MINISTER OF JUSTICE

Author — The Canadian Conference of Catholic Bishops,
          March, 1984

The hallmark of public statements by the Canadian Conference of Catholic Bishops has always been a deep concern for the dignity of each human being and for the well-being of society in general. [1] This same profound respect for life in all its manifold forms urges us as spiritual leaders of a major segment of Canadian society to appear before your timely committee to highlight once again the inherent beauty but also the vulnerability of human nature and to encourage the Federal Government through your efforts effectively to protect and to promote the dignity of all people.

Recognizing the government's responsibility to legislate for believers and non-believers alike we will submit, for the most part, considerations and arguments of universal validity. Indeed, experience tells us that most Canadians share these views. We will begin by highlighting the meaning and inner dynamic of human sexuality as seen by many philosophers, scientists and theologians today. Such a vision of sexuality is in fact central to dealing successfully with the complex legal and social problems of pornography and prostitution.

I — THE MEANING OF HUMAN SEXUALITY

Each human being is marked profoundly by his or her sexuality. The direction of this influence however, is shaped for the most part by the way each of us responds to this precious gift. The multi-faceted reality of sexuality can be a central component of rich and lasting relationships. It can also offer occasion for shameless exploitation and degradation of others, especially of women.

1 — The Ambivalence of Sexuality

Sexuality is sometimes seen as a simple biological function, such as eating or drinking. No doubt biology plays its part. More importantly however, sexuality is a social reality that places us in relationship and possible communication with other people.

This relationship can, however, be abused and perverted into its opposite. Thus the original goodness of sexuality ("In the image of God He created him, male and female He created them... and it was very good" Gen. 1:27-31) often enough leads to domination rather than true encounter between persons (Gen. 3:16). Because of this inherent ambivalence, human sexuality needs the guiding and humanizing influence of culture and civilization. Culture, human history, and Jesus Christ Himself, invite us to move beyond the biological reality of male and female to a truly human relationship of man and woman.

2 — Sexuality as the Experience of Otherness

As men and women we are different from each other. Thus, there is at first the threat of separation and division between people because of this otherness. Inasmuch however, as we accept and appreciate this fundamental and seminal difference, sexuality can lead us to accept others in their newness, and more radical still, enables us to create new life. In this way, sexuality is the basic force that makes possible encounter, communion and new life among people. Thus, in human sexuality we find at once the threat of radical division and the promise of true encounter. Failure to recognize and appreciate this ambivalence would mean failure to live our sexuality as human beings. Whenever we close ourselves to all but our own desires, whenever we treat others as mere means to our own pleasure or profit, we deny their personhood and their fundamental right, guaranteed by numerous charters of rights and freedoms, to be different from us.

Sexuality does include the physical and pleasurable desire of union with the other person, even though it cannot be reduced to instinct alone. Sexual pleasure, however, which in itself signifies joy in life and the grateful acceptance of the gift of life, can also tempt to injury and violence. This threat of violence arises from an aggressivity inherent in sexuality. Even more so however, it stems from the fact that others can threaten our very existence if they fail to welcome us as persons and to accept us in our otherness. Defensiveness, withdrawal from others and even violence towards others can have their origin in this ambivalence of human sexuality.

Pornography and prostitution must be seen in this broad context. Pornography separates our bodies into different segments and is therefore contrary to real enjoyment and acceptance of life. Prostitution, among other things, prevents its participants from accepting the creative risk of sexuality in its deepest sense. Both realities are marked by the rejection of true otherness so that anyone can be partner in this relationship as long as they pay or participate in the play acting.

3 — Sexuality and Pleasure

To seek pleasure can mean many things. It can mean affirming the other person in his or her dignity but it can also mean the denial of personhood. Pleasure can mean withdrawal from others as persons and from true human encounter. It can signify fear of the other in his or her difference rather than acceptance and enjoyment of that individuality. The other thus becomes an instrument of pleasure or profit to be exploited at will.

Once praised as the reward of liberation from social and personal constraints, sexual pleasure can become itself repressive and weaken rather than strengthen our freedom. Pornography and prostitution become in this way "opium of the people", a new enslavement creating a false world of fantasy, unreality and progressive addiction to sexual desire and pleasure.

4 — The Unity of Body and Mind

Against a false dualism that has long burdened Christian tradition, we cannot forget that *we are our bodies* (1 Cor. 6:12-20). Thus, we would be seriously mistaken if we were to believe that we can use our bodies or those of others as simple means without involving at the same time our very personhood or that of others. Physical pleasure as well as pain have an influence on and are influenced by the totality of the person. Sexual activity in all its forms involves our whole person and the very depth of our personality. For Christians, the body takes on even added importance and value as the icon and sacrament of the Spirit of Jesus Christ living in us (cf. 1 Cor. 6:19-20). Such a belief further strengthens our respect and reverence for the integrity and value of our bodies.

Sexual language expresses and determines the totality of our being. Sexuality in its ambivalent potential of openness or separation is at the core of human interaction and communion without which we cannot exist, neither in our childhood nor as adults. True sexuality is meant to be an experience of creative growth. This experience is found above all in the procreation of new life which can become the privileged moment of transforming otherness into communion and therefore of humanizing such encounter.

In our view, the radical evil of pornography and prostitution and hence the urgent need for action against its pernicious influence arises from the very fact that both realities go radically counter to the true meaning of sexuality by decreasing rather than augmenting its humanizing power in our personal and social history. This central point in the debate was already made by Archbishop Pocock in a statement of Dec. 3, 1976, when he said:

It is through our God-given sexuality that we as human beings can reach out to one another in love. It is in sexual union that a couple can express to one another tenderness, intimacy and permanent fidelity. The public and profitable exploitation of the sexual, so common around us, is a direct betrayal of the basic values of sexuality itself... What was intended by the Creator to be most precious is trivialized. What was created to be most deeply personal is dehumanized.[2]

II — PORNOGRAPHY

The term "pornography" comes from the Greek words *porne,* a prostitute, and *graphe,* a depiction or description. Pornography can thus be defined as the pictorial or literary representation, for pleasure or profit, of degrading, often violent, sexual behaviour, real or simulated, for pleasure or profit. Another way of making the same point would be to define pornography as that which exploits and dehumanizes sex so that human beings are treated as things, mere sex objects.

1 — The Perversion of Pornography

Our Episcopal Commission for Social Communications recently summarized the evil of pornography in this way:

> Pornography perverts human sexuality. The marvelous world of interpersonal relationships, human communication and love is reduced to a means by which one human being is exploited by another. This is not an innocent distraction; it is an offence against the dignity and rights of human persons.[3]

Pornography is therefore not only a *personal* moral evil but also a *social* evil. It promotes a vision of sexuality gravely detrimental to life in society.

As we mentioned earlier, our sexuality and its manifold expressions play a major part in the way we become responsible members of society and achieve mature adulthood. Pornography seriously impedes or even blocks this development.

> Pornography in all its forms contributes to a philosophy, a life-style, an attitude towards sexuality, in which another person is seen as an object, a means of fulfilling an urge or desire. It is a selfish sexuality devoid of love. When one human being is sold as pornography all are diminished and offended.[4]

Moreover, pornography often suggests violence as a source of satisfaction and pleasure both for the victim and/or the aggressor. Any serious critic will agree that it is impossible for society to function well and at the same time to condone the presentation of violence as an acceptable and pleasurable means of achieving one's goals. Life in society is predicated on the stringent control of our latent tendency to use violent means to achieve our desires.

It is sometimes said that pornography helps to diminish violence by providing a fantasy release for the aggressive tendencies of its consumers. Available evidence however, points increasingly in the opposite direction. Pornographic material inclines its consumers to accept violence, to devalue and even to deny the dignity of others and to give rein to our tendencies to dominate others, tendencies that are often the effect of affective and sexual deprivation or of economic, political and social powerlessness.

Pornography is socially pernicious as leading us to accept and even to promote attitudes of submission or domination. Such attitudes are indeed latent in all of us, but in our view and in the view of most Canadians they are not to be encouraged. They need effective social deterrence as do any tendencies that might lead to theft or aggression.

2 — Pornography and Social Progress

The recent growth of pornography in our country parallels a disturbing social trend towards greater violence and disregard for people. As a society we can hardly let this development go unchecked, especially in view of the fact that it glorifies the domination of women and children. At a time when society recognizes that the status of women should be acknowledged and their image enhanced, it seems particularly contradictory that pornography should be permitted to propagate a denigrating and especially offensive stereotype of women. Moreover, pornography not only reflects social development but actively influences the evolution of society. Thus we can rightfully ask whether governments can tolerate the risk of giving free rein to an industry which goes directly counter to the perhaps still imperfect but nevertheless significant humanization of the man-woman relationship, an improvement that has been achieved through the efforts of many centuries. To yield to the power of this industry would be an especially crass example of putting profits before people.

3 — Pornography and Freedom of Expression

Freedom of expression is a fundamental right inasmuch as it permits critical comment. It is not meant to serve financial profit, but to prevent governments and other institutions from reducing or denying to others reasonable opportunities for critical questioning. Freedom of expression is a right inasmuch as it serves true progress and humanization. It is not an abstract right without limits. Individual rights such as the right to pleasure or to free expression may be limited by a more fundamental right of others to be different. It is revealing that the right to freedom of expression is often claimed for egoistic personal benefit, especially by those who have the financial means to dominate others.

An important function of the state is to protect the rights of the underprivileged. Freedom of expression must be placed in this basic perspective. The use of censorship may be unfortunate but it is surely a lesser evil than the exploitation or encouragement of hate and dehumanization. All expressions must consider and respect the human dignity of the people to whom they are addressed. Freedom of expression is subject to the more fundamental rights of respect for persons, justice and the need to grow in humanity. Limiting freedom of expression can be a sign of respect for these rights.

4 — The Nihilism of Pornography

In sum then, pornography can only be considered as *anti-life*, harmful to the dignity of persons and to the development of sane and lasting personal relationships as the basis of healthy family life. Because it fails to accept sexuality as a unique gift for understanding and of creating new life in the image of the other person, pornography is *anti-sex*. Because it impedes or even prevents true personality growth and encourages violence and hate, pornography is *anti-social*. Finally, pornography is *anti-culture* because it degrades and destroys rather than ennobles and enriches as does true art and literature.

III — PROSTITUTION

Prostitution cannot be defined simply "as the provision of sexual services for financial reward".[5] Such a limited definition overlooks the fact that at least two people are involved, not to mention the surrounding milieu and the involvement of the police and judicial system. It is rather revealing of the way we perceive the problem that our language has no special name for the other partner of this relationship.

I — The Two-fold Focus of Prostitution

Prostitution should be defined as a transient relationship wherein the actors exchange money for sexual relations. Such a definition recognizes the implications of both the client and the prostitute without denying, of course, the unreal and impersonal nature of this contact. Other factors also come into play, such as one's self-image and one's place in society. The specifying characteristic of prostitution, however, is the exchange of money on the one hand and sexual availability on the other.

Often enough prostitution is explained and excused as a response to physical need. The phenomenon of prostitution goes much deeper however. The client asks for the play acting of another person who offers sexual availability but without the demands and the risks of encounter and mutual self-giving which characterize human sexuality. Thus prostitution, especially legalized prostitution — which we feel to be totally unacceptable — "institutionalizes the concept that access to a woman's body is a right given to men by money, if not by God, and that sexuality is a service women ought not to refuse to civilized men."[6] It may have been possible at one time to claim certain church authorities for such a position. This, however, is no longer possible today if we consider the teaching of the Second Vatican Council.[7] As the Economic and Social Council of the United Nations has stated in almost the very words of Vatican II: "Prostitution as the slavery of women and children is incompatible with the dignity of human persons and their fundamental rights."[8]

2 — The Personal and Social Harm of Prostitution

Predicated on illusion, play acting and a refusal of truly human communication with others, prostitution harms both the client and the prostitute. It undermines the equal dignity of men, women and children. It goes counter to the vision of sexuality as described earlier where each person is enriched and grows through communion with others. Prostitution fails to use sexual relationships as an opportunity for greater humanization and especially denies the highest expression of this humanization, the gift of life to a new person.

Prostitution is a form of consumerism where personal inter-action is reduced to the fulfillment of egoistic needs and fantasies. Like pornography, prostitution disregards the other person in his or her otherness and uses "it" as a thing. The client is reduced to a source of money and the prostitute to a sexual fantasy.

Finally, prostitution is also a form of institutionalized violence wherein some are abandoned to protect others. It is not without reason that prostitutes are often victims of contempt and extortion, of physical violence and even murder. They become the scapegoats for personal, economic, political and social problems. We seriously delude ourselves however, if we believe that sexual satisfaction or even aggression can be the answer to our unfulfilled desires in life and to our need for personal recognition.

IV — LAW AND MORALITY

Governments recognize their responsibility for the conditions of community life in a society. These conditions however, and therefore the responsibilities of government, extend to the conditions of physical life. If we *are* our bodies and if our integration into society takes place above all through our bodies, our physical activities and their presentation in public have an impact on the way we become members of society and therefore on the future of society itself. This reality holds true even more so for sexual activities as sexual relationships ensure the continued survival of a society and have a major impact on the well-being of its members.

In this regard, governments must do more than simply adjust laws to social realities, especially in areas of public disagreement. Such a flight from responsibility would go counter to their very mandate.

Governments have a responsibility to encourage all citizens to promote the common good. Of course, such encouragement will not be by force but relying on persuasion in full respect for the freedom of each individual.

As legislators, governments should not impose on a pluralistic society the moral views of a particular group. Nevertheless, they remain responsible for governing in such a way that the well-being of society and its progress in humanity are served, as defined by the duly-elected government of the day. In this sense then, the role of law and government is to help us do better. It tries to protect and advance specific values, often codified as human rights. It helps us enjoy our freedoms in an increasingly complex world where the protection of the weakest remains a central responsibility of legislators. Hence, the purpose and goal of government remains the protection of the common good; i.e., of those social conditions that help each person, families and other groups to achieve their own fulfillment as fully as possible.

This understanding of the role of government underlies the purpose of criminal law as defined in a recent publication of the Federal Department of Justice itself, namely "to contribute to the maintenance of a just, peaceful and safe society...".[9] In other words, three basic values are identified as central to the well-being of Canadian society and proposed as guiding principles for our legislators and laws. Criminal laws, like all others, are legitimated not of and by themselves, but according to the basic options and goals we have chosen as a society.

This basic question of what are our common goals as a society arises when we try to define the limits of the right to freedom of expression. Is this an absolute freedom or is it meant to protect other rights or realities, such as the right to political dissidence, respect for others, protection of the under-privileged, social progress, justice and others? Freedom of expression is meant to protect our rights from the unjustified needs for security or profit of a small group. And yet we cannot fail to recognize that unrestricted freedom would eliminate all possibility of achieving the goals we have chosen as a society. Government is responsible for defining the rules for our social life and setting the limits of personal and social action that are still compatible with the well-being of individuals and of society. This intervention, especially in the area of criminal law, will be held to the necessary minimum. Nevertheless, legislators may, for example, be forced to choose between the value of some freedom of expression and the survival of society, or between some economic need and the necessity of improving relationships between men, women and children.

These considerations lead us back to the responsibilities of governments with regard to pornography and prostitution. Both of these realities are in conflict with profound human values. As we have seen, they can deform the development of the human person and threaten those human relationships on which society is based. Thus, while religious views reinforce and defend these values, they can in no way be identified and therefore disclaimed as the religious preferences of a certain minority. Recognizing these values and working to protect them remains a central task of government.

V — SPECIFIC PROPOSALS AND COMMENTS

1 — Regarding Pornography

From the preceding reflections, it becomes obvious that there can be no such thing as claim of freedom of expression in the interests of pornography. Pecuniary interests are legitimate as long as they respect the totality of the human person. But they are not meant to be safeguarded by the right to freedom of expression. The right of freedom from government control does not extend to freedom to harm others. Freedom of expression does not include freedom to depict real or simulated degradation, aggression or domination in sexual relations.

It is no doubt difficult sometimes to limit clearly the rightful place of art, critical comment or scientific study. But these disciplines too are subject to the overriding limits and requirements of our common goal of growth in humanity.

Taking into account these multiple considerations we wish to make the following concrete suggestions for criminal law reform:

1) Any presentation, by whatever means, should be considered pornographic or obscene which, for a financial motive, depicts violent or degrading sexual behaviour, real or simulated. As a description of "degrading" one might enumerate certain actions such as enslavement, bestiality, etc.

2) The production, presentation, distribution and exhibition of pornographic material should be considered an offense. In this regard, we request that urgent steps be taken whether by the Minister of Justice or the Canadian Radio-Television Commission to curb the use of pornographic material on television, cable or satellite.

3) Pornography involving children should be considered an especially serious offense, subject to very severe penalties.

4) The words "or sex" should be added to the section of the Criminal Code dealing with hate literature (Section 281, 2).

5) If it should prove impossible further to criminalize pornography, as an absolute minimum there should be severe restrictions on the production and distribution of such material so as to make access as difficult as possible. Pornography must not be allowed to spread its heinous message of sexual aggression, torture and disregard for another and his or her body.

2 — Regarding Prostitution

The Committee's discussion paper proposes three legal options in this regard: criminalization, legalization and decriminalization. In our view legislation — i.e., the official recognition and control of prostitution — would be the least acceptable of these options, especially if we consider today's understanding of the body as described earlier, as well as the increased recognition of the dignity and equality of women.

In line with a now outdated anthropology the Church at one point did support the control of prostitution by the state. This anthropology and understanding of the human body however, has seen development over the centuries, so that it is no longer possible to invoke previous statements without reference to their historical and cultural context, and to the evolution of Christian thought.

We do support a strengthening of the law against procuring and living off the avails of prostitution, especially if it is joined with intimidation or violence. If we continue to prosecute prostitutes, either for soliciting or upkeep of bawdy houses, it seems obvious that their clients should be subject to similar prosecution. Otherwise, we would only maintain an unjust situation, especially with regard to the ordinary street prostitutes who have limited financial resources to defend themselves.

Finally, there is a strong consensus in our country to prosecute as criminals people who solicit minors or who engage them in prostitution. Once again, we encounter the state's primordial responsibility for protecting those who are weakest, be that in their emotional development or in relationship to other adults.

3 — The Need for Education and Other Action

Legal decisions are important but not the only measures to counteract pornography and prostitution. Educational, economic and cultural action is required to respond to our sexual and affective needs, in full respect for the dignity of each person and the demands of true personal encounter. In its resolution of May 19, 1983, the Economic and Social Council of the United Nations made the following concrete suggestions to which we fully subscribe:

a) preventing prostitution through education in ethics (and sex education) and through social formation at school and outside school;

b) increasing the number of women who enter, on behalf of the state, into direct contact with the people concerned;

c) eliminating whatever discrimination exists that marginalizes prostitutes and impedes their reintegration into society;

d) limiting the industry and commerce of pornography and applying especially severe punishment whenever minors are involved;

e) discouraging effectively procuring and living off the avails of prostitution, especially if minors are involved;

f) helping with the retraining of former prostitutes and assisting their integration into society.

Above all however, what is needed in all institutions that serve humanity, and what must be expected from the leaders of these institutions, is the stirring rediscovery of the dignity of men and women, a determined commitment to authentic human values and true human progress. Concern about pornography and prostitution is concern about the broader issues of which these two evils are a part. It is a deep and lasting concern to change the growing disregard and even unawareness of what constitutes true humanness.

VI — THE SPECIAL TASK OF CHRISTIANS

In addition to the foregoing considerations based on universal human values, Christians have specific faith reasons for condemning pornography and prostitution. Thus, on the occasion of this brief, we wish to remind the members of our own Church that pornography and prostitution go counter to our adoption as childlren of God and brothers and sisters of Christ. This faith knowledge will strengthen our personal and community decisions in this regard as Catholic people whether these decisions involve:

1) the refusal to produce, present, distribute or make use of pornographic material;

2) participation in study or action groups on these questions;

3) family and sex education of children and adolescents;

4) support for people with emotional or sexual difficulties;

5) personal and financial assistance for centres that support victims of sexual or emotional violence;

6) support for women in their struggle to achieve economic, social and cultural equality.

There are many possibilities for successful action. Above all however, we need to recognize the pernicious consequences of pornography and prostitution and at the same time to realize in humility that all of us can be tempted to degrade others and to distort the image of God in ourselves.

NOTES

1. Cf. many CCCB statements on social, economic and peace issues, especially *Unemployment: the Human Costs,* January, 1980, in *Do Justice!,* edit. E.F. Sheridan, SJ (Éditions Paulines, Sherbrooke, Qc., 1987), Document 49, also Documents 18, 20, 23, 26, 31, 33, 36, 38, 40, 42, 43, 46, 55 and 56. Cf. also this volume, Section II, Doc. 13, *Ethical Reflections on Respect for Life*; also *New Hope in Christ: on Sickness and Healing,* a CCCB Pastoral Message, from Publications Service, 90 Parent Ave., Ottawa, Ont., K1N 7B1.

2. *An Open Letter of Concern,* to all the clergy and for communication to the parishes, etc., Dec. 3, 1976, in *Letters and Legislation* (Chancery Office, 355 Church St., Toronto, Ont., M5B 1Z8), Vol. 2, pp. 501-2.

3. Letter of Jan. 31, 1983 , to the chairman of the Canadian Radio-television and Telecommunications Commission, Ottawa, K1A 0N2.

4. *Ibid.*

5. Special Committee on Pornography and Prostitution, *Pornography and Prostitution,* Issues Paper, 1983, (Department of Justice, Ottawa, Ont., K1A 0H8), p. 48.

6. Suzan Brownmiller, *Le Viol* (Montréal, *L'Étincelle*), 1976, p. 475.

7. Second Vatican Council, *Constitution on the Church in the Modern World* (1965), n. 27. Editor's note: it was certainly not the intention of the CCCB brief to suggest that church authorities could *ever* have been cited for the reprobated position of the preceding quotation, but only that some might be alleged for the *legalization of prostitution as a lesser evil,* in certain extraordinary circumstances.

8. Resolution adopted May 26, 1983, for the *Suppression of the Traffic in Persons and of the Exploitation of Persons by Others,* UN Association in Canada, 63 Sparks St., Ottawa, K1P 5A6. Cf. Second Vatican Council, *Constitution on the Church in the Modern World* (1965), n. 27.

9. *The Criminal Law in Canadian Society,* quoted in *Pornography and Prostitution* (cf. note 5, above), p. 9.

Section IV, Document 3

SUBMISSION TO
THE COMMISSION OF INQUIRY
ON UNEMPLOYMENT INSURANCE

Author — The Commission for Social Affairs, the CCCB,
February 13, 1986

1 — Introduction

Mr. Chairman, members of the Commission of Inquiry on Un-employment Insurance, we welcome this opportunity to share with you some of our concerns regarding the crisis of human work and the question of unemployment benefits in the context of permanent, large scale unemployment.

As representatives of the Social Affairs Commission of the Canadian Conference of Catholic Bishops, we believe that there are fundamental ethical priorities to be addressed with respect to Canada's Unemployment Insurance program. Implicit in the mandate of your Commission is the fact that basic decisions on goals and objectives for the Unemployment Insurance program involve basic value choices about the kind of country and people we want to become. [1]

As pastors, it is not for us to analyse in a scientific way the technical details of the U.I. program. We believe, however, that the fundamental challenges and problems that need to be addressed are more ethical than technical in nature. We wish to speak to some ethical themes and issues that relate to work and unemployment benefits from the perspective of working people and with a particular solidarity with popular organizations of the unemployed such as *Action chomage,* in Quebec and *The Working Centre* in Kitchener-Waterloo, Ontario.

2 — Unemployment Benefits: a Moral Obligation

The obligation to provide unemployment benefits, that is to say, the duty to make suitable grants indispensable for the subsistence of unemployed workers and their families, is a duty springing from the fundamental principle of the moral order in this sphere, namely the principle of the common use of goods, or to put it in another and still simpler way, the right to life and subsistence. [2]

As John Paul II's affirmation makes clear, the primary objective of an unemployment benefits program is to provide unemployed workers and their families the means to maintain a decent standard of living. It would therefore be misleading to look upon such a program as commercial 'insurance' in the conventional sense. Unemployed workers have a right to these benefits and are not to be thought of as "insurable risks".

3 — Unemployment Benefits Attacked

A number of arguments have surfaced in the debate on the future of Canada's Unemployment Insurance program. It is argued, for example, that U.I. actually is the *cause* of unemployment by reducing the incentive to work. Government and corporate economists further argue that U.I. acts as an impediment to "labour market adjustment" and "labour mobility". According to the logic of this incentives theory, unemployment benefits must be vigorously restricted in order to pressure working people into taking low-wage and demeaning jobs. Taken to its logical end, it is argued that U.I. benefits must be kept below the wages of the worst paying jobs in the country.

The present review of the U.I. program comes at a time when social expenditures in general are being seriously cut back and social programs restructured. The government has designated the "private sector" as the engine for growth. Deficit reduction appears to be the main preoccupation (yet billions of dollars, in the last few months alone, have been handed over to banks, oil companies, wealthy individuals and money markets). The core of this agenda is a renewed vision of "market society" where human beings and social relations are defined in terms of demand-and-supply forces of the market. The dominant tendency is to subordinate human dignity and human needs to the abstract rhetoric of the market.

We believe that these disturbing trends are symptomatic of a moral disorder in this country. In effect, the protection of capital takes priority over labour, over people, over communities.

4 — The Primacy of Work

Ethical considerations are rarely recognized as a constitutive dimension of the public policy-making process. Canada is facing a crisis of work and is plagued with unemployment levels bordering on social disaster, yet there is little or no attention paid to the profound link between human work and the very meaning of human life.

Work is one of the characteristics that distinguishes human beings from the rest of creation, so work in a sense is of the very nature of humanity. Through the activity of work people are able to exercise their creative spirit, realize their human dignity and participate in the development of society. Work corresponds to human dignity, expresses this dignity and increases it.

From this vision of the human person follows a key principle of Catholic social teaching: the priority of labour over capital. This principle concerns the production process, where working people are the subjects of production. All capital and technology are mere instruments or objects as they are, historically, the fruit of human labour and always subordinate to labour.

The basis for determining the meaning and value of work lies in the subjective dimension of work. Work has value because the worker is a *person*. People working are not commodities or objects whose worth is determined by the market.

5 — Human Work and the State

While work is a duty (out of regard for family, society and future generations) it is also a fundamental human right. It is the duty of institutions and persons responsible for the whole orientation of economic policy to provide employment for all who are capable of it.

In the final analysis, the responsibility for full employment lies on the shoulders of the state.

At this point it is important to recall the commitment that was made by the federal and provincial governments of Canada in this regard through the *International Covenant on Economic, Social and Cultural Rights* (1976). [3] Article 6 obliges our governments to recognize the right to work, which involves the right of everyone to the opportunity to gain their living by work which is freely chosen or accepted. Furthermore, governments must take the appropriate steps to safeguard this right and achieve its full realization. In article 7 of the Covenant, the governments of Canada agreed to recognize the right of everyone to the enjoyment of just and favourable conditions of work which ensure, in particular:

a) remuneration which provides all workers, as a minimum, with:
i. fair wages and equal remuneration for work of equal value without distinction of any kind, in particular women being guaranteed conditions of work not inferior to those enjoyed by men, with equal pay for equal work;
ii. a decent living for themselves and their families in accord with the provisions of the present Covenant;
b) safe and healthy working conditions.

Full employment, then, should always be a primary objective of government planning. It is not realistic, nor is it admissible, to expect to provide suitable employment for all who are capable of it, relying on a private sector strategy wherein employment is seen as a possible secondary effect, somewhere down the road. Work is a human right for all, not a privilege for a few.

6 — Unemployment: Widespread and Permanent

Permanent, large-scale unemployment is a fact which clearly demonstrates that there is something fundamentally wrong with the socio-economic order in this country. In not facing its responsibility for full employment, the state in Canada has in effect resigned itself to a social evil which systematically violates the dignity of nearly two million Canadians. [4] In order to accept the unacceptable, technical formulae and elaborate rationale have been developed to legitimate unemployment. Government economists speak of the "non-accelerating inflationary rate of unemployment" (NAIRU). According to the Report of the Macdonald Royal Commission, unemployment is "natural", "normal", "voluntary" and even healthy from an economic point of view.

7 — Unemployment: the Human Costs

The technical language and cold economistic logic that dominate policy discussions will never tell the tale or hide the devastating human costs of unemployment. Behind the staggering unemployment statistics are human beings, families and communities. In the words of an unemployed mother:

> We have to stand back from all (the statistical details) and look at the overall picture of human waste which we're being asked to accept. When we throw a skilled craftman, with perhaps 25 years' service at Massey-Ferguson, onto the garbage heap, with a few weeks' notice and little chance of getting another job before retirement — we've destroyed a vital part of his personality, of his ethical being, just as surely as by chopping off an arm. If we multiply that several hundred thousandfold, we have a sick society. When we deprive a whole young generation of job prospects, a real hope of productive activity, we warp the fabric of future society. When whole towns like Sudbury are shut down for months on end, the roots of decent community life wither... such phenomena raise fundamental questions about social purpose and social morality. Mental illness, marriage breakdown, suicide, racism, sexism, family violence, rape, alcoholism, crime and vandalism, do not stem simply from the "sin" of individuals; the conditions of mass unemployment manifestly breed these social evils. (From testimony before the *Hearing Panel on Ethical Reflections on the Economic Crisis*, Archdiocese of Toronto, 1983).[5]

Unemployment's devastating impact on body and soul is negative proof that work is an essential dimension of human life.[6] The insinuation that unemployment is normal or for the most part voluntarily chosen is perverse.

8 — An Ethical Challenge

Mr. Chairman, and members of the Commission of Inquiry, these are some of our reflections regarding the crisis of work and the ethical challenge of unemployment. Your review of the unemployment benefits program should reflect the basic ethical principles in this area. Indeed, it is imperative that the present Unemployment Insurance program be radically revised in order to reflect the dignity and the rights of working people.

We believe that the major principles found in the U.N. *International Covenant on Economic, Social and Cultural Rights* should serve as an ethical framework for the transformation of the current U.I. program into a benefits program for all who are in need of such assistance.

To repeat, unemployment benefits are a fundamental social right. Therefore, the objective of this review process should not be to "discipline" workers through program retrenchment. Nor should the priority be put on lowering expectations, penalizing workers and encouraging whole communities to relocate. A number of creative recommendations have already been presented to this Commission by trade unions, organizations of the unemployed, women's groups and numerous other community organizations and individuals. Indeed, alternative recommendations and models for the creation of an ethically sound unemployment benefits program are not lacking.

What is needed, however, *is* the *political will* and *creative imagination* to implement changes to the current U.I. system which are inspired by the very nature of human work.

NOTES

1. In recent years we have attempted to stimulate ethical reflections on Canada's socio-economic order. Examples include the following documents: *Unemployment: the Human Costs* (1980), *Ethical Reflections on the Economic Crisis* (1983), and *Ethical Choices and Political Challenges* (1984), a brief to the Macdonald Commission: all in *Do Justice!*, edit. E.F. Sheridan, SJ (Éditions Paulines, Sherbrooke, QC, J1E 2B9, 1987), Documents 49, 55, 56.

2. John Paul II, *On Human Work* (1981), in *The Papal Encyclicals*, edit. Claudia Carlen, IHM (Wilmington, N.C., McGrath Publishing) V, n. 18/82, p. 316.

3. *International Covenant on Economic, Social and Cultural Rights* (1976), United Nations Association in Canada, 63 Sparks St., Ottawa, K1P 5A6.

4. This estimate of real unemployment in Canada is based on the official statistics together with two categories of unemployed which the federal government ignores. These are discouraged workers (people who want work but have given up looking) and underemployed workers (working part-time only because they can't find full-time work).

5. In *Canada's Unemployed: the Crisis of Our Times,* Report of the Hearing Panel on Ethical Reflections on the Economic Crisis (Archdiocese of Toronto, 355 Church St., Toronto, Ont., M5B 1Z8), p. 14.

6. Cf. the study prepared for the Canadian Mental Health Association, *Unemployment: Its Impact on Body and Soul,* 1983 (CMH Association, National Office, 2160 Yonge St., Toronto, Ont.).

Section IV, Document 4

GLOBAL JUSTICE — GLOBAL PEACE: CANADA'S ROLE IN DEVELOPING A NEW INTERNATIONAL ORDER[1]

Submission to the Special Joint Committee on Canada's International Relations

Author — Canadian Conference of Catholic Bishops, Canadian Catholic Organization for Development and Peace, Canadian Religious Conference, *l'Entraide Missionnaire*, March 11, 1986

INTRODUCTION

We wish to thank the members of the Special Joint Committee on Canada's International Relations for the opportunity to present our views on the future directions of Canada's foreign policies. It has been fifteen years since the Government of Canada conducted its last major review of this country's foreign policy. We believe that the signs of the times — the spectre of mass starvation and the growing debt crisis in parts of the Third World, coupled with the constant threat of nuclear holocaust — reveal that this is a critical moment in the history of the world. A serious review of Canada's foreign policy is both timely and imperative.

Pastoral experience

Since the last foreign policy review fifteen years ago, the Canadian Conference of Catholic Bishops (CCCB) has become active in addressing a variety of issues from a Gospel perspective on global peace and disarmament, human rights and economic development. Through pastoral visits to many Third World countries, Canadian bishops have experienced first hand the realities of human suffering, poverty, dependency and repression. Through global events like the international Synods of Bishops, Canadian bishops have encountered the growing concerns of other churches around the world about the international debt crisis, the nuclear arms race and military regimes. In response, the CCCB has persistently addressed these issues through a variety of public statements, pastoral messages, meetings with government officials and numerous education and action programs in dioceses across the country.

The Canadian Catholic Organization for Development and Peace (CCODP) has been one of our major instruments for education and action in international concerns of the Church.[2] Organized in 1967 by the Canadian bishops, CCODP has a twofold program of (a) providing funds for community-based social and economic development projects in Third World countries and (b) increasing public awareness here in Canada regarding the realities and causes of poverty, underdevelopment and repression of human rights in the same countries. Funding socio-economic projects, CCODP has assisted the poor in organizing and developing their own communities. Through its education program, it has brought visitors from Latin America, Asia and Africa to educate Canadians as to their struggles for justice and liberation.

The Church in Canada has also had the opportunity to learn a great deal from the pastoral experience of religious and lay missionaries in Third World countries. During the past fifteen years, Canadian missionaries have served in Africa, Asia and Latin America. In 1985, there were approximately 3,700 Canadian Catholic missionaries active in this capacity. The Canadian Religious Conference and *l'Entraide missionnaire* have helped to facilitate and coordinate this missionary presence. Through this missionary activity, the Canadian Catholic Church has had opportunity to be in direct contact with communities of poor and oppressed peoples in the Third World countries.

At the same time, the Catholic Church has collaborated with other Christian Churches in Canada in the formation of a series of coalitions engaged in research, education and action on global justice concerns. These include coalitions focussed on specific regions such as the *Inter-church Committee on Human Rights in Latin America,* the *Canada-Asia Working Group,* and the *Inter-church Committee on Africa.* Coalitions have also been formed around specific policy and development concerns such as the *GATT-Fly* project on global economic justice, *Project Ploughshares* on peace and disarmament issues, the *Inter-church Committee on Refugees,* the *Taskforce on the Churches and Corporate Responsibility,* as well as the *Inter-church Fund for International Development.* Together these coalitions have proven to be an invaluable source of information and analysis on international issues.

Gospel perspective

As Christians, our perspective is firmly rooted in the Gospel of Jesus Christ and His message of justice and peace for the world. The ancient prophets heralded Christ's entry into human history as the Prince of Peace (Is. 9:6). At the inauguration of His ministry, Jesus announced that He was the message of the prophets come true, "good news to the poor" and "liberty to the oppressed" (Lk. 4:16-10). In His Sermon on the Mount, He outlined the essential elements required for building the kingdom of justice and peace on earth (Mt. 5:1-12). And, in His description of the last judgment, Jesus made it quite clear that acceptance of Him involves loving one's neighbour and seeking justice for the poor, the disinherited and the oppressed (Mt. 25:31-46).

The implications of this Gospel message for the modern world have been outlined by the Church in a series of social teaching documents. A central theme of this teaching is the message — *opus iustitiae pax* — peace is the work of justice. There can be no lasting peace in the world unless the injustices that divide and exploit peoples are eliminated (PT, PP, JW [a key to authorities cited thus is found at the end of this document, preceding the notes]). As long as poverty and oppression persist in many regions, there is no foundation for real and lasting peace. As Paul VI declared, "if you want peace, work for justice" (GP-6). "Development is the new name for peace" (PP).

The Church's social teachings have also criticized the structural injustices and ideological conflicts which undermine the search for true peace in the world today. As John Paul II reminds us, our models of society and systems of international relations — North and South, East and West — are dominated by competition and antagonism in which the strongest prevails. "Political views", he declares, "contaminated by the lust of power, by ideologies, by defence of one's own privilege and wealth must be abandoned". [3] The Cross symbolizes Christ's unifying power to reconcile North and South, East and West. The Church maintains that the establishment of a new international order based on justice and peace is a moral imperative for the survival of humanity on this planet (GP-7). Achievement of these ends requires conversion to new forms of solidarity within and between nations.

Eighteen months ago, John Paul II addressed many of these themes during his historic visit to Canada, 1984. [4] In his pilgrimage across the country, he publicly denounced the growing threat of nuclear war and militarism (Ottawa), the "imperialistic monopoly" that makes the South poor and the North rich (Edmonton), and the international market economy that obstructs food production and causes global hunger (Flatrock). At the same time, he outlined some basic principles for building a new economic order (Toronto) and urged Canada to exercise leadership in the cause of international justice and peace (Edmonton, Ottawa).

Global conflicts

The Church has become increasingly aware of new social forces which have intensified conflicts between North and South, East and West, in recent years (OA, JW, LE, GP-1, GP-2, EC, ER). New forms of capital and technology, coupled with new patterns of ownership and control, have generated major structural changes in both national and international economic and political systems. As a result, a new international environment has emerged characterized by new conflicts and tensions. These realities pose a major challenge for developing a foreign policy based on justice and peace in the world today.

Over the past decade, industrial and financial capital has become organized on an unprecedented geographic scale through the operations of transnational corporations and banks (OA). Today, such enterprises can shift their operations around the globe on the shortest notice, taking advantage of profitable investment opportunities, thereby outflanking workers' demands in various countries (EC). This, in turn, has created new conditions for international competition, as nation states (and regions within nation states) compete with one another for investments of transnational capital. At the same time, the introduction of sophisticated computer technology into the processes of industrial production is having far reaching social consequences (EC). Computerized factories, electronic offices and mechanized farms are expected to be the wave of the future. Using less and less human labour, the new technologies are likely to have serious social impacts in terms of unemployment, underemployment and the marginalization of working people (ER, EC).

This new global economic environment has served to heighten North/South tensions (EC, GP-8). Under the new conditions of international competition, the industrialized countries of the North have accelerated the scramble for control of resources, markets and labour in Third World countries (WJ, EC). The social consequences for the poor majority in numerous African, Latin American and Asian countries have been devastating. In textiles, electronics and auto-parts, for example, several Third World countries have been designated as pools of low-cost, low-skilled labour, wherein average wage levels are 10 to 20% of those in the more industrialized states. In food production, large agro-business firms have managed to re-organize food production for export rather than domestic needs and to drive millions of peasants off the land into urban centres, thereby swelling the ranks of the poor and unemployed (GJ-6). In addition, the relentless build-up of military regimes in the South has led to widespread repression of human rights. In the case of Central America and the Philippines, for example, billions of dollars required for food, shelter, education and health care have been spent instead on military forces and equipment to suppress social unrest among peasants, workers and the poor (GP-1).

The new global economic realities have also served to heighten East/West tensions (EC, GP-1, GP-8). Economic competition between Eastern and Western bloc countries has accelerated, especially for access to strategic resources and new markets. It has become clear that the formerly unchallenged United States economy is now compelled to compete not only with West Germany, Japan and other western nations, but with communist bloc states as well (EC). In order to protect their ideological and competitive positions, both the

United States and the Soviet Union have rapidly expanded their political security systems. As a result, we have seen the massive build-up of nuclear arsenals on both sides — the neutron bomb, the SS-18, the MX missile, the SS-20, the Cruise missile — which has brought the world perilously close to a nuclear holocaust. Indeed, the NATO (North Atlantic Treaty Organization) and Warsaw Pact countries spend 20 times more on their military forces than on development aid to the Third World (GP-1).

Presentation format

As we understand it, the federal government's Green Paper, *Competitiveness and Security: Directions for Canada's International Relations,* [5] has been designed to respond to these new global realities and conflicts. According to this document, Canada's foreign policy is to be organized around two basic objectives, namely, increasing "economic competitiveness" and "political security". We believe, however, that a foreign policy organized precisely for these objectives will only serve to heighten tensions and conflicts between North and South, East and West. As an alternative approach, we shall present a case for reformulating Canada's foreign policy around the objectives of "global justice" and "global peace".

In appearing before this committee, we do not present ourselves as technical experts on international economic and political affairs. We do, however, bring a socio-ethical expertise based on our pastoral experience. Our pastoral methodology involves a number of steps: (a) being present to the daily struggles of the victims of poverty, oppression and war; (b) analyzing the economic, political and social structures that cause this human suffering; (c) making moral judgments on these realities in the light of Gospel principles and the Church's social teachings; (d) stimulating creative thought about alternative orientations, policies and programs; (e) acting in solidarity with concerned groups in Canada and the Third World to build a new international order based on justice and peace (WA, ST, EC).

In applying this pastoral methodology for justice and peace, we use some basic operating principles. For example: the needs of the poor take priority over the wants of the rich; the provision of basic human and social needs over production for military purposes; the rights of workers over the maximization of profits; the preservation of the environment over unlimited industrial or military expansion; the participation of the marginalized over an order that excludes them (GJ-20, ER, EC). In so doing, however, it is not our intention to make moral judgments in an authoritarian or dogmatic fashion. While basic ethical principles are themselves universally valid, their application to concrete realities allows for some diversity in options and application.

Our presentation here is divided into two parts. In Part One, we shall outline some of our concerns about global justice, focussing our attention on policies and programs related to development assistance, human rights, international trade, debt relief, refugees/immigration and corporate investment. In Part Two, we shall go on to outline some of our concerns about global peace, focussing attention on various policies and programs related to nuclear weapons, nuclear strategies, strategic defence, arms trade, militarized regions and military production. Our intention throughout is to urge Canada to adopt a more independent foreign policy, oriented towards the building of a new international order based on justice and peace.

In making this presentation, we realize that other Christian Churches, communities and agencies will also be submitting their own briefs to your committee. A noteworthy example is the brief prepared by the Canadian Council of Churches, *Canada's International Relations: An Alternative View.* While the Council's submission and others of inter-church coalitions, development agencies and nongovernmental organizations are likely to present more detailed analysis and policy recommendations, our presentation here may be somewhat more general. Nevertheless, we expect that it will be complementary to many of these other initiatives.

PART I — GLOBAL JUSTICE

Priorities

Our first set of priorities for Canada's foreign policy has to do with global justice strategies. Through the Church's missionary involvement in the Third World countries and various fact-finding missions to specific regions, we have seen at first hand the human suffering of the victims of poverty, oppression and underdevelopment. These experiences, in turn, have compelled us to analyze the causes which are rooted largely in the economies of industrialized countries and international market structures. For the world economy continues to operate in such a way that the "rich North" exploits the "poor South" (GP-6). A foreign policy, based on increasing economic competitiveness in world markets, is bound to intensify rather than overcome the injustices that exist between North and South.

Over the past decade, the poor nations have consistently called for the creation of a new international economic order (JA, GJ-1, WA). The primary objective here is a redistribution of wealth and power. The nations of the South insist on their right to organize their own economies to serve the basic development needs of their own populations. Instead of organizing for export production, greater emphasis has been placed on developing self-reliant economies (GJ-1). A foreigh policy based on global justice would aim at breaking the bonds of economic domination by industrialized countries, favouring more self-reliant models of development in the Third World. This would mean that cooperation and solidarity with This World people would take priority over economic competitiveness.

We believe Canada could play a significant role in fostering the development of a new international economic order by pursuing a foreign policy based on global justice. The following are some examples of policy concerns and strategies that deserve serious consideration by the Canadian government.

Development Assistance

The Church has become deeply concerned about the increasing commercialization of Canada's bilateral aid program. It is our understanding that approximately 80% of Canada's bilateral aid to Third World countries is tied to the purchase of goods, commodities and services in Canada. Most of Canada's aid, therefore, never really leaves this country but is funnelled directly into Canadian business. Similarly, Canada's Export Development Corporation (EDC), which lends money to foreign buyers (including Third World companies), makes loans which are also tied to the purchase of Canadian goods and services. While it may appear that the EDC is helping to finance Third World companies requiring capital, a closer look sometimes reveals that the companies receiving the loans are subsidiaries of Canadian or American transnational corporations.

More recently, the Canadian government announced its intention to channel a substantial portion of Canada's development assistance funds into an international trade facility. In effect, public funds for development assistance purposes will be used to facilitate exports by Canadian companies to Third World countries. Less Canadian aid will be available for authentic development assistance supplying the basic needs of the poor majority. We believe that this kind of commercialized aid policy will serve to increase the economic hardship of the poor in many Third World countries and further aggravate North-South relations.

We maintain that Canada's development assistance programs must be designed to serve the demands of justice in Third World countries. The experience of the Canadian Catholic Organization for Development and Peace, and that of other Church and non-governmental development agencies, clearly demonstrates that there are alternative models of development assistance. As a primary objective, Canadian aid should be directed in particular to those countries whose governments are seriously attempting to pursue development strategies aimed at serving the basic needs of the poor majority in their societies. This means putting greater emphasis on supporting and promoting independent models of development.

As a step in this direction, Canada should rapidly and progressively untie its bilateral aid, allowing recipient countries to use international tenders for projects financed by Canadian aid. Similarly, Canada's development assistance funds should not be used, directly or indirectly, in the form of export credits to secure capital contracts for Canadian businesses. Finally, we believe that Canada's development assistance funds should be increased to reach the original target of .07% of Canada's Gross National Product by not later than 1990.

International Trade

The Church has become increasingly concerned about the ways in which the trade policies of industrialized countries like Canada, serve to maintain patterns of inequality and dependency between North and South (PP, JA, WJ, GJ-6). In spite of numerous commodity negotiations and agreements, the prices which producing Third World countries receive for their products remain proportionately far less than the prices they have to pay for rapidly rising costs of imported manufactured goods. Proposals to index the prices of Third World commodities, by tying them to increases in the costs of manufactured products, have been resisted by most industrialized countries, including Canada. Moreover, attempts by some Third World countries to process more completely their primary products before export have frequently been thwarted by industrialized countries imposing tariff structures such as import duties (WJ).

In recent years, there has been increasing action by industrialized countries like Canada to liberalize some trade barriers and encourage selected exports from low wage countries (e.g., textiles, clothing, electronics, etc.). While such trade has augmented the export earnings of those countries, it has also served to take advantage of cheap labour conditions and to re-organize the economies of these countries for export production rather than to meet local basic needs. At the same time, the Canadian government's intention to enter into a free trade agreement with the United States could well mean that Canada would end up giving more preferential treatment to U.S. products than to Third World products. This kind of trade policy could well contribute to expanding rather than reducing the development gap between North and South.

We maintain that Canada's trade policies must give much more serious consideration to the demands of justice in Third World countries (PP, JA). A primary goal of our trade policy with them should be to promote economic development strategies oriented towards the basic needs of their populations (JA). In many cases, this means engaging in "planned trade" that encourages greater economic self-reliance in Third World countries rather than export production. Those countries pursuing a basic needs strategy are more likely to engage in trade involving means of production (e.g., natural resources, machinery, technology, etc.) that cannot be found or developed locally or regionally.

At the same time, Canada's trade policy with Third World countries should take more positive and constructive action on prices and markets (JA). Canada should be able to support fairer commodity prices and proposals for indexation in international negotiations. Beyond these measures, Canada should be prepared to negotiate long-term trade agreements of mutual benefit with specific Third World countries committed to economic strategies to supply basic needs of their population. It is also important for Canada to include a fair labour practices code in all its trade agreements. Moreover,

Canadian workers should be effectively represented in any trade negotiations to ensure against massive job losses here in Canada.

Debt Relief

The Church has become increasingly aware of the global debt crisis and its crippling impact on the economies of most Third World countries today (PP, JA). Nation-states like Mexico, Brazil and Argentina are compelled to use well over 50% of their export earnings for debt repayments. Canadian banks alone account for some 25 billion dollars in outstanding loans to countries in the Caribbean and Latin America. Indeed, the debt crisis represents perhaps the single most important roadblock to Third World countries struggling to develop economic strategies to serve their basic needs.

In recent years, we have also become aware of the fact that the terms of rescheduling and renegotiating international loans often involve the imposition of severe restrictions on debtor nations. This has been the experience especially of Third World countries. The International Monetary Fund has consistently called on debtor countries in the Third World to reduce domestic consumption and increase exports. For most this has meant major cut-backs in social services, controls on workers' wages, higher interest rates and increased levels of unemployment. If Canada continues to support this kind of international loan policy, our country will be increasing the burden of debt crippling the economies of so many Third World countries.

We maintain that Canada's financial policies must focus on the international debt crisis and corresponding strategies for debt relief or a debt moratorium of Third World countries (JA). In collaboration with influential Third World countries and other like-minded middle powers in the North, Canada should develop concerted strategies to change the loan policies, priorities and restrictions of the World Bank and the International Monetary Fund. The terms for rescheduling and renegotiating loans should be completely revised to enhance rather than obstruct economic strategies aimed at serving the basic needs of the poor majority. It is also essential that steps be taken to see that special rescue operations to relieve the debt crisis for certain countries do not leave the poor to carry the main burden.

At the same time, it is our understanding that some debtor countries are considering direct negotiations with the governments of creditor nations rather than with the IMF itself. In such negotiations, efforts would be made to seek agreements on the terms of a debt moratorium, the writing-off of certain bad debts incurred for white elephant projects, and the resumption of debt payments only after economic recovery has occurred to provide sufficient surplus for export. If such negotiations emerge, the Canadian government should play a positive and constructive role in favour of a debt moratorium for Third World countries.

Corporate Investment

The Church has also been actively concerned about the operations of transnational corporations and banks which exploit Third World peoples rather than facilitate economic development that serves their basic needs. Today, a significant number of Canadian-based resource companies, manufacturing industries and financial institutions are operating in Third World countries. Close to 80% of all Canadian transnational investment in the Third World is concentrated in the Caribbean and Latin America. There are, however, no social criteria and monitoring mechanisms to ensure that such investment is serving the social and economic development needs of people in these countries.

Case studies reveal serious concerns about the operations of Canadian-based corporations and banks in Third World countries. Some have been involved in the exploitation of cheap labour conditions and have required generous investment incentives from local governments (e.g., tax holidays, lower corporate taxes, low environmental standards, etc.). Canadian corporations and/or banks continue to operate in countriies like South Africa, the Philippines, Chile and other repressive military regimes, thereby serving to strengthen the hand of oppression. The Canadian government's Export Development Corporation often supports these forms of Canadian investment through loans, export credits and other types of financial assistance.

We maintain that measures must be adopted to ensure that Canadian-based corporations and banks operating in Third World countries serve the development needs of the poor majority in those countries (JA). Experience elsewhere has shown that voluntary codes of conduct for transnational corporations have not proved effective. What is required are appropriate social criteria and monitoring mechanisms for evaluating the operations of Canadian investment operations in Third World countries. One way to ensure compliance would be for the federal government to insist that Canada's own Export Development Corporation develop a clear set of social and human rights criteria to be met before licences, credits or loans are granted to Canadian corporations for overseas investment (JA).

A major concern of the Churches has also been the lack of public information about the overseas operations of Canadian companies and banks. Measures are required to ensure that these Canadian enterprises are more publicly accountable. Canadian companies operating in countries governed by repressive military regimes should be required to disclose information on the nature of their transactions in those countries. Canadian banks should also be required to make public information on loans to foreign governments or their agencies.

Repressive Regimes

The Church has also been actively concerned about the build-up of repressive regimes in certain Third World and Eastern European countries where there has been widespread violation of human rights. Each year, representatives of the Churches and related non-government organizations meet with the External Affairs Minister to present case studies of human rights violations and repression in various Latin American, Southeast Asian, Eastern European and African countries. Cases of torture, arrests, disappearances, long-term detentions and massacres are documented. In these situations, the doctrine of national security is generally used to rationalize the use of military force to control civil liberties and thereby provide a "stable climate" for foreign investment and economic growth.

Canada has generally condemned human rights violations in other countries. Too often, however, we have turned a blind eye to these realities. Canada still does not have a comprehensive human rights policy whereby to assess critically relations with countries governed by repressive regimes. The Canadian government tends to rely on foreign governments for internal information on what is happening in countries where Canada has no embassy, depending on the U.S. State Department for information concerning a number of Latin American countries. In regions where U.S. interests are at stake, this has not proved adequate for formulating Canadian policy on human rights violations.

We maintain that Canada must play a more active role with regard to human rights issues in Third World countries dominated by repressive regimes as well as in Eastern Europe. To do so, Canada needs to develop a comprehensive human rights policy as part of its overall foreign policy. Such policy should outline detailed criteria by which human rights situations in a given country can be assessed and indicate the mechanisms necessary for acquiring information from independent observers. A parliamentary committee should also be mandated to conduct an annual public review of the observance of human rights in countries governed by repressive regimes.

It is also essential that Canada apply human rights criteria in its own financial transactions with other countries. The Export Development Corporation, for example, should be required to assess all available information about the human rights records of repressive regimes before any decisions are made to provide financial support for exports to those countries (JA). Similarly, human rights criteria should be applied with respect to Canada's votes in the International Monetary Fund and related international financial institutions.

Refugees/Immigration

The Church has been consistently concerned about Canada's immigration and refugee policies and practices (GJ-4, GJ-5, JA). Canadian immigration policies have been traditionally based on economic rather than humanitarian criteria. Canada's own immigration point system has been largely designed to select people in the prime of life, who are most adaptable to this country's labour force and who will put the least strain on government social services. For the poor South, selective immigration policies like these often mean a serious "brain-drain". Recent federal government initiatives have further intensified this problem by putting a priority on selecting wealthy, entrepreneureal immigrants.

Church concern extends also to Canada's refugee policies. The government has tended to be either slow or inconsistent when responding to the needs of refugees fleeing from repressive regimes in certain regions. Canada responded quickly to political upheavals in Hungary, Czechoslovakia and Vietnam by accepting large numbers of refugees, but was comparatively slow in its response to refugees from political repression in Chile and, initially, in El Salvador. In effect, Canada's refugee policy has tended to favour the victim of the left-wing regimes.

The Church maintains the need to develop more just immigration and refugee policies as part of its overall foreign policy perspective (GJ-4, GJ-5, JA). Greater attention must be given to the importance of sharing the riches of this land with those who have grave need of a new home. Humanitarian criteria should take precedence over strictly economic interests. This requires major changes in Canada's immigration point system to ensure that it is not used to generate a "brain-drain" from Third World countries.

Canada needs as well a more just refugee policy, giving at least equal, if not higher, priority to North/South refugee concerns. More attention and place should be given to the victims of right wing military repression than has been the case heretofore (JA). The annual quota for admission of refugees fleeing from political repression should be increased.

PART II — GLOBAL PEACE

Priorities

The second set of priorities for Canada's foreign policy to be discussed here has to do with global peace strategies. Through Church connections elsewhere in the world (e.g., the United States, Western Europe, Eastern Europe and the Third World) as well as the experience of the Church and Christian movements for peace here in Canada, we have encountered the social fears of militarism in a nuclear age. These experiences, in turn, have compelled us to analyze more clearly the links between the arms race and the global economic and political systems. Today, nation states are not only compelled to compete vigorously with one another for transnational investment but they are further tempted to protect profitable investments through the support of political security systems (GP-1). Hence, the increasing trend toward militarization of nation states and their economies, East and West, North and South (GP-8, EC). The two superpowers, the United States and the Soviet Union, maintain their own political security systems through military alliances (NATO Pact, Warsaw Pact) and through political/economic spheres of influence in strategic regions (Central America and the Philippines for the United States; Afghanistan and Poland for the Soviet Union).

We submit that a foreign policy based on increasing political security will simply end in intensified tensions and conflicts between East and West, North and South. What is needed instead are strategies for global peace which are designed to promote and facilitate a true sense of common security in the context of global interdependence (GP-8). To a large extent, the global justice strategies discussed in the previous section would, if enacted, help to generate the economic, social and political conditions required for common security and global interdependence. At the same time, however, additional strategies are needed to offset the continuing threats of a nuclear holocaust and military repression which obstruct the search for true peace and common security in the world today.

We believe that Canada, which has developed a reputation as a peacemaker in the modern world, has an important role to play in the promotion of global peace and the construction of a new international political order. Indeed, Canada may be in a pivotal position to pursue certain peace strategies. The following are some examples of policy concerns and strategies that deserve serious consideration by the Canadian government.

Nuclear Weapons

The Church has repeatedly expressed its opposition to the continuing acceleration and expansion of the nuclear arms race (GP-1, GP-2, GP-6, GP-7). Nuclear weapons production in both the Soviet Union and the United States appears to have its own built-in technological imperatives. Each break-through in weapons research means a further expansion of the nuclear arms race. Moreover, the development of new weapons technology is fueled by substantial financial resources. In 1986, we are told, weapons research in the U.S. alone is expected to consume $39 billion. The U.S. is expected to spend an additional $30 billion on research related to the Strategic Defence Initiative over the next few years.

As a nation state, Canada has officially rejected the so-called nuclear option. Canada, however, still participates in the production of nuclear weapons systems (GP-1). Through the U.S.-Canada Defence Sharing Agreement, Canadian industries are directly involved in the production of component parts for nuclear weapons systems (e.g., the Cruise missile system , Trident submarines and launchers for neutron bombs). Canadian scientists and high-tech industries are also involved in research and production of components of communication systems and related technology used in nuclear weapons. Many of these projects are funded in part by the federal government under the Defence Industry Production Programs.

We maintain that concerted efforts must be made to reverse the escalation of nuclear weapons production and to curtail its built-in expansive imperative. As an important step in this direction, Canada should re-activate its proposals for a "strategy of suffocation" submitted to the United Nations Special Session on Disarmament in 1978 (GP-1). Based on the recognition that it is difficult to find an effective and verifiable way of limiting nuclear weapons research, the strategy proposes that the place to exercise effective control is at the testing stage of nuclear weapons systems.

To re-activate this "strategy of suffocation", we would encourage Canada to pursue more vigorously, through the United Nations, agreements on proposals prohibiting the testing of nuclear warheads, nuclear weapons delivery vehicles and components for the Strategic Defence Initiative (GP-1). More concretely, Canada could begin by prohibiting the further testing of nuclear warheads delivery vehicles on Canadian soil; e.g., the Cruise missile.

Nuclear Strategies

The Church has also become increasingly concerned about the ongoing development of nuclear war-fighting capability and strategies (GP-1, GP-2). Both the United States and the Soviet Union, through the development of new weapons systems, have moved into more advanced stages with respect to their capabilities for fighting a nuclear war. Neither of the superpowers has thus far been effectively challenged by any of its allies regarding this escalation. As a member of the NATO alliance, Canada's position on these matters remains ambiguous at best.

Canada has yet to call for a change in NATO policy regarding the first use of nuclear weapons. Today, the development of a nuclear first strike capacity and a nuclear war fighting capacity is being rationalized in the West as essential for the maintenance of national defence and security objectives. But it is dangerous confusion of thought to rationalize first-strike weapons *as defensive,* and as such serving military strategy. Nuclear weapons are not military weapons in the normal sense of that term. They are means of massive extermination and destruction, not means of defending or holding territory. In our historical context of extravagantly over-armed nuclear powers, nobody wins a nuclear war. It is a fatal illusion that first use of such weapons can form part of a general military strategy.

We maintain that Canada must develop an independent policy on these issues if our country hopes to reduce rather than intensify East/West tensions (GP-1). To begin, the Canadian government should clarify its own operational understanding of deterrence and identify the types of weapons related to that understanding. Canada could also propose changes in NATO's nuclear doctrine by calling for a declaration of no first-use of nuclear weapons. Further, Canada should actively oppose the deployment of any nuclear weapons systems designed for first strike and war-fighting purposes.

Canada should also support efforts in the United Nations to achieve agreements for more effective controls over the spread of nuclear arms on this planet. These measures include: a resolution calling for a freeze on the production and testing of nuclear weapons; the development of an independent satellite surveillance system to monitor arms control agreements on behalf of all nuclear weapons states; and the establishment of demilitarized zones in the common regions of the earth such as the oceans and outer space.

Strategic Defence

The Church has recently expressed serious concern over nuclear defence strategies such as the Strategic Defence Initiative of the United States, the Star Wars program. As a number of observers have pointed out, the Star Wars program, despite views to the contrary, is a nuclear offensive weapon system. With the Star Wars system in place, the capacity of the U.S. to launch a nuclear first-strike and engage in nuclear war-fighting operations becomes almost credible. At the same time, the Star Wars initiative would undoubtedly lead to an expansion of nuclear arsenals on the Soviet side, thereby greatly accelerating the nuclear arms race.

This U.S. program has opened up new questions about Canada's role and responsibilities in a nuclear age. While Canada has officially declined the invitation to participate formally in the Star Wars program, Canadian participation is likely to come in other ways. Canadian high-tech companies expect to be awarded contracts, perhaps supported by federal grants and incentives. There may well be a direct or indirect link between the program and the rebuilding of the continental defence system in northern Canada. If there is an operational link between Star Wars and NORAD (the Northern Air Defence System), then Canada would become directly implicated in the U.S. nuclear offensive potential (GP-13).

We maintain that Canada should resist giving grants or subsidies to Canadian high-tech firms engaged in research or production of components for the program. Canada should also insist, as a precondition of the renewal of the NORAD agreement, that there will be no operational link between the Star Wars program and the continental air defence system in Northern Canada.

In this connection, it is important to recognize that Canadian territory is situated in a strategic position between the two superpowers (GP-1). Our territory has already been used for the storage of nuclear weapons (e.g., Comox, B.C.), the passage and testing of U.S. and Soviet submarines off the West Coast (e.g., Nanoose, B.C.), as well as the testing of nuclear weapons systems (i.e., the Cruise missile). In the future, there is likely to be even greater pressure on Canada to make its territory available for strategic defence and related nuclear war-fighting facilities. Canada must make a clear moral choice to resist being lured further into compliance with these nuclear war strategies.

Militarized Regions

Church concern has extended to the increasing militarization of certain countries or regions which are considered strategic, both economically and politically, for the two superpowers and related industrialized nations (GP-1). The Soviet Union (e.g., in Afghanistan, Poland, etc.) and the United States (e.g., in Central America, Philippines, etc.) support the development of military regimes in these areas to protect their "back yards" and "spheres of influence" against external threat. Massive military and economic aid is funnelled into these satellite countries in order to secure rights for military bases, develop military and political alliances, and gain access to important sources of new materials and markets.

As a result, major regional conflicts mark the global landscape today, the majority of which are located in the Third World. In most cases, gross economic disparities and social injustices have given rise to greater pressure for social change which, in turn, has led to military takeovers of government to protect the wealthy elites from the poor majority (GP-1). The result is often widespread repression of human rights, increasing social conflict and the eventual outbreak of civil war. Many of these regional conflicts and wars are fueled by military support from one or more of the industrialized powers (GP-1).

We maintain that Canada could play an effective peacekeeping role in relation to some of these regional military conflicts. There is a vital need today for third party intervenors to monitor ceasefires, check on arms flow and create appropriate conditions for a just and peaceful settlement of the conflicts. The crisis in Central America today and the problems encountered by the Contadora peace initiative, illustrate both the challenges and the difficulties of pursuing such peacekeeping initiatives.

Nevertheless, Canada could make a significant contribution based on past experience. Peacekeeping with respect to regional military conflicts in certain Third World "hot-spots" should become a priority for Canada's armed forces. To perform this role, Canada would have to develop a more independent foreign policy. Canada's armed forces would also have to be specially trained and properly equipped for such peacekeeping missions.

Arms Trade

The Church is increasingly aware of how the international arms trade fuels these regional military conflicts (GP-1). It is estimated that over 70% of the international arms trade now involves Third

World countries. Substantial amounts of limited foreign exchange are thus spent on the purchase of arms and related military equipment. Here, military equipment includes both the lethal (e.g., guns, hand grenades, ammunition, explosives) and non-lethal material (e.g., prison gear, surveillance systems, armoured cars, surveillance aircraft, torture devices, riot control equipment).

Canada has not been an innocent bystander when it comes to international arms trade (GP-1). The sale of Canadian manufactured military and police equipment to the Chilean military regime and the Export Development Corporation permits for the sale of aircraft to the Honduran military regime have given cause for real concern. Similarly, Canadian industries have been involved in sales to the South African government, of equipment and technologies that were likely to be used for military or police operations. The sale of Canada's CANDU nuclear technology to military regimes in South Korea and Argentina raises serious questions. More recently, a Canadian manufacturing subsidiary was directly involved in supplying armoured vehicles for the new U.S. rapid deployment force which is expected to be used for military intervention in areas of regional conflict.

We maintain that Canada should actively promote effective measures to control and reduce the international flow of military arms. In the past, international efforts to limit arms trade in the world have been largely unsuccessful. Nevertheless, open reporting or full disclosure of arms transfers would be a major step towards effective controls. In the United Nations, proposals have been made for the establishment of an Arms Trade Register designed to monitor and disclose information on arms transfers.

It is important that Canada actively support the proposal for an Arms Trade Register. In so doing, the Canadian government should call for a public disclosure of all direct and indirect (i.e., via industries in other countries) arms transfers from Canadian industries to Third World countries. At the same time, the Canadian government should take the necessary steps to prohibit the export to Third World "hot spots" of arms or weapons systems that might be used for repression or insurrection.

Military Production

Finally, the Church is deeply concerned about the growing priority of military production and spending in the world economy, particularly of industrialized nations (GP-1). The world's annual military expenditure has reached well over $600 billion, or, in other words, close to two billion dollars a day. Indeed, global military spending accounts for more than the Gross National Product of the continent of Latin America and double that of Africa. As a consequence, the resources of the earth are increasingly mobilized for the "service of death" rather than the "service of life" ,(GP-6, GP-1).

In Canada, military production and spending priorities have been on the rise (EC). In recent years, spending on the part of the federal government has grown significantly to meet NATO commitments (e.g., F-18 fighter aircraft) while social spending has steadily declined along with development assistance for Third World countries. Equally disturbing is the increasing trend to retool Canadian manufacturing industries for the production of military equipment with federal assistance under the Defence Industry Productivity Program. At the same time, there is a clear trend to locate new arms industries and military operations in economically depressed areas as a means of resolving problems of high unemployment (e.g., Cape Breton, Labrador, etc.).

We maintain that Canada needs to re-examine its military spending and production priorities (EC, GP-1). For example, Canada's involvement in the Defence Sharing Agreement with the United States and the federal government's Defence Industry Productivity Program need to be seriously re-examined in the light of concerns presented above. Otherwise, Canada's economy will become more and more closely tied to the arms race.

In this context, the federal government should give serious attention to economic strategies for industrial conversion from military production to socially useful forms of production (EC). In Britain, West Germany and elsewhere, certain labour unions have been directly engaged in transforming arms industries into more socially useful forms of production (e.g., public transportation systems). The federal government could benefit from these and related experiences in developing its own economic strategies for Canada.

CONCLUSION

These are some of the major concerns we wish to bring to your attention as you review the future direction of Canada's foreign policy. It has been our contention here that a foreign policy based on the twin objectives of increasing economic competitiveness and political security will heighten conflicts between North and South, East and West. As an alternative, we have urged Canada to develop a more independent foreign policy oriented towards the two-fold priorities of global justice and global peace. Here, the long range goal is to build a new international economic and political order based on increasing co-operation and solidarity, North and South, East and West.

It should also be understood that the development of an alternative foreign policy along these lines would require structural changes in Canada's own economy and society. As the *Green Paper* put it, domestic and foreign policies are "two inseparable elements of a truly national policy". A foreign policy, oriented towards the priorities of global justice and global peace, would necessitate a greater degree of economic and political self-reliance or independence on the part of Canada as a nation state. While this may not be the time or place to talk about corresponding changes required in Canada's economic and social order, it should be noted that the Church has consistently addressed these concerns in a number of recent statements (ST, ET, EC).

We firmly believe that Canada, through a creative and independent foreign policy, could make a substantial contribution towards building a new international order based on global justice and global peace. It is also clear that there are strong pressures, emanating from some of the more affluent and powerful sectors of our society, urging Canada to respond to the "tough new world" realities by continuing to develop a foreign policy based on increased economic competitiveness and political security. To choose an alternative foreign policy would require considerable moral vision and political courage. But this is the kind of leadership required by nation states like Canada at this moment in history.

During his visit to Canada, Pope John Paul II presented this challenge in dramatic terms in his Edmonton homily at the Canadian Forces Base Namao. Commenting on the last judgment passage in the New Testament where Christ says: "As you did it to one of the least of these my brothers and sisters, you did it to me..." (Mt. 25:40), John Paul warned:

> ... In the light of Christ's words, this poor South will judge the rich North, and the poor people and poor nations — poor in different ways, not only lacking in food, but also deprived of freedom and other human rights — will judge those people who take the goods away from them, amassing to themselves the imperialistic monopoly of economic and political supremacy at the expense of others.[6]

In effect, we are faced with a profound moral disorder in the global economic and political structures that govern our common life on this planet. Current global conflicts could well lead to the destruction of both humanity and a habitable world. The destruction may be a slow process as in the case of starvation or repression in the Third World or it may be rapid as in the case of an exchange of nuclear weapons resulting in a holocaust. In either case, the building of a new international order based on justice and peace is no longer simply a moral imperative. It is essential for the common survival of humanity on this planet!

We hope and pray that the members of this committee will respond creatively and positively to this critical challenge. At the same time, we believe that recent events in the Philippines are a living sign that the spirit of God is alive in the struggles of people who thirst for justice and peace on earth!

TABLE OF SOURCES CITED

Major Social Teaching Documents

The Universal Church

PT John XXIII, *Pacem in Terris* (Peace on Earth) 1963[1]
PP Paul VI, *Populorum Progressio* (Development of Peoples) 1967[1]
OA Paul VI, *Octogesima Adveniens* (Call to Action) 1971[2]
JW Synod of Bishops, *Justice in the World*, 1971[2]
RH John Paul II, *Redemptor Hominis* (Redeemer of Mankind) 1979[1]
LE John Paul II, *Laborem Exercens* (On Human Work) 1981[1]

The Canadian Church

WA   CCCB, From Words to Action, 1976[3]
ST   CCCB, A Society to be Transformed, 1977[3]
ER   CCCB, Ethical Reflections on the Economic Crisis, 1983[3]
EC   CCCB, Ethical Choices and Political Challenges, 1984[3]
JA   Canadian Church Leaders, Justice Demands Action, 1976[3]

Related Church Documents

Global Justice

GJ-1   CCCB 10th Anniversary of Development and Peace, 1977[3]
GJ-2   CCCB To Prime Minister on North-South Dialogue, 1981[3]
GJ-4   CCCB To Parliamentary Committee on Immigration, 1975[3]
GJ-7   CCCB Open Letter to the Bank of Montreal, 1978[3]
GJ-6   John Paul II, Homily, Cndn. Forces Base, Edmonton, 1984[4]
GJ-20 John Paul II, Homily, St. Paul's Church, Toronto, 1984[4]

Global Peace

GP-1   To Standing Committee on External Affairs, 1982[3]
GP-2   CCCB The Neutron Bomb: Enough is Enough, 1981[3]
GP-6   Paul VI, To First UN Special Session on Disarmament, 1978[5]
GP-7   John Paul II, Moral Choices for the Future, Hiroshima, 1981[6]
GP-8   John Paul II, Message for World Day of Peace, 1986[7]

---

[1] *The Papal Encyclicals,* edit. Claudia Carlen, IHM (Wilmington,   N.C., McGrath Publishing), V.

[2] In *The Gospel of Peace and Justice,* edit. J. Gremillion (New York, Orbis Books, 1975).

[3] In *Do Justice!,* edit. E.F. Sheridan, SJ (Sherbrooke, Éditions Paulines, 1986).

[4] In *Canadian Catholic Review,* Saskatoon, v.2, Oct., 1984.

[5] *The Pope Speaks* (Washington, 1979), XXIII, p. 278.

[6] *Catholic Mind* (New York, 1981), LXXIX, June, p. 55.

[7] *Origins* (Washington), XV, 1985, n. 28, p. 456.

NOTES

1. This submission is a response to the Federal Government's Green Paper, *Competitiveness and Security: Directions for Canada's International Relations* (cf. note 5, below), prepared for the hearings of the Special Joint Committee on Canada's International Relations.

The proposal of the Canadian Catholic Organization for Development and Peace for a joint response was approved by the CCCB Executive Committee, on the recommendation of the Social Affairs Commission. The final draft was revised and approved by the President or Executive of the proponent groups.

The actual presentation was made March 5, 1986, by Bishop Adolfe Proulx, Social Affairs Commission; Rev. Wm. F. Ryan, S.J., CCCB Secretary General; Dr. T. Clarke, CCCB Social Affairs Office; Miss Thérèse Bouchard, Executive Member CCODP; R.P. Michel Marcil, S.J., General Council Member, *l'Entraide missionnaire inc.* The presentation was followed by questions from each of the Committee members.

2. Cf. *Do Justice!*, edit. E.F. Sheridan, SJ (Éditions Paulines, Sherbrooke, 1986), Documents 17 and 45; also this volume, infra, Section V, Document 7.

3. John Paul II, *Message on World Day of Peace*, 1986, in *Origins* (Washington), XV, 1985, n. 28, p. 462.

4. All his addresses, homilies, etc., are to be found in *The Canadian Catholic Review* (Saskatoon, 1984), vol. 2, n. 9.

5. Dept. of External Affairs, Ottawa, 1985.

6. John Paul II, Homily, Canadian Forces Base Namao, Sept. 17, 1984, *l.c.* in note 4, above, p. 62/378.

Section IV, Document 5

A NEW COVENANT: TOWARDS RECOGNITION OF ABORIGINAL SELF-GOVERNMENT IN CANADA [1]

Author — Leaders of the Christian Churches in Canada, February 5, 1987

A HISTORIC MOMENT

In the Spring of 1987, Canada's major political and Aboriginal leaders will gather in Ottawa for the final session in the current round of constitutional talks on the rights of Aboriginal peoples in Canada. For the past four years, the various national associations of Aboriginals — the Assembly of First Nations, the Native Council of Canada, the Inuit Committee on National Issues, the Metis National Council — have developed a common approach and are striving to reach an agreement with the Prime Minister and the Premiers on constitutional amendments regarding Aboriginal rights. After three meetings with the First Ministers, the central issue appears to be the entrenchment of the rights of Aboriginal peoples to self-government in Canada.

Over the past four years, the major Christian Churches in Canada have also been working together to promote Aboriginal rights in the Canadian Constitution. Our primary objective here has been to stimulate public awareness and mobilize public support for the recognition and entrenchment of basic Aboriginal rights in the Constitution, particularly the right to self-government. During this period,

Church representatives have attended each of the First Ministers Conferences as observers under the auspices of the various national Aboriginal organizations. They have also held consultations with national and provincial Aboriginal leaders, met with federal cabinet ministers and provincial premiers, participated in joint press conferences with Aboriginal leaders, sponsored public forums on Aboriginal rights, and published popular education materials on the issues.

As pastoral leaders, we believe that this is an historic moment in the life of our country. This round of constitutional negotiations will affect the lives of some two million Indian, Inuit and Metis people and their descendents for generations to come. Many of these Aboriginal peoples, whose ancestors have inhabited this country since time immemorial, are members of our churches. Following the liberating message of the Gospel, we believe that this is a time for new beginnings — a time to rectify ancient injustices and to recognize the rights of Aboriginal peoples in the Canadian Constitution. It is a time to establish a New Covenant with the first peoples and nations of Canada.

A NEW COVENANT

Indeed, the current round of constitutional talks may be the last opportunity for developing a new covenant between Aboriginal and non-Aboriginal peoples in this country. In retrospect, it has become all too clear that the old covenants, including many of the treaties, have not served the demands of justice. Initially believed by Aboriginal people to be instruments of friendship and peace, the treaties were often misused and broken by the newcomers who wanted this land for their own. Dispossessed of their lands, relegated to reserves or marginalized in urban centres, Aboriginal peoples soon experienced the highest rates of unemployment, poverty, alcoholism, suicide, imprisonment and infant mortality in Canada.

The idea of covenant-making has deep spiritual roots which can teach us a great deal about the true purpose and meaning of covenant-making and covenant-keeping among peoples today. In many Aboriginal communities, the leaders remind us of the covenants which their ancestors made with the Great Spirit, the Creator. Similarly, we recall in the Judaeo-Christian tradition the covenant which God made with the people of Israel. This covenant was renewed by Jesus Christ Who proclaimed the equality of all human beings as sons and daughters of creation (Gal.3:28). In the story of Israel God freed the people from oppression and led them to a new homeland where a covenant was established to create a new people, a new nation (Dt. chaps. 7-8). When the people forgot that their land was a symbol of God's generosity, the prophets warned against greedy instincts and recalled the people to their responsibilities under the covenant.

There are, therefore, moral and spiritual dimensions to making and keeping covenants. Such dimensions must be essential to the creation of a new covenant involving Aboriginal peoples in Canada today. The new covenant must recognize the rights and responsibilities of Indian, Inuit and Metis to be distinct peoples and cultures. The new covenant should affirm their rights and responsibilities as self-determining nations and societies within Canada. The new covenant should enhance the identity and dignity of the Aboriginal peoples of this country. These are the major challenges at the heart of the current constitutional talks on Aboriginal rights.

ABORIGINAL RIGHTS

It is established that numerous Aboriginal nations and cultures existed in this country prior to the European occupation some four centuries ago. These societies were self-governing nations with their own self-sufficient economies, characterized by distinct cultural practices, social structures, spiritual traditions and strong family bonds. Today, having experienced cultural oppression and economic dependency for three centuries, Aboriginal peoples are struggling to decolonize themselves and regain the recognition of their historic rights in Canada. These Aboriginal rights are recognized in both international law and the historic documents of this country. We maintain, however, that the rights of Aboriginal peoples are not simply legal or political issues but, first and foremost, moral issues touching the very soul and heart of Canada.

For these reasons, we believe that some basic dimensions of Aboriginal rights need to be recognized and guaranteed as an integral part of the constitution.

1. *The right to be distinct peoples.* Today, as in the past, Aboriginal peoples are steadfastly resisting policies designed to assimilate them into the dominant society and to foster divisions and inequalities among them. Instead, Aboriginal people, Indian, Inuit, Metis have the right to be recognized culturally as peoples and nations. This includes the right to be distinct peoples even with respect to each other.

2. *The right to an adequate land-base.* If Aboriginal peoples are to retain their self-understanding as peoples with their own cultures, land rights are essential. Aboriginal societies are rooted in a special relationship between the people and the land. There is, in other words, a spiritual bond between the peoples and their lands which forms the basis of each nation's unity. A land-base with adequate resources is also necessary to develop and sustain a viable economy.

3. *The right to self-determination.* If Aboriginal peoples are to realize their aspirations as peoples and nations, they must be the architects of their own futures, freely and responsibly. They have the right and capacity to make their own decisions, develop their own lands and economic potential, educate their own children and plan their own future. This means being free to make their own mistakes.

SELF-GOVERNMENT

Taken together, these basic dimensions of Aboriginal rights need actualization in the recognition and implementation of Aboriginal self-government in Canada. Self-government is the necessary means by which Aboriginal peoples can give concrete expression to their identity as distinct peoples, develop the economic potential of their own lands and design their own cultural, social and religious institutions to meet their own needs. In this process, Aboriginal peoples will be empowered to break the bonds of dependency and regain a sense of human dignity and worth as self-determining peoples and nations in this country. This requires the entrenchment of Aboriginal self-government in the Canadian Constitution.

We maintain, however, that it is not sufficient simply to affirm the principle of Aboriginal self-government in the Constitution. All too often, in the past, intransigent governments at provincial and federal levels have found ways either to ignore or resist implementing the rights of Aboriginal peoples. If authentic self-government is to become a reality in Canada, then both federal and provincial governments must be obliged constitutionally to negotiate and implement the terms of self-government with Aboriginal nations and peoples. This demands the recognition of Aboriginal self-government as an enforceable right in the Constitution.

At the same time, we maintain that the diversity which exists between the various Aboriginal peoples and groups in Canada must be recognized and respected in these negotiations. There can be no single, uniform model applicable to all Aboriginal peoples. While recognizing this to be a new, distinct level of government in Canada's political structure, it is important to remain open to a variety of options in response to diverse needs and circumstances. Whatever forms of Aboriginal self-government are negotiated, it is essential that several basic components be ensured. These include an adequate land-base, sufficient fiscal resources and appropriate decision-making powers required for the exercise of self-government at this level.

A CALL TO POSITIVE ACTION

The final session of the current constitutional negotiations on Aboriginal rights represents a critical moment for Canada. As a country, we have a unique opportunity to repair past injustices, heal wounds and develop just relationships in a new covenant. This calls for action to entrench Aboriginal self-government as an effective right in the Constitution. It also calls for action to ensure that constitutional amendments will be realized on related concerns such as: the provision of the basic means (i.e., land-base, fiscal resources, powers of decision) required for the exercise of effective self-government; the recognition of equality between Aboriginal peoples, including sexual equality; measures to prevent the extinction of Aboriginal rights in future land claims settlements; and the assurance that future constitutional amendments affecting Aboriginal peoples will not be made without Aboriginal consent.

As a country, we must not allow this historic moment to slip by without action along these lines. While some of the details may be complex, requiring intense discussion and negotiation, a healthy dose of political vision and will is essential if Canada is to move forward with a new covenant. For these reasons, we fervently hope and pray:

— that the diverse Aboriginal groups throughout Canada will continue working in solidarity to advance their proposals for the entrenchment of Aboriginal self-government and related rights in the Constitution;

— that all governments will respond positively and with openness to the common Aboriginal proposals for constitutionl recognition and protection of their rights;

— that members of the Christian churches, together with those of other faiths and all people of good will, will join us in promoting public awareness and support for the full recognition and implementation of these rights in Canada.

In this way, Canada could become a practical example to the rest of the world, of a society coming to terms with the historic demands of justice to the descendants of its original inhabitants. In so doing, we may be able to recover some of the deeper spiritual meaning of covenant making, essentially involving God, the Creator, the Great Spirit.

NOTES

1. Church initiatives in the area of native rights were largely coordinated by *Project North,* an inter-church coalition of which the CCCB was a supporter. For earlier statements of the Conference, cf. *Do Justice!,* edit. E.F. Sheridan, SJ (Éditions Paulines, Sherbrooke, 1986), Index of Subjects, "Native Peoples". *Project North* seems to have evolved into *The Aboriginal Rights Coalition,* 90 Terrence Ave., Ottawa, Ont., K1N 7B1.

Involved in the production of *A New Covenant* were: The Anglican Church, Council of Reformed Churches, Evangelical Lutheran Church, Mennonite Central Committee, Oblate Conference, Presbyterian Church, Religious Society of Friends (Quakers), Canadian Conference of Catholic Bishops. The document was endorsed by Bishop Bernard Hubert, Pres. of CCCB.

Concerns about constitutional Aboriginal rights were outlined by the churches in 1984, in a pamphlet *You Can Help Write the Next Chapter in Canada's History,* available from *Aboriginal Rights Coalition,* above.

Section IV, Document 6

STATEMENT ON RESTRICTIVE MEASURES AFFECTING REFUGEES

Author — Bishop Bernard Hubert, President, the CCCB,
February 25,1987[1]

We wish to join with other community organizations and church groups in expressing shock and deep concern over the adoption of the restrictive refugee measures, recently announced by the Minister of Immigration.

A large majority of refugees seeking asylum in Canada today are struggling to escape from the realities of death, torture, poverty and misery in their homelands. By substantially altering the entry requirements for refugees coming to Canada, the federal government's measures may well serve to reinforce a fortress mentality in this country.

We realize that there have been some problems recently with false refugee claims and that this phenomenon poses real difficulties for federal authorities. But the solution does not lie in establishing refugee determination procedures which are in danger of confusing the category of refugees with that of immigrants. Nor can these problems be solved by introducing more bureaucratic red tape that ends in penalizing all refugees requesting asylum in Canada.

Among these refugees are individuals and families from the war-torn countries of Central America, threatened with deportation by the American authorities. The U.S. government is said to be ready to deport more than 200,000 people declared "illegal aliens". As a result, thousands of these second time refugees are now at our border crossings. For them, Canada is the last resort and first asylum.

In fact, these Central American refugees are hostages of international politics. Their need for protection is undeniable. Canada's new restrictive measures could well lead to many of these refugees being returned to countries which, according to the Canadian government as recently as last week, cannot guarantee their safety.

All across Canada, Church groups and community organizations are once again opening their doors in response to refugees searching for justice, security and peace. This humanitarian work has recently been honoured by the United Nations Organization with the award of the Nansen Medal to Canadians. We fear that the policy changes, announced last week, may mark a sharp departure by the federal government from this humanitarian tradition in refugee affairs.

Working with very limited resources, these non-governmental organizations have acquired extensive experience which gives them the capacity to intervene effectively in the present crisis. In collaboration with these groups, the churches of Canada have repeatedly called for a refugee status determination procedure which is just, workable, expeditious, respectful of fundamental human rights and freedoms, and in conformity with international conventions. We believe that the recent measures fail to meet these criteria, being unjust and inhuman.

The Government of Canada, having recently affirmed "constructive internationalism as the only appropriate response to interdependence", cannot now abdicate its responsibilities. It must fulfill its commitments and grant asylum to all refugees, as defined by the terms of the Geneva Convention. We hope and pray that the Canadian government will realize that this country faces a new kind of refugee crisis on its own borders, and reconsider these restrictive measures.

The leaders of the Christian communities are following closely the evolution of events and the plight of refugees at our borders. They would prefer to work actively with Canadian authorities in finding a just solution to the current refugee crisis in the humanitarian tradition that has, until now, prevailed in Canada.

NOTES

1. For other statements of the CCCB on immigration and refugees, cf. *Do Justice !*, edit. E.F. Sheridan, SJ (Éditions Paulines, Sherbrooke), Documents 39, 41, 42 and index of subjects "Immigration". Also this volume, Section IV, Document 1, above.

Section IV, Document 7

ON PROPOSED CHANGES
TO GENERIC DRUG LAWS

To The Honourable Harvie Andre,
Federal Minister of
Consumer and Corporate Affairs

Author — Bishop Paul J. O'Byrne, Chairman,
          Commission for Social Affairs, April 22, 1987

On behalf of the Episcopal Commission for Social Affairs of the
Canadian Conference of Catholic Bishops we wish to express our
concern over changes to the Drug Patent Act (Bill C-22).

We have followed the debate on this legislation and have noted
that the pressure to change Canada's generic drug laws has not come
from the people of this country. Indeed, national organizations
representing thousands of Canadians from virtually all sectors of
society have been unanimous in calling upon your government not
to proceed with the proposed legislation.

We add our voice to that call because we believe that this legislation, if enacted, would be detrimental to the interests of average
Canadians, especially of the elderly and the poor. Thanks in large
part to existing drug patent legislation, Canadians enjoy low prescription drug prices and high standards of health care. The proposed
amendments will cost Canadians hundreds of millions of dollars annually in drug price increases. The changes will also have serious
implications for health care costs and for the future of Medicare in
this country.

We urge your government to resist the pressure from the multinational drug industry and from the United States Administration. At the time when your government is negotiating a bilateral free trade arrangement with the United States, the people of Canada are watching vigilantly to ensure that national interests and the common good of the Canadian people are not sacrificed to market interests.

As the federal Commission of Inquiry on the Pharmaceutical Industry declared in its 1985 report, the Canadian compulsory licensing policy "can be thought of as a mechanism to provide socially optimal patent protection in the pharmaceutical industry that other countries might well emulate". Because the people of Canada affirm that this policy is not — and should never beome — a trade issue, we urge you, in the name of Canada's most vulnerable citizens, to withdraw Bill C-22.

Section IV, Document 8

FREE TRADE: AT WHAT COST?[1]

Author — The Social Affairs Commission, the CCCB, May 8, 1987

INVITATION

Across Canada today, people are becoming increasingly concerned about the prospects of a comprehensive free trade accord with the United States. On a daily basis, the media provide a regular dose of news reports and commentaries on various aspects of the current trade negotiations between the two countries. The federal government maintains that a U.S.-Canada free trade accord will have profound effects on Canada's economy and society, not only for the next decade but for the next century as well. While there are no guarantees regarding the outcome of the bilateral free trade negotiations, the people of Canada are being asked to make a "leap of faith".

At first glance, many may well wonder why so much commotion has been stirred up over the current free trade negotiations with the United States. After all, Canada has traditionally been a trading nation and the United States has certainly been Canada's largest trading partner. Over the past forty years or so, the two countries have gradually moved in the direction of freer trade. Moreover, many people likely feel that reducing tariff and non-tariff barriers is a really complex or abstract economic matter having little to do with the daily life concerns of most people in our society.

A closer look, however, reveals that the free trade agenda is more than just another economic policy regarding exchange of goods and services. Today, free trade is combined with other measures designed to deregulate and privatize Canada's economy. In effect, a comprehensive free trade agreement appears to be the centrepiece of a major strategy to restructure Canada's economy and society for a high-tech market future. These changes, in turn, could have a real impact on the lives of people who work in various businesses, manufacturing industries, agricultural enterprises, service industries, cultural activities and the resource sector of our economy.

1. Public debate

The time has come for a nation-wide inquiry and public debate on the question — *Free Trade: At What Cost?* To date, neither the federal nor any of the provincial governments has been given a clear mandate to negotiate a comprehensive free trade agreement with the United States. Nor has there been much in the way of constructive discussion and debate on the issues. While it is important to refrain from making definitive judgments until the details of the negotiations are known, it is nonetheless imperative that people become actively involved in raising ethical questions concerning the economic, social and policital implications of bilateral free trade.

Historically, free trade with the United States has been a highly controversial public issue in Canada. As in the past, it is becoming increasingly clear today that the free trade issue is symbolic of much deeper concerns about Canada and its economic, political and cultural future. Once again, people are reflecting on who we are — as a people, as a nation — and asking what kind of society do we want to be or become. Before making a "leap of faith", it is important that there be serious public discussion and debate of these issues.

As Christians, we cannot stand idly by watching this public debate about Canada's future unfold. Many of the people who make up our own Christian communities — factory workers, small farmers, fisherpeople, business people, working women, people on social assistance and fixed incomes, native peoples, service workers and others — may be directly affected by the implications of a free trade accord. Like the early Church, we must find ways of listening to the concerns of our members and of supporting them as faith communities. Moreover, there are fundamental ethical questions about the values and priorities of our society at stake in the free trade debate.

2. Christian responsibilities

As pastoral leaders, we have a responsibility to encourage members of Christian communities to examine major issues of public policy in Canada from the standpoint of the Gospel and of the Church's social teachings. In recent years, we have actively promoted public discussion, debate and action on some basic values and priorities related to major economic and social policy directions in this country.[2] At the same time, numerous Christian groups and networks across Canada have been actively involved in raising serious ethical questions about a variety of specific economic and social policy concerns at regional, national and international levels.

Indeed, in the tradition of the ancient prophets of Israel, Christians today have a responsibility to raise ethical questions about major public policy concerns. In the name of Yahweh, the living God of Justice, the prophets consistently called on His people to account for their economic and social policies (e.g., Amos, Micah, Jeremiah, Hosea, Isaiah). In this tradition, Jesus Himself announced He was the message of the prophets come true, "good news to the poor" and "liberty to the oppressed" (Lk.4:18,19). Throughout His ministry, He taught us to look upon everyday life from the perspective of those who have become the victims of injustice in society (e.g., Mt.25:31-46).

In this spirit, we invite local faith communities across Canada to become involved in a process of study, discussion and action on some of the social and ethical issues at stake in the free trade debate. By faith communities, we are referring here to parishes, basic Christian communities of religious, social justice groups, organizations like the Catholic Women's League, Development and Peace, and a variety of ecumenical groups or associations across the country. We believe that Christian communities like these have an important role to play in raising ethical concerns about major economic and social policies affecting the lives of people in this country.

I — OBSERVE: SOCIAL ANALYSIS

As Christians, we are called to read the "signs of the times" and to analyze the economic, social and political structures that cause human suffering. This means being present and listening to the con-

cerns of people who may be affected by particular economic or social policies in our society. Today, the free trade debate provides an
opportunity for Christian communities to do some analysis of the
social impacts of a major economic policy in their own regions.

In doing social analysis, it is important to analyse public policies
from the perspective of the various people, groups and interests
affected in our society. Here, it should be understood that peoples'
views on economic strategies like free trade depend a great deal on
where they stand in relation to the economy and society itself. If one
is a bank manager or corporate executive, one's view of free trade
may be quite different than that of an unemployed father or a single
working mother struggling to feed, clothe and house a family of four
children. Each person, however, by virtue of his or her working
experience, has some knowledge of how the economy does function or should operate.

In each community or region, there are likely to be different concerns and viewpoints on the prospects of free trade with the United
States. Here are four categories of concern that have emerged in the
public debate on the social impacts of free trade for Canada.

1. BUSINESS CONCERNS

Canadian business, which has traditionlly been rather cautious
about free trade with the United States, has recently become a strong
advocate of free trade. This shift is due largely to the new economic
realities of international competitiveness, the rise of protectionism
in the United States and the growth of Canadian transnationals who
now have the capacity to compete in world markets. It is argued that
access to the huge U.S. market provides the best hope for expanding economic growth and prosperity in Canada. For example:

(a) Several large Canadian corporations and banks maintain that
bilateral free trade would help facilitate their own growth and expansion through corporate takeovers and mergers;

(b) Several Canadian corporations, which have successful investments in telecommunications, transportation and real estate in the
United States, would benefit from a bilateral free trade accord;

(c) Some segments of the lumber, mining, fisheries, agriculture, energy and manufacturing industries want a free trade accord to secure

existing access to U.S. markets and to offset the rise of U.S. protectionism;

(d) Some parts of Canadian consumer associations and small business associations see free trade as contributing to lower market prices and operating costs;

(e) Some Canadian subsidiaries of U.S. transnational corporations believe they would be able to produce more for export than for the domestic market under a free trade arrangement.

2. WORKERS' CONCERNS

Canadian workers, small producers and people on social assistance and fixed incomes, however, have become increasingly opposed to a comprehensive free trade pact with the United States. In some cases, bilateral free trade is seen as a direct threat to their livelihood and way of life. For example:

(a) Workers in labour-intensive industries such as textiles, clothing, electrical products, leather products, toys and games fear for the loss of their jobs;

(b) Service workers, mostly women, are increasingly concerned about the potential threat to jobs posed by trade in services (e.g., financial services, clerical work, data processing) with the U.S.;

(c) People on social assistance and fixed incomes are alarmed by changes already required by the free trade negotiations concerning Canada's drug patents legislation that will result in massive increases in prescription drug prices;

(d) Many farmers fear the loss of their farms and income due to the gradual elimination of marketing boards and subsidy programs which are alleged to be "unfair trade practices";

(e) Workers in branch plants of U.S. companies in Canada are also concerned about the prospects of more layoffs and plant shut-downs if Canadian subsidiaries are able to shift more production back to their parent corporations under a free trade accord.

3. PUBLIC CONCERNS

The Canadian public is also concerned about the general impact of a comprehensive free trade accord on Canada's economic, social and cultural policies. In order to establish a "level playing field" for free trade, Canada's economic, social and cultural policies will have to become more "harmonized" with those of the United States. Many people are concerned about the eventual effects this may have on policies and programs originally designed to ensure greater equality in our society. For example:

(a) In order to be competitive with southern U.S. states which have adopted lower social welfare standards our federal and provincial governments may be pressured to reduce or even eliminate certain social programs considered to be non-tariff barriers (e.g., unemployment insurance, medicare and collective bargaining measures).

(b) Canadian writers, artists and entertainers are concerned that free trade could result in an even greater flooding of Canada's markets with U.S. television media, publications and entertainment, thereby generating further assimilation to the dominant American culture;

(c) To ensure free market exchange, certain federal assistance programs for regional economic development may also have to be reduced or removed, which could have a devastating impact on poorer provinces and regions;

(d) Bilateral free trade may require other changes in Canada's economic policies (e.g., deregulation of the economy, reduction of consumer protection measures, environmental standards, etc.);

(e) There are also concerns that Canada's public sector tradition, which is distinct from that of the United States, may be further eroded through increased emphasis on privatization measures (e.g., sale of more crown corporations and contracting-out public services to private firms).

4. GLOBAL CONCERNS

At the same time, some people are concerned about the impact of a comprehensive free trade pact with the United States on Canada's capacity to act as a sovereign nation with an independent foreign policy. A variety of international justice and peace organizations in this country fear that closer economic (and political) ties with the United States could put further constraints on Canada's global responsibilities. For example:

(a) Those Third World countries seeking enhanced trade relations with Canada could well face more intense competition for Canadian markets due to preferential treatment for U.S. products and what may amount to a new form of continental protectionism;

(b) Canada could face further restrictions on its capacities to promote human rights in certain repressive regimes, especially in those countries or regions which are in U.S. economic or military spheres of influence (e.g., Central America, Southeast Asia, South Africa);

(c) Canada's immigration and refugee policies could become more restrictive, favouring wealthy entrepreneurs required for a high-tech market economy rather than people struggling to escape from conditions of poverty and political repression;

(d) Canada's responsibilities in promoting nuclear disarmament could be further constrained by increased involvement of Canadian industry in military production for the U.S., resulting from bilateral free trade;

(e) Closer economic ties with the United States through comprehensive free trade also increases the potential for economic retaliation, thus heightening the difficulties of pursuing a more independent foreign policy in these areas.

Finally, it should be noted that the free trade debate reveals different visions of Canada's economic and social future.

On the one hand, the proponents of bilateral free trade foresee an increasingly export-oriented economy for Canada in a high-tech market age. A comprehensive free trade agreement, it is argued, would enable Canada to become more open to profitable transnational investment, more specialized in high-tech production and more competitive in world markets. A U.S.-Canada free trade accord would also set a precedent for expanding international free trade through negotiations on the General Agreement on Trade and Tariffs.

On the other hand, the opponents of bilateral free trade maintain that Canada's economy needs to become more self-reliant and less dependent upon export-oriented production and interests of transnational corporations. More than most countries, it is argued, Canada has the natural resources, capital, technology and, above all, the human skills required to develop a more self-reliant economy designed to produce most of the goods and services needed in our society. What is required is a major reorganization of economic and social policies and strategies, at national and regional levels.

II — JUDGE: ETHICAL REFLECTIONS

As Christians, we are called to view the economic and social realities of our times primarily from the perspective of the Gospel message of Jesus Christ and His concern for the poor, the marginalized and the oppressed. From this faith perspective, we believe there are fundamental ethical concerns to be raised about the values and priorities of our economy and society. The social impacts of bilateral free trade, discussed above, provide some basis for ethical questions about the values and priorities implicit in the future directions of Canada's economy and society.

TABLE OF SOCIAL DOCUMENTS
(Cited in this Section)

The Universal Church

PT[3]   *Pacem in Terris* (Peace on Earth), John XXIII, 1963
GS[3]   *Gaudium et Spes* (The Church in the Modern World), Second Vatican Council, 1965.
PP[3]   *Populorum Progressio* (Development of Peoples), Paul VI, 1967
OA[3]   *Octogesima Adveniens* (Call to Action), Paul VI, 1971
JW[3]   *Justice in the World*, World Synod of Bishops, 1971
LE[1]   *Laborem Exercens* (On Human Work), John Paul II, 1981
CL[1]   *Libertatis Conscientia* (Christian Freedom and Liberation), Congregation for Doctrine of the Faith, 1986

The Canadian Conference of Catholic Bishops

WA[2] *From Words to Action*, 1976
ST[2] *A Society to be Transformed*, 1977
WJ[1] *Witness to Justice: A Society to be Transformed*, 1979
UC[1,2] *Unemployment: the Human Costs*, 1980
ER[1,2] *Ethical Reflections on the Economic Crisis*, 1983
EC[1,2] *Ethical Choices and Political Challenges*, 1984
GJ[4] *Global Justice — Global Peace*, 1986

[1] Publications Service, CCCB, 90 Parent Ave., Ottawa, K1N 7B1
[2] In *Do Justice!: Social Teaching of the Canadian Bishops*, edit. E.F. Sheridan, SJ (Éditions Paulines, Sherbrooke , J1E 2B9), 1986
[3] In *The Gospel of Peace and Justice*, Jos. Gremillion (Orbis, Maryknoll, N.Y.),   1976
[4] In this volume, Section V, Document 2, above

The social teachings of the Roman Catholic Church, inspired by the moral vision of the Scriptures, have outlined some ethical themes, principles and tools for examining the values and priorities of our economy and society (CL, ch. 5). These ethical themes provide some basic criteria for evaluating the free trade option and its implications for our society. It should be noted, however, that it is not our intention here to encourage people to make moral judgments in a dogmatic or authoritarian fashion. While moral principles are themselves universally valid, their application to concrete situations allows for a diversity of options. Our main purpose here is to stimulate ethical reflections on the social implications of the free trade strategy.

We have, therefore, divided some of the relevant ethical themes and principles from the Church's social teachings into four brief categories.

1. ETHICAL ORDER

Through its social teachings, the Church has consistently maintained that there is an ethical order to be followed in developing economic and social policies of nations. In evaluating the social impacts of bilateral free trade, it is important to recall the following ethical principles:

(a) That the value and dignity of the human person lie at the centre of an economy based on justice. All persons are made in the image of God (Gen.1:26-27) and therefore have certain inalienable rights; namely, the right to life and what makes for a truly human life (adequate food, clothing, housing, employment, education, health care, effective participation in decisions) (GS 26; PT 8-27).

(b) That the primary purpose of an economy should be the common good; that is, equitably to serve the basic needs of all people in a given society. "All other rights whatsoever, including those of property and free commerce, are to be subordinated to this principle" (PP 22, LE 14). This principle is rooted in biblical themes like the God of Justice (e.g., Ps. 9:7-12, 18; 94:1-15; 96:10-13) and the Covenant (e.g., Dt. 16:20ff; Is. 42:1-7).

(c) That all nation states have a responsibility to ensure that their economies are organized to serve the basic needs of all their peoples (JW 13-19; LE 18). Governments are responsible for promoting economic and social justice for their peoples (e.g., Is. 32:1-5; Pr. 16:11-12, 29:4, Jer. 33:14-16).

(d) That to be authentic, economic development must be "integral", encompassing the social, cultural, spiritual, as well as economic needs of peoples (PP 14). Economic strategies based simply on maximizing private profits, power or technological growth result in distorted forms of "development" (CL 12, EC, p. 4).

(e) That the global realities of interdependence in the modern world call for new forms of solidarity between peoples and nations in building an international order based on justice and peace (PP 43ff; LE, GJ, EC, p. 6).

2. ETHICAL PRIORITIES

The Church's social teachings further emphasize that some basic ethical priorities should be followed in developing economic and social policies. Thus, in evaluating the social impacts of free trade, consideration should be given to the following ethical priorities:

(a) That the needs of the poor take priority over the wants of the rich in an economy based on justice (ER, EC, p. 5). This does not simply mean increasing hand-outs for the poor but requires instead a more equitable distribution of wealth and power among peoples and nations (WA 3, ST, UC 13). This is the Gospel's "preferential option for the poor" (cf. Lk. 1:46-55; 4:18-19; 6:20-26; 12:13-21; 16:13-15; Mk. 4:18-19; Phil. 2:6-11), which is also reflected in the story of the Last Judgment (Mt. 25:31-46).

(b) That the basic rights of working people take priority over the maximization of profits and the accumulation of capital. Human labour, therefore, is to be the subject, not an object in production, taking priority over both capital and technology (LE 12, ER, EC, p. 5, CL 87). The Scriptures also warn against the exploitation of workers (e.g., Jas. 5:1-6).

(c) That the participation of the marginalized in economic and social planning takes priority over an economic order that excludes them (ER, EC, p. 6). All peoples have rights to self-determination, to participate effectively in economic and social decisions affecting their lives (JW 16, 17).

(d) That self-reliant models of development are essential if an economy is to be organized to serve the basic needs of its population. Through economic self-reliance, peoples' energies are directed towards developing local resources to serve the basic human and social needs of their communities (JW 1, 13-19). The early church also maintained this principle (e.g., Acts 4:32-35).

(e) That, in an economy based on justice, responsible stewardship of the environment takes priority over unlimited industrial expansion (WA 6, EC, p. 6, 12). Economic development, therefore, must take place in harmony with nature (e.g., Ps. 104; Lev. 25:1-19).

3. MARKET VALUES

At the same time, the Church's social teachings have warned against the dangers of emphasizing market oriented values and priorities in developing economic and social policies. Ethical concerns also must be taken into account in evaluating free trade strategies. For example:

(a) The tendency to define human beings and social relations in terms of the demand and supply forces of the market place. As a result, human beings, human labour and human needs are treated largely as commodities to be bought, sold or exchanged in the market place (e.g., LE 7, ER, EC p. 10).

(b) The emphasis on possessive individualism, self-gratification, personal selfishness, material consumption and the accumulation of personal wealth as ultimate values in a market society (EC, p. 15; ST). In the Gospels, the values of the beatitudes (Mt. 5:1-12) are frequently contrasted with these market values (e.g., Lk. 12:13-21; 1 Tim. 6:3-10).

(c) The priority given to competitiveness as the supreme law of economics (PP 26, ST). Here, the doctrine of the "survival of the fittest" prevails. The strong survive while the weak are eliminated (ST, ER).

(d) The emphasis on the maximization of profits, technological expansion and economic growth as "development" priorities in a market oriented society (PP 14). Here, capital takes priority over human labour and the basic purposes of development (ER, EC, p. 4, 5). Scripture constantly warns against the cult of idols such as wealth and power (e.g., Mt. 6:24; Jn. 2:13-25; Lk. 16:14-15; Am. 2:6-16).

(e) The belief that the market contains some kind of built-in system of "natural justice" whereby accumulated wealth in the hands of the few trickles down to the many. Yet experience shows that market structures result in a very uneven distribution of wealth (ER, EC, p. 10-11).

4. DEPENDENT SOCIETY

The Church's social teaching also warns against the dangers of nations and societies becoming increasingly dependent on external powers. These ethical concerns also deserve consideration in evaluating free trade strategies. For example:

(a) The power of transnational enterprises which exercise enormous influence over the economic, political, social and cultural lives of people and nations states (OA, 44). Such transnational powers are not accountable to the common good (WJ p. 36, 37).

(b) The problem of economies failing to serve the basic needs of their own populations because they are primarily export oriented, and dependent on externally controlled means of production (JW 1, 13-19; WJ p. 20, 35-39). As a result, development priorities are determined largely by external interests rather than by the basic needs of the developing communities (EC p. 6, 11; ER).

(c) The danger of not achieving full self-expression and self-realization as a community of people(s) when a nation becomes too economically, culturally and politically dependent on external powers.[3]

(d) The critical need to protect cultural sovereignty, as the "fundamental criterion" of a society or nation, against the pressures of domination by external economic and political powers.[4]

III — ACT: PASTORAL STRATEGIES

As Christians, we are also called to move "from words to action". For faith communities, this means developing pastoral strategies for education and action on the ethical concerns involved in major issues of public policy like free trade. It also means collaborating with other people and associations in bringing about public policy changes and social transformation.

In developing pastoral strategies for action on the free trade issue, it is important to build on the presentations of Parts I and II. In Part I, we observed and analyzed some of the social concerns and impacts of bilateral free trade from the perspective and experience of several sectors of the community and region. In Part II, we reflected on these social impacts, making some ethical judgments in the light of the Church's social teaching. This brings us to the work of developing strategies for action as a faith community on the free trade issue. Even if the details of the trade negotiations and agreement are not readily available, it should be possible to develop strategies for education and action based on the concerns raised above.

1. POSITION STATEMENT

As a basis for action, it is helpful for groups to develop their own position statement or set of resolutions on particular issues of public policy. In developing a position or resolution on the free trade issue, consideration should be given to some or all of the following elements:

(a) A brief reference to the ethical concerns you bring as a faith community in addressing the social impacts of bilateral free trade in your region;

(b) A general expression of your position as a group on the issue, that is to say, whether you are for or against a U.S.-Canada accord on free trade;

(c) A brief listing of particular concerns you may have about the social impacts of bilateral free trade in your community or region;

(d) A list of conditions that should be met before a bilateral trade agreement is made;

(e) A reference to some form of action required on the part of the federal government and your own provincial government on the issue;

(f) A call for democratic processes for public participation on the free trade issue before final decisions are made.

Groups not ready to take a definitive position on the issue may wish instead to develop a short statement of concern.

2. COMMUNITY EDUCATION

To generate support for your group's position, education initiatives are essential in both the Church and the community at large. Despite the considerable attention given to the free trade negotiations in the media, there is still a serious lack of public information, awareness, discussion and debate on the issue. The following suggestions might be considered in developing education initiatives.

(a) Convinced groups could make arrangements for sharing the experience and results of their reflection and study with local pastors, religious superiors and the bishop of the diocese;

(b) Information sessions could be organized for parish councils, religious communities or the provincial meetings of Development and Peace, Catholic Women's League and other concerned church organizations;

(c) These same church groups could also be invited to discuss and endorse the position statement or resolutions developed by a group workshop on the free trade issue;

(d) Education initiatives could be developed in collaboration with Christian churches who share similar concerns about the free trade issue;

(e) Articles on the free trade issue could be written for publication in diocesan newspapers and related church publications, as well as letters to the editor of community newspapers.

3. POLITICAL ACTION

In addressing issues of public policy, faith communities should express their concerns through appropriate forms of political action. In developing action strategies on the free trade issue, the following might be taken into consideration:

(a) A copy of your group's position statement or resolution, along with a covering letter, could be sent to the Prime Minister, the Premier of your province and your members of parliament;

(b) A meeting might be arranged with your local member of parliament to discuss the group's statement or resolution;

(c) Personal letters by individuals and families could be sent to political leaders and representatives at federal and provincial levels expressing your position and concerns on free trade;

(d) Efforts could be made to mobilize support in parishes and other church groups for petition campaigns that coincide with your group's position and concerns on the issue.

4. REGIONAL COALITIONS

Finally, effective action on major public policy issues generally requires collaboration with other community organizations who share common concerns for social and economic justice. This can be done through coalitions around common issues like bilateral free trade. Consideration might be given to the following initiatives:

(a) Identify regional coalitions of community organizations who share similar concerns on the free trade issue;

(b) Meet with representatives of the regional coalition to discuss ways in which your faith community organization might participate in their activities;

(c) Encourage members of your faith community or organization to participate in public meetings or rallies sponsored by the regional coalition;

(d) Arrange for spokespersons from your faith community or organization to speak at public meetings or rallies on some of the ethical issues at stake in the free trade debate.

NOTES

1. Available also (with discussion questions and workshop suggestions in a substantial pamphlet for seminars and group study) from Publications Service, CCCB, 90 Parent Ave., Ottawa, ON, K1N 7B1.

Please note: issued by the Social Affairs Commission of the Canadian Conference of Catholic Bishops, this document is for the purpose of stimulating study and action by local Christian communities. As such it does not represent the official teaching of the Church, except where this teaching is directly invoked.

2. Cf. *Do Justice!*, edit. E.F. Sheridan, SJ (Éditions Paulines, Sherbrooke, QC, J1E 2B9), 1986.

3. Cf. John Paul II, Address to UNESCO, June 1980, nos. 6-16, in *Origins* (Washington), X, n. 4, p. 60.

4. *Ibid.*, nn. 14-16, p. 62.

Section IV, Document 9

PASTORAL LETTER ON THE TWENTIETH ANNIVERSARY OF THE CANADIAN CATHOLIC ORGANIZATION FOR DEVELOPMENT AND PEACE[1]

Author — The Canadian Conference of Catholic Bishops, December 11, 1987

Dear Sisters and Brothers in Christ,

1. This year, 1987, is the twentieth anniversary of one of the great events in the life of the Catholic Church in this country: the launching of CCODP, the Canadian Catholic Organization for Development and Peace.

2. At that time, our Church committed itself to build CCODP as an organized movement whose task would be to help us face up to today's global dimensions of God's ancient command: love your neighbour as yourself. The neighbours on whose behalf Development and Peace challenges us to active love are our neediest sisters and brothers in Africa, Asia and Latin America.

3. They are among the peoples of whom the Second Vatican Council spoke in the opening words of its 1965 *Constitution On the Church in the Modern World*:

   The joy and hope, the grief and anguish of the people of our time, especially those who are poor or in any way afflicted, are the joy and hope, the grief and anguish of the followers of Christ as well. [2]

4. As the bishops of Canada came home after Vatican II, they found themselves involved almost immediately in discussions and plans that led to the founding of Development and Peace two years later. During the same period, by what we can now look back to as an inspiring coincidence, Pope Paul VI was writing one of his most challenging encyclicals. Published in 1967, just a few months before Development and Peace was announced, it was called *On the Development of Peoples.* More daringly than ever before, that letter called on Catholics everywhere to work to close unjust rich-poor divisions in our distorted world. The Pope wrote: [3]

> It is not just a matter of eliminating hunger, nor even of reducing poverty. The struggle against destitution, though urgent and necessary, is not enough. It is a question, rather, of building a world where every person, no matter of what race, religion or nationality, can live a fully human life, freed from servitude imposed by other people or by natural forces; a world where freedom is not an empty word, and where the poor man Lazarus can sit down at the same table with the rich man.

5. In this pastoral letter, we Catholic bishops of Canada wish to celebrate the first 20 years of Development and Peace. Working at its mandate, which so closely parallels Pope Paul VI's challenge, CCODP has accomplished great things. We wish also to reflect on how all of us must continue to work for justice and peace in the years ahead. Conditions still seem to be deteriorating for our neighbours who are poor. We must, all of us together as Church, continue the search for ways to make their struggles for basic necessities central to our shared mission to order temporal affairs according to God's plan for justice and peace.

TWENTY YEARS TO CELEBRATE

6. As we look back on the first 20 years of Development and Peace, one reason for gratitude is the way the internal life of this organization is evolving in our country. Also to be celebrated in a particular way is the growth of CCODP's partnerships and networks with other groups, at home and abroad. What it has done in public education and fund-raising also merits special praise. With these initiatives have come Third World self-help projects and the emergency aid funds

which, for many, have made the difference between despair and hope, and even between death and life.

7. It is important and helpful, we believe, to draw attention to the Church's achievements in and through Development and Peace before reflecting on the grave challenges we face in the brutal fact that world-wide poverty continues, and even worsens.

CCODP's Growth

8. Development and Peace was founded by the Canadian bishops working with Canadian lay people, religious and priests. The leadership of the organization was entrusted, from the beginning, to lay Catholics, but we bishops, with priests and religious, have also continued to work for its growth and success. It has been an organization of and for the whole Church in this country. Every diocese and, indeed, every parish has been reached. Through CCODP's education and aid projects, Catholics everywhere in Canada have been given grace-filled opportunities for insight, openness and generosity. Volunteers in local communities continue to organize local Development and Peace groups which this year reached a total of 230 — a number that will continue growing.

CCODP's Partners

9. At the community, diocesan, regional and national levels, there are groups working for development education and social change in this country. Fortunate indeed are those communities where these groups and CCODP groups find ways to complement and enhance each other.

10. Special mention must be made here of the co-operation offered CCODP by the development and funding agencies of other Christian Churches in Canada. Noteworthy in this collaboration is CCODP's direct involvement in the social justice coalitions that are a special feature of ecumenical solidarity in this country.

11. This network of partners inside Canada now reaches into many Third World communities. The leaders of Development and Peace over the years have built up a complex of partners in Asia, Africa

and Latin America. These Third World partners share in Development and Peace decisions about which projects to be funded in their countries. Of equal, and probably even greater importance, is the contribution these partners make to educating Canadians. Through their experience and understanding of what causes their poverty, they influence the educational work being done across Canada by Development and Peace. For many of us, visits to Canada by CCODP's Third World guests have provided some of our deepest insights into what it means to be a Christian in our strife-torn world.

12. This growing network across Canada and around the globe, of people determined to stand together for justice and peace in social and economic development, is a major reason for hope for all of us.

Funds and Projects

13. While the work of CCODP goes on all year long, it has a particular emphasis in *Share Lent*. This annual campaign has been the focus of CCODP's development education work and its major fundraising action. All across this country, there have been Catholics who have taken *Share Lent* very seriously, making it an event of personal and community importance, for its impact at home and its results abroad. Through *Share Lent* over the past 20 years, CCODP has raised more than $70 million for development assistance and emergency relief. Another $30 million have been added by contributions outside this annual campaign. Important matching grants have come from CIDA (the Canadian International Development Agency). Some provincial governments have added to the total. In sum, the outflow of aid to Third World projects through CCODP has exceeded $162 million.

14. Even this very incomplete inventory of what Development and Peace has accomplished over the years give all of us good reason to celebrate.

THE CHALLENGE OF THE FUTURE

15. When we begin, now, to reflect about the future of CCODP, certain probing questions recur: what have we learned through CCODP

about Third World poverty? How does CCODP's mandate look in the light of today's situations, in the church and in society, in Canada and abroad? What have we discovered in 20 years of engagement in development education and assistance? What are the most urgent challenges facing us as Church in our responsibility to help our neediest sisters and brothers achieve full human development?

Poverty Through Their Eyes

16. When we look at their world through the eyes of those who receive CCODP funds, what do we see? Pope John Paul II, speaking at Edmonton in 1984, gave us a description we must never forget:

> The poor people and poor nations — poor in different ways, not only lacking food but also deprived of freedom and other human rights — will judge those who take these goods away from them, amassing to themselves an imperialistic monopoly of economic and political supremacy at the expenses of others. [4]

17. Poverty in the form of cruel need — the need for decent housing, clean water, land for food, basic health care, appropriate education, participation in the decisions which have the most impact on personal and community life — is a dominant fact of life for the majority of people today. This ugly fact is accompanied by another: poverty is mainly due to the denial to the poor of their basic rights and essential goods. True, natural disasters — droughts and earthquakes — disrupt or destroy communities and plunge their populations into experiences of cruel hardships. The toll of these dramatic natural disasters is not to be compared, however, with that of continuing social injustice, of "servitude imposed by other people," [5] in Pope Paul VI's words.

18. That is why our Third World partners tell us aid, like tears, is not enough. That is why they say it is not enough for us to try to share our surplus with the victims of poverty. Aid is essential, especially after natural disasters. But, always, we must work at ending imposed servitude and deprivation. Always we must learn to see in what ways we, in a rich country, may be involved in making or keeping them poor. That is why our efforts to aid our stricken neighbours must be twinned with initiatives for our own education. We must try to discern why Pope John Paul II could say at Edmon-

ton that we may well stand judged by the poor for taking food, freedom and other human rights away from them. [6]

CCODP's Mandate 20 Years Later

19. By its founding charter, CCODP is committed to promoting active solidarity between Canadians and the peoples of the Third World. To this end, it is to channel donations to Third World socioeconomic development projects and, at the same time, to try to help Canadians understand that obstacles to development often lie within our own mental, social and political structures. There is no question about the basic reasons for this mandate; there is no question about the need to promote self-help projects abroad and development education at home. The only question, surely, has to do with how the intentions of that mandate can be more enthusiastically and fully achieved.

20. The founders of CCODP, we can say, hoped that it would be, over time, not just one organization among many but a gathering of the whole Church in this country in a growing community of love and support for the victims of social injustice. That is not to say that anyone expects CCODP to do this whole job alone, but it is CCODP's job to get all of us involved in building such a community.

Mandate Confirmed by Catholic Social Teachings

21. CCODP's workers and supporters can take heart from the fact that their mandate is fully in line with the Church's social teachings. As Pope Paul VI said in his 1967[7] encyclical: "It is a question of building a world where every person… can live a fully human life." He stressed that there cannot be justice and peace without full human development. The 1971 Synod of Bishops, in turn, affirmed that: [8]

> Action on behalf of justice and participation in the transformation of the world fully appear to us as a constitutive dimension of the preaching of the Gospel, or, in other words, of the Church's mission for the redemption of the human race and its liberation from every oppressive situation.

Pope John Paul II has renewed this same challenge by insisting that central to our vocation as Christians is the call to develop everywhere a civilization of love.[9]

What has been Learned?

22. Twenty years of work by CCODP have brought the success that we noted earlier in this letter. They also show all of us that world poverty is not easily ended, and also that the process of development education in this country is slow and difficult.

23. One of the objectives of CCODP's development education programme is to change mentalities, attitudes, behaviours and structures in such ways that human solidarity can be realized. For this, both personal conversion and social change are required. Each has its own difficulties. People can so easily find excuses for delay, for caution, for resistance when invited to change. New awareness of ourselves and of the world dawns slowly.

24. What is called for is not just a gradual, interior hidden adjustment. CCODP has aimed to encourage more and more people and groups to get involved in action for development. All of us have been called to give moral, financial and political support to changes directed to the development and liberation of people in the Third World. Some argue that this is not Church business; others protest that it is unrealistic and, indeed, impossible.

25. In such objections and difficulties, Development and Peace is experiencing nothing new. All who try to follow Jesus know that He urges us to a self-giving that is as unlimited as His own: an unresting, tireless love that seeks justice and peace for everyone.

To Build Together for the Future

26. It is not our intention in this pastoral letter to propose specific directives for CCODP's future work. Within the organization, its leaders from national, regional, diocesan and parish levels have been active throughout this anniversary year. They have been continuing their efforts to make CCODP always more effective in promoting development and peace. One such initiative has been the recently com-

pleted independent study of CCODP's educational programmes and materials. As part of CCODP's review process, we wish to share some observations that we believe will support and advance what is already alive in the Church in this country.

27. The many workers and supporters of Development and Peace — all those involved in it — are truly Church. You are involved in the evangelizing work of development. Engaged in promoting justice and peace, you are signs, visible expressions, of the baptismal vocation of all Christians. Through Third World partnerships, the universal dimensions of the Church are reflected. As bishops, we see this and welcome it.

28. We also see possibilities of greater growth, and we wish to help CCODP in this area. Increasingly, Development and Peace should become better known and more active in each diocese. This would not be at the expense of CCODP's national and international activities, but in support of them. We wish an ever more clearly visible collaboration of CCODP's diocesan workers with other diocesan workers around each bishop. The confirmation and maturation of CCODP as an expression of evangelization by the local Church can only aid its mission everywhere, including each and every parish.

29. We recognize that our hoped-for diocesan developments will place some new demands on CCODP. Canadian Catholics are astonishingly diverse. We have different ethnic backgrounds, different economic experiences, different political imaginations. There is among us a great variety in our understanding of justice, development and peace. Even our understanding of Church varies considerably. Pervading all this is a common secular culture that beckons us to choose comfort and self-gratification. If the CCODP message is to penetrate each of our local Church communities more deeply, much effort must be given to designing new education materials and methods.

30. CCODP's increased presence and activity in our local Churches will also, we hope, aid in clarifying and deepening the links between faith and social involvement. We think particularly of links of CCODP with faith education and with the celebration of the faith in the liturgy. The concluding message of the 1987 Synod of Bishops confirms the close relationship of holiness and work for justice: [10]

The Holy Spirit leads us to understand more clearly that holiness today cannot be attained without a commitment to justice, without a human solidarity with the poor and the oppressed.

The model of holiness for laity must integrate the social dimension of transforming the world according to the plan of God.

31. To aid in this process, we bishops will examine the formation and training programs for priests and other pastoral agents. We wish all those who serve as animators of our Christian communities to be the best possible collaborators in the work of Development and Peace. As one method for this, we foresee regular local meetings of CCODP leaders with other diocesan leaders, to build understanding and solidarity within each local church around its pastors.

32. From the beginning, CCODP has aimed at drawing peoples together. It has called us to see our neighbour in those we tend to ignore or neglect. It reminds us to love our neighbour in ways that can change our own world. In this, the Canadian Catholic Organization for Development and Peace is a servant of Jesus Christ Who makes us just in new ways, Who enables us to love without limits.

33. We, your bishops, are grateful to the council, staff and volunteers of Development and Peace, and all associated with them, for twenty years of courageous and persevering work. We thank God for the new hope you have been able to plant, in the Third World and also here in Canada. We pray with you for the future of this work. May you continue to help us all grow in courage and hope as, together, we strive to live and act as one body towards all whom Jesus loves.

NOTES

1. Projected at the October Conference of the Bishops in 1966, The Canadian Catholic Organization for Development and Peace was organized in 1967 and announced in a Joint Pastoral Letter of March 14, 1968, cf. *Do Justice!*, edit. E.F. Sheridan, SJ (Éditions Paulines, Sherbrooke, Qc., 1986), Document 17, p. 142; also Document 45, p. 322, marking the tenth anniversary of CCODP. The first letter was over the signature of Bishop Alexander Carter (Sault Ste. Marie), President of the Conference, the second signed by his brother, Bishop Gerald Emmett Carter, Bishop of London and also President.

2. *Second Vatican Council*, edit. Austin Flannery (St. Paul Editions, Boston, 1975), p. 903.

3. In *The Papal Encyclicals*, edit. Claudia Carlen, IHM (Wilmington, N.C., McGrath Publishing, 1981), V, p. 191, n. 47.

4. In *The Canadian Catholic Review* (Saskatoon, Sask., S7N 0W6), Oct., 1984, p. 62.

5. *The Development of Peoples*, 1967, in *The Papal Encyclicals*, cf. note 3, above, V, p. 191, n. 47.

6. *L.c.* in note 4, above.

7. *L.c.* in note 3, above, cf. also, nn. 14-17, 20, 45-55.

8. *Justice in the World*, statement of World Synod of Bishops, 1971, in *The Gospel of Peace and Justice*, Jos. Gremillion (Orbis Books, Maryknoll, N.Y., 1975), p. 514, n. 6.

9. Cf. John Paul II to the Bishops of Germany, Nov. 17, 1980, at Fulda: "Permit me to go back to my appeal to the *Katholikentag* (Catholic Assembly) in Berlin... 'Help me to build a worldwide civilization of love.' " *Orientations* (Washington, 1980), X, n. 25, p. 389. Also his farewell message to Germany, Nov. 19, 1980: "All Europe is awaiting the realization of this civilization of love, inspired by the spirit of the Gospel and, at the same time, profoundly humanist. In fact it responds to the deepest needs and aspirations of man even in the social dimensions of his existence." *Documentation Catholique* (Paris, 1980), p. 1171. This idea of "a civilization of love" is one to which John Paul II returned several times in subsequent homilies, messages, addresses. Cf. also his exhortation to the Pontifical Commission Justice and Peace, Feb. 9, 1980, *Development and the Ideal of Social Love*, in *The Pope Speaks* (Washington, 1980), XXV, p. 173.

10. *Message to the People of God*, n. 2, in *Origins*, Washington, XVII, n. 4, p. 387; also in *Synod of Bishops, 1987*, p. 24, Documentation Service, CCCB, 90 Parent Ave., Ottawa, K1N 7B1.

Section IV, Document 10

FROM COLD WAR TO PEACEBUILDING: A MESSAGE ON THE OCCASION OF DISARMAMENT WEEK 1988

Author — The Commission for Social Affairs, the CCCB, October, 1988

Disarmament Week (October 24-31) is an occasion for the peoples of the world to stimulate and strengthen movements for peace. As bishops responsible for justice and peace concerns we invite members of Christian communities to participate actively in the events of this week and to join with others in the work of peacemaking.

For believers, especially Christians, it is a time to make a visible commitment to be peacemakers, and in deep solidarity of spirit, to work for a world in which justice will flourish and peace abound (cf. Ps. 72:7). The call to be peacemakers does not come from any existing movement but from Jesus the Christ. The Gospel's peacemaking mandate calls us to make hard choices and honest judgments about the arms race in general and Canadian defence policy in particular.

During this Disarmament Week 1988, we wish to refer to the modest but important progress that is being made in the disarmament negotiations between the Soviet Union and the United States. The very fact that cold war rhetoric has been replaced by serious dialogue and negotiation between the superpowers is reason for a new sense of hope in the peace movement. The global effort today for peacemaking is also symbolized in the awarding of the Nobel Peace Prize to the U.N. peacekeeping forces. Canada has made important contributions to the development of international peacekeeping mechanisms. While Canadians have good reason to be proud of this award, efforts should be made to re-establish peacekeeping duties as a priority in Canadian defence policy.

We know, however, that peace with justice among nations lies only at the end of a long road. The forces promoting the arms race are very powerful. Military establishments have sophisticated methods of preventing effective moves towards disarmament. Technological developments seem to have their own self-generating momentum. This momentum threatens global peace by reducing the ability of governments and groups to influence disarmament policy effectively. Our technological civilization is very skilled in preparing and waging war but does not yet know how to build peace.

As Christians, we must examine critically our attitudes regarding Canada's role in the arms race. Some of the Christian community find themselves victims of despair or of a pessimistic indifference. Some question the very possibility of achieving the Gospel vision or of having that vision influence the political order. Others believe that peace and security can be built on the basis of an evil intention of "mutually assured destruction", which lies at the heart of the doctrine of nuclear deterrence. Still others claim that the division of the world into blocs and "spheres of influence" is "natural" and inevitable.

The Church's social teaching, however, rejects these claims. A world dominated by the logic of military and economic blocs is, in the words of Pope John Paul II, an evil rooted in "structures of sin". [1] The exaggerated concern for military security deadens the impulse toward cooperation by all peoples and nations for the common good and for common security. While not proposing a strategy for unilateral disarmament, John Paul II maintains that nuclear deterrence cannot constitute, in a lasting way, a viable base for security and peace. [2]

As Canada's church leaders have noted with concern, the federal government's *Defence White Paper* lapses into "anti-Soviet cold war rhetoric", and prescribes a major increase in defence spending. [3] The White Paper advocates what amounts to security for some, at the price of insecurity for others. The vast majority of Canadians, however, according to a survey by the North-South Institute, implicitly reject both the cold war diagnosis and the prescriptions of the White Paper. [4]

In their open letter to the Prime Minister in response to the *Defence White Paper*, Canada's church leaders outlined principles upon which to formulate an alternative approach. At the core of this alternative is the concept of common security. This means that "Canadian security, in common with the security of the whole human family, should focus on the elimination of the current dangerous military arsenals and the development of a world order that respects the rights of people to determine their own affairs" (Cf. Is. 2:4 "... and they shall beat their swords into ploughshares..."). The search for real security means that a military strategy of nuclear first strike and war-fighting capacity must be abandoned. Real security calls for equitable trade patterns, development assistance, the promotion of human rights, peace-keeping duties and other action that directly promote the common good and foster conditions of social and economic justice. In short, if you want peace, work for justice (Cf. Is. 32:17; Jas. 3:18).

Canadian territory is situated in a strategic position between the two superpowers and can be used either to stabilize or to threaten the international system. Current Canadian defence policy, dominated by the logic of military blocs and alliances, permits the use of Canadian territory to enhance the military capacity of the United States. The pursuit of true security, however, requires that Canada resist the pressure to make its territory available for a de-stabilizing strategic air defence and related nuclear war-fighting facilities. As Canadian church leaders have said, Canadian territory should not be made available to *any* country for the purpose of attacking or threatening to attack a third country.

During Disarmament Week, we encourage all members of the Roman Catholic Church in Canada to pray, speak and act for peace. As believers and as citizens we are called to raise fundamental moral and ethical questions about Canadian defence policies. Indeed, we are called to support policies that reverse the arms race and move Canada into a leadership role in pursuing peace with justice[5]. We encourage members of Christian communities to become more active in the peace movement and to take the modest steps available to each and every one of us. As we become more informed and concerned about issues of peace, we become a more peaceful people, united with others who share a genuine hope for peace.

NOTES

1. In *Origins* (Washington, 1988), XVIII, n. 38, Section V, pp. 653ff.

2. In *Origins* (Washington, 1988), XVII, n. 32, n. 5, p. 549.

3. Cf. *Peacebuilding: The Church Response to Canadian Defence Policy*, Working Paper 881, 1988, Project Ploughshares, Conrad Grebel College, U. of Waterloo, Waterloo, ON, N2L 3G6.

4. Cf. *Review/Outlook*, 1987-88, North South Institute, 55 Murray St., Ottawa, ON, K1N 5M3.

5. Cf. this Section IV, Document 4, above, esp. Part I.

Section IV, Document 11

ON THE IMPENDING BUDGET

To the Honourable Michael Wilson, Minister of Finance[1]

Author — Archbishop Gilles Ouellet, Chairman,
Episcopal Commission for Social Affairs, March 18, 1989

I am writing on behalf of the Social Affairs Commission of the Canadian Conference of Catholic Bishops to express our concerns about the prospect of social spending cuts in the forthcoming budget, as a primary means of reducing the federal deficit.

As pastors, we do not claim to be technical experts on taxation. We do, however, have a responsibility to raise ethical issues about economic and social policy directions in Canada, based on the social teachings of the Church and our pastoral experience of the needs of our people. In this context, we are greatly concerned about the recent demands for deep cuts in federal social spending as a means of reducing the deficit.

As you know, the Church maintains that there is a moral order to be followed in developing an economy and society. From that perspective, the value and dignity of the human person lies at the centre of an economy based on justice. The primary purpose of an economy, therefore, is to serve the common good. This means that the state has a moral responsibility to intervene in the market to ensure that the economy serves the basic economic, social and cultural needs of the people. In the light of these ethical principles, we wish to share the following comments and suggestions with respect to your forthcoming federal budget.

First, we maintain deficit reduction must not be effected by laying disproportionate burdens on the majority of working people. It is difficult to accept the argument that social spending is a primary cause of the deficit. As many observers have noted, the federal deficit has been caused by a number of complex factors including high levels of unemployment, subsidies and tax write-offs for corporations, and unjustifiably high interest rates.

Second, we maintain that Canada's system of universal social programs must be strengthened, not weakened by deficit cutting measures. As we have stated before in relation to your government's de-indexation of family allowances, the principle of the universality of entitlement is a basic right of citizenship. It is essential for developing a sense of shared responsibility and social solidarity. When social benefits are "targeted" for those "most in need", tensions, prejudices and social divisions emerge. In other words, selective social programs inevitably serve to create divisions between those "who pay" and those "who receive". As a result, the poorest sectors of society are further stigmatized, humiliated and in some provinces, even harassed. In contrast, universal social programs are more likely to be fully utilized by all people, including those in need, while selective social programs tend to discourage eligible people from applying for and receiving benefits. Finally, universality ensures that social programs are less vulnerable to political manipulation.

Third, we maintain that the government has alternative policy choices that can be pursued in its efforts to reduce the federal deficit. It could, for example, raise public revenues by increasing corporate taxes and by lowering interest rates.People are becoming very aware that the corporate share of taxes has been steadily declining while personal income tax (especially for low and middle income earners) has been rising. It is therefore an ethical imperative that a new system of taxation be developed to ensure that corporations and wealthy individuals pay their fair share.

As Canada's Minister of Finance, Mr. Wilson, we ask that you give serious consideration to these ethical concerns before steps are taken to finalize the preparations of the federal government's forthcoming budget. In advance, thank you for your consideration and attention to these vital concerns.

NOTE

1. The letter was copied to Right Hon. Brian Mulroney, Prime Minister; Hon. Perrin Beatty, Minister, Health and Welfare; Rt. Hon. John Turner, Leader of the Liberal Party; Hon. Ed Broadbent, Leader of the New Democratic Party.

Section IV, Document 12

ON RESTRICTING FUNDS FOR HIGHER EDUCATION OF NATIVE STUDENTS

To the Right Honourable Brian Mulroney, Prime Minister[1]

Author — Archbishop James M. Hayes, President, Canadian Conference of Catholic Bishops, April 24, 1989

I am writing at this time to express our concerns over the recent wave of protests by Canada's native peoples, against the federal government's decision to curb funds for post-secondary education for native students.

As you know, the Catholic Church has had a long history of direct involvement in the education of native peoples in Canada. In our view, it is essential that Aboriginal peoples have guaranteed access to opportunities for complete education so they can make a significant contribution to their own development as First Nations and to Canada as a whole.

It is our understanding that the *Post-Secondary Education Assistance Program for Native Peoples* has been highly regarded as an effective program, in the Auditor General's Report. Similarly, higher education authorities like the Canadian Universities Teachers' Association have praised it, calling for its continuation.

The Assembly of First Nations has asked for a moratorium on this recent decision in order to develop a joint process for arriving at a mutual agreement between the First Nations and the Government of Canada on educational policy directions before any program changes are implemented.

We are convinced that this is a reasonable request, though Mr. Cadieux, your Minister of Indian and Northern Affairs, has refused to entertain it. In our view it would be highly conducive to maintaining and improving education for the native peoples of Canada. While the whole issue is being debated in the House, we feel strongly that the hunger strike of native students has gone on long enough.

NOTE

1. The letter was copied to George Erasmus, President of First Nations; Hon. Pierre Cadieux, Minister for Indian and Northern Affairs; Rt. Hon. John Turner, Leader, Liberal Party; Hon. Edward Broadbent, Leader, New Democratic Party.

Section IV, Document 13

SUBMISSION TO THE LEGISLATIVE COMMITTEE ON BILL C-21: AMENDMENTS TO THE UNEMPLOYMENT INSURANCE ACT

Author — The Social Affairs Commission, Canadian Conference of
Catholic Bishops, September 25, 1989

Mr. Chairman, we welcome the opportunity to share our views on some of the ethical issues and priorities at stake in the legislation to amend the Unemployment Insurance Act (Bill C-21).

In recent years, the Canadian Conference of Catholic Bishops has issued several public declarations and documents related to the issues being studied by this legislative committee. In 1980, we spoke about the realities and causes of unemployment in our document *Unemployment: the Human Cost.* These themes were further developed in our declaration *Ethical Reflections on the Economic Crisis* (1983) and our subsequent brief to the MacDonald Commission in 1984, entitled *Ethical Choices and Political Challenges.* [1] And, in 1986, we addressed the ethical priorities of an unemployment insurance program in our submission to the Forget Commission. [2]

At the outset, it is important to be clear about the perspective from which we approach Bill C-21 or any other piece of social legislation. As pastors, our concerns about unemployment insurance reform are rooted in the primary principle of the social teaching of the major churches, namely, the dignity of the human person. All persons, in other words, are made in the image of God. This fundamental principle, which is the foundation of solidarity in society, is the source of all other ethical principles. In this context, we wish to underline three more specific principles which are developed in the above mentioned documents on unemployment.

The first principle concerns the common use of goods. The scriptures remind us that the resources of the earth are to be distributed for God's intended purpose, namely, to serve equitably the basic needs of all people for a more fully human life. All other rights, the Church teaches, including those of property and commerce, are to be subordinated to the principle of the common good. There is, in other words, a 'social mortgage' on all means of production (e.g., capital, technology). The state, therefore, has a responsibility to intervene in the market to ensure that the basic needs of all people are being met in the social and economic order.

The second principle concerns the preferential option for the poor. Throughout the scriptures, the needs and rights of the poor, the marginalized and the afflicted are given special attention in God's plan for creation. In a given economy, therefore, the needs of the poor should take priority over the wants of the rich. This does not simply mean more handouts for the poor. Instead, it calls on the state to ensure a more equitable distribution of wealth and power among peoples and regions in a given society.

The third principle concerns the priority of human labour. The value and dignity of human work has a special significance in God's plan for creation. It is through the activity of work that people are able to exercise their creative spirit, realize their human dignity, earn an adequate income and participate in the development of their society. Human labour, therefore, should not be treated as a commodity to be bought and sold in the market place. On the contrary, the basic rights of working people should take priority over the maximization of profits. The state has a responsibility to ensure that this priority of human labour is represented in the operations of the economy.

It is on the basis of these ethical principles that we wish to comment on Bill C-21. As we emphasized before the Forget Commission Inquiry, the federal government has a moral obligation to provide a comprehensive social insurance program for unemployed workers. The primary objective is to provide unemployed workers and their families with the means to maintain a decent standard of living during periods of job loss. This does not call for a commercial insurance program in the conventional sense. Unemployed workers have a right to these benefits and should not be treated as "insurable risks". As Pope John Paul II stated in his encyclical *On Human Work*:

The obligation to provide unemployment benefits, that is to say, the duty to make suitable grants indispensable for the subsistence of unemployed workers and their families, is a duty springing from the fundamental principle of the moral order in this sphere, namely the principle of the common use of goods, or to put it in another and still simpler way, the right to life and subsistence. [3]

From this perspective, the proposed amendments to Canada's Unemployment Insurance Act give us cause for serious concern. Through our own consultations with the popular organizations of working and non-working people, we have heard and seen examples of the human outcry and anguish being expressed in reaction to the government's proposed amendments. While we do not intend to comment on the technical aspects of Bill C-21, we do wish to identify some of the major ethical and social implications at stake in the proposed amendments to the Unemployment Insurance Act. For example:

1. Government Withdrawal: The proposed withdrawal of the federal government's financial obligations to Canada's Unemployment Insurance program is unprecedented in the 50-year history of the program. The U.I. program has been one of the cornerstones of Canada's social security system. The financial withdrawal of the federal government, which represents the contribution of the public at large along with those of workers and employers, undermines the purpose of a "social insurance program" like the U.I. The withdrawal of government contributions may also put the future of the program in jeopardy.

2. Benefit Reductions: The government's decision to cut 1.3 billion dollars in regular benefits (April, 1989) could have the hardest impact on the weakest segment of working people. According to a study by Global Economics, close to a million workers will suffer income losses. Among the 155,000 people who stand to lose their benefits entirely (due to new regulations for qualifying periods, etc.), some 82% will have had jobs paying less than $25,000 a year. Some 400,000 workers who made less than $15,000 last year stand to lose $1,500 each in U.I. benefits.

3. Entrance Restrictions: The proposed introduction of longer entrance requirements and shorter maximum durations may save some $770 million but it could also generate hardship for certain sectors of workers. As noted above, an estimated 155,000 workers would fail to qualify for U.I. and another 620,000 will have their benefits reduced because of these new requirements. Seasonal workers and others with unstable employment patterns will be especially hard hit. These impacts will be felt in all regions, including those regions experiencing high levels of unemployment.

4. Penalty Clauses: The proposal for increased penalties (e.g., reduced weekly payments) affecting workers a) who "voluntarily quit their jobs, b) who are dismissed by their employers, or, c) who refuse suitable employment", could be both severe and discriminatory. The imposition of U.I. penalties on workers who have been dismissed from their jobs serves to reinforce the disciplinary authority of employers over workers. By increasing penalties on those who voluntarily leave their jobs or those who refuse job opportunities, more pressure is put on workers to accept whatever jobs and working conditions are offered by employers.

5. Natural Unemployment: The proposed amendments include a redefinition of what is to be considered an acceptable level of unemployment in Canada (cf. tables 1 and 2 relating to subsections 6.2 and 11.2). The tables imply that higher regional rates of unemployment are expected to continue indefinitely. As a result, 6-8% levels of unemployment are considered to be "natural". There is nothing "natural" about such levels of unemployment (e.g., between 800,000 and 1,100,000 people) when one considers the grief and human tragedy that this implies for the individuals and families involved.

6. U.S. Harmonization: The proposed amendments appear to be designed to avoid countervailing actions by the United States under the Free Trade Agreement. In the past, Canada's Unemployment Insurance program has been declared an "unfair subsidy" in terms of trade with the U.S. The financial withdrawal of the federal government and the subsequent weakening of the U.I. program and its benefits serve to remove the prospects of U.S. countervailing action. In effect, the proposed changes will further harmonize Canada's U.I. program with the much less comprehensive U.I. program of the United States, where 73.6% of workers do not even qualify for unemployment insurance.

From our ethical perspective, we find the proposed amendments to Canada's Unemployment Insurance program unacceptable. As the above data show, the proposed changes would have a negative impact on the lives of close to a million workers and their families in Canada. They include seasonal workers such as people working in fishing, forestry and construction industries as well as other workers who are the victims of lay-offs and plant closures. As a result, unemployed people and those precariously employed will likely be driven deeper into poverty and marginalization. Add to this the corresponding social costs — increased mental and physical illness, alcoholism, suicides, family breakups and violence against women and children — all of which point to a greater moral disorder.

At the same time, the proposed changes to the U.I. program cannot be assessed as a set of independent factors separate from the effects of other economic and social policy directions. The government's own budget papers (April '89) predict a steady rise in unemployment through 1990, when another 100,000 people will be added to the jobless rolls. If the government continues its policy of high interest rates, these unemployment trends will surely continue. Moreover, the budget cuts in regional development programs, transfer payments and agricultural programs will likely increase conditions of poverty and unemployment. These trends could be further exacerbated by the introduction of the 9% federal sales tax in 1991. In effect, the federal government seems to be weakening the U.I. program at a time when it is most needed.

In our view, one of the disturbing assumptions underlying Bill C-21 and its accompanying documents is the notion that human labour or working people are commodities to be bought, sold, retrained, relocated or discarded in the market place. Many of the provisions of Bill C-21 discussed above — the benefit reductions, the entrance restrictions, the penalty clauses, the natural unemployment levels — all have the effect of treating workers as 'objects' whose worth is determined by the market. By treating workers as commodities, the value and dignity of the human person is violated. And when economic policies put more pressure on unemployed men and women to accept low wages and precarious employment, a climate of fear is generated.

As Pope John Paul II reminds us:

The attainment of workers' rights cannot be doomed to be merely a result of economic systems which on a larger or smaller scale are guided chiefly by the criterion of maximum profit. On the contrary, it is respect for the objective rights of the worker — every kind of worker: manual or intellectual, industrial or agricultural, etc. — that must constitute the adequate and fundamental criterion for shaping the whole economy.[4]

In the final analysis, Mr. Chairman, we believe that the basic ethical criterion of economic policy in general, and unemployment insurance in particular, is an institutional commitment to full employment. Suitable employment for all who want to work is a fundamental right, not a privilege for some. While all institutions and sectors of society have a role to play in creating decent jobs, it is the responsibility of the state to ensure that the mechanisms of the economy are used to achieve the goal of full employment. As we emphasized in our presentation to the Forget Commission, it is only in the context of a full employment policy framework that adequate reform of the unemployment insurance system can take place. To amend the unemployment insurance program without an effective government strategy for generating institutional commitment to full employment constitutes a violation of the three basic ethical principles we outlined at the beginning.

We ask Mr. Chairman that Bill C-21 be withdrawn and that reform of the unemployment insurance program be undertaken only in the context of a full employment policy framework aimed at creating decent jobs for all working people in Canada. For we maintain that institutional commitment to full employment is a precondition for building a new society based on economic and social justice.

NOTES

1. Documents 49, 55 and 56 in *Do Justice! The Social Teaching of the Canadian Catholic Bishops,* edit. E.F. Sheridan, SJ (Éditions Paulines, 1987, Sherbrooke, P.Q., J1E 2B9).

2. Section IV, this volume, Document 3.

3. N. 18, in *Origins* (Washington, 1981), pp. 237 f.

4. *Ibid.*, n. 17, p. 237.

Section V

PASTORAL MESSAGES

Document 1

CHARISMATIC RENEWAL

Author — The Canadian Bishops to all Canadian Catholics,
April 28, 1975

INTRODUCTION

Different Reactions to the Charismatic Renewal

1. Rapid expansion of the Charismatic Renewal in the Catholic Church in Canada is quite evident, and you all know what a variety of reactions it has caused. In some cases, it has been received with enthusiasm, in others with caution, in still others with misgivings and even distrust. Many questions are asked in relation to this spiritual trend, and it is increasingly debated. We are in the presence of a religious phenomenon that is arousing growing interest among Christians.

Reason for this Declaration

2. This trend, even if recent, cannot be isolated from the Church. Within the Church and part of the Church, it serves as a new witness proclaiming that Pentecost continues. It has evolved as a means of spiritual renewal, thus becoming linked with one of our principal pastoral responsibilities. It is, therefore, our duty with solicitude and keen insight, to exercise discernment regarding this trend. The good of the Church is involved. Moreover, the present Holy Year emphasizes the importance of spiritual renewal in the life of every Christian. For these reasons, we have decided to share with you our reflections on the Charismatic Renewal.

This Message is Addressed to All Christians

3. Besides conveying our feelings in this regard, our message will help clarify this trend which is spoken about so often. It is important to underline in this regard that our interest in the Charismatic Renewal is not limited to this spiritual movement. Is it not in the Spirit that faith in Jesus Christ is conceived, is nourished and grows in clarity? That is to say, the believer is called to become alert to the call of the Spirit in his or her daily living and to respond generously. There is no doubt that our reflections on the Charismatic Renewal apply to the life of every Christian.

A Subsequent Declaration on Other Spiritual Matters

4. Although we are speaking now only of the Charismatic Renewal, this in no way means that we want to minimize the importance of other spiritual movements in Canada, or their undeniable contribution to the life of the Church in our country. They are many. We have every intention of discussing them extensively in a subsequent statement.

I — POSITIVE ORIENTATIONS
OF THE CHARISMATIC RENEWAL

Charismatic Renewal is Based on the Role
of the Spirit in the Church

5. We know from the many statements received from all regions of Canada, that the Charismatic Renewal is centred on the presence of the Holy Spirit in the Church community and its members. In this way, it strives to sensitize Christians to the meaning of this presence and to its bearing on their lives. Why? In order that such an awareness may open each believer to the Spirit received in Baptism. Everyone knows by experience how people stifle the Spirit, frequently blanking out the manifestations of His presence in their lives. We need only mention such causes as selfishness and the lack of faith.

Relations with Christ in the Charismatic Renewal

6. While placing great importance on openness to the Spirit by a docile response to His entreaties, the Charismatic Renewal aims primarily at strengthening the bonds that unite the believer to Christ. The purpose is to establish an ever greater intimacy with Jesus — a union which allows the Christian to know the Father more intimately.

Relations with the Trinity in the Charismatic Renewal

7. The fundamental goal of the Charismatic Renewal could be expressed as the intensifying of the believer's loving knowledge of the Father, by developing "familiarity" with Christ in an ever growing availability to the action of the Spirit. At the very base of the Charismatic Renewal we recognize the trinitarian structure of the Christian faith — the solidarity of the Spirit with Christ and the Father is not only maintained but also firmly asserted.

Devotion to Mary

8. It is in this trinitarian context that devotion to Mary finds its place. In the Charismatic Renewal, the mother of God is honoured as the one whose "yes" to the plan of the Father perfectly expressed the responsiveness of the human creature to the action of the Spirit.

Relations with Others in the Charismatic Renewal

9. Aware of being inserted into the trinitarian community, a member of the Charismatic Renewal is called upon to discover progressively how life, rooted in the Spirit, quickens all relations with others. It is a life concerned about communion, seeking to be present to others, respecting their otherness, in order to share with them the joy of being united in Christ Jesus. It encourages each person to abandon that depersonalized anonymity that is sometimes a mark of how Christians relate to their community. The Charismatic Renewal seeks to establish between believers interpersonal relations that permit each one to emerge with his or her own identity, style and personal stamp. It is not surprising then to find relaxation and joy at charismatic meetings, each one feeling at ease because he or she is recognized, counted as someone, appreciated and loved. There clearly exists in the Charismatic Renewal the praiseworthy intention of restoring among Christians a personalizing community life, where simplicity and spontaneous behaviour replace the stereotyped forms of communication and exchange characterizing certain Christian communities.

Prayer in the Charismatic Renewal

10. This loving communion in the one Spirit in Jesus Christ is expressed in different ways in the Charismatic Renewal. Prayer is given a special place — ardent prayer especially to praise God and to thank Him for His gifts, to tell Him of our happiness in loving Him and being loved by Him. It is also in prayer that each one gives voice to personal concern for others.

Spontaneity of Prayer

The most striking characteristic of the prayer of charismatics is the manifest joy they experience as Christians being together with Christ. Hence, the spontaneity of prayer which, although it respects traditional forms, is often improvised.

The Sacraments in the Charismatic Renewal

11. In the Charismatic Renewal, prayer is not a substitute for the sacramental life of the Church. On the contrary, it cannot be dissociated from this life.

a) *Relation to Baptism and Confirmation*

Prayer is intended to develop in believers great docility in responding to the action of the Spirit received in Baptism and Confirmation, thus leaving the way open to His manifestations in their lives. Their prayer shows that their whole life is being lived under the sign of these two sacraments. It makes the fundamental role of these sacraments stand out clearly in all that they are becoming. With regard to this, we should make clear that "baptism in the Spirit"[1] administered in Charismatic groups is not a second baptism but a symbolic act signifying a new openness[2] of the believer to the Spirit received in baptism.

b) *Relation to Penance*

Building one's life under the sign of baptism, is a procedure rife with obstacles to be overcome, struggles to be undertaken and temptations to be mastered. It is a slow process in which people are constantly at grips with the powers of sin, hence the importance of the sacrament of reconciliation which helps the believer to overcome weaknesses and failures by opening the heart ever wider to the reconciling action of the Spirit.

c) *Relation to the Eucharist*

However, the summit of praise and gratitude towards God is reached in the Holy Eucharist. It is recognized as the supreme thanksgiving, wherein Christians, despite all trials and sacrifices, express the joy of being with Jesus, of sharing His presence with their sisters and brothers. In this way, the Charismatic Renewal stresses in its own way that availability to the Spirit is the fundamental disposition transforming the life of every believer into a eucharistic offering.

Introduction to Charisms

12. By insisting as it does on self-abandonment to the action of the Spirit, the Charismatic Renewal aims to make more room in each Christian soul for the Holy Spirit to reveal Himself. This surrender helps each believer to radiate the presence of the Spirit.

Precisely what is meant here? The answer to this question is of major importance. It will render possible the explanation of the meaning of the term charismatic and indicate precisely the place held by charisms in the Charismatic Renewal.

a) *The gift of the Spirit*

13. We should state clearly at the outset that this spiritual movement asserts without hesitation or ambiguity, just as the Apostle Paul teaches, that the Holy Spirit is the supreme gift that God freely offers us (Rom. 8:9; 1 Cor. 12:3; Eph. 2:18; Acts 19:5-7). It recognizes no less clearly that charity is the fundamental sign (1 Cor: 13:1-13; Rom. 12:9-21) and irreplaceable witness of the presence of the Spirit in the Church community and in its members.

b) *Definition of Charisms*

14. If such is the case, just what is the purpose of charisms (1 Cor. 12:4-11, 27-30; Rom. 12:4-8; Eph. 4:11-12)? They are manifestations of the Spirit which are obedient to the exercise of charity. Given for the use of all, they are intended for the good of each and every one, to build and develop the Church community. Their role can be summed up in one word — service. Thus they have a ministerial function if we give the word "ministry" its true meaning which is "service" (Eph. 4:11-12; Rom. 12:4-8). And so it is that there are charisms which earmark those who receive them for the service or

ministry of the word, others for that of governing. Examples could be extended indefinitely.

c) *Charismatic Dimension of the Church*

15. One of the merits of the Charismatic Renewal is to recall intentionally the importance of charisms in the life of the Christian community and its members. Their presence in the Church is neither unusual nor secondary. It is one of its essential characteristics, for the Church community is, by its very nature, charismatic (1 Cor. 12:4-7). As it was stated in Vatican II, the Holy Spirit is still building the Church and guiding it by His "various gifts both hierarchical and charismatic".[3] The fact that these charisms exist in the Church shows the inexhaustible riches of the Spirit Who makes His presence felt among Christians through their individual and collective charity. This is why charisms are the inseparable auxiliaries of charity. They act in concert wherever they are found. Their role is to help the Church exercise its "diaconate" of love, that is to say, the ministerial function of dispensing to all persons the love that the Father manifested to them in Jesus Christ. To this end, their expression takes on a variety of forms. Consequently, it is as vain as it is arbitrary to think it possible to draw up an exhaustive list of charisms or to limit their number to those mentioned by the Apostle. He simply gives some examples drawn from the experience of the Christian communities of his day (1 Cor. 12:28; Rom. 12:48). We might point out that the gifts of tongues and prophecy that we hear about in certain charismatic groups are explicitly mentioned by the Apostle.[4] Opinions differ as to the significance of these gifts but this does not affect their authenticity. It is arbitrary to consider them dubious without examination.

d) *Diversity of Charisms*

16. Insistence on such and such a charism in certain groups of the Charismatic Renewal in no way implies that the movement, taken as a whole, neglects or denies others that do exist. On the contrary, emphasis is rightfully placed on the unlimited diversity of charisms. While acknowledging that certain of them stand out more clearly, the Renewal is well aware that most of them abound in ordinary ways in the life of the Church.

e) *Attitude of the Believer towards Charisms*

17. Given to the Church to help Her fulfill Her ministry of love, charisms are free. They cannot be exacted from God nor sought for themselves. In this matter, a Christian must simply thank God for His gifts and be disposed to receive those God sees fit to give for the good of His people (1 Cor. 12:11). Such is the teaching of the Charismatic Renewal.

f) *Discernment with regard to Charisms*

18. Aware that appearances are frequently deceiving, the Charismatic Renewal justly insists on the need for exercising "discernment" where charismatic manifestations of the Spirit are concerned.[5] The fundamental criterion is always charity, accompanied by humility, joy, serenity, simplicity and patience, to mention only a few of the fruits of the Spirit (1 Cor. 13:1-3).

Place of the Scriptures

19. The acknowledged importance of charisms in no way diminishes the importance of Scripture in the Charismatic Renewal. It is from the revealed word of God that the movement draws the substance of its prayer, the themes of its reflection and the matter for its meditation. Scripture serves as a very privileged spiritual source that cannot be dissociated from prayer and sacramental life in the Charismatic Renewal. The basic orientations of the Charismatic Renewal are positive — of that we are certain. In his allocution of October 10, 1973 to the leaders of the Catholic Charismatic Renewal, Pope Paul VI summarized these orientations in the following terms:

> We rejoice with you, dear friends, at the renewal of spiritual life manifested in the Church today, in different forms and in various environments. Certain common notes appear in this renewal: the taste for deep prayer, personal and in groups, a return to contemplation and an emphasis on praise of God, the desire to devote oneself completely to Christ, great availability for the calls of the Holy Spirit, more assiduous reading of the Scripture, generous brotherly devotion, the will to make a contribution to the service of the Church. In all that, we can recognize the mysterious and discreet work of the Spirit, Who is the soul of the Church.[6]

II — NEGATIVE ASPECTS

Introduction

20. There are, however, shadows in the picture. Here and there, sporadically there are excesses, though we must be careful not to generalize about their presence in the Charismatic Renewal in Canada. We must not, on the other hand, minimize the harm they do to the movement and its members. We realize that this is a cause for concern for the movement as well as for us. It seems fitting then to review the negative aspects that call for adjustments.

Seeking Marvels

21. The Charismatic Renewal indicts as false any seeking after exclusively extraordinary manifestations of the Spirit. The desire for "marvels" for their own sake is what is commonly called "sensationalism". It exists in some groups. Here, all the attention is fixed on certain striking or dazzling charisms, such as the gift of tongues, of prophecy or of healing, whereas very little is made of other gifts of the Spirit that appear rather modest.[7] Testimonies about these "marvels" abound. Their many details are recounted to the point of eclipsing for hearers the fundamental importance of charity in the life of a Christian. The balance established by faith between the gift of the Spirit and its charismatic manifestations is destroyed. It is not surprising that fixations of this nature cause many illusions and counterfeits of the gifts of the Spirit.

Exaggeration of "Belonging" to the Movement

22. Another excess that should be pointed out is centred on one's belonging[8] to this spiritual movement. Here and there, the impression is given that one must belong to be a complete Christian. Such a pretension rightly disturbs the believer's conscience. Need we recall that the only criterion for assessing Christian behaviour is that charity

which comes from the Spirit Who gives life to the Church community? Underlying this pretension is the idea that the Charismatic Renewal has the monopoly of charisms, or is at least the only rightful witness thereof. This we know is wrong, for the Church Herself is the place where the Spirit manifests Himself. As we have seen, that is one of the fundamental assertions of the true Charismatic Renewal. Thus it is not necessary to belong to a charismatic group in order to receive the gifts of the Spirit. He breathes where He wills.

Sensationalism

23. The exaggerated importance placed on the emotional experience[9] of God in certain charismatic groups should also be examined. It is disturbing. We cannot deny that it is in his or her affective life that the believer meets with God to learn to know Him better and to enjoy His presence. Jesus speaks to us as we are, in our bodies; the salvation He offers goes even that far. His victory over death was precisely to deliver us in His flesh from the power of sin. We must not, however, conclude from this that the life of faith is measured by the intensity of emotion of the believer's religious experience. Such a criterion would be deceiving. The Spirit awakens the entire person to the presence of Christ in his or her life. It would be arbitrary, therefore, to limit His action to the sphere of emotions only. The Spirit also acts on our intelligence, our powers of reflection and our will.

Detriments of Emotionalism

24. The emotionalism against which we should struggle ignores the importance of the intellectual experience of God in the life of faith. It naively contests its value. Devotion engendered by such an attitude is bound to be short-lived, since it dies out with the emotion that gave rise to it. Another consequence, no less serious, flows from the primacy given to feelings. It causes a systematic distrust of both biblical and doctrinal reflection. We see this wherever emotionalism prevails. There results a taste for the "immediate" to which one gives priority over all concern for deep reflection that would reveal still hidden treasures.

Fundamentalism

25. There is also question of the vogue among certain charismatic groups for an exclusively literal interpretation of Scripture. This method, commonly called "fundamentalism", reduces practically to nil the role of reason and, more particularly, that of reflection for understanding the Bible. Everything is evident at first sight, because it is expressed by the literal meaning of each word. [10]

Remedies

This is why it is urgent to multiply the efforts to read Scripture in a way that goes deeper than the over-simplification of fundamentalism, and to open the mind to scientific methods of interpretation. In like manner, it is important to stimulate theological reflection wherever it is lacking. It is a matter of the very essence of the Charismatic Renewal — does it not aim to deepen in believers a living knowledge of the Spirit in their lives? How can this be attained without penetrating by reflection the teaching of Scripture and that of the Church?

Self-centeredness of Certain Groups

26. Likewise, we should question the indifference — even reluctance — of some groups to take an active interest in the needs of those around them. [11] Their predominant tendency is to self-centeredness. The joy they experience from togetherness gives rise to a sentiment of personal satisfaction that transforms their groups into ghettos. Such groups become closed circles, providing a few hours of escape from reality, rather than being as they should be — spring-boards for plunging into the world.

In such circumstances, openness to the Spirit and to His charisms can easily degenerate into an unacknowledged desire to seek compensation for the disappointments of everyday life. This same sort of danger threatens their prayer life. These pitfalls are indeed very real and good intentions are not enough to eliminate them. More is required. The Holy Spirit calls us to go beyond the limits of self-interest. It is He Who urges the Church community to put self aside to go out and meet the world. This means that to make every Christian understand the need to listen to the Spirit, the Charismatic Renewal must take an active part in the Church's involvement with the world, cooperating with Christ in the liberation and integral development of people. Wherever such a concern is lacking, every effort must be made to arouse it, in view of the service to which all aspire who are open to charisms. It is up to each person to discern the form of involvement to which the Holy Spirit is calling him or her in the light of the needs of the world.

The Formation of Leaders

27. The formation of group leaders is for us of particular importance. The excesses described clearly show that leadership formation must receive careful and active consideration. Yet this does not always happen. We have noticed that it is of unequal caliber and in some cases leaves much to be desired. As a result, some leaders are little prepared for their duties. Their knowledge of Scripture is superficial, their theological information very scant. These deficiencies render a disservice to the movement. Yet means do exist for remedying the situation. Make sure, therefore, that every leader has the thorough basic training needed for performing his or her duties competently.

False Ecumenism

28. A number of charismatic groups include as participants, numbers of other denominations. It is our opinion that this laudable initiative may contribute to bringing Christians closer together. This sometimes deviates into a false ecumenism. For example, one sees groups here and there with a pronounced tendency to smooth away the differences which still divide Christians. This is done in the hope of strengthening the bonds of union, solidarity and communion in Christ. Despite the good intentions, this behaviour is deceptive. By playing down the differences that separate Christians, it establishes among them relations from which no one emerges with a true iden-

tity. Under such conditions, there can be no authentic togetherness nor any true exchange. This is a world away from authentic ecumenism.

Conclusions as to Negative Aspects

29. Without depreciating the positive value of the Charismatic Renewal in Canada, we must admit that it also has negative aspects. They are the inevitable price to be paid for anything new. Their existence reminds us that this spiritual movement is still in its infancy. Like every living organism, it has growing pains and this should not surprise us.

III — COOPERATION OF THE CHARISMATIC RENEWAL WITH THE CHURCH

Positive Values

30. As we understand the Charismatic Renewal, it emerges as a growing call to the Christian conscience, urging it to in-depth renewal. It springs from the heart of the Church community like a hymn of whole-hearted trust in the all-powerful presence of the Spirit in the world. Its expansion across our country casts the light of hope on new horizons towards which the Spirit is irresistibly drawing the Church in Canada.

Dynamism

31. The Charismatic Renewal calls you to work at building the future for such is its orientation. While focussed on prayer, its centre is action. Are not charisms intended to assist the Church community in exercising its function of ministry? Thus membership in the Charismatic Renewal should aim to be in the service of the Church for the building of her future. It commits one totally to action.

Mission of the Renewal in the Church

32. That is why we must work together in the mission that we share. Are we not all sent by Christ to serve the Father among all? Openness to the Spirit makes one forgetful of self. Those dedicated to Christ, like Him, should be totally given to others. Joy in the presence of the Risen Lord in our lives does not belong to us. It is destined to shine out all round us bringing joy to others.

The Renewal as Leaven in the Church

33. We are sure of the aptitude of charismatics to act as leaven in their own community. Many proofs of this have been given us. Thanks to their example and zeal, many Christians have rediscovered a taste for prayer, the joy of belonging to Christ and a sense of religious community. In short, there are many fields of action open to their apostolic aspirations. For example, an increased involvement in animating liturgical, catechetical and pastoral programs would be appreciated. Similarly, we would like to see intensified involvement in various parochial and diocesan activities. We have in mind especially organizations dealing with young people, couples having difficulties and the aged. Cooperation could also be extended to all aspects of social affairs, a vast range of areas which are calling out for help.

IV — COMMUNICATION BETWEEN PASTORS AND THE RENEWAL

34. Projects for collaboration abound. The more, however, they develop in a climate of cordial dialogue, the more their success will be assured. Hence, the need to establish regular channels of communication. Their main purpose will be to keep us in constant contact, to develop some common projects, to make known the needs of the Church at all levels, and to be of help as the circumstances indicate. In several dioceses, the bishop has already appointed an official representative to facilitate this dialogue.

35. This permaent communication network will open the way to fruitful exchanges and cooperation. The ever present good will and the filial regard which the Charismatic Renewal has always shown for pastors are, for us, guarantees that it will be so.

GENERAL CONCLUSION

36. Remain attentive to the Spirit. He alone can bring to completion, in ways no human hand can trace in advance, our common efforts to build tomorrow's Church.

NOTES

1. Cf. G.A. Sullivan, *Baptism in the Spirit,* Gregorianum (Rome, 1974), lv, pp. 48-68; H. Carrafel, *Faut-il parler d'un Pentecostisme Catholique)* (Paris, Éditions du Feu Nouveau, 1973), pp. 56-58; also D. Ranaghan, *Baptism in the Holy Spirit* (Dove Publications, New Mexico, 1970), p. 63ff.

2. G. Guttierrez, *Lumen Vitae* (Brussels, 1974), n. 3, pp. 384-386.

3. *Dogmatic Constitution on the Church,* n. 4.

4. 1 Cor. 12:10; cf. *Lumen Vitae, op. cit.* in note 2, above, pp. 397-99.

5. Cf. 1 Thes. 5:19-22; also Second Vatican Council, *Dogmatic Constitution on the Church,* n. 12.

6. *Osservatore Romano* (Vatican, October 18, 1973).

7. *Op. cit.,* note 2, above, p. 390.

8. *Ibid.,* pp. 388f.

9. *Ibid.,* pp. 389-90.

10. *Ibid.,* p. 395.

11. *Ibid.,* pp. 390-92.

Section V, Document 2

FULLNESS OF LIFE: BASIC ELEMENTS OF A CHRISTIAN SPIRITUALITY

Author — The Canadian Conference of Catholic Bishops, Pentecost Message, April 5, 1978

INTRODUCTION

The active presence of the Spirit gives reason for great hope.

1. Having become one of us so that we might have life and have it to the full (Jn. 10:10), Jesus has never abandoned us. When He returned to the Father, He sent His disciples the Spirit He had promised. This Spirit is always present and active in the Church and in the heart of every Christian. In every age, the same Spirit enables believers to make present anew Jesus and His life-giving message of love and peace.

2. As your bishops, we are encouraged to see the extent of the renewal the Spirit has brought about in the Church in recent years. This renewal is expressed in so many diverse initiatives and movements that it would be difficult to describe them fully. For many people, particularly the young, this renewing action of the Spirit leads to a fresh discovery of the mystery of faith and religious values.

The presence of the Spirit is also evident in society at large. He is at work in the efforts of all those who attend to the needs of others and who work towards a society that is more human, just and loving.

3. Nevertheless, we also see present in society today certain destructive elements which reflect the forces of evil, neglect of God, selfishness, injustice, violence and oppression. We are aware, too, that the Church community itself is divided by internal tensions and shaken by changes in the society within which the Church must be present. But the Spirit is vigilant. His action gives reason for great hope. It is this hope that we wish to share with you, brothers and sisters, through this message to all Catholics in our country.

The Spirit's presence calls for discernment and guidance

4. Faced with times similar to ours, St. Paul recommended perseverance and vigilance. He tells us: "Never try to suppress the Spirit or treat the gift of prophecy with contempt; think before you do anything — hold on to what is good." (1 Thes. 5:19-21)

We recommend this same perseverance and discernment today as we offer you some broad outlines of Christian spirituality. Without going into full detail, we believe that any movement and experience of renewal may be evaluated by using five basic criteria:

I   — encounter with God in living prayer;
II — communion with the Church;
III — witness by the whole Church;
IV — patient commitment to the service of others;
V — continuing conversion of heart and life.

I — ENCOUNTER WITH GOD IN PRAYER

5. Authentic Christian life and spiritual renewal are rooted in a personal, loving meeting with God in prayer. In this way we come to know who God is and what wonders He has worked. In prayer we experience a communion of love with the Father, aided by the Spirit Who shows us that we are children of God (Rom. 8:15-17). Prayer animated the Christian's entire life, developing the awareness that all things are renewed in Christ.

Prayer requires effort and the support of a faith community

6. St. Paul tells us that even if we do not know how to pray, the Spirit pleads for us in our hearts (Rom. 8:26). Even so, acceptance of this gift of the Spirit demands that we make a serious, constant effort. This implies a freely imposed self-denial. Respect for moral values and self-discipline are needed to control inner drives and maintain a salutary harmony.

Secondly, in order to hear the voice of the Spirit within us and to speak heart to heart with God, we must create moments of solitude and silence in our daily lives.

Moreover, in today's culture which tends to over-emphasize rationalism, we should be aware that the whole human being, physical, psychological and spiritual, is involved in prayer. By appealing to our senses, gestures and symbols play an essential role in helping us to prepare our hearts for prayer and to express it.

Finally, the Christian tradition, like all other great religious traditions, reminds us of the need for experienced spiritual directors to lead us to an ever more faithful and deeper relationship with God.

7. We note with joy that in recent years, here and elsewhere, the Spirit has awakened a great thirst for spiritual experience. More and more groups and houses of prayer are being established. There Christians discover or rediscover prayer and learn to share their spiritual experience with brothers and sisters in faith. Through such prayer groups and prayer meetings, the Christian people may, by means of wise discernment, find once again in prayer that spontaneity which is the goal of our liturgical renewal. Gatherings of this kind can also help us to praise God with joyful enthusiasm. They may even help us rediscover the true value of pious practices once so popular but lately discarded as routine actions with little or no significance.

8. The present attraction of contemplative communities, especially for the young, is another indication of this spiritual thirst. These communities have great responsibility in this spiritual renewal. Having consecrated themselves in full freedom to the praise and service of God, the primary role of the Church, they give a powerful witness to the totality of God and the relativity of all earthly things.

II — COMMUNION WITH THE CHURCH

9. The disciple of Christ is called personally, by name, to bear witness to Jesus and His message. But each has also been called in company with others. All those in whom the seed of the Word of God has taken root make up that vast family of Christ's disciples called the Church. Together they learn to pray. Joyfully recognizing the love of God in Jesus Christ, believers praise the Father in communion with their brothers and sisters in faith. With their pastors, they try to discern the message of the Gospel and to discover in it dynamic meanings for today's world.

10. The liturgy celebrates Christ's salvation of all people for all times. Because of this, it represents the privileged source and expression of this fraternal communion. In the sacraments, particularly the Eucharist, we are called to experience and express the bonds by which God unites us in faith, hope and love. In the earthly liturgy, by way of foretaste, we share in the heavenly liturgy and journey as pilgrims toward the eternal kingdom. [1]

The faith community cares for all

11. Assembled in the Lord, Christians are called to go into the world to share the riches of faith. Believers are called to care in a special way for those who, for various reasons, have strayed from the Church. These must feel that the Church community still cares for them. It is through contact with an authentic Christian community, which welcomes them and helps them believe in God's love for them, that they will be able to renew or resume their membership in the People of God.

12. This supposes that there are real Christian communities within the Church. Indeed, in order to give their faith a more personal and communal dimension, many Christians have felt the need for new types of community. With brothers and sisters around them, they seek to live and express more concretely and fully the salvation brought by Jesus Christ. If these communities live in sincere communion with the great family of the Church and its pastors, they can contribute considerably to its renewal and be eloquent witnesses to the Gospel.

III — WITNESS BY THE WHOLE CHURCH

Jesus' followers continue His mission by witness

13. Jesus, son of the Virgin Mary, was consecrated by the anointing of the Spirit to announce the Good News to the poor (Lk. 4:18). He entrusted to His disciples the task of carrying on this mission, of taking the Good News to the ends of the earth and to all sectors of humanity.

The entire Church is responsible for witnessing to Jesus Christ at every moment of history and to all peoples of the earth. Every Christian, whether bishop, priest, religious or lay person, each according to his or her own vocation, is responsible for this mission: to help other brothers and sisters discover and share God's love for them in Jesus Christ.

14. Witness cannot be authentic unless it is based on attitudes that are truly lived: understanding and openness, a sharing of life and destiny with others, solidarity in striving together for all that is good and noble. In short, we must radiate a simple, spontaneous faith and a hope which surpasses all human aspirations. All this is required of Christ's witnesses because "modern man listens more willingly to witnesses than to teachers, and if he does listen to teachers, it is because they are witnesses."[2]

To grow, faith must be shared

15. But witnessing demands even more. It should lead to a sharing of faith and religious experience. We are called by the Spirit to a "spirituality on the move", not to a ghetto attitude which dares not reach out beyond itself for fear of being challenged. We are called to share our spiritual experience with those who are close to us as well as with those who are far away; with those who have placed their hope in Christ as well as with those who profess other religious beliefs or who call themselves non-believers.

16. The fact is that faith grows through sharing. In sharing their knowledge and experience of Christ, believers together make the gifts of the Gospel their own. Their faith becomes more personal and com-

munal. In this way they bring about a deeper transformation of the milieu in which they live. This milieu then becomes itself a place where faith is learned. In such a milieu, believers are always in a state of apprenticeship , of progressive growth, because faith as a gift from God demands an ever-renewed acceptance in order to remain living and dynamic.

**Faith education begins in the family
and takes root in life and the Word of God**

17. The Second Vatican Council reclaimed for the family the beautiful name, "domestic church". It is here that spiritual experience begins. In the family the child, supported by parents, learns to love God, to pray in common and to serve God by serving brothers and sisters. Within their own homes children learn how to establish contacts with the world and to relate to others.

This early formation in the family must find continuity and confirmation when the young go on to complete their formal education. Collaboration among the various agencies responsible for this development becomes necessary. Bridges must be built between the family, the school and the Christian community. Otherwise the faith of the child will not find sufficiently receptive soil to take deep root.

18. This is also true for the adult, whether lay, priest or religious. Each of us needs the support of a community if we are to encourage the growth of God's gift within us and to share it with others. We see here the importance of constantly rebuilding Christian communities so that they may remain faithful to the life and to the Gospel. Sunday sermons reflecting the Gospel and its practical application, life-related liturgical celebrations, the care of the poor and others in need, establishment of groups for reflection and action, are indispensable for keeping the faith community alive and radiant.

19. However, all initiatives to foster the growth of faith bear fruit only in the measure that they are rooted in the Word of God. There is no end to discerning the profound meanings of the Word. It is a nourishment for life that is accessible to everyone. This is why we can never encourage too much those initiatives by which Christians may acquire a sound knowledge of Sacred Scripture. In doing so, believers can explore together their life experiences in the light of God's Word and the tradition of the Church.

IV — THE SERVICE OF OTHERS

Spiritual renewal leads to action

20. Our faith-life cannot remain solely interior and individualistic. Our beliefs must issue in concrete acts of service to others. Christ awakens in our hearts a desire for the age to come. Yet by that very fact, "He animates, purifies, and strengthens also those noble longings by which the human family strives to make its life more human and to render the whole earth submissive to this goal. [3]

21. The age to come will be shaped not so much by spectacular action, but through the activities of everyday life. Indeed, all those who strive to do their best in the ordinary circumstances of life participate in building up a better world.

Hope in God's kingdom transforms personal and social life

22. Through His death and resurrection Christ delivered the world from the bonds of sin and re-established it in grace. Hence, the daily work of the Christian is never just temporal activity. Be it domestic, scientific, technical, political or cultural, it also has a religious dimension. When Christians bear the confusion, mediocrity, tensions and contradictions of our time, they give witness to the new life Jesus gave to the world.

23. Our hope is directed to the future coming of the Kingdom when the lame will walk, the deaf hear, the blind see and the poor receive the Good News. Strengthened by this hope, Christians do not passively await the realization of this ideal. Rather, believers help to make it happen even now.

Dedicated to the transformation of selfish mentalities and unjust social structures, Christians seek to remedy scandalous social and economic inequalities in our country as well as in the rest of the world. In this way, believers exercise authentic, Gospel-inspired influence and give witness to their hope. [4]

24. Jesus not only gave first place to the little ones and the underprivileged of society, He identified with them personally. That is why the disciples of Jesus must work for liberation from all sorts of mis-

ery and the abolition of all forms of exploitation (Mt. 25:31-46). But in a society in which conflict tends to become permanent and in which violence has become a strategy for change, Christians have a mission to witness personally to the transforming strength of love and the non-violence of the Gospel.

In struggles for liberation which Christians share with others of different ideologies, believers need to be inspired by the example of Jesus to be free from all forms of slavery. Thirst for power, the frenetic race for success and comfort, racist tendencies, unrestrained eroticism: all these forms of domination can imprison, alienate and eventually destroy us.

The Spirit of the Beatitudes, on the contrary, calls for an attitude of detachment, especially with regard to material wealth. But can this attitude, which is part of the freedom of the children of God, be authentic unless it is translated into a style of life that is simple and poor in the manner of the Master?

V — CONTINUAL CONVERSION OF HEART AND LIFE

The Cross: sign of all suffering and source of renewed life

25. In every aspect of life the Christian is marked with the seal of the Cross which the Lord freely accepted. For believers, the Cross of the risen Christ is not simply a memory of the past. They accept to bear it in their journey knowing that this same Cross is the very source of life. The Christian also recognizes the Cross in all personal suffering and in that of others: in social injustice, in the humiliation which is too often the lot of the aged, the handicapped, the unemployed, the undereducated, those on low salaries and on social assistance.

When a Christian becomes aware that these social problems are collective sin — that is, social evils for which all bear responsibility — then the believer is already on the road to conversion.

In fact, the agonizing discovery of collective sin often leads Christians today to rediscover a sense of personal sin. Then the believer recognizes personal sin as a refusal to love one's fellow humans as well as a refusal to love Him Who loved us so much that He died to deliver us from the prison of sin.

Genuine conversion requires courage and dedication

26. Conversion is at the heart of the Gospel message. It is a constant and profound transformation of heart, attitudes and habits. Jesus, like John the Baptist, called for such conversion from the outset of His preaching: "Repent, for the kingdom of heaven is close at hand." (Mt. 4:17)

To be genuine, this conversion of heart must transform one's whole life. Conversion consists in knowing how to say no to everything that separates our personal and social life from God, making it less human.

The Christian, therefore, renounces everything that smacks of exploitation or compromise with injustice. In many cases this conversion will lead to discovery of new forms of collective life that are in conformity with the radical demands of evangelical poverty and simplicity.

27. The Church as an institution is also called to constant conversion. We see, however, some resistance to change at this time. Such an attitude is not compatible with the Spirit of God. Today, as in the days of Abraham, the Spirit calls us to follow Him as daring pilgrims. Everyone is invited to participate in the continuing renewal of the Church, so that it may present to God and to the world a countenance "without wrinkle or stain" (Eph. 5:26-27).

Experiencing conversion in the sacrament of reconciliation

28. Only the Spirit can bring about this conversion in individuals and institutions. He alone, according to the words of the Prophet, can change our hearts of stone into hearts of flesh and write upon them the law of love (Ez. 11:19).

All can experience, within the Church, this same law of merciful love in the sacrament of forgiveness. In this sacrament we can know the solicitude of the God Who seeks the sheep that has strayed. We are confident that rediscovery of the sense of collective and individual sin, and renewal of the image of a loving God, will permit Christians to grasp the riches of this sacrament.

CONCLUSION

Fullness of Christian life for every believer

29. Every believer should seek fullness of Christian life. This becomes possible when we strive to live according to the five general criteria we have just described. Particular vocations may lead groups or individuals to place emphasis on one or the other of these aspects, but no one should so emphasize one aspect as to ignore or neglect other necessary elements.

For example, those who feel called to the charisms of prayer and contemplation must also develop their social conscience. On the other hand, those engaged in social action should remain open to the contemplative dimension of life. In this way, we strive together towards fullness of life, sought not only for ourselves but also for our brothers and sisters. "I have come," said Jesus, "that they may have life, and have it to the full" (Jn. 10:10).

No individual or group in the Church can claim to have a monopoly on the Spirit. Therefore, let each one try to do his or her part to build up the Kingdom of God, remaining open to the influence and the call of others. Each should respect the diverse actions of the Spirit in motivating different members of the people of God. The gifts we are given are without number, yet there is but one Spirit.

NOTES

1. Second Vatican Council, *Constitution on the Liturgy* (1963), n. 8.

2. Paul VI, Apostolic Exhortation, *Evangelization in the Modern World* (1975), in *The Pope Speaks* (Washington, 1976), vol. 21, p. 22, n. 41.

3. Second Vatican Council, *Constitution on the Church in the Modern World* (1965), n. 38.

4. Cf. Pope John Paul's homily, Front Mountain Road, Moncton, N.B., Sept. 13, 1984, nn. 7-9, in *The Canadian Catholic Review* (Saskatoon, Sask., Oct., 1984), pp. 353f.

Section V, Document 3

TO ELDERLY MEMBERS OF THE CHURCH: A PASTORAL MESSAGE

Author — The Canadian Conference of Catholic Bishops, June 9, 1980

Introduction

At Pentecost 1978 the Canadian bishops published a pastoral letter, *The Fullness of Life.* In it they reaffirmed that the heart of the Gospel message is a call to Christian hope and creativity. This is a message which is constantly pertinent and worthy of our attention. This is why your bishops wish to develop and deepen some of the aspects of this message that have particular applications to the older members of our society and to their irreplaceable mission in the Church.

Our present reflection is closely linked to the pastoral project of the Canadian Conference of Catholic Bishops, *Growth in Faith in and Through the Family.* [1] Who have taken a deeper interest in family life and its customs and traditions than our senior generation? Who have had more influence on the spiritual and material prosperity of families? The family is one of the inestimable values of our heritage which they bequeath to the younger generation, together with the witness of their own faith journey.

To be Alive

We all experience the joy of being alive. Life is dear to us. It is a priceless gift. Our happiness and contentment spring from life, for life gives us the joy of knowing and loving, of relating to others, of learning, of sharing in the world of persons and of things, of experiencing wonder and delight.

Today you can experience the thrill of life and the satisfaction it brings in new and different ways. Although your outlook on things may have changed with the years, the change should mean not a lessening but a deepening appreciation for life. Indeed, your present situation gives you time for leisure, for creativity and new activities — a time in which each individual can live life with a sense of fullness and accomplishment. Your life takes on a new direction as you realize that your past with its rich memories and experiences is a door to the future.

Sickness, suffering, loneliness and lack of funds may be burdens for you and overshadow your declining years. The light of faith, however, illuminates this latter stage of your earthly pilgrimage. It is not an ending but a passage leading to the beginning of another way of being and living. Faith in this "new heaven and new earth" (Rev. 21:1-5) is a source of hope and consolation for us.

Christian Fulfillment

The human life which you love so dearly is transformed, enriched and renewed by our faith in the Risen Christ. Your Christian experience has enabled you to know the gift of God the Father, who permits us to share in His divine life and adopts us as His children (Rom. 8:16). His divine Fatherhood is a source of new life for all. This life is given to us that we may foster its growth and bring forth fruit (Jn. 15:8) in accord with Jesus' promise: "I have come so that they may have life and have it to the full" (Jn. 10:10).

God's precious gift is offered to everyone of good will. You have been blessed by it. You share in it to the extent that you live in close union with Jesus Christ. From Him, through Him, you have received a renewal and transformation of your life. As He Himself says, He is the Bread of life (Jn. 6:35), the life within the vine (Jn. 15:4), the pledge of eternal life (Jn. 6:51), the way to the Father (Jn. 14:6). His Paschal mystery invites you to an ongoing and growing conversion, to a trustful abandonment of yourself to God our Saviour. Your long life gives you special insight into the profound meaning of St. Paul's words: "The reason He died for all was so that the living should

live no longer for themselves, but for Him Who died and was raised
to life for them" (2 Col. 5:15).

Your living Christian faith is therefore a cause of joy, of thanksgiving, of encouragement. It is a real source of strength to you as
you grow older.

Solidarity in Faith and Love

Because of the saving grace of Jesus' redemption, and the spiritual
relationship which makes us all the Father's children, our Christian
life unites us mysteriously, yet truly, to all believers and to the saints.

At the Second Vatican Council, the Council fathers affirmed that
the Church is "truly and intimately linked with mankind and its history".[2] This interaction includes both the work of our Christian salvation and the development of the entire Christian community.

This is why the Church speaks to us of the communion of saints.
This is that mysterious relationship, that participation in the life won
for us by the saving act of Jesus Christ — a life which transcends
all frontiers, all limits, and gives us access to the blessings of salvation, to the help of the saints and to the worship Christ and His Body,
the Church, offer endlessly to the Father.

On May 1st, 1974, Pope Paul VI appealed to the members of *Vie
Montante*, an apostolic organization of the elderly, to

> ... live this dogma of the Communion of Saints. May we all dis-
> cover in it that vital impulse which as our faith affirms, will some
> day blossom in the fullness of eternal life. Thanks to this invisi-
> ble spiritual communion, many people today can count on the
> witness of the members of this movement — in other words, on
> your witness as senior members of the Church.
> First of all, there are the men and women of your own age who
> are looking to you for support, friendship and apostolic concern,
> at a time when retirement often gives them an opportunity to
> rediscover the one thing necessary. Your families, your parishes,
> the local church — in other words, your diocese — can appreci-
> ate the many services which are made possible by your availabil-
> ity, your wisdom, your experience and the example of your faith
> and piety.[3]

You should be firmly convinced that your life of faith and of prayer play an important part in the extension and growth of the Father's Kingdom. Paul VI also emphasized this.

As you are well aware, there is no retirement age for doing the will of God. His will is that we become saints. Every stage in life has its own way of responding to the love of Christ and of witnessing to Him. The Church, on her part, has the grave duty and responsibility of insuring that everyone find in her the proper place to answer this call.

If the close of life never quite fulfills the ideal of its beginnings, this should help us recognize how mysteriously all is grace, and all ends in God's grace. The essential thing then becomes, in the words of St. Paul, to "make up all that still has to be undergone by Christ for the sake of His Body, the Church" (Col. 1:24).

Spiritual action at its best, the building up of the Mystical Body of Christ, lies in sanctification through prayer, sacraments and fraternal charity. [4]

This is the work to which you are called. Your very age commits you to it. In your own particular environment, you are witnesses to Jesus. No one else can give this witness in your place. Your character, your gifts, your age, indeed your very sufferings, give your witness a special stamp. If you did not exist, certain features of the Father's face, certain aspects of the Church, would remain forever undisclosed and unknown. Rejoice that you have been chosen to be the special witnesses of the goodness, the wisdom and the tenderness of God.

Collaborating in your Bishop's Pastoral Activity

You can help us, and we need your help. We count on you to help us in our task, for as you know, the bishop is the successor of the apostles serving the People of God within a local church. As the one who has the primary responsibility of proclaiming Jesus Christ to the members of his diocese, the bishop has a mission to establish communion among the faithful, and to encourage priests, men and women religious and lay people to be his collaborators.

It is readily understandable that the pastoral concern of the bishop and his collaborators should turn first of all to the generations to whom you have handed over the work of building the world today, and to those preparing to assume similar responsibilities tomorrow. Your mission as the older members of the diocesan Church is to support the apostolate of your bishop and his helpers on behalf of those who come after you.

Let us share with you one of our great pastoral concerns — vocations in the Church. How will the young people who are so dear to you grow in the Christian life if there are no new priests and religious? Jesus urges us to "ask the Lord of the harvest to send labourers to His harvest" (Mt. 9:37). Urgently we confide to you, in a special way the ministry of prayer for priestly and religious vocations and for the equally important vocations of lay people to share in the apostolic activity of the Church.

You exercise this ministry of prayer whenever you take part in the eucharistic celebration, where the joys, the sorrows and the sufferings of your age and state of health are clothed in the infinite merits of Christ our Saviour.

Meditation on the mysteries of the Rosary, which is in a way the divine office of the elderly, is another effective means of uniting yourselves to the prayer of Our Lady, and to that of all those who have given themselves to the Lord in the monastic life.

Dear senior members of our dioceses, we wish to remind you that the success of our pastoral mission depends largely on your determination to persevere in your Christian commitment to living the Christian life to the full. The Lord has given you to our parishes in the cities and the rural areas, to play a role as quiet, yet effective collaborators of inestimable value.

We appeal specially to the older members of spiritual movements or associations and to those who belong to social clubs or leisure-time groups, asking them to reflect in the light of the Gospel on their responsibilities as senior members of the Church in these particular groups or movements.

We ask older priests and religious, whose vocation called them to share in a special way in the evangelizing mission of the Church, to continue to share with us in this mission by exercising a role of spiritual leadership with the elderly laity. You can thus serve the Church not only by prayer, but also by participating in spiritual renewal sessions for the elderly in parishes, senior citizens' residences, or nursing homes whenever it is reasonable and your health permits.

Conclusion

As a final word we ask the senior members of the Church to discuss with your pastor your role in spiritual and apostolic renewal particularly as it applies to the elderly. You have a unique message to give which arises out of your experience of a life that knows God as He reveals Himself in both the old and the young.

It is with deep appreciation that we thank you for your witness to Christ, your fidelity to life and your continued service to the Lord.

NOTES

1. As a Canadian sequel to the General Synod of 1977 (*Catechetics in Our Time*), the Canadian bishops inaugurated a program of pastoral animation of family life, as a preparation for the General Synod of 1980 (*Role of the Christian Family in the Modern World*). A first phase produced a substantial study, *Marriage and the Family,* in three parts: Sociological Considerations, Biblical and Theological Considerations; Pastoral Considerations (192 pp.)

This was followed by *Faith Grows First in the Family* (36 pp.), and in turn by *What Does it Mean to be a Family?* (48 pp.).

The second phase of the project was a set of five booklets (51-140 pp.), *The Family: Growth or Alienation* (A. April); *Family and Society* (A. April and B.M. Daly); *Responsible Parenting* (H.W. Daigeler); *Responsible Procreation* (A. Guimond); *Building Christian Families* (J. McCarthy, RSCJ, and L. Rochon). All these are available from CCCB Publications Service, 90 Parent Ave., Ottawa, K1N 7B1.

2. Second Vatican Council, *The Church in the Modern World* (1965), n. 1.

3. French text, in *Osservatore Romano* (Vatican, May 2-3, 1974).

4. *Ibid.*

Section V, Document 4

MESSAGE OF THE CANADIAN BISHOPS IN PLENARY ASSEMBLY TO ALL PRIESTS IN CANADA

Author — The Plenary Assembly, the CCCB, October 28, 1981

Dear fellow priests:

The bishops of Canada have just completed their annual plenary meeting. Once again we were called upon to discuss and make decisions about a variety of issues affecting the inner life of our Church as well as its relationship to Canadian society. As we did so, you, the priests of Canada, were very much in our minds. Our thoughts were above all those of recognition and gratitude.

The last fifteen years have not always been easy. The wide-ranging changes initiated by the Second Vatican Council's summons to renewal were reinforced in our own country by dramatic developments of a social and cultural nature. Although these varied from region to region, the overall effect has been very much the same. The Church and world in which we exercise our ministry today are markedly different from those in which many of us were ordained twenty or more years ago. That we, as a community of faith, have been able to respond as well as we have to the challenges of our recent history is due in large part to your fidelity and effort.

It is good from time to time to pause and take stock of all that has been accomplished. The liturgical renewal, to take the most obvious example, has been on the whole a positive experience in our country. The vernacular, the new rituals, the development of lay ministries, the rediscovered sense of the ecclesial dimension of baptism and confirmation; all these have deepened our appreciation of the liturgy as involving the active participation of the whole community. What has been experienced in the liturgical assembly has spilled over into other areas of Church life. On parochial, diocesan and national levels, the laity are more involved than ever before.

Beyond these and other changes that have transformed our experience of the inner life of the Church, the recent past has witnessed a marked shift in the way we relate to the world around us. Our entry into the ecumenical movement has already borne considerable fruit. It will continue to be one of our priorities. In the area of social justice, too, we have together begun the difficult but essential task of communicating to our people something of the Gospel challenge to reach out in a special way to the poor and the oppressed, both here and around the world.

For us bishops to recall all this is to be reminded how grateful we ought to be to you for the unique contribution you have made towards its achievement.

Priesthood and community are all but inseparable. As we think about the life of the Church in our land, we cannot help but think of you and of your role in that life. Conversely, when we think of you, the community, within which and for which you exercise your ministry, is never far from our minds.

In the priesthood, as in so much else in the Church, there is much that is old and much that is new, much that is constant and much that changes. Now as always, to be a priest means to accept a ministry or service of leadership within the community of faith, a ministry of word and sacrament, of example and pastoral care. To be a priest today in our country does not change that. It simply demands a concrete form of priestly ministry, reflecting and responding to our own situation.

The agenda in the coming decade for our Church and therefore to a large degree for your ministry, will be deeply influenced by our continuing efforts to implement the Council's vision of what the Church is and ought to be. It will also necessarily reflect our struggles to be creatively present to the life experience of our people. As we try to do both, there will inevitably be tension and conflict. For you, as for us, St. Paul's reference to a "ministry of reconciliation" will take on new meaning (2 Cor. 5:18f).

Of the many specific issues that one could evoke, I would like to mention only one, lay involvement. Here is something that will, I think, have a considerable impact on our Church in the years ahead. The shortage of the clergy, but even more the Council's sense of the Church as the People of God and the Body of Christ, is leading to a remarkable awakening among many people of a desire to exercise genuine Christian ministry both in the world and in the Church. We are beginning once again to understand the New Testament teaching about the one Spirit and the many gifts.

Here is scope for a new emphasis in priestly ministry. Priests should be among their people as those who inspire, call forth, coordinate and sustain their multiple and varied gifts. All signs indicate that it is in this direction that the Spirit of Christ is at present calling the Church. To put one's priesthood at the service of that call will enhance the vitality of our communities. It will also be a source of great personal satisfaction.

Let me end with a simple expression of my prayer and my hope for you, a prayer and hope in which all the bishops of Canada join with me. May you become ever more deeply convinced of the unique worth for the Church and for the world of your priestly ministry. May your own prayer and reflection, your liturgical celebrations and pastoral involvements enlighten and deepen your commitment. May we all continue to serve and to build up the Body of Christ.

Section V, Document 5

CHRIST THE REDEEMER, YESTERDAY, TODAY AND TOMORROW: MESSAGE FOR THE JUBILEE OF REDEMPTION

Author — Bishop Henri Legaré, O.M.I., President, the Canadian Conference of Catholic Bishops, February 25, 1983

1. *Inauguration of the Jubilee of Redemption*

On March 25th, the Feast of the Annunciation of Our Lord, Pope John Paul II will open the Holy Door at St. Peter's Basilica just as the successors to St. Peter have done for the past seven centuries as they marked the beginning of Holy Years and the great Jubilees of the Church. By this simple yet significant gesture, the Pope invites all of us to "open our doors to the Redeemer" and to celebrate the 1950th anniversary of our Redemption through Christ's death and resurrection. We invite all Canadian Catholics to make this Jubilee a special time of spiritual renewal and openness to the Redeemer of humanity, from the opening ceremonies to its conclusion at Easter, 1984.

2. *Jubilee — a Tradition from the Old Testament*

Long before the coming of Christ, the people of Israel marked the great events of their life during a Jubilee Year. This was first and foremost a sacred time, a time sacred to God; at the same time it was a period of rest for the land, and during the Jubilee, social and economic measures for the common good were initiated. With the appearance of the Prophets, the Jubilee Year became a sign of an age to come, an age to be inaugurated and realized by the Messiah, the Christ. For it was He Who would proclaim the age of freedom, the abolition of oppression and the year of grace (Is. 61; Lk. 4:18-22). It was He Who would bring universal salvation through His death and resurrection (Acts 13:30) and thus free humanity from sin, forming a new people in whom there would be no Church, past, present and future; it is the People of God, baptized in the Risen Christ and strengthened by the Spirit.

3. *An "ordinary year celebrated in an extraordinary way"*

Throughout the centuries generations of believers have remembered and relived the Redeemer's saving actions. Today, the People of God continue to come together to relive in the midst of salvation history, Christ's death and resurrection, to celebrate with hope and love, in faith and repentance the event which changed human history into an era of reconciliaition, forgiveness and freedom. The Jubilee of the Redemption calls us then to intensify that which we live every day:

> ... this next Jubilee is an ordinary year celebrated in an extraordinary way: the possession of the grace of Redemption, which is ordinarily lived in and through the very structure of the Church, becomes something extraordinary through the special nature of the celebration which has been decreed.[1]

4. *Calling the world and our country to reconciliation*

The Jubilee of the Redemption takes place as the whole Church prepares for the international Synod of Bishops. The Synod's topic of Reconciliaiton: our personal reconciliation with God, ourselves and others; reconciliation between peoples, Churches and nations; peace through the eradication of hatred, hostility, rivalry, the use of weapons and all types of violence and injustice. This quest for reconciliation and peace is a profound sign of the victory of Christ over personal and collective sin and becomes "... a special form of fidelity to the mystery of Redemption, its application in the concrete life of man and of nations."[2] Fidelity to Christ places us in solidarity with our suffering brothers and sisters who face the cruel realities of poverty, persecution, internment, exile, the violation of their human rights, sickness and despair.

Our country shares in the severe problems of our world. A harsh economic crisis dramatically affects our people, particularly, families, the poor and the young. The divisions caused by the Constitu-

tional debate are far from healed. Our society is pulled in conflicting directions suffering from a loss of moral conscience caused by
a growing individualism. We are beset by dehumanizing ideologies
without respect for the human person, hostile to any sense of personal and collective responsibility, and to the quest for justice and
equality. These ideologies are gradually permeating society, threatening human life through abortion and euthanasia, and the family
through the increase in divorce, laws and attitudes that are anti-
family. The Christian cannot remain unconcerned or indifferent. We
are deeply challenged by the call of Christ: "He refused to support
their supposed absolute personal rights claimed at the expense of
the weaker and innocent. He came as a proclaimer of justice and
peace. He encouraged reconciliation, peace-making and non-
violence."[3]

We are to make real in our time Christ's message of good news
to the poor, freedom for captives and liberation for the oppressed
(Lk. 4:18-20). The salvation He promised is for today. As the people
of God, the Church, we are called to recreate the saving presence
of Christ in our time, in our community. We can do so because
"Christ set us free that we might remain free and might share the
gift of His sacramental Body for the building up of His ecclesial
Body".[4]

As we build the Church, we also contribute in a particular way
to the building of society, for it is in the midst of life that we are called
to experience and share the fundamental values of human existence
that are according to the plan of God.

5. *Together on the path of Redemption*

Pope John Paul II, whom we will welcome joyfully to Canada next
year, invites us to respond to God our Father's call to conversion and
reconciliation. This Jubilee Year should be a "year of welcome for
the Lord". In our hopes, our commitment, our daily joys and sorrows we hear again God's call to all humanity to be redeemed. The
Cross hangs in our homes, and stands on our church steeples as
a symbol of our faith. Raised over the world, the Cross reminds us
that Jesus Christ has opened for all the gates of the Kingdom.

NOTES

1. John Paul II, *To Cardinals and Members of the Roman Curia,* Dec. 23, 1982, in *The Pope Speaks* (Washington, 1983), 28, pp. 143-44.

2. John Paul II, *ibid.,* p. 150.

3. *Jesus Christ, Centre of the Christian Life,* a pastoral reflection of the Canadian Conference of Catholic Bishops, n. 46, available from CCCB Publications Service, Ottawa, K1N 7B1.

4. John Paul II, *Open the Doors to the Redeemer,* (on the Holy Year of 1983), in *Origins* (Washington, 1983), 12, p. 565, n. 5.

Section V, Document 6

NEW HOPE IN CHRIST: A PASTORAL MESSAGE ON SICKNESS AND HEALING[1]

Author — The Canadian Conference of Catholic Bishops, September 1, 1983

INTRODUCTION

1. The good news of salvation proclaimed to the world by Jesus Christ sheds its light over the entire span of human history. Nothing, whether it be joy or sorrow, sickness or health, riches or poverty, lies beyond its transforming power. This promise of a new and more abundant life, when all tears will be wiped away and weeping, death and pain will be no more (Rev. 21:4), lightens the burden of all who suffer in this world. And yet, freely accepted suffering does not paralyze our efforts for health. The expectation of a new earth, strengthening though it be in times of trial, also calls us here and now to heal people and bring wholeness to God's creation.

2. Jesus, Who won the final victory over suffering and death, was Himself born in poverty and abandoned to a criminal's death on a cross. For the rest of us, weak and strong, there is no exception: some degree of suffering will surely mark our lives. We may refuse to accept it, to yield with humility — still it remains a challenge. How do we bear suffering and at the same time seek healing as we move towards the total, God-given health of eternal salvation?

3. Here, in the two-fold question of why we suffer and how we are healed, is a mystery beyond our complete understanding. Yet we do know that in attempting to respond to this challenge, we are plunged

into the very mystery of salvation symbolized by that life-giving opening in the side of our Saviour (Jn. 19:34), and referred to by St. Peter when he says: "Through His wounds you have been healed" (1 Pet. 2:24).

4. In sharing these pastoral reflections with you on caring for the sick and working for health, we know that we are speaking to every heart, for everyone knows suffering and desires healing. If you are sick, disabled or infirm through age, we especially wish to bring you hope. If you have a particular call to heal or alleviate suffering, we mean to support and encourage your efforts. But we also wish to invite all of good will to work towards that fullness of life which God has prepared for us.

5. In offering these reflections, we will first draw inspiration from the Word of God as it has been revealed in the Bible. We will then consider how the Christian community has lived out its mission to heal. Finally, we shall offer some guidance on how Christians in Canada today might respond to Jesus' invitation to new life.

PART I

SUFFERING AND HEALING IN THE BIBLE

6. The first pages of Genesis present a picture of serene well-being whose foundation is intimacy with God. This overflows into the idyllic relationship of man and woman with each other and with the creatures of Eden. Through sin, suffering and alienation invade that world of peace. The Lord, however, does not withdraw His merciful and saving grace but promises to restore the original wholeness of His creation.

7. The Book of Deuteronomy reaffirms that belief in the life and health-giving power of God Who remains faithful forever to the Covenant with His people and Who will place a new law in our hearts so that sin and suffering will be no more. In the Book of Exodus, too, we read that the God of Israel is a saving God coming freely and sovereignly to the aid of His people. Israel chants, "Yahweh[2] is my strength, my song... my salvation", and God responds, "It is I, Yahweh, Who gives you healing" (Ex. 15:2,26). Ezekiel's beautiful vision of the ever-broadening stream emerging from the Temple, flowing down to the Dead Sea and bringing health and teeming

life wherever it goes, speaks of the Lord's health-giving presence among Israel His chosen people and announces His plans to heal all people of the world in the new age (Ezek. 47).

8. *Yeshe*, the Hebrew word for "salvation", sums up this life — and health-giving vision of God. Literally, it means being brought into the open, being rescued and liberated, whether from sin or slavery of the heart, from prison or poverty, from sickness or death. However, this salvation implies a faithful relationship with a protector, a liberator Who restores to freedom and wholeness of life. This healing Saviour is the Lord Himself Who gave the law to the people of Israel saying: "I am Yahweh your God Who brought you out of... slavery" (Ex. 20:1). Thus, according to the Bible, salvation is an action of total healing whereby both sin and suffering are taken away by God's health-giving power for those who follow His Word.

9. In the prophet Isaiah we learn for the first time how God often heals and brings fullness of life in ways that go counter to our own expectations. The remarkable Servant Songs show the Lord's chosen servant as someone who gives witness to God by his very sufferings and brings healing even to those who afflict Him: "On Him lies a punishment that brings us peace, and through His wounds we are healed" (Is. 53:5).

10. Throughout the New Testament, we find the same unity of salvation announced in the Old Testament where God's saving Word is joined to His healing action. Jesus' very name speaks of healing: "You must name Him Jesus, because He is the One Who is to save His people" (Mt. 1:21). The healing ministry of Jesus commands a place of great prominence in the Gospel. Matthew affords a good example of this emphasis on healing in Jesus' mission:

> That evening they brought Him many who were possessed by devils. He cast out the spirits with a word and cured all who were sick. This was to fulfill the prophecy of Isaiah: "He took our sicknesses away and carried our diseases for us" (Mt. 8:16-17).

11. With Jesus, healing of mind and body becomes the clear sign that the Kingdom of God is already present. When Jesus heals a leper or proclaims the parable of the Good Samaritan, it is an obvious sign of His compassion for those in suffering. But even more it points to the new life of the Kingdom: the total and permanent healing of the human person in all its dimensions and relationships. Jesus' healing Word of power reaches the whole person. It heals the body, but

even more important, it first restores those who suffer to a healthy relationship with God and with the community. Many of the healing miracles have this double perspective: "Your sins are forgiven" and "pick up your stretcher and go home" (Lk. 5:23,25).

12. Jesus, however, does not resolve the impenetrable mystery of suffering, which afflicts even the innocent. When asked about the man born blind, whether his sin or that of his parents had caused the blindness, Jesus replied that it was neither, but "so that the works of God might be displayed in him" (Jn. 9:1-3). The story of the rich man and the poor Lazarus helps us understand that suffering is not necessarily a result of our own wrong-doing but a condition of our broken human existence. Suffering offers to Lazarus the opportunity for personal acceptance of God's will and to the rich man the opportunity for a concrete expression of love. Lazarus rose to his vocation, and the rich man did not (Lk. 16:19-31).

13. Jesus' own life was interwoven with many forms of suffering. He knew fatigue, hunger and thirst. He experienced opposition, rejection and loneliness. He not only tolerated, but freely entered into the hidden design of suffering and healing foretold by Isaiah. He accepted suffering while turning in humble submission and trust to this beloved Father (Heb. 5:7-9). Peter was rebuked and called "Satan" for seeking to dissuade Jesus from suffering: "The way you think is not God's way but man's" (Mk. 8:33). At the high point of the Last Supper, linked indissolubly with Calvary, Jesus' own spirit of voluntary sacrifice was summed up in stark simplicity: "This is my body... given for you. This cup is the new covenant in my blood... poured out for you" (Lk. 22:19-20).

14. Thus through healing and sacrifice Jesus triumphed over suffering and rose to new life in glory. The startling feature of the Good News is that suffering has become a way to overcome suffering. God shows His power over suffering and death not only by curing or raising, but by entering into our suffering and thus overcoming it from within. By taking it upon Himself, He heals it. The cross now calls to much more than stoic acceptance of pain or evil — it signals our triumph over them — death has become the gateway to new life. Such a message presents an insurmountable obstacle to some; to others it is pure madness, but to those who have faith in Christ, it is central to understanding Him as "the power and the wisdom of God" (1 Cor. 1:23-24).

15. The Gospel's emphasis on new life and health continues to mark the days of the infant Church. From the very moment of their first mission by Jesus, the Apostles shared in His authority to heal (Mt. 10:1). At the time of their final sending, Jesus confirmed this power as a witness to the truth of their proclamation (Mk. 16:17). At the temple gate from which Ezekiel saw the life-giving river flow, Peter invoked this healing power of Jesus, when He said to the lame man: "I have neither silver nor gold, but I will give you what I have: in the name of Jesus Christ the Nazarene, walk!" (Acts 3:6). Twice Paul lists the charism of healing among God's gifts to the people of Corinth (1 Cor. 12:9,28-30), and James includes anointing and prayers for the sick among the official actions of Church authorities (Jas. 5:14-16).

16. But suffering too is always present. Three times St. Paul begged the Lord to remove "a thorn in the flesh" but the Lord did not remove it (2 Cor. 12:7-10). Nonetheless, suffering has received a new meaning in the symbol of the cross. Freely accepted suffering participates in the work of the redemption. "It makes me happy to suffer for you, as I am suffering now, and in my own body to do what I can to make up all that has still to be undergone by Christ for the sake of His body, the Church" (Col. 1:24). So too, in their trials as followers of Jesus Christ, Peter and the other Apostles rejoiced "to have had the honour of suffering humiliation for the sake of the name" (Acts 5:41).

PART II

THE HEALTH CARE TRADITION OF THE CHURCH

17. The powerful concern of the Bible for the healing of the whole person and of all persons has continued throughout the history of the Church. It is impossible in this short message to give a full account of this proud tradition. We simply wish to highlight a few examples that show how caring for the sick and curing illness where possible, are an essential dimension of Christian service.

18. Hippolytus, writing in the second century, testifies that Christians continue to exercise the gift of healing just as they did in the time of the Apostles. *The Apostolic Constitutions,* a fourth century liturgical document reflecting much earlier practice, provides for the

stallation of exorcist and healer, and includes a prayer for the power of healing in the ordination of the presbyter.

This concern for health that brought about physical restoration but more often the inner healing of love, made the emperor Julian the Apostate exclaim in grudging admiration in the fourth century: "Now we see what makes Christians such powerful enemies of our gods. It is the brotherly love which they manifest toward strangers and towards the sick and the poor". [3]

Among its manifold actions of healing, this love led the Church to establish the special ministry of deacons for the service of the Eucharist and of the sick and underprivileged. The shrines of Aesculapius, the ancient Greek god of healing, were re-dedicated to saints and their tradition of service to the sick continued in the name of the Lord. The Church's mission to heal inspired the fourth century Church Father, St. Basil the Great, to found and maintain at Caesarea a vast charitable institution which became the model of Christian hospitals. His contemporary, Gregory of Nazianzen, refers to this institution as a place where illness becomes a school of wisdom, where disease is regarded in a religious light, where misery is changed to happiness, and where Christian charity shows its most striking proof. [4]

19. This marvelous synthesis of wholistic healing which Jesus left to the Church continues through the centuries. Throughout Europe and later on in the New World we find special places of devotion where weary pilgrims search for spiritual as well as physical healing. Many early hospitals were associated with cathedrals and monasteries. This pattern of helping service is a significant sign in itself. Hospitals were built near the cathedral, a witness in stone to Christian faith in the two-fold presence of Christ: the real under the eucharistic bread and the mystical in sick or needy brothers and sisters.

20. The Knights Templar and later on many other orders of religious men and women, both Catholic and Protestant, were founded to nurse the sick. St. Catherine of Genoa (1477-1510) is considered a founder of modern hospital work. More humane treatment for the insane was innovated at St. Boniface Hospital in Florence in 1784. The hallmark of Christian missionary efforts was and continues to be medical service to the people of other countries. Great Christians — John Wesley, Louis Pasteur, Florence Nightingale, Albert Schweitzer, Tom Dooley — have led the way in the healing arts and

in caring for those who suffer. Charismatic figures such as Mother Teresa and Jean Vanier continue to emerge from within the Church today, responding with new insights to the health care needs of our time.

In our country as well, many outstanding Christians have worked in the health apostolate — Catherine de Saint-Augustin, Jeanne Mance, Mère d'Youville, Father Albert Lacombe, and others. How many Canadian cities owe their first medical services to a religious order or movement!

21. These great individuals and the communities they founded reveal for us the source and power of Christian service to the sick. They responded to Jesus' call for new life and served the suffering and deprived through healing and compassion.

Their concern for the broken was often the result of a life-long struggle to cope with suffering in their own lives and to transform it into an experience of growth. In this way the lives of these eminent men and women show us how suffering can help us to accept God's healing influence. They do not teach us to find happiness in pain. Suffering remains a sign of brokenness that should be resisted. When, however, it is recognized and accepted as a basic condition of life in this world, we can integrate it into our search for wholeness and spiritual growth, as many Christians before us have done.

PART III

OUR ATTITUDES AND PRACTICES AS FOLLOWERS OF THE SUFFERING HEALER

22. The history of Christianity is a record of service to the sick and of commitment to health. How are we today to receive that tradition, to appropriate it and to pass it on enriched by our own contribution?

a) *For Individuals*

23. The Bible has clearly taught us that our God is a God of life Who desires healing and health of body, mind and soul. Thus, all of us are called to preserve, protect and even enhance our health. In this

way we will not only avoid being an undue burden on others but, more importantly, share in restoring the original goodness of God's creation.

This responsibility for our own health includes our duty to care for the well-being of others and thus for the social, political and economic policies that make personal health possible. More will be said about this global challenge later. Suffice it to say for now that many illnesses today are a direct consequence of our life style, such as excessive use of tobacco, alcohol, drugs and junk foods, a lack of exercise, over-activity causing stress — all of these factors that are under our immediate personal and community control.

24. Even if we are sick, we maintain particular and even privileged responsibilities within the Church and society. For one, we always remain to some degree responsible for our own health and healing. Thus, as far as possible, we should participate through action or attitude in our own integral healing rather than submit passively to treatment.

More important, suffering people, including the chronically or terminally ill, can give a special service to others if they exemplify how salvation, the fullness of life for ourselves and for others, is often mysteriously bound to the way of sorrow. Many people who suffer or have suffered are richer and wiser for it, experiencing the truth of St. Paul's word that we become "heirs of God and coheirs with Christ, sharing His sufferings so as to share His glory" (Rom. 8:17).

Thus, if you are presently sick or infirm, you can, in new or deepening realization of always being loved by God, inspire others and give them courage to assume their own burdens. Still more, in your own body you can share in the great mystery of suffering for the sake of Christ's body, the Church (Col. 1:24). In your very suffering you can bring healing to others. For us Christians, you can paradoxically be at once cared for and caring for, ill and yet life-giving.

25. To all of you who are called to a special ministry of healing or caring — physicians, administrators, nurses, people in paramedical services, hospital chaplains, pastoral care workers and volunteers — we wish to express our special gratitude. We encourage you always to deepen your compassion in Christ, and at the same time to increase your professional competence. As Pius XII said so beautifully in an address to health care professionals:

> To recognize Jesus in the invalid and to act yourself like Jesus with him — here is the ideal of every Christian nurse! In this way, it

will come about that the image of Christ will be reproduced twice at every bed of pain: in the sick person, the Christ of Calvary expiating and resigned; and in the one assisting, the compassionate Christ, divine Doctor of soul and of bodies.[5]

Such service will let you see and accept your own vulnerability and need for healing. This sharing in suffering will strengthen your resolve and ability to give and heighten your sensitivity for the dignity of the people entrusted to your care. In this way, you will enter ever more deeply the life-giving mystery of human suffering.

26. The healing gifts in the Church are varied but all are needed to bring new life in Christ. Some bring wholeness to others by carrying their own suffering. Others, building on nature, contribute their medical skills in the imitation of Christ. Still others have received the rare gift of charismatic healing. All of these gifts are celebrated and summed up, as it were, in the sacrament of the Anointing of the Sick where the Church's ministry of healing is joined with its ministry of reconciliation. "By the sacred anointing of the sick and the prayer of her priests, the whole Church commends the sick to the suffering and glorified Lord, asking that He may lighten their suffering and save them."[6] In this sacrament the Christian community brings to the sick the healing reassurance that they are not abandoned but supported in their time of trial by the life-giving presence of the Lord and His people. In this way the anointing of the sick helps Christians in spite of and through their illness to follow and identify with the suffering and risen Lord.

b) *The Family*

27. A special word must be said about the family and its role in health care. The family is the source of a joyous and healthy attitude towards life. It is also a well-spring of courage in the face of trials and of Christian compassion towards others who suffer. Modern research indicates that many illnesses are caused or aggravated by strained and tense relationships, especially in the family setting. Conversely, peace and harmony within the family promote health. Health too can be contagious. Healthy communities, especially families, make for healthy persons and they in turn strengthen the well-being of a community.

28. With the healing power of the family in mind, more emphasis is being placed in recent years on home-centred, rather than

institution-centred care. Being cared for at home where possible enables the sick, and even patients for whom there is little or no hope
of recovery, to enjoy the immediate support of their families and
friends. At the same time, these opportunities for loving compassion and reconciliation can bring new wisdom and love to everyone
involved, gifts that may be more difficult to acquire in the less personal surroundings of a hospital. In addition, the immediate contact with suffering can remind family and friends of life's true
meaning and strengthen their humility and desire to grow in the
Lord.

c) *The Parish*

29. The whole Christian community is called to overcome the burden of suffering in all its forms, not only to alleviate it but to prevent
it where this is possible. All of us are gifted with the responsibility
accepted at Baptism to continue Christ's healing mission. But parishes also have a major role in helping people to understand, accept
and transform their suffering. As an extended community of support, the parish must seek to integrate in its worship and its activities the suffering of its members so that it becomes authentically
life-giving. Those who are well thus enable the sick, disabled or
infirm to feel needed and to experience their suffering as life-giving.

30. The sick and suffering people in our communities can be prayed
for by name at the Sunday Eucharist and through the help of special ministers can even participate in the same Eucharist by receiving the Lord's Body. These ministers become visible signs of the
community's concern for the sick when they participate in the reces-
sion at Mass as they take Communion to the sick. In this way, all
of us are reminded of the sick, both home-bound and hospitalized,
and made aware and responsible for their spiritual, physical and
emotional needs.

31. The Sacrament of Anointing of the Sick might be celebrated at
least once a year during the Sunday Eucharist. This enables all to
appreciate the community nature of the sacrament as the whole parish realizes its own need for healing and its ministry to heal others.
These parish celebrations should not be merely isolated events when
the community passively waits for God to heal. They are really
opportunities for the whole parish to renew its commitment to be
God's healers. For healing it is important to know that the community needs and cares for us.

32. Pastoral care of the home-bound or hospitalized makes this concern real. Fortunately, many parishes are already setting up Pastoral Care Teams whose members — clergy, religious, or lay — are given special formation in ministry and training in listening skills. These volunteers can do much through careful listening to make available the professional help that is needed. Moreover, through their words and actions they can help the sick to see their situation in the light of Christ and to be nourished by His sacraments.

Another type of parish service is accompaniment of the dying in their final journey and to help them experience approaching death as the gateway to new life. The recently bereaved, too, need the support of the community. Grief Recovery Teams help people move through the stages of grief so that the process can be one of growth in faith, rather than crisis. They can also help to plan funerals as authentic Christian celebrations.

33. Finally, amidst the wide-ranging parish or diocesan responsibilities for health care that we carry collectively, we must not forget the structural and legislative changes necessary to help the sick and infirm, especially those who are poor or marginalized. Working together to reduce high fees in nursing and other homes or to safeguard and strengthen our Medicare system are but two examples of such involvement. Making parish churches and other public buildings fully accessible to the disabled is another way of making this commitment real.

d) *Catholic and Other Health Care Institutions*

34. Catholic health care facilities — whether hospital, nursing home, personal care home or long-term care in general — fulfill a unique role in witnessing to the Christian attitude toward suffering and healing. Catholic institutions share goals similar to non-denominational health care facilities. However, the institutional approach to the ministry of healing offers Catholics a privileged opportunity to supply the best possible care in a manner and atmosphere fully inspired by the Gospel and to work for exemplary standards of hospital care.

35. Traditionally, these facilities were seen as religious institutions expressing a particular charism of the founding religious congregation. More and more, they are seen today as Church communities participating in an integral way in the apostolic responsibilities of the whole diocesan Church. We encourage this shift in perception and we call upon all the baptized working in these institutions to

continue to develop in them this Christian attitude of concern for the whole person. The entire staff, professional and volunteer, skilled and unskilled, need constant growth in spiritual maturity for this service. Thus both patients and staff should receive ongoing pastoral care and education in faith.

In recent years, governments have assumed increasing responsibilities for health care. Caring for the sick, however, remains an important Church service as a witness to Christ's life-giving message and as a sign of His healing presence. Moreover, there remain sectors in our country and elsewhere, where public care is incomplete. In line with the Church's preferential option for the poor, Catholic health care facilities should continue to serve especially the most needy, the most vulnerable and the weakest.

36. We also encourage Catholics working in non-denominational health care institutions. We urge you to reflect prayerfully alone or, better still, together with other Christians in your daily work, on being with the suffering and with other healers. Remember always how closely your daily concerns touch what was at the heart of Jesus' ministry: to heal the sick and to comfort the suffering. Care for all people equally, according to their need but independent of creed, colour or income, for each person is created in God's image and has unique importance in His creation. In your reflections you will draw even deeper inspiration from the knowledge that it is Jesus Himself Who meets us in the sick and suffering: "I was sick and you visited me" (Mt. 25:36). *"Our Lord, the sick"* was a catch phrase for the patients in the mediaeval *Hôtel-Dieu* (Hostel of God) institutions. What better way to instill profound respect and love for the suffering?

37. Hopefully all people of good will working in health care facilities would see their work as a noble vocation. It entails the responsibility to ensure that the principle of loving concern for people, originating in God's love for humanity, should penetrate this privileged work place. Such love is always patient and kind. It is never rude or selfish. It is always ready to excuse, to trust, to hope and to endure whatever comes (cf. 1 Cor. 13:4-7).

Hospitals and other health care institutions should always serve the sick and never the reverse, as happens when the sick cease to be persons, becoming mere objects in an impersonal process of medical technology or helpless victims of labour conflicts. In an age when the technological often takes precedence over the spiritual, and efficiency over true compassion, it is vital to recall the supreme impor-

tance of person-centred care. Such care should include consideration for the spiritual needs of people. Healing takes place best in
an atmosphere of love and understanding which includes reconciliation with oneself and with others. To rely on faith without medicine would be irresponsible, but to rely on medicine without faith
would be also inadequate.

c) *The Social, Economic and Political Community*

38. Certainly, today there are new marvels of the healing arts but
there are also new dimensions of suffering which the world has never
known before. Science and technology, especially in the field of bio-
genetics, continue to make dramatic advances in the diagnosis and
treatment of illness. The new discoveries, it is true, can open the
way to impermissable manipulation of human life and favour the
false expectation of a man-made world without suffering. There is,
however, much promise for the control and even elimination of many
diseases, in a way not dreamt of only decades ago. Public health services prolong life. Infant mortality has decreased in most countries
and even the unborn child can be treated for certain deficiencies.

39. Here again, however, there are new threats of illness and harm
as nuclear radiation and industrial wastes menace the air, soil and
water of our planet and new technologies are employed to kill the
unborn. Often enough the curious paradox arises that people try
by all means to prolong life, while on the other hand they hasten
to extinguish it in its beginning and sometimes towards its end. One
could well ask then whether advances in healing have kept pace with
the growth of suffering, especially if we consider that improved
methods of health care are often unavailable in poor and developing countries. As Pope John Paul II reminds us in his 1980 Advent
Encyclical *On the Mercy of God*:

> The state of inequality between individuals and between nations
> not only still exists, it is increasing. It still hapens that side by
> side with those who are wealthy and living in plenty there exist
> those who are living in want, suffering misery and often actu-
> ally dying of hunger, and their number reaches tens, even
> hundreds of millions.[7]

40. The pace and demands of modern life have given rise to a tide
of emotional and nervous disease. Medical services are strained to
the limit because of the way we organize our lives, individually and

collectively. Doctors report that many patients require medical assistance for problems that relate more to their social or physical environment than to their own body structure. Small babies and children are admitted to hospital for days at a time, not because their physical condition is so severe but because their families cannot cope or there is no extended family to give support. Some hospitals have wards filled with elderly patients left to themselves. Sometimes their families have ceased to care; in others, there are not enough senior citizens' homes available or we fail to provide the community support that would allow elderly and infirm people to remain in their own homes.

41. Christian health care must include a critical analysis of our attitudes, lifestyles and of the structures of society that inflict suffering on powerless people. For instance, are the vast expenditures of money on remedial medicine justified, when basic housing, nutrition, education and sanitation policies multiply unnecessary illness, especially in Third World countries? Christians need to explore and change the roots of ill health found in the way we organize our society. Inadequate but expensive housing is a health threat to the poor. In the field of education we find exaggerated competition among students and staff that places needless strain on people. Unfair and unsafe labour practices threaten the health of workers and of their families. Economic policies that increase automation at the cost of rising unemployment neglect people's basic need to find recognition and dignity in work.

The healing of these social ills and the provision of fully adequate health services to all people in our country and elsewhere may be beyond the reach of individual persons, but they are not beyond the reach of people working together. They are within the reach of governments and therefore of the political process. This process involves each of us and calls for our active and untiring participation, be that at the parish, diocesan, regional or national level. [8]

CONCLUSION

42. We have tried in this pastoral message to probe the hidden meaning of suffering, but even more to see through it the healing light of Christ's victory over evil in His cross and resurrection. Just as the self-giving life and death of Jesus Christ was taken up and trans-

formed in His risen state, so we too as persons and as people pass through the way of service and suffering to a new and fuller life.

43. This hope of final healing, far from diminishing our concern for health, stimulates our individual and collective efforts to overcome suffering in this world "for it is here that the body of a new human family grows, foreshadowing in some way the age which is to come". [9] It calls us to love and serve our suffering brothers and sisters in the image of our Lord Jesus Who gave His own life to save us, He Who "did not cling to His equality with God but emptied Himself to assume the condition of a slave... even to accepting death, death on a cross" (Phil. 2:4-8). When we follow the example of the Lord Jesus Who "went about doing good and curing all" (Acts 10:38), we obey His command to cure the sick (cf. Mk. 16:18).

44. In this way, our new life in Christ is already made manifest through our own manifold efforts for personal and social wholeness. But even where our efforts fail, we do not lose heart but are encouraged by St. Paul's admonition:

> Though this outer man of ours may be falling into decay, the inner man is renewed day by day. Yes, the troubles which are soon over, though they weigh little, train us for the carrying of a weight of eternal glory which is out of all proportion to them (2 Cor. 4:16-17).

NOTES

1. Available from Publications Service, CCCB, 90 Parent Ave., Ottawa, ON, K1N 7B1.

2. It is debated whether the divine name is correctly pronounced in this way. Without taking sides, we make use of the translation of the Jerusalem Bible.

3. *Quae Supersunt Praeter Reliquias apud Cyrillum Omnia*, edit. F.C. Hertlein (Teubner, Leipzig, 1875), vol. 1, p. 391f. The translation (?) provided in the document is very free and of unknown origin. In the passage cited Julian writes: "The negligence and unconcern of our (pagan) priests with regard to the poor suggested to the Christians the idea of applying themselves to works of charity, and they have succeeded in the worst of their enterprises thanks to the seductive appearance of their practices... In this way the Christians begin with what they call *agape*, hospitality and serving meals... and so draw masses of people into atheism (disbelief in the Roman gods)." Editor's note.

4. St. Gregory Nazianzen, *Funeral Oration for St. Basil*, n. 63, in *The Fathers of the Church*, vol. 22 (Catholic U. of America Press, Washington, 1953), p. 88f.

5. Pius XII, in *The Pope Speaks* (Washington, 1954), 1, p. 55.

6. Second Vatican Council, *Dogmatic Constitution on the Church* (1964), n. 11.

7. In *The Papal Encyclicals,* edit. Claudia Carlen, IHM (Wilmington, N.C., McGrath Publishing, 1981), V, p. 289, Section 11, n. 114. Cf. also our Labour Day Message, *Sharing Daily Bread,* nn. 6, 13, 15, in *Do Justice!* edit. E. F. Sheridan, SJ (Éditions Paulines, Sherbrooke, P.Q., J1E 2B9, 1987), p. 258.

8. Cf. our 1976 and 1977 Labour Day Messages, *From Words to Action,* and *A Society to be Transformed,* documents 5 and 16, in *Do Justice!,* cited in note 7, above. Also *Ethical Reflections on the Economic Crisis* (1983), *ibid.,* Document 55, nn. 4, 5, 6.

9. Second Vatican Council, *Constitution on the Church in the Modern World* (1965), n. 39.

Section V, Document 7

A REFLECTION ON MORAL LIVING [1]

Author — The Episcopal Commission on Theology, the CCCB,
approved by the Administrative Board, May 23, 1985

INTRODUCTION

1. In our Pastoral Reflections on Jesus Christ [2] we have tried to renew and strengthen people's faith in Jesus as the centre of the universe and of history. We answered some of the questions and concerns about Jesus which they have shared with us as bishops, with their parish priests or with religious educators. In this present message on the challenge of moral living we wish to continue these efforts of helping and supporting through our teaching the work of all those who have a special part in the proclamation of the Gospel.

These reflections are addressed in a particular way to priests, catechists and other pastoral workers. We share these thoughts as elements of reflection for our pastoral collaborators. What we say here is not all that can be said about this vast and crucial question. It is our hope that, encouraged and enlightened by our reflections, these pastoral leaders, in turn, will help all Catholics understand and appreciate better the call of moral goodness. In this way, all the people of God will reach fullness of life with greater clarity and commitment.

2. In a time of widespread indifference about right and wrong, we must recall clearly and reaffirm forcefully the need for moral values and their central role for true happiness in life. In a time of deep moral confusion we wish to point out once again how to find and follow the path of goodness and truth. As the Holy Father said to us bishops during his recent visit in Ottawa:

If the world no longer dares to speak about God, it expects from the Church, and especially from the bishops and from the priests, a word which witnesses to God with strength and conviction, in persuasive and adapted language, never reducing the greatness of the message to the expectation of the listeners. [3]

3. Our reflections will first show how the norms for moral living are given for our own good. Our God is a living God Who gives life and guides His children to glory. As human persons we walk this road towards life in freedom. It is a road difficult to follow and sometimes unforeseen. We must search for it with care and sincerity.

As we shall see in Part III, however, we are guided on our journey by the wisdom of past generations. They have left us universal values and norms that enlighten our conscience and prompt us to do right. All can learn from the lessons of history but as Christians we receive added strength and guidance through the work of the Holy Spirit. Strengthened by His light we are enabled to follow Jesus with greater love and in more complete truth.

PART I

MORAL LIVING: PATH TO FULLNESS OF LIFE

Humanity's quest for happiness

4. The desire for happiness and fulfillment is a basic thrust in the life of all people. This longing for ultimate self-realization and success drives us on even if we experience failure and frustration. Indeed, many psychologists today base their theories of personality development on this desire for self-fulfillment and many philosophers see self-realization as the criterion that determines the goodness of our actions.

Such an analysis of morality is not a new phenomenon for the Church. Christian tradition has always looked at personal fulfillment as a central goal of moral living. No doubt, there is a need to recall this basic insight of our own tradition but it must be done in a way that spells out its true meaning. The Christian notion of fulfillment is very different from any egoistic pursuit of individual happiness.

Christian self-realization calls us to grow in self-discipline and to reach out to others and especially to God, Creator of heaven and earth and Father of Jesus Christ.[4]

A call to fullness of life

5. At times, moral discourse, especially Catholic moral teaching, has been perceived as contrary to our deep-felt desire for happiness. This false impression may have been reinforced by certain presentations of morality that were overly concerned with laws and duties. In reality, however, and in the eyes of faith, it is clear that this inner force and desire for fulfillment and happiness is something beautiful and basic. God Himself has placed it in our hearts. Sin often tempts us to pursue false and misleading aspirations, but God's original design remains unchanged. He wants all of us to be happy, free from every bondage and perfect according to our own highest abilities. Many years ago, St. Irenaeus of Lyons expressed this very teaching in his magnificent phrase: "It is the living human being who is God's glory",[5] i.e., the glory of people who radiate wholeness and who reach "the fullness of their being".[6]

A reality taught by the Bible

6. The very first pages of the Scriptures speak of this divine plan in the splendid account of humanity's creation. Having called Adam and Eve into being, God blessed them and said: "Be fruitful, multiply, fill the earth and conquer it. Be masters of the fish of the sea, the birds of heaven and all living animals on the earth". And the text concludes: "God saw all He had made, and indeed it was very good" (Gen. 1:26-28).

At the heart of the Gospel, Jesus' own message is one of good news, a good news of salvation and wholeness. His promise is happiness and fulfillment. "How happy are the poor in spirit, theirs is the kingdom of heaven... Happy those who mourn: they shall be comforted..." (Mt. 5:3-11) Nor should we forget the Book of Revelation and its great vision of the new Jerusalem where God's original design will come to completion. Here God lives among humanity. "He will make His home among them, they shall be His people, and

He will be their God, His name is God-with-them. He will wipe away
all tears from their eyes, there will be no more death, and no more
mourning or sadness. The world of the past has gone" (Rev. 21:1-4).

Fullness of life and life's short-comings

7. Each of these texts in its own way confirms the Bible as a message of salvation, a truly real and concrete salvation that is intimately linked with our aspirations and affects every dimension of our
innermost lives.[7] True, perfect happiness cannot be achieved in this
world. At times the trials of life slow our journey and suffering threatens to overwhelm our hopes. Yet we are always sustained by our
faith in the Creator's unfailing desire for our fulfillment and joy. Indeed God's intervention in history by entering a covenant with His
people, the sacrifice of His own Son on the Cross, and the Son's
triumph over death in the resurrection, the mission of the Church
through the outpouring of the Spirit at Pentecost, all of these saving
actions are meant to confirm our deepest yearnings and bring us true
and everlasting joy and happiness through communion with God
Himself.

PART II

FINDING THE PATH TOWARDS LIFE

We take the road to life in freedom

8. As human beings we are free to follow or reject the path of goodness. Animals are driven by instinct not reason, but humans are left
free to make their own decisions (cf. Sr. 15, 14). As St. Paul says,
we must strive "to discover the will of God and know what is good,
what it is that God wants, what is the perfect thing to do" (Rom.
12:2).[8] In other words, we must accept the grave challenge of finding the meaning of true happiness and discovering the path to it.
God offers Himself to us in our freedom, a call we can accept joyfully or refuse at our peril. We can draw closer to the fountain of

life that will quench our thirst for happiness or we can neglect it and move away from the true fulfillment of our deepest desires. In sum, we are called to take charge of our lives and to answer for our actions.

A road difficult to follow and sometimes unforeseen

9. No doubt, self-realization and self-fulfillment, "achieving the fullness of one's personal being", [9] are noble but also eminently difficult tasks. There are many roads we can follow, some leading to life, others to frustration. There are many choices we can make, but not all are equally valid. From experience we know that some decisions bring an immediate satisfaction and yet, in the long run, they endanger our well-being because, at root, they attack family life, promote injustice or spread ill-health. Other examples would be the actions of people who use narcotics, of people who deliberately break their promises or those who use others for their own profit.

Again other decisions seem at first to negate our desires but, in the end, they bring a more authentic fulfillment to our lives. Such is the case, for example, of people who spend much of their leisure time on community work or of couples who give up many comforts to welcome a new child in their home.

Some decisions are morally right in themselves and others wrong

10. All through our lives and often in difficult and complex circumstances, we must strive to discover that which leads to real growth and that which leds to deterioration. In other words, we must discover what is morally good and what is morally evil. The distinction, however, is not an arbitrary one. As Vatican II teaches:

> In the depths of our consciences, we detect a law which we do not impose on ourselves, but which holds us to obedience... For human persons have in their hearts a law written by God. To obey it is the very dignity of persons; according to it we shall be judged. [10]

Some choices, by their very nature, are conducive to the human growth of persons and of society. Others are negative and destructive in themselves even though those who take these decisions may do so in good faith and with a right intention.

Moral good promotes growth. Moral evil destroys

11. This is the very point moral philosophers affirm when they speak of objective moral good and evil. The moral good is what preserves life and leads to its fullness. It allows people as individuals and as a society to grow and to find true fulfillment. Moral evil, on the other hand, hinders people's authentic development and that of their society.

As human persons we have a clear and special destiny in God's plan. Our growth as people depends, therefore, on specific forces and structures that can be discovered. As Pope John Paul II said recently:

> Human persons are gifted with a truth of their own, with an intrinsic order of their own, with a make-up of their own. When their deeds are in harmony with this order, with the make-up proper to a human person created by God, they are good deeds "which God prepared for us in advance (Eph. 2:10).

And the Holy Father continued:

> The goodness of our acting springs from a deep harmony between our personal being and our acts, while on the contrary, moral evil signals a break, a profound division between the person who is acting and his or her actions. The order inscribed in our being, that order which is our proper good, is no longer respected in and by our actions. The human person is no longer in his or her truth. Moral evil is precisely the evil of the person as such; moral good is the good of the person as such.[11]

The need for careful and critical reflection

12. Reflecting on these affirmations we realize with even greater clarity how important our decisions are and how grave is the responsibility that flows from this reality. This teaching also highlights our basic and vital duty to question our own spontaneous aspirations

and to ask in truth: is the action I am about to take morally good? Will it help me grow as a person and advance the growth of people around me? Does this action lead to greater service of others? Will it really respond to the depth of my being or am I giving in to fleeting and superficial desires? Does it make life more human? Will my decision reflect God's plan for my life? All of these considerations are moral questions of the highest order. The answers we give will influence profoundly our own existence and happiness and, indeed, the future of people around us.

The danger of "doing what others do"

13. To pursue this critical analysis of our actions is not an easy task. Often enough we would like to remain shallow in our scrutiny and simply follow the behaviour of others. In recent years, standards of conduct, formerly authoritative and accepted, have been rejected or challenged. This may make us feel more liberated, more autonomous and adult than before, but reality is different. Our moral decisions are under enormous pressures from social trends and the media. Sports figures, entertainers, TV stars all exercise a subtle or not so subtle influence on conscience. Consider the hidden but pervasive impact of slogans, stereotypes and of the standard "that everyone does it". An especially powerful example is the myth that only the young, athletic, beautiful and rich are worthy of our attention and esteem, only people who are "cool" and free from cumbersome commitments. No doubt, if we seriously studied the influence of this stereotype on our lives, we would find a surprising impact on our attitudes and decisions.

Our desire for immediate satisfaction

14. A second threat to our freedom is the unbridled desire for immediate gratification. Often the prospect of instant pleasure hurries us to avoid serious reflection and analysis. This danger is especially prevalent in our consumer society, a society of impulse and impatience where our wishes must be realized as quickly as possible. It almost seems as though we were caught up in a race to have everything at once. "Wait no more", we are told. Buying on credit, catch-

ing up with fast-changing fashions, racing against the clock are all
symptoms of our haste to have.

The need to form and renew conscience daily

15. Faced with these pressures from within and from without, we
need to reflect and meditate constantly on our actions. We must learn
how to resist and become free from trends and forces that promote
instant pleasure and shallow fulfillment. "Become free" means probing our heart and listening quietly to its message to discover our
deepest goals and how to achieve them. It means being open to all
aspects of life, becoming aware of the real powers active in society
and within ourselves. It means forming and renewing our conscience
daily, discovering what makes us grow as individuals and what
humanizes the world around us. This is our first moral duty if
we wish to follow the Lord's call.

PART III

THE LIGHT OF MORAL VALUES AND NORMS

Values express the wisdom of history

16. As we have seen, the challenge of moral living is central for our
fulfillment as human persons. It is a difficult task but we need not
face it alone. We can benefit from the experience of history which
has identified for us the moral values that are essential for integral
human development and happiness. Dignity of the person, respect
for life, justice, goodness, unselfishness, honesty, sincerity, loyalty,
fidelity, truthfulness, moderation, courage, participation, solidarity, forgiveness: these are some of the values we must strive for and
be guided by if we want to be faithful to ourselves and to achieve
wholeness. These values serve as guideposts for our actions and,
at the same time, challenge us to grow in goodness.

Whoever disregards these values recommended by the wisdom of generations — and confirmed by the Word of God — will become a slave to his or her environment and instincts. Disrespect for these basic principles of human living can lead in the end only to failure and despair. The same principle holds true for communities and nations. As soon as a society loses its sense of justice, its respect for human dignity or its sincerity, decadence and corruption take hold. We cannot lead truly positive and constructive lives and at the same time fail to honour these fundamental guidelines. Moral values sharpen the call of our conscience to do good.

Norms translate values into practical terms of action

17. Several times in history, these values have been set down in clear charters of rights and duties to signify their vital importance for personal and community living. For example, if we read the Ten Commandments in this light we realize how much these norms serve to protect and promote our humanity. Most of the prohibitions they express signify in negative form some very central and positive values: "Honour your father and your mother... You shalll not kill... You shall not commit adultery... You shall not steal... you shall not bear false witness against your neighbour... You shall not covet your neighbour's house" (Ex. 20:12-17). Committing such acts means destroying one's community and thus destroying one's own being. Humanity has had this unfortunate experience all too often in the destructive horror of wars and of other social evils.

Some values and norms are universally valid

18. Thus it is easy to see why, after the dark years of World War II, we felt the need to enshrine these values in the *Universal Declaration of Human Rights* of the United Nations. The forceful preamble of this declaration affirms the need to base all our collective and individual decisions on a deep respect for the dignity of each person. As the text says,

> Whereas recognition of the inherent dignity and of the equal and inalienable rights of all members of the human family is the foun-

dation of freedom, justice and peace in the world, Whereas disregard and contempt for human rights have resulted in barbarous acts which have outraged the conscience of mankind; and the advent of a world in which human beings shall enjoy freedom of speech and belief and freedom from fear and want, has been proclaimed as the highest aspiration of the common people,

Hence, beginning with Article One, there is a claim of universally valid rights and duties:

All human beings are born free and equal in dignity and rights. They are endowed with reason and conscience and should act towards one another in a spirit of brotherhood/sisterhood. [12]

Values and norms protect and promote humanity

19. Our search for happiness will be in vain unless we accept these universal norms and the values they promote. Moral values protect humanity in people and help us discover our true inner destiny. They help protect against violence, pride, distrust, selfishness and hate. They prohibit us from destroying people, using them as mere means.

PART IV

WALKING THE PATH OF LIFE GUIDED BY THE HOLY SPIRIT

Only communion with God brings true fulfillment

20. Moral values and norms help our search for happiness. There is, however, another dynamic at work in our world that stirs our hearts and leads us towards true self-realization. It is the dynamic of salvation and grace which reinforces our deepest aspirations and brings fulfillment that goes beyond the inherent powers of nature. St. Irenaeus not only links God's glory and humanity. He goes on to say human life is the vision of God. [13] In this way we come to know what reason alone could not have discovered: that only in communion with the living God do we find true fulfillment and real hap-

piness. Life's meaning and the road towards it have thus been revealed more clearly. We realize with certainty that concern for our
own fulfillment means following our deepest desire for communion
with God, but through the way of the cross.

The Holy Spirit guides us and God's love surrounds us

21. This path of life was charted for us by Jesus Christ Himself.
Renewed and reborn as Christians by the waters of baptism, we can
rely on the presence of the Holy Spirit in us. He is our light and
strength. He helps us find the right path as by instinct, a prompting
of grace, and gives us courage to walk this road. The Holy Spirit
introduces us into the mysteries of God and helps us discover this
extraordinary message that changes our whole outlook on life: God
is truly Father to us all and we are His children. "Because you are
His children, God has sent the Spirit of His Son into our hearts"
(Gal. 4:6; cr. 1 Jn. 3:1-3; 5:1-5). And elsewhere St. Paul writes, "This
hope is not deceptive, because the love of God has been poured into
our hearts by the Holy Spirit which has been given to us" (Rom.
5:5). Our whole life has been transformed by God's love which has
been revealed to us, and our desire for happiness has been strengthened by it. Joyfully we realize: we are not left alone in an absurd
and meaningless universe but led and held by God's love, whatever
our sin, weakness or limitation. Thus we learn how to wonder at
our own life, how to receive it with gratitude and to trust.

We respond in love

22. Then, from the depths of our being and supported by the
action of the Holy Spirit, that fundamental attitude arises which en-
livens our actions and transforms our judgment, namely love. We
begin to realize and appreciate the central message and deepest call
of the Gospel:

> You must love the Lord and God with all your heart, with all your
> soul, and with all your mind. This is the greatest and the first
> commandment. The second resembles it: you must love your
> neighbour as yourself. On these two commandments hang the
> whole Law, and the Prophets also. (Mt. 22:37-40)

From now on, love will be at the heart of all our actions.

A self-giving love

23. Christian love means following God on a path that is often unforeseen. We know there will be suffering and the cross. The demands on us are radical. They will require self-denial, the gift of self and forgiveness, in the example of Jesus Himself Who, on the cross, gave up His own life for our salvation. Love of God and of neighbour is the basis of moral life and of human fulfillment but a love that is true and total, that welcomes others and is truly open to them. Such love seeks and accepts peace and reconciliation. At moments when we are truly resolved to give ourselves in the service of others, we will find, to our surprise, the self-realization and wholeness we desired. As the Gospel says: "Anyone who wants to save his or her life will lose it; but all who lose their lives for my sake, they will save it" (Lk. 9:24). In a culture marked by desperate striving for pleasure and money, security and power, we must recall clearly the challenge of the Gospel, a challenge whose truth is confirmed by our own deepest experiences. In the bond of true love and lasting commitment we find our very freedom. In active solidarity and sharing with others, we find that joy which led Mary to exult in the work of the Spirit (cf. Lk. 1:35ff and 46ff).

A path of daily renewal and growth

24. The challenge is clear, but we all know the experience of weakness, of being lax in our commitment and of selfishness. As St. Paul reminds us, evil continues to pursue us, even though we have received the Spirit's pledge and been marked by his seal (2 Cor. 1:22). Thus we need to distinguish carefully between the work of the Spirit and that of sin. "When self-indulgence is at work," says St. Paul, "the results are obvious: fornication, gross indecency and sexual irresponsibility, idolatry and sorcery; feuds and wranglings, jealousy, bad temper and quarrels; disagreements, factions, envy, drunkenness, orgies and similar things". And St. Paul adds the terrible admonition: "I warn you now, as I warned you before: those who

behave like this will not inherit the Kingdom of God". On the other hand, the shining fruits of the Spirit are: "Love, joy, peace, patience, kindness, trustfulness, gentleness and self-control. There can be no law against things like that, of course" (Gal. 5:19-23). If we reflect carefully on our actions and the fruits they bring forth, we will realize ever more clearly where change is needed and that without it true love cannot grow.

Listening to the Word of God

25. In this journey of moral growth we need to rely heavily on the Word of God, especially the Gospel. The Gospel is first a message of hope but also of radical challenge. Probing the depth and quality of our innermost thoughts, it forces us to drop our illusions and face reality. It makes us look at people and events in a new light and to work for justice. For example, reading the Sermon on the Mount we will realize the need for our own conversion. How will we respond to the words of Jesus Who exhorts us:

> But I say this to you: anyone who is angry with his brother will answer for it before the court... But I say this to you: if a man looks at a woman lustfully, he has already committed adultery with her in his heart... If anyone hits you on the right cheek, offer the other as well... But I say this to you: love your enemies and pray for those who persecute you, in this way you will be children of your Father in heaven, for He causes His sun to rise on the bad as well as the good, and His rain to fall on honest and dishonest people alike" (Mt. 5:22,27,39,44-45).

These words do not tell us exactly what to do in every situation, but they point the way. They disturb our complacency and in this way open the way to conversion and growth. Only if we reflect deeply and prayerfully on the challenge of the Gospel will our hearts be transformed, our wills take the right decisions.

**Guided by the teachings of the Church
and the example of the Saints**

26. The Bible text is not the only guide for our conscience in the complex and ever changing circumstances of our lives. God's word lives on throughout the ages in the community of those who believe in Jesus Christ. As His Church, they are together guided by the Holy Spirit. Catholics can rely on the teachings of the Holy Father and the bishops — Council documents, encyclicals, messages of the Bishops' Conference or of individual bishops — as they exercise their ministry of proclaiming "the truth which is Christ" and "the principles of the moral order which spring from human nature itself". [14] These messages — just as the example of the saints who lived before us and the witness of Christians today, who base their whole lives on Christ — probe the specific call of the Gospel for each generation and help us follow the road towards Christ. The whole Church, as the community of believers, must listen to the Spirit of God and in this way discern what is good and worthy of praise.

CONCLUSION

27. Let us conclude and affirm once again: the final glory of our lives cannot be left to chance, to our fleeting desires or the vacillations of social trends. We must take charge of our own lives and exercise freely the responsibilities we have received.

28. This central challenge of moral living implies the need always to refine our conscience. For this we must learn how to pause in silence and reflect critically on our actions; we must free ourselves from fascination by public opinion and learn how to withstand the tempting desire for easy and instant pleasure. In tranquility and openness to the values and norms offered by the wisdom of history we must search for what is best in us and for us. In prayer we must open our hearts to the call of God's word as it frees us from sin and enables us to love in all truth. We must search together as a community of believers, especially with those who suffer, and welcome the guidance of the Church's pastors. In the final analysis: we must welcome Jesus in our lives.

29. "Fear not: open your doors wide for Christ Jesus". [15] These words of our Holy Father are central because God's design is fulfilled in Jesus Christ. He reveals for us the true meaning of life. Through the gift of His Spirit He frees us from ourselves, widens our hearts and opens us to the fullness of life.

Then the way towards happiness and the glory of God will become clearer. Then we will build on a firm and everlasting foundation, just as Christ's own deeds remain with us forever, He Who died on the cross but rose again in the light of Easter morning: "I have told you this so that my own joy may be in you and your joy be complete" (Jn. 15:11).

NOTES

1. Available from CCCB Publications Service, 90 Parent Ave., Ottawa, ON, K1N 7B1.

2. *Jesus Christ, Centre of the Christian Life,* Canadian Conference of Catholic Bishops, 1981, CCCB Publications Service, 90 Parent Ave., Ottawa, K1N 7B1.

3. In the *Canadian Catholic Review,* Saskatoon, Sask., Oct., 1984, p. 76.

4. Second Vatican Council, Constitution *The Church in the Modern World,* n. 24.

5. Irenaeus, *Against Heresies,* Bk. IV, C. 20, N. 7, *Ante-Nicene Christian Library,* edit. A. Roberts and J. Donaldson, Edinburgh, 1868,
For the glory of God is a living man: and the life of man consists in beholding God. For if the manifestation of God made by means of creation, affords life to all living on earth, much more does that revelation of the Father, which comes through the Word, give life to those who see God.

6. John Paul II, General Audience, July 27, 1983, in *Osservatore Romano* (Vatican, Aug. 1, 1973), 3.

7. In our recent message *On Sickness and Healing,* we spoke at length of the health and life-giving power of God our Father. Cf. Document 6 of this section, Part I.

8. Cf. Second Vatican Council, *The Church in the Modern World,* n. 17.

9. In Audience cited in note 6, above.

10. *Op. cit.,* note 8, above, n. 16.

11. John Paul II, General Audience, July 20, 1983, in *Osservatore Romano* (Vatican), July 25, 1983, p. 3.

12. *Universal Declaration of Human Rights* (United Nations), Preamble and Article 1, in *The International Bill of Human Rights* (Office of Public Information, United Nations, New York, 1978), pp. 4f.

13. Irenaeus, *l.c.* in note 5, above.

14. Second Vatican Council, *Declaration on Religious Liberty,* n. 14.

15. John Paul II, Homily during Mass of Inauguration, Oct, 22, 1978, in *The Pope Speaks* (Washington, 1979), 24, p. 24.

Section V, Document 8

BEYOND FEAR:
A PASTORAL MESSAGE ON AIDS

Author — The Canadian Conference of Catholic Bishops,
    March 16, 1989

INTRODUCTION

1. Since the beginning of the decade the infectious and communicable disease called AIDS has spread through a large number of countries at a terrifying rate. Canada has not been spared, with 2,323 reported cases, 1,259 resulting in death, between 1980 and January 1989. It has also been noted that the number of persons in a given region who have this disease tends to increase alarmingly: in fact, recorded cases double from year to year. In many sectors of the population this is causing panic or provoking so great a fear that people feel paralyzed.

2. Initially at least, Christians cannot avoid being caught up by this sometimes exaggerated fear whose expansion keeps pace with the spread of the disease itself. Moreover, are they not called by the Second Vatican Council, to share the fears and sorrows of their contemporaries as well as their joys and hopes?

3. The joy and hope, the grief and anguish of the people of our time, especially of those who are poor or afflicted in any way, are the joy and hope, the grief and anguish of the followers of Christ as well. Nothing that is genuinely human fails to find an echo in their hearts. [1]

4. Though we may initially share this fear, we must not surrender to it. On the contrary, we must do all we can to overcome it since

there is danger that fear will sap the energies needed to face the challenge. In a spirit of hope, we would like to see Christian communities, and all people of good will, transcend this fear in three ways:

— by effective compassion for those infected by the virus or suffering from AIDS;
— by clear-sighted assessment of the situation;
— by promoting a spirit of solidarity among care givers.

It seems to us that these responses follow directly from our fidelity to the example and teaching of Jesus, as well as from true appreciation of the worth of every person.

COMPASSION TOWARD THOSE WITH AIDS OR CARRYING THE VIRUS

5. If there is one thing that marks Jesus' conduct, it is His compassion for the sick and broken, and His obvious unconcern for contamination by disease or evil. Contrary to the practice of His time, Jesus touches lepers (Mt. 8:3; Mk. 1:41; Lk. 5:13); shares a meal with people officially unclean (Mt. 26:6; Mt. 9:10; Mt. 11:11; Mk. 2:15-16; Lk. 5:30); disdains the recriminations of the self-appointed judges of the adulterous woman (Jn. 8:1-11); converses calmly with a woman currently living with her sixth "companion" (Jn. 4:1-42). Was it bravado that moved Him, or was He showing us how to surmount the barriers of sickness or moral failure, to encounter the wounded person and to be present to his or her misery?

6. We ask whether it conforms to the Gospel — or even to acceptable human behaviour — to ostracize individuals suffering from AIDS by depriving them of housing and jobs, to refuse them certain kinds of health care, to subject them to humiliating attitudes and treatment, or to go to the extreme of placing them in quarantine? Too often AIDS patients are demoralized by contempt and rejection, smug judgment and moralizing, humiliating inquiries and hasty presumptions, which even extend to children stricken or believed to be infected.

7. Fortunately, despite these negative attitudes towards the victims of AIDS, we encounter wonderful examples of individuals, believers and others, who have listened to their minds and hearts. Many, in

fact, friends of the sick, health care professionals and volunteers have not hesitated to be in contact with the sick, to care for them, to show sympathy and see that they are supported by a warm human presence in their difficult moments. We thank the Lord for these witnesses of His love and we are challenged by their example. We invite our brothers and sisters in faith and all people of good will to develop a similar attitude and to become involved so our society may provide those suffering from AIDS with the help they need and the respect and care to which they are entitled as human beings.

8. We warmly invite Christians to strive, in accordance with the teaching of Jesus, to have more faith in the contagious power of good than in the infection of evil or disease. It seems to us that Christians should do all they can that no one suffering from AIDS feels rejected by his or her brothers and sisters or by God. Surely of those who are present to persons with AIDS, the followers of Jesus should reflect in very special ways the tenderness and saving will of a God whom Jesus calls Father. With others who help, Christians who believe in the Resurrection can help those suffering from AIDS to transform their ordeal into a path to life and rebirth.

9. Such compassion is not easy to practice. Some may regard us as utopian or pious dreamers. We are convinced, however, that compassion, so different from sentimental pity, is the light of Jesus' example helping us to walk His way and to conquer fear.

A CLEAR-SIGHTED ASSESSMENT OF THE SITUATION

10. Our compassion for those who have AIDS should, however, prompt us to look ahead and to think of those who might be infected or become so. Overcoming fear of AIDS should lead us to the second step which we have labelled a clear-sighted assessment of the situation. Initial victory over fear would be only temerity and imprudence if it led us to trivialize the real situation, that so infectious a disease is presently uncontrolled and spreading rapidly in our midst. We must take a clear, intelligent and informed look at this fact.

11. People are led to such a sound and insightful approach through the information published in responsible media. It is of crucial importance that specialists make generally available clear and simple information about how the disease is transmitted and how to avoid

it. All should have this information so that their conduct toward those suffering from AIDS may be guided by reason and not by disgust or irrational fear.

12. The initiatives of public authorities to curb the spread of this disease are also part of this sound approach, and especially their efforts to provide resources for proper care of the sick. Need we mention the positive contribution of the commitment of the Christian community to help society develop an open and responsible attitude toward what is happening, by supporting professional care givers, by being sensitively present to the sick, etc.?

13. We would still be taking a short-term view if we were to confine our attention to the phenomenon itself without concern about its origins and the possibility of attacking its causes. According to current scientific knowledge, the AIDS virus (HIV) cannot survive outside the human body. Reported cases in this country show that the virus is sometimes spread to a child by an infected mother during pregnancy or at birth, and there are a number of cases of infection through blood transfusions. However, recent epidemiological studies in Canada show that in the great majority of cases, the virus is spread principally in one of two ways: either by sexual (homo or hetero) relations or through use of infected syringes by drug addicts. One of the most effective means, therefore, to stem the disease would be to change personal behaviour both in the intravenous use of drugs and in sexual relations with infected persons or carriers of the virus.

14. To this end, some public health services have set up programs for free distribution of sterile syringes to drug users and urged systematic use of condoms as protective devices. They have said, in effect, that these technical means would be best suited for the high-risk clientele with whom they are dealing. They believe, it seems, that these means would be relatively effective in reducing the rate at which the disease is spreading, especially in the case of persons whose irresponsible behaviour involves disastrous consequences for society as a whole.

15. We are fully aware that public health officials must look for the most effective means to counter this epidemic. However, we would, for our part, observe that the two suggested preventive measures do not touch the real causes of this problem. They do not go to its roots. In a tradition that is not limited to Christians, we believe that the problem should be set in a more human context. In the final

analysis, one must call upon the moral and spiritual values of human love and sexuality.

16. A clear-sighted and informed look at this disquieting situation invites men and women of good will to question contemporary sexual attitudes and practice. Efforts to control AIDS which are limited simply to more effective use of technical means and to a frantic search for an anti-AIDS vaccine are obviously insufficient. Is not this to be content to reduce or to check the symptoms of a disease without remedying its cause? Permissivity in intimate relations holds in store some nasty surprises. The rapid spread of AIDS now forces our society to take a second look at the whole tendency to trivialize sex.

17. We believe the human quest for happiness requires or presupposes a considerable measure of self-control, an openness to life and an interpersonal love which goes beyond a simple desire for physical pleasure. These are truths which a hedonistic civilization has largely forgotten or considers obsolete. It is precisely in this forgetfulness or rejection that we discover the fundamental reason for the rapid spread of AIDS. In turn, the real remedy for this tragedy of our declining twentieth century is to be found in a rediscovery of sexuality lived in a chaste, complete and more personal relationship of love, in the context of a stable marriage. Fraternally, we invite all men and women who have the well-being of humanity at heart to accept the challenge of a life which does not shrink from basic moral demands.

PROMOTION OF A SPIRIT OF SOLIDARITY AMONG CARE-GIVERS

18. We have already suggested the third way to overcome fear aroused by the spread of AIDS: human solidarity, in which individuals stand together without regard to differences of religion or philosophy. We invite members of the Catholic communities for which we are responsible to work whole-heartedly at one or other of the tasks to which men and women of our time have committed themselves in an effort to slow the spread of this plague — tasks such as fundamental research in biology and medicine, epidemiological studies of infected populations, philosophical and sociological research on our culture, research in pastoral psychology, moral support of those suffering from AIDS, involvement in specialized

social services, educational programs for youth, detoxification programs, etc.

19. We are determined to support those who accept involvement with victims of AIDS. We invite members of Christian communities not to refuse such commitment in a spirit of solidarity. We believe that we can help our brothers and sisters, desperately fighting this fatal disease, to discover a new quality of life, even as they face death.

CONCLUSION

20. In conclusion we repeat our belief that the challenge of AIDS is to be faced as we face other challenges: we must not let panic paralyze action or press us towards solutions that disregard the dignity of the human person. We are thinking here, specifically, of measures to ostracize AIDS victims and of campaigns limited to simple technical means to fight the spread of the disease. We recall what Cardinal Basil Hume, the Archbishop of Westminster, wrote recently:

21. The fact to be faced is that all of us in society have to learn to live according to a renewed set of values. That will not be easy. How can any appeal for faithfulness and sexual restraint be heeded when there is on all sides explicit encouragement to promiscuous behaviour and frequent ridicule of moral values? Society is in moral disarray, for which we must all take our share of blame. Sexual permissiveness reflects a general decline of values.

22. Some might question whether any consensus on values is possible in a society which has so lost touch with its cultural, religious and spiritual roots. Nonetheless I am convinced that there are untapped reserves of goodness and idealism in many individuals and communities. [2]

23. Indeed, we believe so firmly in the goodness and wisdom the Lord has placed in the human heart that we dare hope we will succeed in meeting this sudden challenge. Because of what happened on the first Easter, we reaffirm our faith in the possibility of the transformation of apparent death into a seed of life!

NOTES

1. *The Church in the Modern World* (1965), n. 1.
2. *The Times,* London, Jan. 7, 1987, p. 106.

Section V, Document 9

A LETTER TO CATHOLICS ON THE RECENT SEXUAL ABUSE CASES

Author — Archbishop James M. Hayes, President, the Canadian Conference of Catholic Bishops, July 10, 1989

When sin is committed, the whole community becomes the victim of its consequences. Bishops across Canada have shared with me the shock and pain they, priests, and all Catholics are suffering in the face of the charges of sexual abuse brought against some priests and religious brothers.

This pain reaches all levels of our Canadian Catholic community as we become acutely aware of the anguish endured in silence for years. This needs to be faced with compassion and understanding. First in our compassion must be those who have been sexually abused. They need and have a right to the acceptance and understanding of the community to further their restoration to wholeness.

Such insight is not quickly or easily found. A variety of over-simplified theories are being put forward by individuals via the media, but experts tell us that a number of different causes or complex combinations of causes can lead to sexual abuse of children and adolescents. In addition, it is usually impossible to detect any predisposition to such conduct before an act is committed. Each case has to be evaluated and treated in the light of its own special circumstances.

As a community, we must listen to those who have been abused and clearly hear their pain. We must offer them human and Christian support, making clear to them that we are sensitive to their special needs and that we seek reconciliation.

As for the guilty, we must remember that we are dealing with an illness as well as a person who has committed a crime. Willful immorality cannot be condoned and criminal action certainly should be punished, but punishment alone is not the answer.

While in no way diminishing the seriousness of these crimes or excusing those who have committed them, each charge must be carefully investigated in a way that avoids creating more suffering. Victims often abhor the glare of publicity and they have a right to privacy. Charges should be proven before the accused is condemned in the court of public opinion. The more than 11,000 priests in Canada, who are faithfully trying to live their commitment, should not be brought under suspicion, ridicule or judgment because of the sins of a small number.

This tragedy of sexual abuse challenges every member of our Catholic community. We are called to strengthen the bonds of faith and charity needed to provide support and to live as a loving, forgiving community. Priests are called to mutual solidarity and to the support of their people. Each of us: bishop, priest, religious and lay person, is called to be mature in our faith, to recognize our own sinfulness but to realize that the darkness of sin need not blind us to the light and truth of the Gospel. The suffering the Church is now experiencing must be illumined by the message of the Cross. It is through faith in the Paschal Mystery of death and resurrection that we will find hope and new life for the whole People of God.

We must all pray earnestly for faith and the strength born of grace and mutual good example, to overcome our anguish and anger, moving to the compassion and forgiveness so necessary for the reconciliation of our communities. I ask your prayerful and human support for the people, priests and bishops of those dioceses facing these tragic situations and for the spiritual good of the whole Church.

Section V, Document 10

TO SPEAK AS A CHRISTIAN COMMUNITY: ON INCLUSIVE LANGUAGE

... for you are all one in Christ Jesus. Gal. 1:28

Author — The Bishops President of the Six National Episcopal Commissions, [1] August 16, 1989

Introduction

As Christians, we are called to witness to the fundamental equality and dignity of all people. This involves diverse actions for social justice which protect and promote human life and dignity. One relatively simple but effective action is the use of inclusive language.

Inclusive Language Defined

Inclusive language, in the broadest sense, means using words which affirm the equality and dignity of each person regardless of race, gender, creed, age or ability. Most people associate it, however, with language which includes women and men in contexts where the message is directed to, refers to and affects both and which avoids stereotypes when speaking about either sex. This understanding of inclusive language is the subject of these reflections.

Signs of the Times

Inclusive language was introduced into society by the contemporary women's movement. As a result, some people feel it may be only a cultural question. The Second Vatican Council, however, reminded us that the Church exists in the world and that Christians have a responsibility to read the "signs of the times" and interpret them in light of the gospel. [2] One of the signs of the times identified by the Council and recent popes is the changing role of women in society. [3] There is, therefore, a special duty to listen to what women are saying about the need for inclusive language. Through listening and reflecting, it becomes apparent that there are significant theological reasons for using and promoting inclusive language.

Language Expresses Our Beliefs

Language is an important matter for the whole Church because it is through language that we express our belief in God and proclaim the Good News of salvation of the world. Throughout our history, great care has been taken in choosing words to reflect our beliefs. For example, at the Council of Nicea in 325 new language was introduced the better to express our understanding of Jesus. Today, the use of inclusive language indicates care is being taken to ensure that words reflect our belief in the equality of men and women, our understanding of the gospel and our affirmation of the Church as a communion.

Fundamental Equality of Men and Women

For Christians, language which is inclusive recalls the original harmony of creation as seen in Genesis (Chap. 2). It also gives verbal expression to the Good News that through the life, death and resurrection of Jesus we are reconciled with God and a new creation is initiated where we are all one in Christ. At its most profound level, inclusive language is a sign of our respect for the fundamental equality of men and women, and a means of proclaiming the gospel message of inclusiveness.

The Church as a Communion

Concern about inclusive language is also rooted in a theological understanding of the Church as a communion. This understanding of the Church was a central insight of the Second Vatican Council[4] and was reaffirmed by the Extraordinary Synod of 1985.[5] When the Church is described as a communion, it means that Christians are in union with God and with one another, through Jesus Christ, in the power of the Holy Spirit. In this sense, the Church is a sacrament or sign of the unity to which the whole of humanity is called. "Hence, there is in Christ and in the Church no inequality on the basis of race or nationality, social condition or sex."[6] This passage from the Council also recalls the fundamental equality and partnership of all the baptized who are united in Christ.

Implementation — Long Term

The theological reasons for using inclusive language are powerful. Yet, implementation of inclusive language in the daily life of the Church will take time. More work is required on the part of specialists and there are different levels of awareness among members of the Church community.

Biblical and Liturgical Texts

All translations of the bible and all texts contained in the Sacramentary and other liturgical texts are protected by copyright. Biblical translations and liturgical texts are revised periodically and efforts are being made to be attentive to inclusive language. It is a long process, however, because the biblical translator must communicate the message in a way that is both faithful to its original meaning and understandable to today's reader. The translator must also work with other specialists such as theologians, historians and archeologists in order to produce good translations of ancient texts. The revision of liturgical texts involves a lengthy approval process culminating in confirmation by the Vatican. Other specialists such as composers of hymns and linguists also have a role to play in the smooth transition from exclusive to inclusive language.

Evolution of Language

The rules of grammar also affect the use of inclusive language. There is sometimes tension between the desire to respect the rules which protect the beauty and clarity of a language and the reality of a living language which is evolving to recognize effectively the equality of men and women.

Levels of Awareness

Another reason for slow implementation of inclusive language is the different levels of awareness among members of the Church. Some believe that a word such as "man" is already inclusive of women and therefore reflects the theological principles which have been outlined. Others believe that over the years the meaning of "man" has narrowed to the point that it no longer includes women and therefore no longer expresses these theological principles. And still others may not appreciate the linkage between language and theology or the important role that language plays in reflecting our beliefs. The diversity of views sometimes makes for lively debate but if discussion continues in a spirit of openness and respect, it will contribute to increased awareness and understanding.

Implementation — Short Term

Action can be taken while awaiting the completion of the work of specialists. Initiatives can be taken to introduce inclusive language at home, at social gatherings and on the job. Parishes can commit themselves to using inclusive language in the prayers of the faithful, in their choice of hymns, in written materials such as parish bulletins, in announcements from the pulpit, at parish gatherings, etc. They might consider forming discussion groups or inviting experts (e.g., theologians, linguists, historians, liturgists) to assist them in deepening their awareness of the need for inclusive language. All those who preach should also be attentive to inclusive language. And everyone can read more on the subject, listen more sensitively and be more responsive to women who do not see themselves included in our language. As the Presidents of six national Episcopal Commissions, we undertake to pay special attention to inclusive language in all our communications.

Conclusion

Using inclusive language is one way of emphasizing the Church's responsibility to take a stand against one of the widespread forms of discrimination found in our society. As sensitivity to the inclusion of women grows, there should be a corresponding increase in awareness of the need to include all, regardless of race, gender, creed, age or ability. By seeking to overcome discrimination wherever it is encountered, we live more fully as a communion, respond more fully to the gospel and speak as a Christian community.

NOTES

1. Most Reverend Bertrand Blanchet (Theology Commission), Leonard Crowley (Ecumenism), Charles A. Halpin (Ministries and Apostolate), Louis Langevin (Canon Law — Inter-rite), John A. O'Mara (Missions), Gilles Ouellet (Social Affairs).

2. *Constitution on the Church in the Modern World*, n. 11.

3. *Ibid.*, nn. 9, 29, 60.

4. *Dogmatic Constitution on the Church*, Chaps. I, II, VII.

5. Final Report of Synod, II, C, *The Church as Communion*, in *Twenty Years Later*, (CCCB Publications Service, 90 Parent Ave., Ottawa, K1N 7B1), p. 54; also in *Origins* (Washington, 1985), 15, p. 448.

6. *Op. cit.*, note 4, above, n. 32.

Section V, Document 11

MESSAGE ON THE INTERNATIONAL EUCHARISTIC CONGRESS IN SEOUL

Author — Archbishop James M. Hayes, President of the Conference, October 8, 1989

An event of great importance to the Church will be held in Seoul, Korea, next October 5-8: the 44th International Eucharistic Congress. On this occasion, we invite Catholics in Canada to live in solidarity and communion with the Church of Korea. We wish, for example, that meetings of prayer and reflection on the theme of the Congress, *CHRIST, OUR PEACE,* be organized locally.

Peace, a need profoundly felt in the world today, is much more than the simple absence of war. Mostly, it is life in harmony with oneself, others and with the Lord. Thus, for the disciples of Jesus, Christ, Our Peace, has come to knock down the wall of separation and hate (cf. Eph. 2:14), a wall which continues to divide so many persons and nations, sometimes within a same country. Korea itself is a painful example of such separation and division.

To reflect on peace and try to promote it is, first of all, to analyse the different ways we build the wall of hate. St. Paul pointed out in his own time: we begin with prejudice and fanaticism, go on to intolerance, and end up in armed conflict. Even if in Canada the wall of hate does not take the form of armed conflicts, we do have prejudice, racist behaviour and intolerance which so often poison relations among citizens.

If we want to build peace in Canada, we must change our outlook and behaviour towards the main victims of our discrimination and intolerance: immigrants, refugees seeking a country willing to receive them, foreign workers seeking employment, native people cut off from their roots, minorities unjustly treated. Such a conversion is required both by the Gospel and by simple respect for the rights of all rooted in their human dignity.

To become builders of peace where we live and work is also to fight against irrational fear of others who are perceived as threats because they are different. We even risk bringing this fear into our relationships with our brothers and sisters of other Churches, and sometimes of our own Church. In a positive way, to be builders of peace is to be able to accept others as different and to respect them in their differences: colour of skin, ethnic origin, religious belief, social condition.

All of our efforts to build peace, to become artisans of peace, are inspired by the example of Jesus of Nazareth; they have to do with the power of reconciliation and the forgiveness of the Lord, Christ, Our Peace. Christ remains the Living One, always present by the Spirit He left us and under the humble signs of bread and wine. It is particularly this link between peace and Eucharist that the Seoul Congress will evoke. The risen Christ, Who is present, offered and given in the Eucharist, continues to tell us: "Peace be with you" (Jn. 19:21): "I leave you peace, I give you my peace" (Jn. 14:27).

We therefore invite Catholics of Canada to lift their arms in prayer to the Father, in unity with our brothers and sisters assembled in Seoul in a mighty demonstration of faith:

— that, one day, "nations will not lift the sword against each other and that we will not train for war" (Is. 2:4);

— that, tomorrow, countries will make declarations of peace;

— that, tomorrow, Canadian society will renounce its will to dominate, its feelings of superiority, its mechanisms of discrimination, so that, "peace and justice embrace each other" (Ps. 84:11);

— that, tomorrow, the sign of bread and wine, in its very precariousness, may teach Catholics the way of peace built by abandoning oneself and loving the Other totally to the point of giving one's own life.

Section V, Document 12

LETTER TO THE PEOPLE OF GOD: THE MINISTRY OF PRIESTS

Author — The Episcopal Commission for Ministries and the Apostolate[1], the CCCB, January 18, 1990

1. Priests have had a special and important place in the history of Catholicism in Canada, from its beginnings to the present. Thanks to their untiring devotion and missionry zeal, the Gospel has been proclaimed from sea to sea and in the farthest regions of our immense country. Their dedicated efforts have always been acknowledged by the People of God who, in response, have generously given the Church the workers needed for its mission.

2. More than twenty years ago the Second Vatican Council often reminded the world of the importance of priests to the life of the Church. The Council emphasized the "most important and increasingly difficult role" of priests in the renewal of the Church.[2]

This reminder is even more urgent today as the Church in Canada and many western countries is experiencing serious difficulties in the face of a shortage of vocations to the priesthood. Now is a unique time for all members of the People of God to take up this vital question, as the Church prepares for a Synod of Bishops in the fall of 1990 to deal with the formation of diocesan and religious priests, before and after ordination.

3. As members of the Episcopal Commission for Ministries and the Apostolate, we are deeply aware of the importance of the ministerial priesthood to the life of the Church in our country. We wish to share our convictions and hopes with all the members of the People of God, because all of us, laity, religious, deacons, priests and bishops, are responsible for the life of the Church. We ask you to

reflect with us on the essential role that has been confided to priests as collaborators of the bishops and as pastors of the Church in Jesus' name. The importance of this invitation is further emphasized by a recent study of the Canadian Church's human resources. The findings of this study challenge all the members of the Church to prepare realistically for the future and to recognize and affirm the ministry of priests in an ever changing world.

A Situation of Urgency

4. The survey revealed two clear trends. The first is a source of consolation and hope: the number of laity assuming leadership responsibilities, either as volunteers or as paid staff, is significantly on the rise. The second trend, which concerns the priesthood, poses an enormous challenge. In the last twenty years the number of diocesan priests has fallen by 26% and the average age of priests continues to climb. In 1987, 34% of priests were 65 years of age or older; only 26% were under 50 years of age. If these trends continue, it can be expected, that ten years from now, less than 15% of priests will be under 50 years of age. The situation is almost the same among religious communities of priests.

5. A great number of factors play a role in this phenomenon. Among these are declining birth rate, a certain indifference towards religion, family breakdown, the trend to secularization in our lifestyle, the difficulties involved in proclaiming the Gospel in the modern context, and some questions about the exact role of priests relative to the development of new ministries in the Church.

6. As might be expected, the current situation is a source of concern to priests. At a time when they are fewer in number and advancing in age, they are being called upon to meet greater and increasingly complex challenges in their ministries. We need only cite the wide variety of spiritual situations that require personal or group involvement, the need to develop new approaches to sharing the Gospel message, the increasingly numerous and varied expectations of the faithful in our parish communities, the need to adopt new methods in order to promote co-responsibility, the conflict between the demands of the Gospel and certain aspects of modern lifestyles, and so on.

7. As laity you are led by your Christian convictions and your involvement in the Church and the world to live your daily responsibilities with Gospel insight. We are well aware that many times you have to adapt to new jobs and face new challenges and, at the same time, remain faithful to your obligations. Because of this, you have a personal understanding of what priests are facing as they strive to meet the challenges of our changing times. You understand this even better because you know their mission is unique and irreplaceable. Furthermore, you know you can call upon their help.

Some Fundamental Convictions

8. We are convinced that Christ continues to be the pastor of the Church. He does this through those who have received the Holy Spirit through ordination: bishops, priests and deacons. Reflection on this initiative of Christ leads us to a full appreciation of the scope of the presence and action of priests. They are there to make significant and fruitful the presence and action of Christ as pastor of his Church. Through them, the good news of the Kingdom continues to be proclaimed with authenticity; its work of liberation continues effectively, primarily through the celebration of the sacraments; and the coming together of all Christians in ecclesial communion becomes a reality. It is this never ending celebration of the paschal mystery centered on the Death and Resurrection that empowers the People of God, throughout all time, to let the Gospel enlighten their hopes, their joys, their sufferings and to become builders of a better world.

9. We believe that a Church without priests is unthinkable. It is Christ Himself who commands priests to act in his name as pastors. Together and in union with their bishops, priests represent Christ the Pastor. In Christian communities, a new division of responsibilities among priests, deacons and lay people is beginning to appear. This is a cause for rejoicing! Nevertheless, no one can act in the name of Christ and manifest his presence as pastor without first being called, consecrated and sent by him.

10. We are sure that you share these convictions with us. The time has come to seek ways together to create a priestly ministry that is appropriate and rich, one that fully fulfills the expectations of the Lord.

The Challenges We Face

11. The challenges of our modern world call on us to strengthen the gift of priesthood in our Church. All members of the Church share the responsibility to encourage vocations, to discern true calls, and to support those who have been and will be ordained to the priesthood.

12. We therefore ask you to deepen your understanding of the true meaning of priesthood within the diversity of ministry. In the Spirit of the Second Vatican Council, we encourage you to assume your own responsibilities as active members of the Church, so that priests can better realize their proper mission. We urge you to expect from your priests only what Jesus truly intends their ministry to be.

13. In addition, we invite you to be attentive to the basic human needs of those called to give their lives in the service of the ministerial priesthood as celibates. It is both desirable and normal for you to support and encourage your priests in their mission and in their daily lives and especially when they face personal difficulties which could harm their ministry.

14. Similarly, we urge priests to recognize that the challenges of our modern world also call them to deepen their life of prayer, to reflect more on God's word, and to share their convictions with brother priests and lay people more often. It is when priests live as brothers among the People of God that their ministry can lead them to fulfillment and peace. It is in sharing both their inner lives and their responsibilities that they find happiness in their mission.

15. Finally, we want to express our gratitude to priests for the generous gift of themselves. We need to celebrate the magnificent accomplishments and faithful service given by so many priests. Far too often no words of thanks and encouragement are addressed to those whose tireless efforts have touched the lives of so many.

Conclusion

16. We want you to know that we bishops consider priests to be our indispensable collaborators. As we invite you to reflect on the role and person of the priest today, we also ask our brother bishops to do the same. Together, laity, religious, members of secular institutes,

deacons, priests, bishops, we must continue to seek better means of fulfilling the mission of evangelization to which each of us is called at baptism; but, at the same time, we must gratefully acknowledge God's gift of the ministerial priesthood.

17. At this time, when the universal Church reflects upon the formation of priests for our modern world, we invite you in your parishes to reflect on the following questions:

— How are you able to encourage and develop vocations to the ministerial priesthood?

— What does Jesus call priests to be and do today?

— How can parishes help to make it possible for priests to do what Jesus intended them to do?

— What signs of support and appreciation can your parish and family offer your priest?

— How can a movement towards a greater co-responsibility in the Church help the priesthood find its fulfillment?

As you consider these questions personally or as a group, recall the message St. Paul sent to the young community at Thessalonica:

> We appeal to you to be considerate of those who are working amongst you, who guide and instruct you in the Christian life. Treat them with the greatest respect and affection for them because of the work they do. (1 Thes. 5:12-13)

NOTES

1. The Bishops of the Commission are: Most Reverend C.A. Halpin, Chairman, A. Ambrozic, A. Gaumond, J. Gratton, A. Penney, M. Veillette.
2. *On the Ministry and Life of Priests,* n. 1, and cf. citations given there.

Section VI

AT THE WORLD SYNODS OF BISHOPS[1]

SYNOD OF 1971 – PRIESTHOOD – JUSTICE[2]

Document 1

THE GENERAL ORIENTATION OF THE SYNOD

Archbishop George B. Cardinal Flahiff, C.S.B., October 1, 1971

As we begin our third Synod we must agree that, in the short span of four years, we have gained a great deal of experience. We have seen improvements, in particular, in the Synod preparations. No one can say, however, that this new institution has as yet fully discovered its way. That is why our Canadian Conference of Bishops considers it important, at the very outset, to speak of the temptations which threaten us and to indicate some approaches which should guarantee the success of this third Synod.

Starting with a correct orientation appears even more important when we look at the subjects to be treated, the ministerial priesthood and justice in the world, subjects of really major importance.

These touch the very lives of all God's people, which is why they have already evoked the intense interest of the mass media during the time of preparation. We have therefore a common responsibility: if the Synod is to maintain its credibility it must not fall short of the expectations so widely aroused. Even though the time to treat such important questions is short, we must not fail those who look to us.

Two major temptations face us. The first is to see the Synod implicitly as an ecumenical council. As the Holy Father, the President of this Synod, rightly remarked during the first Synod, "We cannot regard a Synod as an ecumenical council; it has neither the same composition, nor the same authority, nor the same objectives." [3] The Holy Father added, nevertheless, that the Synod does bear some resemblance to a council and can, by the grace of God, attain the same wisdom and charity as a council. This wisdom, this charity, requires that we prudently set aside dogmatic probing since this belongs properly to a council. It would be most unfortunate if, in the absence of our priests, and, I dare to add, in the absence also of the poor, we were to devote precious time to theoretical discussions of truly difficult issues. If ecumenical councils have not chosen to define the specific quality of the priestly character, the apostolic origin of the three orders of the hierarchy, the precise distinction between the royal priesthood of the faithful and the ministerial priesthood, relative to their respective roles, we must not attempt to do it here. Let us rather make use of the wealth of truths that the Church now holds as certain and apply them.

The second temptation before us is to consider this consultative and, occasionally, deliberative institution as an instrument for the collegial preparation of an encyclical or pious exhortation. This manner of proceeding has been rejected by the consultations already carried out in regard both to the ministry and to social justice. We are not asked for pious exhortations. Decisions are needed, changes at the level of concrete action and lived experience.

This is why the Canadian bishops make the following urgent proposal: let us direct this Synod towards adapting to the life of our people today, the doctrinal teachings of Vatican II. Far be it from us however, to divorce pastoral decisions from the teachings of the Gospel. But I repeat: let us consistently avoid abstract considerations, lest we lose touch with the people who, in our presynodal consultations, have manifested their agonies and the daily burdens that they have to bear. Let us not have easy recourse to historical considerations or to age-old customs. Let us remember that discipline has often to be determined in the light of actual conditions as well as of doctrines. Let us likewise recall that the opposition and the hostility that we face arise more from the social and historical image projected by the Church's ministers and by those who are active in the field of justice than from the doctrine they preach.

We have come to Rome as bearers of the wishes and the demands of our various Conferences, as well as of our priests and of the People of God. Let us not lose sight of this. As St. Paul said, "If one member suffers, all members suffer." (1 Cor. 12:26) Let us not forget the suffering of those we represent. At the first Synod the Sovereign Pontiff said: "We must take into account the proposals that your Conferences have made and of which you are the interpreters." [4] And I would add, if I may: let us be the interpreters not only of their proposals, but also of their experience and of their sufferings. It is only then that "collegiality will be charity". [5]

To avoid abstractions and to consult closely the proposals and the experience of the episcopal Conferences, the better to adapt to changing circumstances of priestly ministry and of social justice, will have an added advantage: we will avoid the illusion that things will work out automatically with the mere passage of time. In our day especially, postponements are fatal. The accelerated tempo of history relentlessly destroys dead structures and, alas, it also destroys those who live in them. If we address ourselves resolutely to the vital questions, we shall readily see the futility of simply reaffirming the *status quo* at a time when salvation history is so rapidly accelerated. Think, for example, of the recent report of the Sacred Congregation for Catholic Education of the decline of vocations to the priesthood[6]: this fact and the projection of still further decline, show us that this trend cannot be modified merely by the passage of time nor pious exhortations. What is needed is a new vision of what a "vocation" is, and the possibility of discerning vocations in all walks of life.

In closing may I express a wish: that our work be carried out in a positive spirit if we wish to offer some hope; hope for priests who are troubled, hope for the young in our seminaries who are confused, hope for all who labour in the field of social justice. In our world, so sadly characterized by fear and despair, true hope will image Jesus Christ Himself, the Saviour and the Liberator. Again I repeat: this is not the place for mere theory or exhortation. Rather let us see what can be done to adapt the teaching of the gospel and of the Church to the actual life of today. To be sure, this is a way that calls for courage, but it is also the way of creativity, the way of faith. And it is essential for the credibility of our Synod.

NOTES

1. The Second Vatican Council in its decree *On the Pastoral Office of Bishops in the Church*, n. 5, provided for the creation of the Synod of Bishops, established as a permanent structure by Paul VI, Sept. 15, 1965. Its office is to inform and advise the Pope who calls the meetings, determines agenda, confirms election of delegates and presides personally or through a representative.

Delegates are elected by the national bishops' conferences; ten representatives of religious orders are elected by the Union of Superiors General. Attending *ex officio* are the patriarchs, metropolitans and major archbishops outside the patriarchates of Eastern rite Catholic churches, as also the cardinal heads of bureaus of the Roman Curia. Those named by the Pope may constitute up to 15% of the Synod members.

Synods are:

— *General (Ordinary)*, dealing with subjects concerning the good of the universal Church;

— *Extraordinary*, for similar matters requiring prompt attention;

— *Special*, concerned with matters important for the Church in some particular region.

The Synod has met eleven times: as General Synods, 1967, 1971, 1974, 1977, 1980, 1983, 1985, as Extraordinary Synods in 1969, 1985, and in two Special Synods, in 1980, with regard to the development of the Church in Holland and for legislative structures within the Ukrainian Catholic rite.

The General Synod of 1967, besides deciding certain questions of its own structure, included in its agenda the revision of Canon Law, Seminaries, Liturgy, Doctrine of the Faith and Mixed Marriages. Canadian delegates were: Archbishops P.-É. Cardinal Léger, P. Pocock, G.B. Flahiff, and L. Lévesque. Maurice Cardinal Roy attended as Pres. of the Council of the Laity and of the Pontifical Commission *Justice and Peace* and Archbishop M. Hermaniuk as Metropolitan of Ukrainian Catholics in Canada.

The Extraordinary Synod of 1969 was called by Pope Paul VI to promote cooperation and communication between episcopal conferences, among themselves and with the Holy See. An important result was the establishment of a Synod Council of fifteen bishops to assist in the preparation of future Synods, twelve elected by the delegates to the Synod, three named by the Pope. The Canadian delegate at this Synod was Bishop A. Carter, Pres. of the Conference. Maurice Cardinal Roy and Metropolitan M. Hermaniuk attended *ex officio* as above.

2. The General Synod of 1971 had two themes, *The Ministerial Priesthood* and *Justice in the World*, its statement on the latter being enormously influential throughout the Catholic world. Canadian delegates were Archbishops/Bishops A. Carter, J.-A. Plourde, G.B. Cardinal Flahiff, P. Grégoire. Maurice Cardinal Roy and Metropolitan M. Hermaniuk attended *ex officio* as above. Besides the presentations of Canadian members published here, three presentations appeared in *Do Justice!* (Edit. E.F. Sheridan, SJ, Éditions Paulines, Sherbrooke, QC, 1987), Documents 27, 28, 29, by Archbishop J.-A. Plourde, G.B. Cardinal Flahiff, and Bishop Alexander Carter, respectively.

Other presentations by Canadian members (on the *Priesthood,* by Cardinal Roy and Archbishops Grégoire and Hermaniuk; on *Justice,* by Cardinal Roy, Archbishop Hermaniuk) are available from the Archives of the CCCB, 90 Parent Ave., Ottawa, ON, K1N 7B1.

3. Paul VI in *The Pope Speaks* (Washington, 1967), XII, 383.

4. *Ibid.,* p. 385.

5. Paul VI, *Opening Address* at the Synod of 1969, in *Catholic Mind,* (New York, 1969), LXVII, Nov., p. 3.

6. *Basic Program for Priestly Formation,* in *The Pope Speaks* (Washington, 1970), XV, pp. 264 ff., 274 ff.

Section VI, Document 2

THE THEOLOGY OF
THE MINISTERIAL PRIESTHOOD

Archbishop Paul Grégoire, October 4, 1971

It is without doubt the profound wish of this Synod to examine the very real problems of the ministerial priesthood today, to speak to priests in a way which truly touches their situation, and to formulate the principles of a solution to the difficulties they face.

The doctrinal text which has been given to us can certainly contribute, at least in some measure, to the pursuit of these objectives. It helps us clarify certain essential reference points of Catholic theology concerning the ministerial priesthood. From this perspective, we must be grateful that such a text has been presented. It is, however, necessary to consider some dangers associated with the approach taken.

We are working towards a definition of the ministerial priesthood in abbreviated formulas, and we are separating the theological analysis from the study of the concrete problems which new contexts are posing for today's priests.

First Danger

The first danger is certainly to move into the realm of abstraction and to formulate a theological definition of the ministerial priesthood which would seem to be satisfactory to a theoretical theology but which would not take adequate consideration of the real causes of the identity crisis of the priest in the Church and world of today.

For this reason it is regrettable that the text proposed, artificially isolating the theological problems from those of lived experience, is out of touch with the life situation. It is not surprising then, that it settles for formulations which are very general and so other-worldly that they do not respond to the questions which are raised by the new life and work situation of the priest.

This new situation arises from certain phenomena which are either new or more pronounced than formerly:

— the articulation of the theology of the priesthood of the faithful;

— the desire and need for a presence in the world, raised by Vatican II, which naturally leads priests to define their ministry positively and adequately in relation to the major developments and objectives of culture, of civilization, of justice and of peace;

— the progressive phasing out of priests from several of their former fields of activity and competence;

— the evident resistance which priests are experiencing from the faithful towards any governing or teaching authority, based on anything other than competence.

It seems very clear to us that any "definition" of the role of the priest not attentive to these new realities and which does not take them into realistic account, strongly risks becoming a part of the very questions being asked today, when we speak of the identity crisis of the priest.

Second Danger

The second danger is to some extent a consequence of the first. It is to produce the kind of document unlikely to meet priests in their concerns and incapable of communicating by precise articulation the concrete concept of their mission, and that hope and confidence without which they cannot serve with joy and generosity. More than anything else, however, it is this realistic and clear confidence in the irreplaceable character of their service that this Synod must be able to give to priests.

Priests and those thinking of becoming priests, will not be reached by propositions not addressed to anyone, the role of the priest in other-worldly and abstract terms. New realities are questioning the very role itself, presenting it as under siege rather than as a great living experience and challenging to sevice. It will not be sufficient merely to repeat without deepening — risking perhaps distortion for the sake of brevity — the teachings of Vatican II.

The authors of the working paper on the ministerial priesthood seem to have foreseen the dangers mentioned, since they did not themselves determine the use which the Synod might make of the propositions contained in the text given us. Here, then, is a suggestion which I make to this assembly.

The Synod should discontinue the present attempt to set out the theology of the priesthood in terms of propositions which are separated from concrete problems and which pretend "to define" things. It should undertake rather to present its theological reflections, well founded in Sacred Scripture, in a text which analyzes and treats in depth, the key problems which the ministry and life of the priest are posing today. Doubtless many of the theological principles presented in the working paper or by the Synod Fathers will then be most helpful. I propose a brief list of these major questions:

1. the role of the priest in today's world, seen in the spirit of the Second Vatican Council, especially of the Constitution on the Church in the Modern World.

2. the problem of permanence, raised by the departure of many priests and by the increasing instances of inability to exercise the ministerial priesthood effectively;

3. the problem of the distinction between the priesthood of the faithful and the ministerial priesthood, which distinction should be formulated in more complete and explicit terms;

4. the problem of concrete relationships between bishops and priests;

5. the problem of celibacy, to be studied in all its fullness;

6. the application of subsidiarity to the responsibilities which Episcopal Conferences should take in what has to do with certain aspects of the life and ministry of priests.

An approach of this kind, asking theology to address questions arising from our new life situations, would meet the first of the wishes unanimously expressed scarce ten days ago by the Assembly of the bishops of Canada.[1]

NOTES

1. The statement of that Plenary Assembly, Sept. 20-24, 1971, verbatim but slightly abbreviated, follows.

The role of the priest to gather and build the community by proclamation of the Word of God and by the sacraments was thoroughly studied. His duty is to inspire Christian hope by his life and teaching and his role in communal prayer was stressed.

The more controversial problems of celibacy and of the eventual admission of women to various ministries were also given serious consideration.

The advisability of ordaining married men where there is real need was supported by the majority of the bishops. The broadening of the present discipline for the whole Church, beyond the situation of real need, won the support of a small majority.

A large majority of the bishops favour the maintenance of the present discipline as to the return to the ministry (prohibited) of married priests who have been dispensed. A larger majority disapprove the ordination of candidates who do not wish to accept the obligation of celibacy.

As for presently ordained priests, the bishops are agreed that no retroactive law should be contemplated granting permission to contract marriage while remaining in the ministry.

The study of ministry for women is much less advanced. The delegates to the Synod will recommend the immediate striking of a mixed commission of men and women, to initiate effective study of this question.

In several of these matters, particularly those concerning the quality of priestly life, the promotion of vocations, political participation of priests, the Conference insisted on greater freedom in the initiatives of the (local) church in various countries. It was felt that the unity of the Church is not synonymous with uniformity since we are dealing here, not with doctrinal, but with disciplinary questions.

The bishops delegated to the Synod now have an accurate reading of the mind of their colleagues on these points, a firm position taken which will permit the Canadian delegation to contribute to the success of this collegial meeting.

We are happy to note that on many points the decisions of the bishops are in accord with the wishes of the priests.

Section VI, Document 3

PASTORAL PLANNING AND RELATIONS BETWEEN BISHOPS AND PRIESTS

Archbishop J.-A. Plourde, October 8, 1971

A week before the opening of this Synod the Canadian Bishops met in Plenary Assembly to make known to their Synod delegates their opinions on the subjects to be studied, as well as their wishes and expectations for the Synod. For this purpose they voted on a series of propositions which had been raised principally in the pre-synodal schema.

We are delighted to find in the Working Paper (*Relatio*) on Practical Questions, the majority of these propositions in one form or another, with two exceptions: (1) the ecumenical dimensions of ministry and of justice in the world, and (2) the ministries of women in the Church.

I do not intend to cover here all the Canadian proposals. We will give the Synod Secretariat a written report on the position of the bishops of Canada regarding each. My colleagues and I will speak on the points which, in our opinion, are most pressing. Today I wish to treat two of these: pastoral planning and the relationships between bishops and priests.

A. Pastoral Planning

The Working Paper (p. 13) tells us that pastoral action "is an expression of ecclesial communion" and is directed towards "the substantial unity of the People of God". We are in complete agreement with this affirmation, but it would be helpful to specify what we mean by "the substantial unity" of the Church. If it is a question of preserving at all costs the unity of the faith and doctrine necessary for salvation, which is one of our fundamental responsibilities as successors of the Apostles, there can be no question. But it seems to us that we must avoid giving the impression that this fundamental unity requires a uniformity of discipline throughout the Church, that "communion" implies "making everything the same".

Very much to the contrary, this very Synod demonstrates a reality of which we are, perhaps, not sufficiently aware: uniformity in discipline is no longer possible in the Church. Let us start with an historical reality that is already very old — the existence of the Oriental Churches. What does this imply? That political and cultural reasons have led Christian communities to develop in an original way, with their own liturgy, their own canon law, their own structures, their own theology and their own forms of spirituality. Far from being a misfortune in the Church, this is a richness. In the West, uniformity has been achieved and preserved for a long time and, by colonization, has been extended to entire continents: America, Africa, Asia. On the other hand, recent decolonization has supported the birth of truly national hierarchies. In this Synod, these hierarchies are making it clear to us that they have their own needs, their own cultural and missionary requirements, which are different from those of the Western Churches. In other words, this Third Synod can no longer speak only the language of the North Atlantic Treaty Organization (First World).

Even in the West, needs which differ according to countries show that what is really at stake in this Synod is the credibility of leadership. And this leadership, in our respective countries, will not be genuine, will not respond to the real needs of our Churches unless greater freedom of decision is left to Episcopal Conferences which are prepared to assume greater responsibilities.

In concluding this first part, I think that only a genuine application of the principle of subsidiarity can:

(1) assure the Church a pastoral program which is fundamentally one — again we stress that! — but, at the same time, diverse enough in its expression to respond to the actual needs of peoples, extremely different in culture, mentality and life style;

(2) foster the creativity which characterized the work of the Church in the past. I am thinking of the splendour of the Eastern liturgies, of the varied missionary approach to native peoples, of the diverse

forms of religious life. Our times demand this continuing creativity in the Church, so that one of the memorable phrases which might emerge from this Synod may be "unity in diversity and creativity".

B. Relationships between Bishops and Priests

The Second Vatican Council wrote well of the relationships between priests and bishops, particularly in its decree on *The Life and Ministry of Priests* (cf. n. 7). Still, six years later, we must admit that the pre-synodal inquiries show fairly serious discontent in this area. Why not ask why? Is it not because the nature of authority in the Church, in spite of the very clear texts of the Council, is not correctly understood or, if it is, is not carried into practice?

The Working Paper itself provides the key which should direct our reflections and recommendations, when it says, on the authority of the Second Vatican Council, [1] that authority in the Church is a ministry, a service. There is here a truth that is not easy to understand, like so many others in the Gospel, because it goes contrary to a basic tendency of our human nature.

It is significant that although the New Testament speaks of authority in 79 places, there are also 58 texts which warn us about the dangers of power. And this brings us to the two concepts of the Church to which the doctrinal Working Paper refers (pp. 8f.). If we do not balance the schema Christ — Apostles — Church by the schema Christ — Church — Ministers, giving us a triangular representation of the action of the Spirit, exercised simultaneously at the base and the top of the hierarchy, we fall back into an imperial notion of power, valid enough in certain forms of civil society, but one rejected by Christ. "The Kings of the Gentiles exercise lordship over them; and those in authority over them are called benefactors. But not so with you; rather let the greatest among you become as the youngest, and the leader as one who serves." (Lk. 22:25-26)

Authority in the Church is not in itself an absolute; it must not only take on a spirit of service; it *is* service, the service of freedom. It does not have that meaning unless it unifies and channels liberty towards the common good. If it does not do this, it becomes *power,* one of the three great forces of evil and pride which St. John identifies as the abuse or selfish use of money, of sex and of authority (1 Jn. 2:16). It is clear that these three subjects are central to the two themes of our meetings.

The situation seems the more serious today when youth have come to distrust power more than money. As long as a structure holds a monopoly on values, using freedom instead of serving it, they will try to destroy it. And our young priests belong to this generation. They know better than ever how to distinguish authority-service from power, whether it is instinctively exercised or used in a calculated way. We must recognize here a prophetic insight: in the Kingdom of Heaven there will be no more power, but only freedom open to love. We are on the way to that final state. May our way of acting demonstrate it. But this will require changing structures. It will also require a change of attitudes based more on earthly power than on the freedom of the Gospel. Today values are believed in only as long as they are lived in freedom.

In my humble opinion, if the Synod can show unequivocally that the Church is resolutely committed to the path of subsidiarity, which is the road to communion; if the Synod can say clearly that authority is at the service of human liberty, and stops there, it will have opened a window of hope. In a world where everyone is struggling for liberation from servitudes, they will recognize in the Church the image of Jesus Christ, an image which no ideology, and no human power can imitate.

NOTE

1. Cf. *Dogmatic Constitution on the Church* (1964), n. 32.

Section VI, Document 4

THE MINISTRY OF MARRIED PRIESTS IN THE LATIN RITE

Bishop Alexander Carter, October 8, 1971

I wish to speak to Article Four of the Working Paper, *Priesthood and Celibacy.*

The present discipline of celibacy in the Latin Church is not one of the central or basic issues in this Synod's examination of the ministerial priesthood. We all know, however, that it is an issue which continues to provoke ardent discussion especially in Europe and the Americas, where over 85% of the priests of the world are found. Hence it is an issue to be faced honestly and frankly, and which can hardly be termed peripheral. It is not surprising therefore that the Canadian bishops, in preparing for this Synod, gave adequate attention to this subject.

In the Working Paper (Art. 4, p. 24), Cardinal Tarancon wisely says that the question of celibacy must be faced with the greatest honesty and serenity of soul. Unfortunately I do not think that the seven propositions in this article fulfill this noble purpose. We look in vain for any arguments against the present discipline on celibacy. Only in n. 6, p. 26, is there an indication that in extreme circumstances one might be obliged to ordain a married man and even here other remedies are proposed. I fear that the suggestion that it is preferable to experiment by giving more offices to laymen and deacons denotes an unhealthy obsession with celibacy. It would be dangerous to become so preoccupied with saving the present discipline that we would risk eroding the very nature of the priesthood rather than admit married men to Holy Orders. Such a process would effectively deny what we have been saying about the necessary role of the priest in the Church since the beginning of this Synod.

Like all the bishops in the world, including our brother bishops of the Eastern rites, who have already spoken here from their own lived experience, neither our bishops nor our priests in Canada question in any way the great value of the charism of celibacy. Our research shows, however, that many of our priests are living celibate lives for motives which are considerably inferior to those traditionally advanced by the Church. The theological foundations on which the life of celibacy is to be based must be better articulated and more effectively incorporated into our programs of priestly formation. We must cease to consider celibacy as an absolute good and show it in its intimate link with poverty and obedience as an act of ultimate freedom, of total commitment to Christ; otherwise it may easily become not a sign but a countersign.

Secondly, when we and our priests discuss a change in the discipline of the Church regarding celibacy, we do so in full confidence that the charism will always remain. It is an evangelical gift which comes from the Holy Spirit and which is of fundamental value to the Church. The Spirit will not be wanting.[1]

In Canada, bishops and priests have worked together on this subject for two years. I shall try to give a brief picture of our findings. Since it is our duty to inform and advise the Holy Father, I wish to echo the thinking of the whole Church, not just that of the bishops. Since the priests have no active voice in this Synod it is our duty to advance their position as well as our own. We considered four propositions.

The Ordination of Married Men

Canadian bishops are nearly unanimously in favour of ordaining mature married men where there is need, and a small majority are in favour of changing the present discipline to provide for the ordination of married men independently of need. And 90% of our priests are of the same mind. We favour the ordination of married men because we are convinced that married men who have the experiences of family life, and of life in the heart of the secular world, have a new and valuable dimension to bring to the priesthood. To speak of *The Church in the Modern World* implies the reality of the priest being in the modern world. We are still restricting our candidates for Holy Orders largely to men in their mid-twenties who have spent most of their adult lives in schools, colleges and seminaries. We still need such candidates but our world and our churches may now need other types too. When we in Canada speak of this need, we do not restrict it to cases of numerical shortage. There are forms of ministry which could profitably use married priests, not because there are not enough celibate priests, but because of the nature of the ministry itself; e.g., university chaplaincies, family apostolates, catechetics, etc.

The Reinstatement of Priests Properly Dispensed and Married

For us this is a pastoral, not a theological question. Until our people learn to see that married men can be priests, and come to realize that there is no essential connection between celibacy and priesthood, we do not consider it feasible, from a pastoral point of view, to readmit to the full exercise of the ministry those who have been dispensed and married. A minority of our bishops, however, and probably a majority of our priests do not accept the validity of this position. I would add that if some day it should be decided to readmit dispensed priests, we would expect from them the same evidence of suitability, after a period of probation, as we would from married men.

The Conference does not Approve Ordination of Single Men who Refuse Commitment to Celibacy

The reasons again are pastoral. A minority of our bishops and many of our priests do not agree with this position. Ongoing dialogue and continued research are necessary, in our situation of social and cultural change. All freedom should be given to the Conferences to pursue their research in this matter. After all it is their responsibility, in communion with the Holy See and their sister churches, to discover how the Gospel can best be preached and how the Church can be made most relevant to their people.

The Conference Opposes any General Retroactive Law Providing a New Option for those Ordained with Commitment to Celibacy

Regarding this our bishops are almost unanimous, as are also the great majority of our priests.

These are four propositions which we in Canada have considered at great length and very thoroughly, and in all these considerations we have included not only our priests but our laity to the fullest extent possible.

I present to this Synod not only the majority will of the Canadian bishops, but also the convictions of our priests, many of whom wish for more than their bishops. I present also, and with equal sincerity, the wishes of not a few of our bishops who express dissenting opinions. Many priests do not oppose celibacy for selfish reasons, but they feel that mandatory celibacy does not serve as a sign to the People of God and especially to the young as well as would a free election of celibacy, especially in a society where the passionate desire for freedom has taken on a new dimension.

We bishops are here not only to present the conclusions of our Conferences, reached in open discussion, but to express also the opinions of our minorities, and, above all, to reflect the suffering, even agony, of some bishops and many priests in the face of the present discipline regarding celibacy.

In closing, I express the regret that we do not have the opportunity to hear, in plenary assembly, the voices of our priest auditors, many of whom, I am sure, could share with us in a more realistic way the concerns of their fellow-priests, our brothers, in this regard.

NOTE

1. Cf. Second Vatican Council, *Dogmatic Constitution on the Church* (1964), n. 43.

Section VI, Document 5

MINISTRIES OF WOMEN IN THE CHURCH

Archbishop George Cardinal Flahiff, October 11, 1971

I intended to speak of the diversification of ministries in the Church today, but the subject was well covered on Saturday, particularly in the excellent interventions of Archbishop Etchegaray, of Bishop Tepe and Bishop Degenardt. I refrain from adding anything, but limit myself to a question, mentioned by Archbishop Plourde in a previous presentation, but not yet raised in our discussion.

We have spoken of the ministry of the whole Church. Several speakers have dealt with the increasing diversification of the priestly ministry and also with the new ministries that may be proper to the laity. But no one has raised the question of the possibility of a ministry of women in the Church. The question is: are new or changing ministries to be limited to men?

1. A Brief Historical Recall

It is not my intention to deal extensively with this subject. Twenty years ago, the standard answer was:

(a) Christ was a man, not a woman;

(b) He chose twelve men as His first ministers;

(c) Saint Paul has clearly said that women must keep silent in the Church; therefore, they cannot be ministers of the Word (1 Cor. 14:34-35);

(d) Paul also said that woman, having sinned first in the Garden of Eden, can have no authority over man (1 Tim. 2:12-15);

(e) the Church had feminine ministers, especially in the Oriental Church, up to the sixth century, but they were not really ordained ministers.

The conclusion: ministry is a man's work. Let women be content with the part of the Blessed Virgin and of the women around Jesus and the apostles: let them be faithful and obedient servants.

As you are aware, this historical argument cannot be considered valid today. We know that the priesthood of the Old Testament was all-male because of a legitimate reaction against fertility cults in Canaan, whose ministers were mostly feminine. We know that Jesus could not change so radically the social perception of men and women, although Paul would insist later that there are no longer male and female before God (Gal. 3:28). We also know that many of Paul's statements concerning Church discipline are sociological, not doctrinal, as when he insists on women wearing a veil on their heads in church (1 Cor. 11:3-16). As far as I know, therefore, there is no dogmatic objection to reconsidering the whole question today.

2. Women after Vatican II

Texts of the Second Vatican Council (especially in the *Constitution on the Church in the Modern World,* and the *Decree on the Apostolate of the Laity*) made categorical statements against all discrimination against women in the Church. But we must recognize that many excellent Catholic women in particular, and other persons as well, find that no notable effort has been made to implement this teaching. They patiently await, as a gesture of authenticity, the revision of the Code of Canon Law and the elimination of all passages which reflect some inferiority on the part of women.

The change in the position of women in contemporary society, a change partly due to the influence of Christian thought, makes it necessary to deal with this honestly and seriously.

But I am not speaking specifically about this. Perhaps this question will be raised when we treat of *Justice in the World.* I raise only the question of a possible role for women in the ministry or better, in the ministries of the Church.

3. Women and Ministries

In view of what has been said of a growing diversification of ministries, I do not see how we can refrain from raising the question of the possible role of women in these. We would be failing in our duty towards more than half of the Church if we did not at least open the subject.

I recognize that the position of women has not evolved at the same pace in all parts of the world and it may be difficult to have a universal view or perception of this evolution. But it has changed enough in many countries to oblige us, as representatives of the *whole* Church, to pose two questions regarding the possible ministry of women in the Church.

4. First Question

Given the growing recognition, both in law and in fact, of the equality of women with men and the recognition likewise of the injustice of all discrimination against women, should we or should we not raise the question whether women too are to have a place in the sacred ministries of the Church as they now exist or as they are developing?

5. Second Question

With the emergence of new forms of ministries, under the direction of the Holy Spirit, to serve a society developing so rapidly, can we foresee or at least allow for ministries of women, even better adapted than the traditional ones, to their nature, gifts and competence, both in society and in the contemporary Church, of which *The Church in the Modern World* spoke so eloquently?

6. A Practical Answer to these Questions

To my mind the question is too important and too urgent for our Synod to pass over in complete silence. On the other hand, a cursory or superficial treatment would be harmful, and interpreted as another assumption of male superiority.

After informal consultation, extending over several months, the bishops of Canada invited highly qualified representatives of Canadian Catholic women from all parts of the country to discuss the question. Their views and their aspirations were presented clearly, constructively and respectfully. In a General Assembly which was held only three weeks ago, our Episcopal Conference almost unanimously adopted the recommendation which, in the name of this same Conference, I hereby submit to this Synod.

That the representatives of the Canadian Catholic Conference urge the forthcoming Synod of Bishops to recommend to the Holy Father the immediate establishment of a mixed commission (i.e., composed of bishops, priests, laymen and laywomen, religious men and women) to study in depth the question of the ministries of women in the Church.

We do not wish to prejudge the question. We do not know if further action should follow. We certainly have no recommendations regarding the time or the mode of such action. But despite a centuries-old social tradition against a ministry of women in the Church, we are convinced that the signs of the times (and one of these is that already many women perform many pastoral services with great success) strongly urge at least a study both of the present situation and of the possibilities for the future. Unless such a study is begun at once, we may find ourselves behind the course of events. This and this only is the intention of the recommendation that the Canadian Bishops make to the Synod.

Section VI, Document 6

SINS OF CHRISTIANS AND INJUSTICE IN THE WORLD[1]

Archbishop Paul Grégoire, October 22, 1971

The text presented to us is far-reaching. It challenges the world seriously about its injustices and their causes. It invites the Church to examine critically her own life, her witness, the quality and efficacy of her work, her teaching, the education she is giving. I would like to reflect further upon this theme of Christian education for justice.

The text deplores the fact that the Christian social message is neither known nor practiced by the community of the faithful. With this awareness the text asks that the Church do something to change the situation. It suggests explicitly that we explore the possibilities for education found in the liturgy. It is this invitation which prompts me to make several comments and to add some concrete proposals.

We must acknowledge that serious deviations persist in the moral conscience of many Christians, even among some of the most fervent. We continue to consider our *peccadillos* serious, without ever asking ourselves about our responsibilities in matters of justice, particularly social justice. We seem to have lost the sense of what Christ regarded as serious fault. The sense of serious sin seems restricted to certain areas, most often of a sexual nature, while the witness of Paul and of John underlines clearly and vigorously that love of neighbour is the very kernel and fullness of the Christian law (cf. Rom. 13:8-10; 1 Cor. 13:13; John 15:10-17, 13:34).

This is an intolerable situation, a scandal to non-believers. It shows that Christians do not assume their reponsibilities in accord with the demands of the Gospel. For many, especially the young, it is not so much the consciousness of sin that is in question, as the acceptance of a concept of sin that does not square with that of the Gospels. Yet we must frankly admit that such a persistent and widespread situation must have deep and hardy roots in the very institutions of the Church.

Without denying the existence of other causes which contribute to this situation, it seems to me that the use of the sacrament of penance, as defined and lived in the Church, is one cause of these deviations. At the very least, the practice of penance has become inadequate to respond to the social dimensions of Christian responsibilities, particularly in regard to justice.

It tends to accentuate confession and its associated humiliation to the point that personal conversion, the reparation of injury and the correction of unacceptable situations are neglected.

In actual practice, the sacrament of Penance today offers little room for a serious formation of conscience; it provides no occasion for an awareness of collective responsibilities; it leaves the Christian practically alone before his or her conscience, sometimes simply before a list of stereotyped sins, where the hierarchy of authentic Christian values is hardly respected.

This situation explains, in large part, the present disaffection towards the sacrament of Penance. And so it happens that the liturgy, which ought to be a powerful means for Christian formation in justice, is not used to advantage. If this sacrament is to contribute to an effective formation to justice, the Synod must affirm the need to integrate into its celebration these new dimensions of Christian conscience and express the hope that, without delay, a courageous reform of practice will be inaugurated.

It is not a question of envisaging reform in a way that would neglect the personal aspect of responsibility and guilt, or which would tend simply to do away with the private use of the sacrament. Rather this reform ought to promote community celebrations of Penance which would be pastorally visible and valuable, and which would permit an adequate education for today's Christian responsibilities, particularly in matters of justice.

If the urgency of education to justice is great, and we know that it is, and if the present educational deficiencies which debilitate the Church are grave, which our Working Paper recognizes, we must be creative. By doing just this, we could correct the deviations mentioned, further develop among Christians their sense of duty, make them conscious of their collective responsibilities and even contribute to their awareness of the role which structures play in injustices for which we are responsible.

Let me point out that the Canadian Catholic Conference, like other conferences, has already sent to the Roman authorities a study on Penance and has proposed solutions. We are happy that the occasion has been given us to find in the Working Paper confirmation of the pressing need for reforms such as we suggest.

If the Church undertakes an enlightened reform of the sacrament of Penance, it will place at the service of justice a powerful instrument of spiritual help. The Church would thereby lead all to reflect frequently on their lives, in order to analyse their responsibilities, identify sins against justice, acknowlege them before God and resolve on amendment.

NOTE

1. The General Synod of 1971 had two topics: *The Ministerial Priesthood* and *Justice in the World*. Three other presentations of the Canadian bishops on this second theme may be found in *Do Justice!*, edit. E.F. Sheridan, SJ (Éditions Paulines, Sherbrooke, QC, 1987), Documents 27, 28, 29 (cf. also Doc. 26), by Archbishops/Bishops J.-A. Plourde, G.B. Cardinal Flahiff and A. Carter.

Section VI, Document 7

SYNOD OF 1974 — EVANGELIZATION[1]

UNITY AND PLURALISM IN
THE CONTEXT OF EVANGELIZATION

Bishop G. Emmett Carter, October 7, 1974

1. Born of the mystery of the personal love of the one God, the universal Church is herself a communion of local churches sharing the love of Christ, in and through His Spirit. Rooted in trinitarian plurality, proclaimed through the four Gospels of the one Lord and Saviour Jesus Christ, enriched through the Pentecostal Epiphany of the one Spirit, she embraces, in the universal pluralism of catholic unity, peoples of all nations and cultural expressions.

2. Speaking in the name of the Canadian bishops I am privileged to share with you some observations about unity and pluralism in the context of evangelization. Canada is experiencing the first tremors of a potentially explosive cultural upheaval. The placid self-assurance of an affluent democracy is giving way to probing self-analysis and deep concern about the survival of Confederation. As the first traits of post-industrial secularized humanity appear on the screen of history, Canadians are seeking to clarify their identity and to restore a national consensus around our common future purpose.

3. Immigrants from many cultures flocked to Canada as to a land of promise. Their influx altered substantially the social and cultural balance of our youthful nation. Many of these new Canadians found themselves without priests and drifted away from the practice of their faith. The establishment of a Ukrainian hierarchy eventually overcame in part the losses among immigrants of oriental Rites. The

Canadian Catholic Conference is now enriched by the fraternity of six Ukrainian bishops and one Ruthenian. We note with respectful admiration the courageous presentation of the needs of the Oriental Rites in the Church presented in this assembly by Archbishop Maxim Hermaniuk.

Unity and Diversity

4. A pilgrim gazing at the splendour of St. Peter's Basilica is impressed by the tremendous contribution an earlier culture brought to the expression of Christian faith. But even from the oasis of St. Peter's Square the visitor cannot ignore completely the roar of traffic which recalls the temporal preoccupations and priorities of the new Rome surrounding the old. Two cultures coexist, compenetrate and raise a haunting question. What does a culture born of the Roman Empire have to say to the turmoil of contemporary Italian society on the eve of the twenty-first century?

5. As Pope Paul stated at his general audience August 28, 1974,[2] "Pluralism is an ambiguous word... There is a true and a false pluralism." The question of pluralism is indeed a difficult and complex one. Keeping in mind the possible ambiguities inherent in the term, we must nevertheless come to grips with the reality underlying it. Otherwise our evangelization will lack that impact which comes only from a realistic incarnation in the modern world.

6. The main issues linked with pluralism seem to centre around the two poles of unity and diversity. For some, unity demands uniformity. For others, diversity takes priority even over solidarity. Some see pluralism as a source of conflict and contradiction. Still others accept it as a necessary condition of human progress. It might profit our synodal discussions to study the issues in a broader context.

The New Pluralism

7. Pluralism as a contemporary phenomenon manifests itself at several levels:

a) Politically, the bi-polarity of a world society dominated by two major blocks is evolving towards a pluralism of major world powers, as witnessed by the increasing ascendancy of certain peoples of the Third World and by recent developments at the United Nations.

b) Minority groups in several countries are striving with increasing determination to express their relative autonomy both socially and politically. This applies to racial or ethnic minorities, social, political and ideological groups, etc.

c) Another political issue is the vertical pluralism of social classes and the disparity between their socio-economic levels.

d) Economically, recent crises centred on primary resources, food, nuclear and fuel energy, finances, etc., point to the increasing need for world solidarity in the midst of pluralism.

e) Geographically, pluralism manifests its problems in regional disparities, the contrast between urban ghettos and affluent suburbs, or a rich metropolis ringed by zones of misery, etc.

f) Demographically, we face the challenges of clashes between cultures, the dramatic increase in population, exploding and imploding urbanization, etc.

g) Socially, modern societies are becoming extremely complex, with an increasing pluralism of sub-cultures and sub-systems.

h) Increasing mobility and emigration force individuals and peoples of many origins to communicate and live together in new ways.

i) Ideologically, an increasing variety of models for human society is proposed. Individualistic liberalism and collectivistic socialism are challenged by new models based on different readings of history and of social reality.

j) Religious pluralism is also increasing, with the growth of ecumenism, the dialogue of the great religions, the proliferation of new sects, the search for new spiritualities, the renewed religious quest of millions of young people, etc.

Criteria for Evangelical Discernment

8. Faced with these phenomena, several criteria for evangelical discernment are available to us:

a) Unity and Pluralism of Pentecost
There is one Lord, one faith, one baptism. But the Holy Spirit endowed the Church with the capacity to embrace all languages, cultures and peoples. Cornelius became a Christian without circumcision (Acts: 10).

b) Unity and Pluralism of the Eucharist
The sacrament of sacraments assembles and unites master and slave, weak and powerful, races of many colours. Beside its power to build the Church, the Eucharist proved from the start its ability to modify radically the patterns of society and to overcome many inequalities or barriers between persons and peoples.

c) Unity and Pluralism of the Gospels
Four Gospels emerged from the one proclamation of faith in the Lord Jesus Christ, in different communities of the primitive Church. We must recognize more effectively this original pluralism of the universal Christian community where unity is enriched and strengthened by diversity.

d) Unity and Pluralism of Grass-roots Christianity
"What good can come from Nazareth?" (cf. Jn. 1:46) Jesus identified Himself with the least of His people and His followers demonstrated that salvation would indeed come from the poor. The basic human solidarity would indeed come from the poor. The basic human solidarity of those whose only possession is their common human dignity is the privileged soil in which the union of the children of God is expressed and realized. Acceptance of the Good News heals all divisions to find its radical inspiration and strength at this level.

e) Unity and Pluralism of Prophecy
History reveals the natural tendency of all human systems and societies to become exclusive. The Old Testament prophets fought against this inclination. Even after Jesus had commissioned His disciples to baptize *all* nations, Paul had to confront Peter on this issue. The Church is not beyond temptation today. We must re-discover that prophetic dynamism of the Resurrection which eliminates all barriers of race, colour, sex or class while respecting those same differences (cf. Gal. 3:28)

The New Pluralism: A Sharing

9. A new pluralism is emerging in the global village. Modern humanity searches for meaning in a secular society. The dichotomy between this secularized world and the cultural faith experience of most Christians results from our inability to distinguish the essential Gospel message from the cultural accretions which yesterday facilitated its incarnation. The Second Vatican Council's recognition of the hierarchy of truths paved the way for a liberating experience. We can root the Gospel once more in the new cultural pluralism of the technological era.

10. We will prevent the formation of more Christian ghettos by avoiding both polarization and exclusivism and by bringing to each culture the deeper judgment or critique of the Gospel together with the universal enrichment which it provides. Realistic cultural insertion requires a mutual evangelizing of local Churches sharing their manifold experiences of the paschal mystery.

11. An apologetic era identified oneness with uniformity. To be realistic, a church which numbers half a billion people and spans five continents in the most diverse historical context must face a twofold challenge. She requires first a strong central authority with leadership capable of orchestrating the creative energies of the People of God immersed in the global family of humankind and leading it towards total unity. At no time do we need the Pope more than today. But secondly, the Church must simultaneously strengthen the other pole in this dynamic relationship by respecting the pluralism, initiative and legitimate autonomy of the local Churches. They need the freedom to proclaim the one Gospel in a language comprehensible to each different culture. Incapacity to accept new cultural understandings and expressions would make our evangelization a foreign language.

Approaches to Authentic Pluralism

12. With a view to the praxis of Church life we suggest some approaches through which authentic pluralism can be further incorporated:

a) A more trusting recognition of the diverse evangelical expressions proper to various spiritual traditions and groups in the Church. The strength of the centre always depends on the strength of the units. And the units will only be strong when they are challenged by confidence and responsibility.

b) In our secularized milieu people no longer move directly from the street to worship in church. We must recognize that conscience and faith mature progressively, and this requires various forms of belonging to the Church. For example, a Gospel discussion group is not necessarily ready for the Eucharist. Pastoral experiences with the young, with non-practicing Catholics or with unbelievers, bear this out.

c) This openness to various expressions of faith and to more diversified fields of evangelization must be based on a certain minimum consensus among all the apostolic forces in the local Church, a consensus, for instance, about priorities of means as well as of objectives. Sharing the same mission of evangelization, we must share precise common orientation at the local level.

13. We leave the following problems to your further consideration:

a) Canada is not an old country as are many others. Yet we have just celebrated the foundation of the diocese of Quebec, the first in North America, which took place three hundred years ago. We are not a colonizing nation, although we have to examine our conscience about our share in economic domination and oppression. But in general we have had to struggle out of colonial status and now seek to adapt two major cultures and many smaller groups in our own midst.

Hence we hear the voices of our brothers and sisters of Africa and Asia calling for understanding and trust and a chance to adapt the Gospel message to their indigenous cultures. The Holy Father himself, in his speech in Kampala, recognized this need, and we lend our support.[3]

b) We raise the question whether matters of pastoral practice and discipline are not so socio-culturally conditioned that it is increasingly difficult for a central organization, however necessary, to take exclusive responsibility for overseeing them, without in practice violating the relative and rightful autonomy of the local churches and episcopal Conferences. Is not the sharing of this responsibility with the bishops the normal consequence of an ecclesiology which acknowledges the diversity and the important role of the local churches?

c) We consider the Synod an excellent example of unity and pluralism. It should be strengthened to make it a truly collegial body. It should meet with sufficient frequency to cope effectively with the demands and expectations placed on the Church in an ever more rapidly changing world.

Conclusion

We are at a point when perhaps for the first time in history, we perceive the signs of the human community emerging into a true and unified family. Signs are not yet reality, but they must not be neglected. What an opportunity for the Church, raised as a sign of unity among nations, to anticipate the gathering of the Kingdom and to set an example of oneness. It alone has the grace from the Lord to draw all people to itself, even the least and the most helpless.

NOTES

1. The deliberations of the Synod strongly influenced Pope Paul the Sixth's *Apostolic Exhortation on Evangalization* of 1975. Besides the presentations given here, other Canadian delegates were heard: Archbishop J.-M. Fortier, on *The Apostolic Formation of the Laity* and on *The Renewal of Christian Life in Canada*: M. Hermaniuk, *On Pluralism in the Church of Christ with Reference to the Eastern Churches*; Bishop W.E. Power, *Evangelization and Daily Bread.* These are available from the Archives of the CCCB in Ottawa.

2. *Osservatore Romano* (Vatican), English ed., Sept. 5, 1974, n. 36, p. 336; French version, *Documentation Catholique* (Paris, 1974), LXXI, p. 801.

3. Paul VI, to assembled bishops of Africa, July 31, 1969, in *The Pope Speaks* (Washington, 1969), XIV, p. 214 ff.; French version, *Documentation Catholique* (Paris, 1969), LXVI, 763.

Section VI, Document 8

EVANGELIZATION: TASK OF THE WHOLE CHURCH

Archbishop Henri Legaré, O.M.I., October 11, 1974

INTRODUCTION

1. When we address ourselves to the question of the place of the laity in the Church, and more particularly in the Church's mission to evangelize, we are basically dealing with the place which the Gospel has in the lives of those who are baptized-confirmed. It is imperative that this question be understood in terms of the need to develop a Gospel spirituality "for all seasons", for ordinary people. It is our task as bishops to assist, to authenticate, to give leadership to the many ways in which Christians give hands and feet to the Gospel today, ways in which they build a Church based on the life and the faith they share.

Witnessing Power

2. In the light of the Church's task to evangelize we are legitimately inclined to speak here of the witnessing power contained in a life style that really radiates the Gospel. Where the influence of the Church and its institutions may be decreasing, we may happily be forced to insist more on the enormous potential for evangelization contained in the lives of those "living stones" (1 Pet. 2:5), the believers themselves. When Christians let the Gospel feed their lives, whether in their family relationships or in their wider social responsibilities, they become its living witnesses.

3. The question we now ask is: what place do we assign to this witness in the overall task of the Church to evangelize? We draw attention to two points which prevent this living witness of the baptized-confirmed from receiving its rightful place in the Church's mission.

Word and Deed

4. First, there is the tendency to consider witness as secondary when compared with the verbal proclamation of the Gospel. In the first preparatory document for this Synod, evangelization was practically reduced to verbal proclamation. In the final working document the element of witness has been introduced but in such a way that no doubt was possible as to the priority given to verbal proclamation. In the recent synthesis of the Synodal proceedings, Part One, we see again the tendency practically to equate evangelization with verbal proclamation. We feel that whatever new insights may be gained as to the way the Gospel is to be lived in everyday life, there will continue to be a major stumbling block as long as there remains any tendency to consider witness as a secondary element of evangelization.

5. It is important to see evangelization consisting in two indispensably complementary activities: proclaiming in word and bearing witness in deed. The one cannot do without the other. Word and deed belong together as one proclamation; they nourish each other and together constitute evangelization. Action gives credibility to the word. Word clarifies any ambiguity or anonymity in the action. Evangelization is not only a matter of the spoken word but also of the concrete life style, a *praxis,* the spoken word lived (cf. James 2:14-26; Gal. 6:2).

6. As Pope Paul pointed out in an audience to the Council of the Laity, Oct. 2, 1974,[1] contemporary humanity is better disposed to witness than to the word, or at least more inclined to listen when the speaker's word is authenticated by action. It is a matter of seeing how this greater contemporary responsiveness to actions than to words may help us to restore the constitutive place of witness in the Church's task to evangelize.

Laos: the Whole Church

7. But there is a second difficulty, which unfortunately stands in the way of giving witness its rightful place in evangelization. This difficulty is at the level of ecclesiology. Why is it necessary to speak of the place and role of the laity in the Church and in the Church's task to evangelize? What is it that makes us almost immediately think of the laity in terms of the non-ordained membership of the Church? What is it that makes us think of ordained members as having prior responsibility in evangalization? Does this not indicate a tendency to understand and define the Church first in relation to its hierarchical ministry and only afterwards in relation to the rest of the baptized-confirmed people? But does this not violate a fundamental insight of the Second Vatican Council's *Dogmatic Constitution on the Church*? Drawing from the scriptural and patristic sources, the Council insists that the term *laos* applies first and foremost to the body of the faithful as a whole which in its entirety is a spirit-filled and priestly people.[2] On the basis of their baptism-confirmation, all Christians belong to the *laos*. Are we prepared to accept the implications of the fact that the entire *laos* — as one people of God — is commissioned to bring the Good News to the world in word and deed? If we do not wholeheartedly accept this understanding of the Church, we cannot help but end considering the lay apostolate as simply auxiliary to the mission of the hierarchy. Unfortunately, this seems to be the position described in the synthesis of the Synodal discussions on Part One. Such a position is an affront to the priestly dignity of the baptized-confirmed.

Dislocation

8. Here are some observations which may explain the ecclesiological impasse preventing us from respecting the evangelizing thrust of ordinary people living the Gospel. Our starting point must be that the Church, the community of believers, has a ministry or mission to the world, to bring it the Good News. This is a ministry, a mission or responsibility shared by all Christians. Surveying the history of the Church, we see how within the *laos* itself — the people — a dichotomy has developed between the laity and the ordained ministers. This dichotomy resulted in a dislocation of the ministry

or mission of the whole Church. The clergy appropriated all ecclesial ministry; the laity tended to project all ecclesial ministry onto
the clergy. This dislocation has led to a two-class system in the
Church: an active, dominating clergy and a rather passive laity. When
initial attempts were made to re-activate the laity (now understood
or misunderstood as non-ordained Church-members), we tended
and still tend to speak and think of laity in terms of assisting and
participating in the mission of the hierarchy or as having almost
exclusively a specific mission in the secular order.

9. There is an urgent need today to correct this dislocation, both
in our common consciousness and in actual fact. Unless this correction is made, we fear that the laity will continue to be perceived in
a framework that reduces them to second-class members of the
Church. The correction of this dislocation goes beyond having them
participate in the decision-making process in the Church, or assign-
ing them a role in liturgical celebrations, or simply spelling out their
task in the secular realm. No doubt these aspects are a legitimate
concern. But there is the danger that concentrating on these alone
means leaving the basic dislocation untouched.

Conclusion

10. What we are really speaking of here is our understanding of
the Church, her salvific mission to the world, shared by all the
baptized-confirmed. What must be recaptured is the awareness that
it is the body of the faithful as a whole, the whole people of God,
anointed as they are by the Holy One, which has been charged with
the continuation of Jesus' messianic mission to the world.

11. It is impossible to conceive a more basic vocation to ecclesial
ministry or mission than that of being baptized-confirmed. When
Christians permit their everyday life to be inspired by what is contained in their baptism-confirmation, their lives become spiritual
sacrifices acceptable to God and salvific for the world. Then, the
whole Church is indeed evangelizing.

NOTES

1. *Acta Apostolicae Sedis* (Vatican City, 1974), LXVI, 568, quoted in Paul VI's Apostolic Exhortation, *On Evangelization* (1975), in *Origins* (Washington, 1976), V, n. 29, p. 464.

2. Second Vatican Council, *Dogmatic Constitution on the Church*, nn. 9-17, esp. 12; *Decree on the Laity,* esp. nn. 5-22.

Section VI, Document 9

SYNOD OF 1977 — CATECHESIS TODAY[1]

THE CULTURAL CONTEXT OF CONTEMPORARY CATECHESIS

Bishop G. Emmett Carter, October 1, 1977

The Canadian delegation, in whose name I speak, is constituted, as you are aware, of two linguistic cultures. With your permission and by agreement of the President I will speak in my own tongue, but my presentation reflects the common opinion of our delegation and is based on the opinions which we have sought not only from the bishops of our country but also from a good number of young people. (If I may be permitted to speak a word from my own personal experience, I sent out to the young people of my diocese 3,000 letters and received 2,000 replies.) Our intervention is based on enquiries of this kind.

The exchange of ideas and the quasi-seductive pull of values are no longer confined to specific agencies as in the past. Education now takes place in a total cultural milieu, a world milieu made possible by electronic communication, a milieu that is swept by all ideologies and interests. It is in this enormous global milieu, complicated and totally new, that future Christian formation will succeed or fail, where it will catch its second breath or else be seen as an anachronism. Our thought and action, then, must have direct bearing on the structures and values of the modern world; we must bring discernment, initiative and inventiveness. We must not appear nostalgic but rather as bearers of realistic hope.

For this reason we feel strongly that this Synod must not limit itself to a technical discussion of instruments and agents of catechesis in a formal framework. We, as much as anyone, are enthusiastic about the importance of Catholic schools. We recognize this privileged milieu of communicating the value of the Gospel. But of what use is the greatest catechist if there are no students? And of what import is the teaching if the students are totally unprepared or already hostile to the message proposed — or, as in the gospel parable, when the seed sown is eaten before it has a chance to germinate (Lk. 8:5).

In a world where materialism, sensuality, sexuality run wild, and secularism, with its many aspirations of the modern world, contradict the fundamental values of Christ's message, we would make ourselves objects of ridicule if we were to limit discussion to questions of methodology and techniques.

We do not deny the importance of the attempt to reach the young. But our conviction is that the pressures on the young are the same pressures as are felt in every age and that it would be a mistake to concentrate on any particular age group since the whole world is under the influence of a veritable culture shock. What the young can teach us is the freshness of their approach to the ancient problems of Christianity. They are in a sense the prototype of the reaction which all feel in the presence of this struggle.

Our New Universe

We have not yet fully assimilated the newness, the power, the influence of the universe within a universe that technology has created.

As a result of the development of the physical sciences, but also by the rather subtle contributions of psychology and sociology, we have woven a web of relationships, a framework in which we have enclosed the world, or, perhaps, in which we have built a new world. An undreamed of experience has come into existence which has radically changed the relationships of persons to reality, a situation in which adults as well as the young are novices. The world has become what radio, television, motion pictures, the press, illustrated magazines and recordings make of it; the automobile and air travel have introduced new realities of space and time.

The many shapes of the media, in their inter-relationships, strengthen and multiply their effects. Striking at the level of the senses, their effect on us is immediate and total.

The media teach everyone simultaneously and constantly. Different ages and different classes of people are reduced to a single mass. These media impinge on us from the awakening of consciousness to the moment of death, and without respite.

Its Darker Character

This new world has a spirit in which old or present pedagogical methods would hardly recognize themselves. The cultural milieu is an organic whole where structure and values, techniques and ideologies are closely linked. Within this whole, Christian formation finds obstacles and supports.

Supported by money and power, the great technologies of the modern world seek the largest possible clientele. Such an undertaking, relying on humanity's lowest common denominator, aims at our most primitive appetites, favours complacency over development, settles for little intellectual effort and ends up with a doctrinal neutrality rather than an energetic quest for truth.

We see the materialism of our civilization obsessed by a quest for comfort and pleasure, for "instant" action — the characteristics of a destructive consumer mentality. If we grasp voraciously for the improved and constantly dispose of the old, we find ourselves in a vacuum and in a state of increasing frustration.

Such a civilization, devouring and frustrated, generates violence and death. Yet the Gospel calls us to initiate such a world to openness, to search and growth, to fidelity and hope.

We are also in a time of secularism, when absolute values are lost to sight. Because contemporary men and women are interested in reaching as many people as soon as possible, they relate religious and moral convictions to subjectivity, to impulsive and arbitrary thinking. Transcendental values are repressed and in so doing, institutions and laws are banished from their domain. There is, then, the tendency to forget or even deny the existence of such values, yet the Gospel urges us to introduce and support justice, truth, love and liberty in all matters.

Lastly, a world dazzled by its recent accomplishments, that shuns what is not empirically verifiable, does not speak of God. God is thought of as folklore that is not relevant and, therefore, is notably absent in this world of our making. Because it is considered to be of our making, it is hard for us to believe that it comes from Another. We no longer discern the presence of the Unique and Absolute in all our quest and longing. The Gospel, on the other hand, aims to give life through our contact with the Source of truth and love.

Brighter Aspects

Even though we may find ourselves threatened by materialism, secularism, spiritual poverty, there are forces at work in a world where so many human qualities are active, where at least the material conditions for union and communion have been established, forces that bring to the person of today social unity, integration and a sense of dignity. Christian education, likewise, must draw strength from values of solidarity, concrete social involvement and authenticity, all of which are characteristics of our era. By our contact and personal exchange the world over, we have come to a sharper understanding of our common condition and destiny. We have acquired a deeper sense of our fundamental equality and a new repugnance for injustice and discrimination. Obviously this repugnance is not untarnished, yet it does at least arouse our sense of guilt. We find, also, a renewed sense of communion in the defence of our cultures, the improvement of working conditions and the protection of our natural resources. Finally, we note a greater sense of responsibility with respect to others and to our unfolding history.

Paralleling this social growth, an integrity of person can be noted: a taste for involvement and concrete action is more evident than before. In this age of technical know-how we see the will to put words into action. We are no longer satisfied to look at the world, we wish to transform it. A certain eagerness, rash at times and not without the will to power, often makes this desire for involvement aggressive.

The taste for authenticity, for sincerity and liberty that many young people display and communicate, seems to be one of the avenues by which we discover and develop a sense of human dignity in this new and inventive world. Involvement calls for unity of conviction and action; authenticity demands that conviction be autonomous and not imposed from without. And whereas reaction against institutions and systems may reveal immaturity and a lack of realism, the fact remains that this reaction is healthy. It stimulates organisms within the Church, as elsewhere, to ensure their service to humanity rather than simply their survival and growth.

New Directions

The unlimited expansion of the media of communication and education, and of global cultural forces, urge the Canadian delegation to request that the discussion of Christian formation and catechesis be of great breadth, reaching as far as possible in as many directions as the present nature of our world requires. Otherwise, we will be talking of a catechesis of the past, of a formation as passing as snow in the sun.

1. We ask that Christian education interest itself deeply in the media, principally (a) in forming a critical attitude in the use of the media, and (b) in seeking to discover how to express the Christian message in the new language of the media.

2. In great openness, we must seek the co-operation of all Christians and of all people of good will, in the protection and improvement of the cultural milieu where Christian education takes place.

3. Christian formation must respect and follow the lead of continuing education in our constantly developing universe. Teacher and pupil alike must see themselves as constantly in a state of learning, called by a world where discovery is perpetually the order of the day.

4. We must be concerned with a constant striving to integrate our teaching and our celebration with a clear involvement in action; a deep understanding of its nature followed by concrete practice. This action which should be, as far as possible, a communal one, must aim at the development of persons and the improvement of the structures of social life.

NOTE

1. Canadian members of the Synod of 1977 were Archbishop M. Hermaniuk, *ex officio* as Metropolitan of the Ukrainian Catholics of Canada; Archbishops/Bishops G. Ouellet, H. Légaré, G.E. Carter, W.E. Doyle, W.E. Power, delegates of the Conference. Besides the presentations here, other addresses were made by Archbishops/Bishops M. Hermaniuk, *Catechesis and Human Rights*, Gilles Ouellet, *The Renewal of Moral Catechesis*, W. Emmett Doyle, *Spiritual Renewal and Renewal of Catechesis*. These are available from the Archives of the CCCB in Ottawa.

Section VI, Document 10

REQUIREMENTS FOR
CONTINUING EDUCATION IN FAITH

Bishop Bernard Hubert, October 5, 1977

Recently in a meeting of Christians and bishops, a layman, involved in the labour world, called us to a serious examination of conscience.

> You bishops give us excellent social teaching. We are happy with what you say about the struggle for justice, but when Christians take this teaching seriously and act in accordance with what they see as necessary for the concrete achievement of justice — strikes, demonstrations, certain political moves — we feel you show reserve, a timidity and hesitation concerning the choices and moves they judge best adapted to their commitment to justice.

Since the opening of this Synod, we have been speaking of catechesis. We have been saying fine things about it. We have emphasized the necessity of offering adults as well as the young, a continuing catechetical formation. Until now, however, we have hardly touched or reached a consensus on the ecclesial consequences of the catechetical renewal we hope for. As a synodal body, we have stayed away from certain important decisions. For example, we have equated catechesis of adults and continuing education in the faith. This seems to lead to an ambiguity that clouds the radical insights of contemporary continuing education and tends to make us ill at ease and perplexed with regard to the options and methods of our own collaborators, the catechists.

I would like, as well, to draw the attention of my fellow bishops to three points that have direct bearing on our pastoral mission. First,

our attitude towards the modern world; secondly, the Christian formation of believers today and tomorrow; lastly, the role of Church
members, responsible for Christian formation, conceived as continuing education in the faith.

Our Lord Calls Us to Go Forth

Our episcopal language in catechesis is often seen as a closed communication among bishops. I am not at all sure that modern men
and women, be they engineers, industrial workers, electronic tech-
nicians, or workers in large plants, understand much of, or are even
interested in our problems concerning education in the faith. Yet they
are directly concerned. In fact, in all matters of concern to them, they
actually expect to be among the main agents of decision. Within this
Synod it is important that we try to see how our Church, in its
catechesis, may communicate more effectively with the modern
world. Perhaps we shall have to revise our former way of speaking
to traditional Christian communities and learn a language enabling
us to go out to others and be understood by them.

As a work of the Church, catechesis shares in the missionary vocation of the Spouse of Christ. It is the Church, not the world which
is sent on mission. We cannot count on that world taking the initiative to approach the Church, seeking a catechesis that makes no advances. The Church is the more obliged to turn to the world, since
humanity is continually changing before our eyes. We are faced with
a heretofore unknown person, with self-image of a free subject, socially solidary and responsible — like the methods of future pedagogy — put in motion by his/her own dynamisms, rather than by
recourse to external agents. This presents us with a new *kind* of person to be catechised. True, many obstacles hamper the realization
and generalization of such behaviour and still alienate many
moderns, but these are the realities we face, realities which are
promising for humanity and signs of the times for Christians.

Further, the world in which we were formed is ended. At least
in the west, we are at a turning point in our history, and the catechesis
we present today bears this mark. It is up to us now to show whether
we choose to close ourselves off in the ghetto of a pedagogy of the
past or to associate ourselves, courageously and sympathetically, with
the movements of our times in which we must strive to proclaim

the Gospel. Youth, prototype of this new world, relays to us the prayer of the Macedonian in Paul's dream: "Come over into Macedonia and help us." (Acts 16:9) Youth extends us an invitation like that of Jesus to Nicodemus, to be reborn in the Spirit really to know the Reign of God. (cf. Jn. 3:5-6)

The Believer of Today and of the Future

Of what sort will be the believer of tomorrow, whom we already see developing before our eyes? Though there will surely be a variety of Christians, we may expect to find certain common traits. Their spiritual experience will be one of free adherence to Jesus. Undoubtedly they will still want reasons for accepting and believing a message, but they will be sensitively aware of the element of free engagement inherent in faith, and of the personal dimension of their relationship with God revealed in Jesus. The call of God will be seen as addressed to men and women in their capacities of autonomy, initiative, creativity and interpersonal reciprocity. Faith and response will be more consciously linked to those dynamisms, already communicated in baptism and the totality of sacramental life. It will grow rather by internal or organic development than by recourse to contributions from without.

The conditions for growth will correspond to the new character of this faith life. This spiritual experience will rely on a sacramental practice, in which the entry into intimate communion with God and with sisters and brothers will express itself in a personal way, lively and inventive. It will need to be lived in groups of human scale, small groups where intimacy and friendship are possible, where members can mutually enlighten, encourage, stimulate and correct each other. Belonging to the great Christian community of diocese and universal church, it will be strongly marked by the lived experience of one of these small human groups which must be neither a ghetto nor a refuge for anonymity. It is to be desired, finally, that a faith in a God Who is our Friend, would go with bold courage to the rescue of humanity, working especially to construct a social order more concerned for justice and liberty.

Such a pedagogy of the faith, so intimately linked to autonomy of the person and individual dynamisms, proper to each, supposes

that we accept for the future the structures and principles of continuing education; that we must accept, then, a progression in the
appropriation of the Word of God; diversity and adaptation in this
pilgrimage, both with respect to its beginning and to the rhythm of
development; that the responsibility for this growth in faith be with
the believer who must not be pressured but allowed and even
challenged to mature his/her own motivation.

The Church in this Continuing Formation in Faith

The acceptance of this model of continuing education in faith,
calls for new attitudes among those responsible for Christian formation. Attentive to awaken but to let mature the proper concern
for the dynamisms of the believer, those responsible for education
in the faith have essentially to welcome, listen, invite, challenge,
stimulate. Authority, as recommended in the Gospel, will express
itself in service, support, in helping to discern, rather than in
imposing obligation. The Church will see herself mainly as working in people's hearts, supporting a spiritual enterprise, rather than
as dispensing help from the summit to the base, paternalistically or
administratively.

In this new type of education in the faith, the responsibility of
ministers will be in the creation and development of a community
where personal faith experience may find nourishment and growth.
In particular, ministers will be concerned to present profoundly but
with clarity, progressively with sensitive adaptation, the truly constitutive data of the faith, always aware of the hierarchy of Christian
truths. Great care should be taken, too, to create an educative faith
environment, especially in preparing real and moving liturgical
celebrations and in suggesting a positive and constructive moral
praxis, especially in the area of social involvement.

In this perspective the role of the bishop in his diocese, of the
Conference of Bishops in their region, of the Holy Father in the
universal Church, can be seen as that of promoters and guarantors
of Christian communion.

If the Christian community turns to the world and seeks there
"the seeds of the Word",[1] placing itself in the service of Christ and
of the human family, so that the latter, taught by their lived experience, are led to faith, prayer and the practice of justice, that com-

munity will be a source of hope for all. It will make possible conditions under which our times can become an era, not of atheism, but of faith.

In the contemporary world, the Lord calls the Christian community to identify and proclaim the genuine human values and dynamics of human nature and to support all in their journey towards freedom. To the degree that the Christian community performs that task with love, confidence and daring, with realism and critical sense, in that degree all will feel loved by that community and securely guided by it. All will be able to discern, in such a community, "the Light of nations" (Acts 13:47; cf. Is. 49:6).

NOTE

1. Reference is to a phrase of Second Vatican Council, "seeds of the Word" (*semina Verbi*), in the *Decree on Missions* (nn. 11, 15). The Council meant all those elements of truth and goodness found in non-Christian religions and secular cultures, in all times and places. St. Justin Martyr (second century) did not hesitate to attribute these gracious inspirations to the Eternal Word, the Son of God, "the true light that enlightens every person" (Jn. 1:9). Cf. St. Justin Martyr in *The Fathers of the Church* (Christian Heritage Inc., N.Y., 1946), *First Apology,* c. 46, p. 83; *Second Apology,* cc. 10 and 13, pp. 133 ff. In the latter chapter he uses the phrases "seminal divine Word", "seed of the Word". Though obscured by prejudice at times and in places, this view of God's saving grace, offered to all, is part of the theological tradition of the Church.

Section VI, Document 11

SYNOD OF 1980
THE CHRISTIAN FAMILY TODAY[1]

TOWARDS A THEOLOGY OF
MARRIAGE AND THE FAMILY

Archbishop Henri Légaré, September 30, 1980

The family is at a turning point as is society itself. This Synod is a privileged opportunity for us as pastors to look at, study and support the thousands of women, men and children who are seeking a new balance in life.

As my colleague has emphasized, attention to the situation of families in Canada has convinced us that any undertaking in family ministry which does not pay particular attention to the condition of women is doomed to failure. Further, the growth and development which we have had the opportunity to observe in many families has also convinced us that family ministry takes place through families. Finally, we note that many involved Christian families are becoming ever more aware that they are the Church, that they constitute the ecclesial reality and that they can find strength and support in various groups or communities which help them become agents of change in society.

It is obvious that this search by the families of our country for a new equilibrium is not without difficulties. Although many, in spite of the demands and the sufferings inherent in all progress, do commit themselves to the pursuit of human and spiritual growth, many also experience failure.

In either case, a great deal of re-evaluation is taking place. This re-evaluation, whether springing from a new vision of married life or from personal choices in meeting marital and familial problems, demands a re-examination of our pastoral ministry and the theology upon which it rests. As I reflect upon this situation, I would like to share with you some of the questions raised.

I believe that for a large number of young people today in the industrialized countries, marriage and the family no longer mean what they did for previous generations. For many the social and ecclesial institution of marriage seems to have lost its normative role. For them, the couple relationship is based only on love. Love is readily taken as an absolute which, without reference to other values, justifies sexual relations and pre-marital cohabitation.

Who is not impressed by the prevalence and force of tainted misconceptions of sexuality including fertility control, feminine and masculine roles, human interactions and the functions of the family in modern society? The issue in conduct is at times rich in promise, at others very ambiguous.

It may be said that many aspects of the current situation have something of value while at the same time none is free of risk and often suffering. Taken as a whole are they not an expression of the search for a new balance between personal love and institutional constraint, between conjugal communion and the longing for autonomy, between marriage and the natural right to marry, and marriage as sacrament instituted by the Church? Do they not show the efforts required to establish a new relationship between women and men in the family and in a wider society, as well as a new way of situating oneself in the Church?

As the Second Vatican Council said "The Church has always had the duty of scrutinizing the signs of the times and of interpreting them in the light of the Gospel".[2] How then should we assess the current developments which call in question the very meaning of marriage and the family? We must encourage a creative theology beginning from today's experiences, without however, neglecting the riches of the past.

The following questions relate to some specific situations.

1. Validity of Marriage

The first question, one becoming ever more painful, is that of divorce. The fact that divorce has increased dramatically is, in itself, a reason for re-studying requirements for a valid marriage, taking into account the findings of modern psychology, especially regarding the conditions for freedom, maturity and commitment to fidelity. Attention must also be paid, in a socio-cultural perspective, to the situation of the couple and of the family in today's world.

2. Indissolubility of Marriage

This leads us to the deeper question of the indissolubility of marriage. We must re-examine certain aspects of doctrine upon which the indissolubility of marriage is based, taking as our point of departure our pastoral ministry to the divorced and remarried. Our method of studying this question has not been adequate, even if some of the pastoral insights gained may point the way for the future.

The indissolubility of Christian marriage is based on a number of realities: the necessity of faithfulness inherent in human love, the good of the children, the good of society, and the design of God; "What God has united, man must not divide" (Mt. 19:6), but the ultimate foundation upon which the Church's doctrine rests is the symbolism of the union of Christ and His Church (Eph. 5:25-33).

Christian marriage thus becomes the image, the sign and the witness of this indissoluble union. In short, the indissolubility of marriage is based largely on the irrevocable fidelity of Christ to His Church. This teaching, which is undeniably rich, leaves some questions unresolved.

The first, which is theological, is linked to the experience of the people of God, a people saved in Jesus Christ but still a pilgrim people, who welcome salvation in a history where grace and sin are mixed. How does one speak of marriage as a privileged sign of the covenant between God and His people? How to express the difference between the relationship of Christ to the Church and the relationship of the Church to Christ? If the faithfulness of Christ to His Church is absolute, we know very well that the reality of the Church's relationship to Christ is different, and marked by human frailty. Can we then, clearly and simply, equate Christ's relationship to the Church and the Church's relationship to Christ?

The essentialist philosophy within which the theology of the sacrament of marriage evolved, can lead one to think that the Church is already in a state of perfection, that it has in some sense arrived at its end. That approach, however, tends to forget that the Church is truly a pilgrim Church, being constructed in history. Should we not, therefore, rethink the theology of marriage in a more existentialist and personalist framework? Such an approach calls us to take into account reality as it presents itself historically, while still affirming (but in a different way) the indissolubility of marriage.

A pastoral problem arises from the situation of the divorced and remarried. Present pastoral ministry does not pay enough attention to the situation of those who after experiencing the death of a first love, live a second in fidelity, are committed in faith and to the Church, and wish to enjoy full participation at the Eucharistic table.

Re-examination of doctrine on the sacrament of marriage is therefore demanded by a ministry of mercy, which continues to welcome people trying to walk the path of conversion, without denying the evangelical demand for conjugal fidelity. Indissolubility is maintained; but is it not possible to discover a pastoral approach more attentive to the situation that faces us?

3. Baptized Non-believers

A final situation we would like to mention is the marriage of baptized non-believers. This involves the denial of sacramental marriage on the grounds of incapacity, since marriage in the communion of the Church is a profession of faith. The consequence of reducing them to the condition of public sinners seems to imply a denial of their right to a natural or civil marriage. First of all, what is the relationship between the marriage-sacrament and marriage-natural-institution, insofar as the latter is anterior to the former, as the place within which God bestows His gift? And then what is the relationship between baptism, faith, intention and sacrament of marriage? In other words, is it not time to rethink our teaching which links the marriage contract and the sacrament in the case of baptized non-believers?[3]

4. Conclusions

These are admittedly difficult questions. But we think also that to face them in this assembly would be an act of confidence in the Spirit Who does not cease to guide His Church. "Thus, in language intelligible to each generation, she can respond to the perennial questions which men ask about this present life and the life to come, and about the relationship of the one to the other."[4]

NOTES

1. The subject of the Synod of 1980 was *The Christian Family in the Modern World.* Canadian members of the Synod were: Archbishop Maxim Hermaniuk, *ex officio,* as Patriarch of the Ukrainian Catholics of Canada; Archbishops/Bishops G.E. Cardinal Carter, H. Légaré, R. Lebel and J.N. MacNeil, delegates of the Conference. Besides the presentations included here, the following addressed the Synod: Gerald E. Cardinal Carter, *The Christian Family and Moral Education*: Archbishops/Bishops M. Hermaniuk, *The Social Function of the Family*; H. Légaré, *Bio-medical Developments and the Future of the Family*; J.N. MacNeil, *Towards a Theology of Sexuality and the Family, The Apostolate of Families, On Proclaiming the Good News to Families*; R. Lebel, *The Family in the Church of the Poor.* These are available from the Archives of the CCCB, Ottawa.

2. Second Vatican Council, *The Church in the Modern World,* 1965, n. 4, par. 1.

3. Cf. this Section IV, Document 12, n. 6.

4. *Op. cit., l.c.* of note 2, above.

Section VI, Document 12

TOWARDS A SYNTHESIS
FOR GROUP DISCUSSION

The Delegation of the Canadian Conference, October 3, 1980

This presentation wishes to indicate some points that our delegation believes should be included in the synthesis to be discussed in small groups. It is our conviction that these points emerged clearly and strongly in the general discussion of the first week. They should be retained on the agenda for further discussion by study groups. The following questions all have direct pastoral consequences and need to be clarified or at least moved forward at this Synod.

1. *Decision-Making by Episcopal Conferences*

One overarching question is the greater discretion or autonomy of regional or national Episcopal Conferences in some matters touching marriage and family life. Whether it be with regard to cultural adaptation of sacramental rites to indigenous customs or to prudential judgments in the pastoral care of difficult marriages, there are pastoral situations that can best be handled close to the families involved. The Synod should study how an efficacious decentralization can be realized in these matters, according to the principle of subsidiarity and without jeopardy to the universal teaching of the Church.

2. *Validity of Marriage in Modern Conditions*

There is need of further development of the pastoral treatment of marriages that are invalid because one party or both lacked true

and full freedom as now understood in the light of modern be-
havioural sciences. It is not new that the Church gives priority to
free choice as a criterion of a binding marriage. What is new is the
social situation which conditions free choice. Clarification of the consequences of this is urgently needed for the work of tribunals and
for pastoral care generally.

3. Mixed Marriages and the Eucharist

Ours is a country where the presentation of Cardinal Willebrands
has great relevance because of the frequency of marriages between
Catholics and other baptized Christians. This Synod should make
some progress in the study of how "our real, though not perfect communion with other Churches" can be reflected in our pastoral care
of mixed marriages, and so respond in compassion to Christian families who ask that they may receive holy communion together.

4. A Pastoral Style for Family Life

Our delegation's first intervention called for reflection on the
pastoral style or language that would give today's families a clear
sense that they are truly the Church and called by God to be "agents
of history, not its victims".[1] Our small groups should study what
can be said to all pastors about how "to listen to what the Lord says
through families, and also multiply throughout the Church the
opportunities for family members to hear and express the Lord's
call".[2]

5. A Pastoral Approach for the Divorced and Remarried

The dramatic increase in divorce and the consequent number of
second marriages invite us to re-examine the pastoral practice which
excludes them from receiving the Eucharist. It seems important to
us to reflect further on this question. Can we not devise a compassionate pastoral procedure without denying the Gospel demand of
conjugal fidelity and without placing in question the indissolubility
of marriage?

6. The Marriage of Baptized Non-believers

The situation of baptized non-believers who wish to marry
obliges us to question the present pastoral practice. A pastoral prac-

tice which, in order to meet the demands of the faith, is forced to deny the possibility of a valid civil marriage for these people and in turn places them in the category of concubinage or common law unions, is difficult to accept. We believe that it is necessary to pursue the studies already begun on this question.

How do we understand the relationship between the institution of marriage in its original state as a human right and gift of God, on the one hand, and on the other, marriage as a sacrament? How do we establish the connection between baptism, the faith and access to the sacrament of marriage?

7. *The Moral Problems of Responsible Parenthood*

Fertility is a demand of conjugal love. Spouses are called, to "undertake this task in a responsible, human and Christian way".[3] Since the publication of the Encyclical *On Human Life* (1968)[4], the question of the means of contraception and their morality has been the object of continued debate among theologians and pastors. It troubles and divides our Christian communities. It has contributed seriously to creating a negative understanding of the thinking of the Church.

In addition, many couples do not regard natural birth control methods as definitively the only morally acceptable way for them to exercise their responsibility for family planning. One cannot simply dismiss these couples as people who cannot rise above human frailty, for they are often Christian men and women of remarkable faith and commitment.

These facts oblige us to reconsider this question in this Synod. It would seem to us important to reflect on the way in which we present the thinking of the Church.

8. *Youth: Builders of the Families of the Future*

Young people today are being asked to create a "civilization of love"[5] in the midst of an unprecedented crisis of civilization wherein they are being torn between multiple and often contradictory forces.

They are searching for a vision and values which will give meaning to life. One of these is the authenticity of love. In this they meet with many stumbling blocks. While many choose the route of human and spiritual progress, a great number are committed to ambiguous paths. The phenomenon of pre-marital co-habitation is only

534 *Section VI*

one example. Another is that it is difficult for them today to meet God in Jesus Christ.

It seems to us of primary importance that this Synod should clearly reflect to young people that we also share their preoccupations, their searching, their suffering, as well as their hope. Could we not stand by them more sympathetically while the call echoes within them, beckoning them further on the road of love and sharing so that they may build the families of the future?

9. *Theology of Sexuality in Marriage*

It cannot be denied that most Christians perceive our theology of sexuality, marriage and the family in a negative way. In the troubled times in which we now live, families find themselves completely on their own, pulled about by opposing currents, involved in a search for meaning and visions. This situation presents a major challenge for the entire Church.

That is why it seems important to us that this Synod give impetus to the search for a new language, a renewed theology to respond to this need.

In this sense, would this not be the place to reflect upon a theology which integrates human sciences, taking advantage of the new insights into human sexuality? The Wednesday talks of the Holy Father provide an admirable example. Is this not the place to reflect upon a theology which affirms the total significance of human love, of responsible parenthood in relation to fecundity and to the mastery of human fertility which itself marks a turning point in history?

10. *Women Seek Equality*

This Synod must respond to the efforts being made to allow women to come to full dignity and recognition, personally and socially. We must explore how pastoral leaders can do more to bring this movement to full realization in the Church and in the world.

11. *The Church and the Poor*

In a world torn by the injustice of poverty and hunger, and in which humanity's very future depends on its ability to establish a new international economic order, poor families constitute a dramatic challenge to the conscience of the entire people of God. Through the indispensable concrete experiences of solidarity, sharing and sacrifice, are not poor families in a privileged position to incarnate the Gospel?

We also believe the Synod should give an important place to the poor families of the world by study of their concrete situation, and by action for social justice, but chiefly by the significance and import of their presence as a forceful challenge to the People of God.

NOTES

1. Presentation of Archbishop Joseph N. MacNeil, President of the Conference, Sept. 3, 1980.
2. *Ibid.*
3. Second Vatican Council, *Constitution on the Church in the Modern World,* nn. 50 f.
4. Pope Paul VI, in *The Papal Encyclicals,* edit. Claudia Carlen, IHM (Wilmington, N.C., McGrath Publishing, 1981), V, pp. 225 ff., nn. 10-14.
5. Paul VI, cf. Section V, Document 7, Note 9.

Section VI, Document 13

WOMEN IN FAMILY MINISTRY AND THE LIFE OF THE CHURCH

Bishop Robert Lebel, October 14, 1980

1. The submission and oppression to which women are subject in our world is a sinful situation, the result of original sin and of the actual sins of generations — a sinful situation to be corrected. In his presentation Cardinal Ratzinger said, "The Creator's design for woman was expressed to man in these words: 'I must make him a helpmate like himself' " (Gen. 2:18). Further, in the economy of redemption and among those who have "clothed themselves in Christ," "there are no more distinctions between slave and free, male and female" (Gal. 3:27f.). "If, then," says the presentation, "there is an insistence in our time on equal rights and dignity for men and women, this is in full accord with the intent of scripture."

2. The Church therefore, in fidelity to the word of God, must recognize the modern feminist movement as a positive reality. We are dealing on the whole with an advance in civilization. It is a forward step in the establishment of the Kingdom.

3. If there is any place where women's call for liberation should be heard, it is certainly in the Church of Jesus Christ, where the word of God has shed its light. The Church must not be towed along by secular forces of civilization and culture, making excuses for her delays in hearing calls for liberation, on the ground that secular society is doing no better. The Church must be prophetic in words and practice in promoting every form of liberation. It must denounce and endeavour to correct everything in law, custom and cultural expression which embodies any form of discrimination or bondage.

4. The Church has already shown herself in many ways prophetic in the advancement of women, but her message must become clearer and unobscured by any reserve. The presence and influence of the Mother of God permeate the Church, but we are still far from having drawn from Marian dogma all the consequences in ecclesiology and Church practice, regarding the equality, liberty and dignity of womanhood. Far too from completely humanizing the presence of God and His salvation. But the desire to achieve what remains to be done should not prevent us seeing what has been accomplished.

5. A very positive sign has appeared in our times, full of promise that our hopes will be fulfilled. Women have found in Christian marriage and in the Christian family full recognition of their dignity and equality with their male partners. That at least is what the Second Vatican Council proclaims.[1]

6. How can we refrain from hoping to see the consequences of what has now become a reality in the family, "the domestic church," one day realized in the Church as a whole? If this does not result, the analogy between the "domestic church" and the Church as a whole remains imperfect. I leave my hearers to decide who, in that event, may be guilty of delaying that realization. How can we bring the Church as a whole to better assimilation with the "domestic church"? The problem is huge.

7. Part of the answer, it seems to me, lies in a family ministry in which families themselves are responsible for the evangelization which is their concern, internally responsible within the family but also co-responsible on all levels of the Church's ministry, right up to the largest organs of action. And when I speak of co-responsibility, I intend also goal-setting and decision-making.

8. The life, prayer and thought of that basic cell of the Church which is the family must influence the entire life of the Church. This will not happen automatically, by osmosis. Families must have the right to enter into the Church's pastoral organization and must possess the means of exerting influence in it. If families have an influence on the life of the Church, women will have an influence on it, because they comprise at least fifty percent of family membership. Nothing could be simpler to understand.

9. One must not, however, limit woman's role in the Church to her influence through the family. A woman is more than a wife and mother, even if these roles embody an immense human and supernatural reality. How can women, by virtue of what they themselves

are, as human persons, play a role in the Church which is just as important as men's? This is not the place to discuss the concrete forms that this role can take, for example in ministries.

10. What women want is to see in the Church a serious desire to have them assume responsibilities. Certain negative attitudes in matters of no great importance in themselves, are nonetheless very indicative. Why the desire to keep women and girls far removed from the altar? I grant that it is not cruet-carrying that will enable women to attain equality in full religious service, but it is to them a serious matter that they are denied even that. The prohibition has every appearance of a sexist attitude. It even takes on an anti-family tone, since it is the couple or the whole family which could assume the service of the altar, as is shown by a practice which is becoming more widespread in our country and undoubtedly elsewhere. Let us spare ourselves the embarrassment of trying to convince the faithful of the relevance and good sense of such prohibitions.

11. We have a long road to travel in answering our sisters' legitimate desire to employ all their abilities in the service of the Church. We should, or course, avoid embarking on futile projects and must not arouse false hopes. We must have, however, a basic, positive attitude toward their demands, even those which, expressed out of suffering, are resentful, and we must be profoundly convinced that the desire of our sisters for a larger place in the ministry of the Church is an opportunity offered to the Church herself.

NOTE

1. Second Vatican Council, *The Church in the Modern World*, nn. 9, 29, 48-49, 60.

Section VI, Document 14

SYNOD OF 1983[1] — RECONCILIATION

MALE-FEMALE RECONCILIATION IN THE CHURCH

Archbishop Louis-Albert Vachon, October 3, 1983

Number 41 of our *Working Document* proposes that in certain areas, dialogue must take place first within the Church, before being established with the world. One sees immediately the importance and urgency of promoting the dialogue between men and women in the Church itself as an essential place for mutual recognition and reconciliation.

Nature of the Problem

Just as the evolution of the condition of women influences life in society as a whole, it also influences, and will inevitably continue to influence, the life and future of the Church. The United Nations' *Convention on the Elimination of All Forms of Discrimination Against Women,* [2] is a clear indication of the progress of civil societies on this issue. That progress is, of course, not uniform, and differs from place to place, but it is real and is encouraged by the Church.

In fact, since John XXIII's encyclical *Peace on Earth* [3] (1963), and since the Second Vatican Council issued its *Constitution on the Church in the Modern World* [4] (1965), a number of episcopates have acted unceasingly to sensitize public opinion to the difficult — in fact, oppressive — cultural condition of women.

These appeals of the Church to the world for the advancement of the status of women are, however, on the point of losing all impact, unless the recognition of women as full members becomes, simultaneously, a reality within the Church itself.

Theological Perspective

The very theme of this Synod invites us, as men and women of the Church, to join in undertaking a journey of reconciliation arising from the nature of our baptism in Jesus Christ; for "He is our peace: out of what was divided, He has created unity. In His flesh He has broken down the wall of separation which is hatred" (Eph. 2:14-15). "Thus there are no more distinctions between Jew and Greek, slave and free, male and female; for all of you are but one in Jesus Christ" (Gal. 3:28). A new humanity is being realized in Jesus Christ, in which internal conflicts of racial, social and sexual origin are abolished, a new humanity, responsible for promoting its own historical and cultural perfection. In this humanity, man and woman must come to be and to recognize each other as equal in origin and destiny, equal in mission and involvement.

Historical and Present Context of Reconciliation

Women in our country invite us to join them in re-examining certain fundamental attitudes and assumptions and in establishing effective structures of dialogue within each of our local churches. A first step on our path of reconciliation between men and women is listening to one another.

In Canada, an ever-increasing number of women are speaking out and revealing their thoughts and feelings. The dualist vision of flesh-and-spirit and the sexist prejudices resulting from it, have strongly marked their past and continue to mark their present, identifying them with "the occasion of sin". They have experienced and experience alienation, marginalization and exclusion in many forms. Other women have taken a position of silence. Words or silence, both express their suffering and their desire to be understood, recognized, taken seriously for what they are on the most fundamental level.

Increasingly, experience has already shown the rich resources available in an egalitarian partnership between men and women for the extension of the Reign and of the growth of humanity.

As for us, let us recognize the ravages of sexism, and our own male appropriation of Church institutions and of numerous privileged positions in Christian life. Need I mention the example of the masculine language of our official — and even liturgical — texts?

In our society and in our Church, men have often come to think of themselves as the sole possessors of rationality, authority and active initiative, relegating women to the private sector and dependent tasks. Our recognition, as Church, of our own cultural deformation will help us transcend the archaic concepts of womanhood which have been inculcated for centuries.

The history of our country and our Church has already shown our ability to place proper value on the ingenious creativity and inventive participation of women in collective endeavours. Today women are more and more numerous in all areas of public life. They are experiencing and demonstrating a remarkable qualitative upsurge, promoting a notable change in our way of conceiving humanity. This should encourage us to live out with them, as Church, the relationships of equality demanded by our fundamental identity as persons and our life as sons and daughters of God.

Reconciliation in the Light of the Gospel

A second step on our path of reconciliation is to allow ourselves — both men and women — to be confronted by the Spirit of God. We need, as a group, to have our individual and collective attitudes and behaviour illumined by the Gospel. At the heart of the Gospel, the beatitudes will help us identify those aspects in our institutions which are unjust and demeaning. They will enable us to discover what we must change to bring about the recognition of women as having the same status of full membership as men.

Recommendation

The recommendation of the Canadian bishops, therefore, in the light of this intervention, concerns all ecclesial bodies, whether familial, professional, regional, diocesan or other. Let there be organized structures for dialogue which serve as meeting places for mutual exchange and recognition, and effective implementation of new bonds of equality between men and women in the Church.

NOTES

1. The theme of the General Synod of 1983 was *Reconciliation and Penance* (understood primarily as the *sacrament* of penance). Canadian members of the Synod were, Archbishops/Bishops M. Hermaniuk, Metropolitan of the Ukrainian Catholics of Canada, A. Exner, L.-A. Vachon, B. Blanchet, M. Gervais as delegates of the Conference. Besides the presentations included here, other addresses of the Canadian members were: *The Idea of Sin in Today's World*, by Archbishop Hermaniuk; *The Problem of Sin and Signs of Hope*, by Archbishop Exner; *The Wounded of the Church*, by Bishop Blanchet. *Complementarity of the Three Forms of Sacramental Reconciliation*, by Bishop Marcel Gervais. These are available from the Archives of the CCCB, Ottawa.

2. The Convention was adopted by the U.N. Assembly in 1979 and entered into force Sept. 3, 1981. Available from U.N. Association, 165 Spadina Ave., Toronto, Ont., M5T 2C4.

3. Pope John XXIII, *Peace on Earth*, in *The Papal Encyclicals*, edit. Claudia Carlen, IHM (Wilmington, N.C., McGrath Publishing), V, n. 41, p. 111.

4. Nn. 9, 29, 60.

Section VI, Document 15

SACRAMENTAL RECONCILIATION: A THEOLOGICAL ASPECT

Bishop Bernard Blanchet, October 5, 1983

The Church as Sacrament

One can speak of sacramental reconciliation only within the framework of the Church as a whole, considered as a sacrament of salvation. This is the perspective of the Second Vatican Council: "The Church is, in Christ, a type of sacrament: that is to say, the sign and instrument of intimate union with God and of the unity of the entire human race". [1] The seven major acts specifically named sacraments are, therefore, realities within this vast sacramental economy as particular realizations and applications of the wider sacramentality.

This is the case with the sacrament traditionally called the sacrament of penance, which the new Ritual also calls the sacrament of reconciliation, the better to express the central and properly sacramental import of the penitential act. The Christian salvation of which the Church is sacrament can, in fact, be summed up as: a reconciliation (intimate union with God) springing from the absolutely free love of God and bearing fruit in a reconciled humanity (the unity of the entire human race).

The Mystery and Ministry of Reconciliation

Saint Paul writes of the work of salvation accomplished in Jesus Christ: "Everything comes from God, Who has reconciled us to

Himself through Christ and has entrusted to us the ministry of reconciliation" (2 Cor. 5:18). These words speak at one and the same
time of the mystery of reconciliation and what the ministry of this
mystery, in Church, must be.

The apostle forcefully stresses the fact that the initiative of reconciliation comes, not from us, but from God. God reconciles. He grants
reconciliation to the world, as a free gift. This change in a person's
situation before God, which is accomplished through the death of
Jesus precedes all changes in personal dispositions: "while we were
still enemies of God, we were reconciled with Him by the death of
His Son" (Rom. 5:10). Nevertheless, Paul invites everyone to "be
reconciled to God", appealing for a response on our part, to render
effective this reconciliation which has already been given. This
response of conversion (change of heart) and of penance is necessary, but it follows only in response to the divine initiative (2 Cor.
18-20). This is the mystery.

The ministry of reconciliation must be in harmony with this mystery and accentuate its two great coordinates. In the first place, there
is its total gratuity. This we emphasize by first proclaiming, not the
human action, the call to penance, but the Good News of salvation
freely given in Jesus Christ. This ministry must, in the second place,
emphasize the demand for a human response, for there is no reconciliation without encounter. Pardon and repentance must go together.
The sacramental ministry of reconciliation must recapture and express, in the very forms in which it is conducted, both God's free
and loving initiative and the human response of those who have experienced pardon. It is only in this way that the Church will be a
true sacrament of the mystery.

Forms of Celebration

Since the promulgation of the new Ritual by the Latin Church
in 1973, it seems that there are two forms of celebration which fulfill
the requirements of this mystery.

There is, first, the personal form of individual penitent confessing to individual confessor. This form gives priority to the encounter between priest and penitent. This is not, in the format given in
the Ritual, a revival, pure and simple, of "confession" as we have
known it since the twelfth century and practised it since the Ritual

of 1614. Priest and penitent now exchange greetings, listen together to the Word of God, proclaim His love in the very confessing of sin, and pray together to receive God's pardon (effectively signified by absolution) and to be able to give witness to this pardon by making satisfaction in suitable penance and reform of life. They conclude in giving thanks together. This manner of administering the sacrament allows for a more detailed expression of the human response to God's initiative, a more complete expression of the penitent's activity in conversion. It witnesses to the fact that God's pardon comes to each on the most personal level, speaking His Word this very day. Similarly, the act of penance, suggested and accepted in dialogue, can be the beginning of a new life, symbolized in a very concrete manner. This form is thus irreplaceable.

The second form, the reconciliation of many penitents after a common penitential celebration, but with individual confessions and individual absolutions is theologically related to the first. Since confession and absolution occur within an individual encounter of priest and penitent, this form of the sacrament preserves an unchanged theological structure. We will not discuss it here, giving emphasis to a third form, which constitutes a truly new form of the sacrament.

This form, in which a number of penitents are reconciled after a common general or non-specific confession, with but a single absolution to the group, emphasizes the communal dimension of reconciliation and is conducted as a true celebration; the communal dimension is highlighted in the Concil's *Constitution on the Liturgy.* [2] It has the advantage of promoting a collective awareness of sin and its social and political dimensions. It gathers together the people God re-creates in their baptismal calling. It invites them to come together and accept each other as a people of pardoned sinners, to renew strained or broken bonds of union, to live communally the mystery of reconciliation — in brief, to experience the very nature of what the Church is.

Official Church documents have hitherto been rather reticent about this form of the sacrament. We believe, however, that actual Church discipline and *praxis* of this form must be re-evaluated, for the following reasons:

1) History, which reveals the existence throughout the ages of three forms of penance in the Church, gives ample evidence that this sacrament, in its manner of administration, is in the jurisdiction of the Church. The Church has received the sacraments from her Lord,

but she has always been keenly aware that the particular manner in which they are administered has been confided to her responsibility. It belongs to her to define and adapt the ritual forms of the sacrament according to the times and the needs of the people of God. The Church can therefore confidently turn to a new form of celebration of penance without detriment to the sacramental ministry of reconciliation. On the contrary, the very newness of this ministry would be the expression of its fidelity to the mystery.

2) It must be remembered that the Oriental Churches, which also lay claim to apostolic traditions, have both communal and individual forms of this sacrament. Whereas in the Byzantine Church the penitential discipline requires the specific confession of sins in the private form, the Churches of Egypt and Syria began to use the individual form only in the 12th century; and the Nestorian Church employs only the communal form. We would add that, in many Churches, especially in the medieval period, individual confession did not always have the same importance as communal celebrations and that the complete confession of sins, as well as the juridical obligation to confess grave sins, was never as clearly determined as in the west. It is well known that the Catholic Church recognizes the validity of the sacraments in the Oriental Churches.

3) This leads us to suggest that the difficulties experienced in the Latin Church are tied to the declaration of the Council of Trent, proclaiming the necessity of a detailed confession of all grave sins as a requirement of divine law. The Canons of the Council of Trent have to be interpreted in the context of the Protestant Reformation which had challenged the private form of the Sacrament. Trent cannot be cited as an authority for invalidity of a form of penance with general confession and absolution.

4) This form, which includes all the elements necessary for the sacrament, change of heart and its expression in the confession of sins — although general and collective — with absolution, and satisfaction, should not be preached and presented in oposition to the personal form which we consider irreplaceable. The communal form is complementary to the individual form and has its own strengths and advantages. In point of fact, these celebrations allow a large number of the faithful to discover the free nature of God's gifts and to proclaim and celebrate, in this feast of pardon, His unconditional love. The mystery proclaimed by the Gospel is that God doesn't measure His forgiveness sparingly or by rule, but loves us freely.

From a theological viewpoint, these reasons are so cogent that we present the following recommendation:

— that the bases of the present discipline of the Church regarding general confession and absolution be studied with a view to broadening this discipline.

NOTES

1. *Dogmatic Constitution on the Church,* n. 1.
2. N. 27.

Section VI, Document 16

RECONCILIATION AND NON-BELIEVERS

Archbishop Louis-Albert Vachon, October 5, 1983

1. *The Mission of the Church: the Salvation of the World*

Reconciliation with non-believers is part of the universal mission of the Church. To accomplish this mission the Church must situate herself where humanity is at work, living its hopes and its disappointments; that is, in the world, to manifest her close solidarity with the entire human community. This reconciliation can occur only in a meeting of two histories: that of salvation and that of the world. Depository of the gifts of Christ, heir to His death/resurrection and led by the Spirit of Pentecost, the Church must keep alive the work of her Founder, Incarnate in this world to give witness to the truth and to restore a universal family. "For the human person deserves to be preserved... human society deserves to be renewed."[1] There is nothing truly human which escapes the plan of Jesus,

> ... because God wanted all perfection to be found in Him and all things to be reconciled through Him and for Him, everything in heaven and everything on earth, when He made peace by His death on the cross. (Col. 1:20)

2. *Contemporary Atheism: a Giant Challenge for the Church*

Atheism has become, in the space of a few decades, a mass phenomenon growing on ancient Christian soil, overcoming Churches and penetrating the hearts of believers. Though manifest in many ways, in essence it spreads the concept of a world which is self-sufficient, with no need of God.[2]

But lo, in a gigantic challenge, modern humanity, since the Renaissance, has risen against this message of salvation, and has begun to reject God in the very name of the dignity of the human person... atheism has become today a mass phenomenon which besieges the Churches. What is more, it penetrates them from the inside, as if believers themselves, including those who claim to follow Jesus Christ, found in themselves a secret intrigue that destroyed their faith in God, in the name of human autonomy and dignity.[3]

This phenomenon of the direct negation of God, or complete disregard of Him as irrelevant, whether it arises from secularism, materialism, exclusive humanism or other ideologies, has shaken the world on all sides and in various ways.

None of the ages of life escapes it, from young adolescence, a prey to doubt, to skeptical old age, passing through the suspicions and rejections of adulthood. And there is no continent that has been spared.[4]

Atheism must be considered the spiritual tragedy of our time, since it sets up a world without God.

3. *Dialogue: a Path to Reconciliation*

If only for the defence and the affirmation of the human being and the promotion of humanity, the Church must privilege dialogue with culture. She must re-establish existentially the culture of faith in the various cultural domains of today and courageously re-affirm the values of Christian humanism. She must prove to the world that Christianity, far from mutilating the human person, brings to it a concept of life which frees and supports an integral education of the physical and spiritual being of every individual. At the same time, Christianity offers a vision of the world and of society which contributes to the social and moral reconstruction of the human community. This is an imperative of the Incarnation as well as an indispensable condition for the establishment of Church credibility.

Entering into dialogue with culture, the Church will be enriched and can attempt to humanize the dehumanizing elements of culture. It is through such mediation that the Church will respond to the expectations of humanity and will find points of anchorage for faith in Christ, Centre of the cosmos and of history. This is the route the

Church must travel if she wishes to develop a true pastoral of the intelligence.

4. *The World Meeting Place: a Haven of Reconciliation*

This is not a case of being present to counter the evil influences and impact of the new means which societies today adopt for their development, but rather to be in concert with and support those who define, decide and influence the re-orientation of science and technology at the service of the human being and of all humanity. Examples could be: the technology of modern war, biological experimentation, radical change in the fields of communications and information, etc.

5. *Recommendation*

The Church must seek to re-educate faith, through the promotion of the values of Christian humanism at the level of personal and collective living, based on human and secular values, where there is possibility of consensus:
— in respect for life and for the other;
— in justice, human solidarity, fraternity, charity, sharing;
— in the search for truth and beauty;
— in effort for the integral personal development of all and each, a pedagogy of body, spirit and heart;
— in concern for the environment;
— in the struggle for a just society, political and economic, everywhere;
— in the quality of family life.

These are areas which lead one rapidly to a choice of values and in which both Christians and non-believers can work together. If the Church believes in the person, this in turn will allow man and woman to believe in the Church.

NOTES

1. Second Vatican Council, *The Constitution on the Church in the Modern World,* n. 3.

2. *Op. cit.,* nn. 19 f.

3. John Paul II, to participants in *International Congress* (Rome) *On Evangelization and Atheism,* Oct. 10, 1980, *Osservatore Romano,* Vatican, English edition, Nov. 17; French version, *Documentation Catholique* (Paris), LXXVII, p. 967.

4. *Op. cit., ibid.,* p. 968.

INDEX OF SUBJECTS

Achevé d'imprimer sur les presses de
Imprimerie H.L.N. Inc.,
2605 Hertel, Sherbrooke, Qué. J1J 2J4

Printed in Canada — Imprimé au Canada